Ukrainian Nationalism

UKRAINIAN
NATIONALISM

Politics, Ideology, and Literature, 1929–1956

Myroslav Shkandrij

Yale

UNIVERSITY

PRESS

New Haven & London

Published with assistance from the foundation established in memory of Amasa Stone Mather of the Class of 1907, Yale College.

Yale University Press books may be purchased in quantity for educational, business, or promotional use. For information, please e-mail sales.press@yale.edu (U.S. office) or sales@yaleup.co.uk (U.K. office).

Permission is granted by *Canadian Slavonic Papers* to reprint material from Myroslav Shkandrij, "A Change of Heart: Iurii Klen's 'Adventures of the Archangel Raphael,'" *Canadian Slavonic Papers* 51.4 (2009): 513–24.

Permission is granted by *Harvard Ukrainian Studies* to reprint material from Myroslav Shkandrij, "Dokia Humenna's Representation of the Second World War in Her Novel and Diary," *Harvard Ukrainian Studies* 30 (forthcoming). Copyright by the President and Fellows of Harvard College.

Set in PostScript Electra with Trajan display types by IDS Infotech Ltd.
Printed in the United States of America.

ISBN: 978-0-300-20628-9 (cloth)
Library of Congress Control Number: 2014948704

A catalogue record for this book is available from the British Library.

This paper meets the requirements of ANSI/NISO Z39.48–1992 (Permanence of Paper).

10 9 8 7 6 5 4 3 2 1

He who seeks the salvation of the soul, of his own or of others, should not seek it along the avenue of politics, for the quite different task of politics can only be solved by violence. The genius of politics lives in an inner tension with the god of love.

—*Max Weber, "Politics as a Vocation," 1918*

CONTENTS

Acknowledgments

This book is the product of discussions with many friends and colleagues, too numerous to list. I would, however, like to express thanks to Andrij Makuch, Serhy Yekelchyk, Marta Olynyk, Roman Koropeckyj, two anonymous reviewers, and my wife Natalka Chomiak, who read parts of the book in early drafts and offered helpful advice. A number of scholars provided information and suggested sources, among them Orest Martynowych, Kateryna Kryvoruchko, Antov Shekhovtsov, Halyna Hryn, Andrzej A. Zięba, Serhy Cipko, Frank Sysyn, Yuri Shapoval, Gulia Lami, Bohdan Klid, Jars Balan, John-Paul Himka, Olga Bertelsen, Danylo Yanevsky, and Raisa Movchan. Several archivists and librarians shared their expertise with me and helped to locate materials. I would especially like to thank James Kominowski and Vladimira Zvonik of the University of Manitoba's Dafoe Library, Ksenya Kiebuzinski of the Petro Jacyk Central and East European Resource Centre at the University of Toronto's Robarts Library, Sophia Kachor of the Ukrainian Cultural and Educational Centre (Oseredok) in Winnipeg, Oksana Radysh and Tamara Skrypka of the UVAN (Ukrainian Academy of Arts and Science in the United States) in New York, Vasyl Lopukh and Ostap Kin of the Shevchenko Scientific Society in the United States (NTSh), and Natalia Makovska of the Central Archives of Higher State Organs and Government of Ukraine (TsDAVO) in Kyiv. I am also grateful to Petro and Halyna Danyliuk, who allowed me to use their collection of books, periodicals and archival materials, much of which is now housed at the University of Manitoba.

Acknowledgement is due to *Canadian Slavonic Papers* for granting permission to reprint an earlier version of "A Change of Heart: Yurii Klen's "Adventures of the Archangel Raphael" (1948), *Harvard Ukrainian Studies* for permission to use "Dokia Humenna's Representation of the Second World War in Her Diary

Acknowledgments

and Archive," and Mrs. Halyna Levytsky for permission to use the graphic by Myron Levytsky. I also gratefully acknowledge both the Social Science and Humanities Research Council of Canada and the Office of the Dean at the University of Manitoba for providing the financial support that enabled me to conduct archival research.

NOTE ON TRANSLITERATION

Names of people and places have been transliterated from the Cyrillic alphabet according to a modified Library of Congress scheme, although in a few cases, established usage in the English language has been followed (Galicia, Volhynia). Modifications include dropping the apostrophe that marks a soft sign, giving the initial letter in Ukrainian names as "Ye" rather than "Ie," and ending surnames with "-y" instead of "-yi" so as to approximate English pronunciation. These adaptations have not been made in the bibliography or in the citations, where the Library of Congress spelling "E," "Ie" and "-yi" have been retained. The general practice has been to transliterate place names in Ukraine from the Ukrainian language, and in Russia from the Russian.

ABBREVIATIONS

Cheka   Extraordinary Commission. Short for VCHK or All-Russian Extraordinary Commission for Fighting Counterrevolution and Sabotage (1917–22), the Soviet secret police; later renamed GPU, OGPU, NKVD, MVD, KGB

DP   Displaced Persons

GPU   State Political Administration (1922–30), Soviet secret police

MUR   Ukrainian Artistic Movement

NKVD   People's Commissariat for Internal Affairs (1917–46), Soviet secret police

OUN   Organization of Ukrainian Nationalists

OUN-B   Organization of Ukrainian Nationalists—Bandera faction

OUN-M   Organization of Ukrainian Nationalists—Melnyk faction

OUN-Z   Organization of Ukrainian Nationalists—Abroad

SB   Security Service of the OUN

SVU   League for the Liberation of Ukraine

UHA   Ukrainska Galician Army

UHVR   Ukrainian Supreme Liberation Council

UNDO   Ukrainian National Democratic Association

UNR   Ukrainian People's Republic

UPA   Ukrainian Insurgent Army

UVO   Ukrainian Military Organization

ZUNR   Western Ukrainian People's Republic

INTRODUCTION

After the Soviet Union broke up and the Iron Curtain was removed, new nationalisms emerged in Eastern Europe, sparking political and scholarly debates. Few topics have been more fraught with controversy than Ukrainian nationalism. In both the political and academic worlds, exchanges have taken place over the actions of nationalists during the Second World War, over how to characterize the Organization of Ukrainian Nationalists (OUN)—the radical right-wing movement founded in 1929—and over decisions to erect monuments to its leaders. The OUN is admired by many contemporary Ukrainians, including the Svoboda Party, as a national liberation movement that fought against both Nazi and Soviet oppressors. It is described by others as "fascist" and "antisemitic." Its leader, Stepan Bandera, was made a Hero of Ukraine by President Viktor Yushchenko, but the decision was promptly revoked by the incoming President Viktor Yanukovych in 2010. The Lviv Regional Council, which was dominated by the Svoboda Party, then decided on 16 March 2012 to introduce a regional Hero of Ukraine Stepan Bandera Award (Khromeychuk 2012, 455–56). In October 2012, Svoboda, which is often described as "ultranationalist," won over 10 percent of the vote in Ukrainian parliamentary elections. The response of the ruling Party of Regions to this perceived nationalist "ascendancy" was to orchestrate in May 2013 a so-called "anti-fascist" demonstration, which provoked violence in the streets of Kyiv. These controversies had an international resonance. In 2010 the Polish government denounced Yushchenko's decision to designate Bandera a Hero of Ukraine, and convinced the European Union to urge its revocation. In June 2013, the Polish Senate officially described the attacks by Ukrainian nationalists against the Polish population of Volhynia in 1943 as "ethnic cleansing with elements of genocide."[1] Then, from November 2013 to February 2014 came the Euromaidan, a civil-rights movement that turned into a revolution and overthrew Yanukovych. The Russian president Vladimir Putin immediately began a massive, relentless propaganda campaign, which claimed that "nationalists" and "fascists" had come to power in Kyiv and that the lives of Russians were endangered. These accusations provided the pretext for his invasion of Crimea, a move that was given unanimous support by the Russian Duma (parliament).

Although frequently invoked in both political and academic exchanges, "Ukrainian nationalism" remains a poorly understood concept. The term is often used without contextualization. It is frequently forgotten, for example, that the Ukrainian national movement in the nineteenth century and first two decades of the twentieth century was democratic and liberationist, whereas the OUN in the 1930s was authoritarian. What, then, happened in the interwar period to make authoritarian ideology so attractive to young people in Western Ukraine? What made interwar nationalist mythology so potent that it continues to attract loyalty? And should nationalist leaders of the thirties and forties be celebrated or condemned? The present account attempts to provide some answers to these questions by examining the OUN's politics and ideology from its founding to its postwar decline. The organization played a key role in Western Ukraine (Galicia, Bukovyna, and Transcarpathia) and in émigré communities during the 1930s and the Second World War. Its actions are still the subject of controversy. In exploring this history, this account draws on recent scholarly literature but also introduces new materials culled from archives in Ukraine, Poland, Canada, and the United States, from the correspondence of the organization's ideologists, and memoirs. It also analyzes the creative literature produced by the seven major writers sympathetic toward the OUN. In this way the politics, ideology, and literature are allowed to illuminate one another, and prominence is given to the mythmaking aspects of the movement's ideology.

To avoid confusion, some terms are worth explaining. As Alexander Motyl has reminded us, the key distinction among nationalisms and nationalists "concerns not the goal (they all agree that national liberation and nation-state is their goal), but the means. Whereas legally, democratically, and unconstitutionally inclined nationalists will employ legal, democratic, and constitutional means, illegally, undemocratically, and unconstitutionally inclined nationalists will employ illegal, undemocratic, and unconstitutional means" (Motyl 2013, 14 June).

This distinction is related to another important fault line in discussions of nationalism, which runs between those who emphasize its democratizing, liberating potential and those who view it as a form of xenophobia. According to Greenfeld, the early concept of "nation" that arose in sixteenth-century England "presupposed a respect toward the individual, an emphasis on the dignity of the human being. One was entitled to nationality (membership in a nation) by right of one's humanity [. . .] The love of nation—national patriotism, or nationalism—in this framework meant first and foremost a principled individualism, a commitment to one's own and other people's human rights" (Greenfeld 1992, 31). It has similarly been argued that the liberationist, romantic nationalism of the nineteenth century represented struggles for individual enfranchisement, popular enlightenment, and political unification, struggles that were often conducted in the face of foreign domination and imperial rule. In Ukraine the democratic nationalist tradition came to prominence in 1917–18, when, after the fall of tsarism, the Ukrainian People's Republic (UNR) instituted a parliamentary form of government and granted extensive rights to minorities. In these years, support for the UNR came from a wide range of parties, including most Jewish parties.

In contrast, the authoritarian concept of nation that emerged in the twentieth century insisted on sovereignty being exercised not by the nation as a whole but by a select group. In this collectivist ideology the nation is imagined as a single individual, and a leadership group, qualified to interpret the nation's will, is seen as entitled to impose its dictatorship on the masses.

In order to indicate the fundamental difference between a democratic and authoritarian nationalism, the present account writes nationalism with either a small "n" or a capital "N." The first refers to supporters of an independent Ukraine or an autonomous Galicia who generally favored a Western-style parliamentary system and democracy. The second refers to integral nationalists, who were members of the OUN and who adhered to an extreme version of authoritarian nationalism. Oleksandr Zaitsev has characterized integral nationalism as demanding "the unreserved subordination of the individual to the interests of his or her nation, which are placed above the interests of any social group, other nations, and humanity as a whole" (Zaitsev 2013b, 13). In the interwar period Ukrainians in Western Ukraine and the emigration were overwhelmingly "small-n" nationalists and belonged to various parties. The leading Lviv daily newspaper, *Dilo* (Task), for example, represented the moderate nationalism of the largest Ukrainian parliamentary party within Poland, the Ukrainian National Democratic Association (UNDO). However, toward the end of the 1930s the OUN began to win the allegiance of many young radicals. On the eve of the Second World War it had an estimated eight thousand to nine thousand members in Western Ukraine (Wysocki 2003, 337).

This does not mean of course that all those who use violence should be termed "fascists." For the distinction between nationalists and fascists, according to Motyl, we should look at the fact that fascists do not build a state or type of regime de novo. In contrast to fascism, "nationalism cannot and does not presuppose an existing type of regime, political system, or state. Quite the contrary, nationalism presupposes the *nonexistence* of an independent state and therefore concludes that the existence, or creation, of such a state is imperative" (Motyl 2013, 14 June). Since nationalism is interested primarily in creating a state, and not in the type of state to be created, it is not surprising that different nationalisms have adopted various political ideologies, fascism among them. This political flexibility, which includes the ability to change political ideology whenever circumstances demand it, in Motyl's view is not opportunism: "Nationalism and nationalists can be so chameleonic precisely because their ideology is fundamentally indifferent to the type of regime, political system, or state that emerges within the newly created state" (ibid., 25 June). He therefore sees the interwar OUN as most usefully compared to other nationalist movements that have aspired to national liberation and the creation of nation-states, such as the Palestine Liberation Organization, the Algerian National Liberation Front, the Irish Republican Army, the interwar Croatian Ustashe, and the Vietnamese National Liberation Front, and not to fascist regimes or movements. There were elements of fascism in the OUN's ideology, but these are not the determining factor. As will be seen, the OUN itself consistently used a similar argument when it objected to the fascist designation.

The term "nationalist" can also be used in confusing ways. In the 1930s, Polish authorities applied the term indiscriminately to any Ukrainian who supported autonomy or national rights in Galicia. In the Soviet Union, demands for cultural rights, or even linguistic assertiveness, were frequently seen as nationalist. Yurii Sherekh has recalled that a teacher who, after lecturing on the Ukrainian language, continued to speak this language with students during the break, was considered a nationalist by the NKVD (Sherekh 1948, 14). At the root of the problem—Walker Connor has called it "terminological chaos"—is confusion of the terms "nation" and "state" (Connor 1994, 89–117). Connor suggests that nationalism should refer only to an identification with and loyalty to a nation, not to a country or state. And what constitutes a nation? Connor views it as a group of people who feel ancestrally related (ibid., 202). Azar Gat, on the other hand, prefers to emphasize the concept of kinship: "Common descent is only one, albeit prevalent, subcategory within the broader category of shared kinship or 'blood relation.' This is a subtle but important and generally overlooked distinction. It is the notion of extended family which is typical of an ethnos and ethnicity, and this notion often, but not always, includes common descent. In many cases there is a strong sense based on tradition that the ethnos was originally made up of separate groups that came together and amalgamated into one" (Gat 2013, 19).

The Romans, for example, are perceived to have originated from the fusion of Latin and Sabine groups. The English have a strong sense of having descended from Angles, Saxons, and Normans, who achieved complete fusion in language, culture, identity, and "blood" (ibid., 20). The French have their own traditional belief in having descended from Gauls, Romans, and Germans. A perception of shared ethnic identity may therefore rest not so much on common descent as on a belief that intermarriage among founding groups has resulted in a common culture and sense of kinship. In Gat's view, ethnicity, "overwhelmingly tends to combine *both* kinship and a common culture" (ibid., 21).

A stateless people who wish to be recognized as a nation often affirm their deep roots in history in this manner. However, one group of historians who study nationalism sees nations as the products of modernity and dismisses claims of distant origins. Nations, according to "modernists," emerged mostly in the nineteenth century as a result of the social integration and political mobilization caused by print technologies, capitalist economies, urbanization, mass education, mass politics, and state building. This approach emphasizes the role of state authorities and elites in manipulating national sentiment and assigns a passive role to the masses. It tends to see nationalism as something contrived. Ernest Gellner, a strong proponent of such an instrumental view, holds that "[c]ontrary to popular and even scholarly belief, nationalism does not have any very deep roots in the human psyche" (Gellner 2006, 34). He offers the following description as typical of nationalism's development in Eastern Europe: these populations are "still locked into the complex multiple loyalties of kinship, territory and religion. To make them conform to the nationalist imperative was bound to take more than a few battles and some diplomacy. It was bound to take a great deal of very forceful cultural engineering. In many cases it was also bound to involve population exchanges or expulsions, more or less forcible assimilation, and sometimes liquidation, in order to attain that close relation between state and culture which is the essence of nationalism" (ibid., 97).

Anthony Smith, Walker Connor and Azar Gat are among those who have challenged such an approach. They tend to see the roots of ethne (the plural of ethnos), peoples, or nations as reaching into the deeper past. Gat, in particular, regards all these groups as long predating modernity and stretching back to the dawn of history (Gat 2013, 23). He has objected to the view that nationalism is an "artificial" historical construct erected "on older and more natural feelings of love for one's place, language, and customs" (ibid., 8). Instead, he prefers to see modern nationalism not as the manipulation of sentiments by an elite, but as "a function of old popular sentiments empowered by democratization" (ibid., 16). In his view, the idea of nations as "imagined" (Benedict Anderson's idea of collective consciousness) or "invented" (Hobsbawm's idea of invented tradition) has obscured the fact that reprocessing of tradition is not fabrication ex nihilo: "Rather, it primarily involved selective reworking of existing historical materials and folk memories which often had at least some basis in reality" (ibid., 17).

The downplaying of ethnic and national phenomena can be attributed to the failure of dominant social theories like liberalism and Marxism to provide explanatory conceptual frameworks. But Gat also comments: "it is probably not a coincidence that the pioneering modernist theorists—Kohn, Deutsch, Gellner, Hobsbawm—were all Jewish immigrant refugees from central Europe (and Elie Kedourie from the Middle East) during the first half of the twentieth century. All of them experienced changing identities and excruciating questions of self-identity at the time of the most extreme, violent and unsettling nationalistic eruptions. It was only natural that they reacted against all this" (ibid., 16–17).

Although Gat accepts that the state created the nation more often than the other way around, he maintains that in the case of state-ethnos relationships, in most instances "ethne tended to predate the state (and quite often proved highly resistant to its intrusion), with their existing formation sometimes stretching far back into prehistory" (ibid., 19). Liah Greenfeld is also convinced that historically the emergence of nationalism predated the development of "every significant component of modernization" (Greenfeld 1992, 21). In interaction with other factors, nationalism shaped economic forces, political organizations, and a culture of modernity: "It is nationalism which has made our world, politically, what it is—this cannot be put strongly enough" (ibid.).

Sometimes civic and ethnic nationalisms are juxtaposed. Civic nationalism is often viewed as based exclusively on common citizenship and shared political institutions. In reality, however, it cannot be sharply separated from its ethnic twin. In Gat's opinion "there have been very few nations, if any, whose existence was divorced from ethnicity, that is, which did not share cultural and at least some kin affinities" (Gat 2013, 7). In fact, civil nationalism in particular generates assimilation into an ethnonational community, either as an explicit requirement or as a tacit assumption (ibid.). But neither should ethnicities be thought of as homogeneous or hermetically sealed. They are always punctuated by differences and influenced by interaction with other groups.

Major nationalisms differ substantially, as Greenfeld has shown in an analysis of English, French, German, Russian, and American nationalism (Greenfeld 1992). She has demonstrated that they appeared at different times under different conditions and were driven by different social groups. Each contains within itself tendencies that wax and wane, traditions that become dominant for a time, then

recede. Some embrace heterogeneity more than others; the degree of homoge-
neity in a nation or state cannot be used to predict tendencies toward democracy
or dictatorship. It should also be noted that nationalistic appeals to ethnic purity
have been made by democratic leaders and by Marxist-Leninist regimes: "political leaders of the most diverse ideological strains have been mindful of the
common blood component of ethnonational psychology and have not hesitated
to appeal to it when seeking popular support. Both the frequency and the record
of success of such appeals attest to the fact that nations are indeed characterized
by a sense—a feeling—of consanguinity" (Connor 1994, 202).

The power of nationalism in today's world is widely recognized. In Eastern
Europe Soviet patriotism or the feeling of loyalty to the USSR proved to be "no
match for the sense of nationalism demonstrated by nearly all of the peoples of
the Soviet Union" (ibid. 197). However, the nature of the ethnonational bond,
its psychological and emotional hold upon a group, remains under-studied.
Since nationalism is primarily a matter of psychology and self-definition, an
attitude, it has been suggested that in this matter "[t]he poet, as an adept
expressor of deep-felt passion, is apt to be a far better guide here than the social
scientist has proven to be" (ibid., 76). If we are to understand the strength of
ethnicity and nationalism, it would be useful to study the feelings and images
invoked by national poets, the speeches of national leaders, and the pamphlets
and programs of ethnonationalist organizations: "Too often these speeches and
documents have been passed off as useless propaganda in which the authors do
not really believe. But nationalism is a mass phenomenon, and the degree to
which the leaders are true believers does not affect its reality. The question is
not the sincerity of the propagandist, but the nature of the mass instinct to
which the propagandist appeals" (ibid., 76).

The early studies of the OUN's politics and ideology were done by John
Armstrong (1963) and Alexander Motyl (1980). They have been built upon by
recent Polish, German, and Ukrainian scholarship that has used archival
evidence made available in the 1990s. Polish scholarship has long been interested in the interwar Polish state's treatment of national minorities in general
and the Ukrainian in particular. Early research into Poland's nationalities policy
produced studies by Andrzej Chojnowski (1979) and Ryszard Torzecki (1989,
1993). After the fall of communism, materials in Warsaw's archives were used by
a number of scholars to rethink the history of interwar Galicia and of wartime
Ukrainian nationalism.[2] German scholars have produced important studies of
the OUN during the wartime period.[3] Recent Western scholarship has examined the wartime years in Ukraine in several synthetic studies that include
explorations of the OUN's activities. All have delved into the archives to

compose their narratives of life under Nazi rule.[4] A number of scholars, have focused on the involvement of the OUN's members in the Holocaust or the organization's actions during the Second World War.[5] Changing perceptions of the OUN have been the result of the newer findings and the commentaries they have stimulated.

In Ukraine a number of scholars have made contributions to the history and politics of the OUN. Valuable studies of the armed underground during the Second World War have been produced. Known as the UPA (Ukrainska Povstanska Armiia—Ukrainian Insurgent Army), it came under the control of the Bandera faction of the OUN in 1943.[6] Our understanding of life under German occupation has been enriched by a range of studies.[7] The brief existence of Carpatho-Ukraine in 1938–39 has been discussed in several works.[8] Some recent histories have attempted to paint broader pictures of life in emigration and in Western Ukraine: Andrii Portnov has looked at the Ukrainian emigration in Europe (2008); Maria Mandryk has produced a history of nationalism in the interwar years (2006); Oleksandr Zaitsev, Oleh Behen and Vasyl Stefaniv have examined the OUN's relationship with the Ukrainian Greek Catholic Church (2011); and Oleksandr Rublov and Natalia Rublova have discussed interwar nationalism in the light of Polish-Ukrainian diplomatic relations (2012). Recently, Zaitsev has produced an excellent study of the ideology of both the OUN and of Ukrainian integral nationalism as a whole (2013a).

In the nineties, scholars in Ukraine began to make use of secret-police files. This has led to a flood of information and a concerted effort to publish documentation, some of it on Web sites. Since 1994, research accomplished in the archives has been reported in the journal *Z arkhiviv VUChK, GPU, NKVD, KGB* (From the Archives of the All-Ukrainian Cheka, GPU, NKVD, KGB), a serial publication that also reprints documents. Some archival materials have been published in anthologies.[9] Scholars have examined the secret-police archives in connection with the arrest and sentencing of Soviet citizens accused of nationalism in the 1920s or membership in the OUN in the 1930s. Many of the accused were from Galicia or had spent time in the West. These studies have demonstrated the falseness of almost all accusations by drawing on archival sources and providing key documents.[10] Publishing documentation on the OUN and UPA, including memoir literature, has also been the goal of the multivolume *Litopys Ukrainskoi Povstanskoi Armii* (Chronicles of the Ukrainian Insurgent Army), a project begun in 1978 by Peter Potichnyj. Fifty volumes have appeared in the West. Since 1995, another fifteen volumes of a new series have been published in Kyiv. This new series includes documents from archives in Ukraine.[11]

Our understanding of the OUN's history and politics has been enriched by new memoirs.[12] Some histories produced after the war have long been integrated into research, including an account of the OUN's expeditionary forces by Lev Shankovsky (1958), and histories of the OUN by Volodymyr Martynets (1949), Petro Mirchuk (1968), and Lev Rebet (1964). These works generally take a partisan approach, defend a particular faction within the organization, and often avoid discussion of darker pages in the organization's history. The information they provide is now being integrated with the new archival research and more-recent memoir literature.

Surprisingly little research has been devoted to the OUN's ideologists themselves. Critics who have aimed to demonstrate that elements of fascism, racism, or antisemitism existed in the organization have tended to present impressionistic, often dismissive accounts of these figures. Several important individuals remain completely unstudied and, in some cases, are practically unknown. The present study draws both on the published writings and unpublished correspondence of the organization's inner circle to examine the thinking of key strategists: Dmytro Andriievsky, Volodymyr Martynets, Yevhen Onatsky, Mykola Stsiborsky, and Yuliian Vassyian. It focuses on their evolution during the interwar period in the context of political developments. Even Dmytro Dontsov, whom many contemporaries considered the most important ideological influence not only on the OUN but on the entire interwar generation, has hardly been analyzed. Since Mykhailo Sosnovsky's study (1974), there have been few serious attempts to understand him or even examine his works.[13] The present account explores his conflicts with the OUN's ideologists and various literary figures, a subject that has not as yet been investigated by scholars. The argument here is that Dontsov, who was never a member of the organization, represented a different variant of integral (authoritarian) nationalism. His views differed in a number of ways from those of the OUN's chief ideologists. Unlike the OUN, he did not refuse the epithet "fascist," and he paid special attention to mythmaking and the role of literature. He used the journal *Vistnyk* (Herald, 1933–39), which he edited, to present his views.

The present account is divided into three sections. The first describes the OUN's rise, its relations with the interwar Polish state and with Ukrainian society. The focus is on what made authoritarian politics attractive to many contemporaries and why the organization was able to grow. The second section examines more closely the OUN's ideology and the importance of Dontsov's ideas.

The third section, which constitutes approximately half the study, is devoted to creative literature, without an understanding of which it is impossible to explain how the organization developed a potent mythology. This part of the analysis is concerned with the mythic thinking that animated fiction, poetry, and essays. The seven major writers who helped to forge the organization's vision of a new political community were Yevhen Malaniuk, Olena Teliha, Leonid Mosendz, Oleh Olzhych, Yurii Lypa, Ulas Samchuk, and Yurii Klen. In the postwar emigration, Samchuk and Klen rejected much of the interwar legacy. They became part of the literary organization MUR (Mystetskyi Ukrainskyi Rukh—Artistic Ukrainian Movement), which in the years 1945–48 was active in Western Europe's Displaced Persons (DP) camps and mounted a sustained critique both of the OUN's prewar ideology and of Dontsov. The final chapter discusses Dokia Humenna's *Khreshchatyi iar* (Khreshchatyk Ravine, 1956). Like most other émigrés from Central and Eastern Ukraine, she was a strong critic of the OUN. Eastern Ukrainians, although nationalists in the sense of being independentists, rejected talk of dictatorships or führers, which their Soviet experience had taught them to detest. The publication of Humenna's novel-chronicle, which is based on a diary she kept during the German occupation of Kyiv, had a wide resonance in the émigré community, as the many letters she received from readers indicate.[14] A discussion of her book is included because it indicates how "Eastern" Ukrainians conceptualized the war and how they produced a critique of the OUN. In this way the book provides a "mainstream" perspective on the organization, one that is useful to recall in light of attempts to idealize the organization in contemporary Ukraine.

The year in which Humenna's book appeared, 1956, is symbolic in a number of ways. In that year Lev Rebet and Zynovii (Zenon) Matla, two leaders of Stepan Bandera's wing of the organization, the OUN-B, formed a new party, which they named the OUN-Z. Members of the new party were popularly known as the Dviikari (followers of the duumvirate, or dual leadership). This party adhered to an entirely democratic platform and accused Bandera's supporters of developing a leader cult (*vozhdism*) and using the dictatorial methods that were a throwback to the 1930s. The New York Group, a young generation of modernist writers, also began to publish their first works in 1956. They focused on personal experience and the individual imagination. Their disregard for politics represented an implicit rejection of authoritarianism and the ideology of integral nationalism.

The lack of serious research devoted to the seven writers close to the OUN (there are almost no studies in English) has resulted in a serious gap in the understanding of interwar nationalism. The present account integrates recent studies of individual figures with earlier accounts produced by émigré critics like Yurii Sherekh (Shevelov) and Volodymyr Derzhavyn, who after the war found themselves in the West.[15]

The interwar generation came out of the brutal experiences of 1914–20, the First World War, the struggle for independence, and the establishment of bolshevik rule. It witnessed the growth of authoritarian movements throughout Europe and the rise of communist and fascist regimes. A sense of epochal upheaval encouraged contemporary intellectuals and writers to develop political myths. These served a double purpose: they created reassuring links to the past, but also encouraged transcendence of the past by projecting visions of a modern nation. The seven writers who are examined in this study are associated both with the "Prague School" and the Lviv journal *Vistnyk* (Herald, 1933–41). They extol patriotism and heroism, and express fascination with the "golden ages" of Kyivan Rus and the Cossack state of the seventeenth and eighteenth centuries. They also often exhibit a fierce anti-traditionalism when they criticize the past with a view to transforming the present.

These seven writers were influenced by Dontsov, who promoted the necessity of violence and called upon literature to forge a new modern individual. His *Natsionalizm* (Nationalism, 1926) demanded a break from the mainstream humanist tradition, which he regarded as saturated with sentimentality, sweetness, and pity. Invoking Friedrich Nietzsche and Georges Sorel, he encouraged the creation of a literature infused with irrational yearnings and the "barbaric" philosophy of myth and legend. He favored a dynamic writing that reflected a time of conflict and change, and that portrayed the individual in revolt against established norms and peace-loving ideals. Initially he was well disposed toward futurism, expressionism, and romanticism, but because he later shifted his ground and began attacking modernism, the debt he and the entire interwar generation owed to literary and artistic modernism has gone unrecognized.

The present account argues that the work of these seven figures represents a contribution to modernism. In doing so, it challenges conventional critical wisdom, which has drawn a firm distinction between postwar modernism (which is associated with democracy, pluralism, and formal experimentation) and the literature of the 1930s (which is associated with populism, traditionalism, and outmoded forms of literary realism). In Ukrainian literary scholarship, this dichotomous picture has solidified into a dogma that has only recently been challenged. The interest in modernism among contemporary Ukrainian critics has drawn them to the work of post–Second World War émigrés, to the work of the Cultural Renaissance of the 1920s in Kharkiv and Kyiv, and to the Europeanizing trends that preceded the First World War. The missing link in this genealogy of modernism is the body of writing produced outside the Soviet Union in the 1930s, which has been overlooked or dismissed as retrograde.

To develop this view of a 1930s modernism, the present account draws on the writings of scholars like Emilio Gentile, Peter Fritzsche, and Lutz Koepnik, who have indicated the intimate kinship between modernism and nationalism. Roger Griffin's recent work (2007, 2008) and the groundbreaking anthology edited by Brandon Taylor and Wilfried van der Will (1990), which describes fascism's involvement with modernism, have proven useful.[16] Griffin, for example, has described fascism itself as form of political modernism, a "maximalist" reaction to Western modernity, but one that was revolutionary and focused on overcoming what it saw as modernization's "disaggregation, fragmentation, and loss of transcendence with respect to premodern societies" (Griffin 2007, 10).

Modernist aesthetics, especially the focus on rupture and renewal, influenced many writers on both the extreme left and extreme right. They directed their anger against "bourgeois" ideology (the rationalism of the Enlightenment and liberal democracy), and developed violent forms of the palingenetic myth (the idea of a regeneration of ancient characteristics). Right-wing versions of this myth often incorporate a fascination with Rome, pagan health, barbarian strength, and sudden transformations that reveal an individual's true nature when a link is discovered to the distant past. Such mythmaking played an important role in the literature of authoritarian nationalism.

This generation, whatever its political colors, exhibited a remarkable enthusiasm for, and faith in, political struggle. It refused to reconcile to the existing political situation and continued to dream of a independent state, even when the odds against such a state emerging seemed overwhelming. In the seventies, three decades after the war, Mykhailo Horyn met some OUN members who were still serving their sentences in the Gulag. The imprisoned dissident, like other Ukrainian and Jewish prisoners of conscience who at this time found themselves in the camps, came to admire the steadfastness of these old prisoners, their discipline, solidarity, and commitment to national rights. He wrote: "To this day I cannot fathom how we succeeded in educating those kamakazis—not hundreds, but hundreds of thousands of people who were ready to die for the Ukrainian idea. [. . .] The thirties developed the idea of a state as the primary value in the system of values. No one asked what kind of state it should be; no one delved into economics, the social structure that had to emerge in that state. Everyone simply agreed: we will win a state, and then everything will fall into its required place" (Horyn 1991, 38). This account aims to provide some insights into the faith and fanaticism that drove this generation.

A number of commentators have been drawn to an unproblematic glorification or denunciation of the OUN as a whole, in all its phases and at all times. This account attempts to avoid doing so by distinguishing the various views and concerns voiced by individuals within the organization and by reminding readers of the constantly changing context that was shaping events. The Nationalists argued that force counted in the modern world. They were motivated by the threat to national survival and what they saw as the need for violent struggle. They drew on revanchist sentiments nurtured by defeat in the struggle for independence in the years 1917–20 and by a sense of their country's unjust treatment at the hands of Western powers. They praised authoritarian forms of government and sometimes adopted pagan ideals, along with a contempt for weakness and for qualities of tolerance and compassion, which they thought these ideals implied. However, although a shift occurred in the years 1937–41, Nationalism differed from Nazism in not cutting its ties with religion, in rejecting racial theory, and in focusing on independence—a direct challenge to the Nazi idea of *Lebensraum* (living space for the Germans). An internal debate took place over fascism, racism, Italy, and Germany throughout the 1930s and 1940s.

In *Mein Kampf* (1925–26) Hitler described the German nation as responsible for civilization's most important achievements, and the Slavs as subhuman. He imagined Europe as a Greater Germany ruled by a master race of 250 million Germans, to whom the Slavs, including Ukrainians, would be enslaved. The threat was real, and many considered the creation of a competing political mythology a matter of vital urgency. However, at this same time—and particularly in the two years that preceded the Second World War—it appeared to many observers that Germany was contemplating the establishment of a Greater Ukraine, a state that would stretch from the Carpathian Mountains to the Caucasus. One commentator wrote in 1939 that the Ukrainian question was Europe's "greatest unsolved problem in nationality," and the potent ferment of nationalism led him to believe that there could be no permanent solution to the politics of Eastern Europe that did not permit "a reasonable realization of Ukrainian nationhood" (Kirkconnell 1939, 89). He continued: "A Ukrainian puppet-state would [. . .] provide the greatest colour of justice and legality to any Hitlerian seizure of southern Russia, and there seems little doubt that such a state would be set up if the *Drang nach Osten* should ultimately reach Kiev" (ibid., 74). Like many others at the time, this informed Canadian scholar expected the scenario played out in 1918 to be repeated and Germany to establish a Ukrainian state. Ukrainians therefore had to reflect upon the threat of slavery and the promise of statehood in a potential new order. Interwar Ukrainian politics and literature capture the dilemmas of this situation, a nation's hopes, fears, and anxieties.

POLITICS

1

———◆◆———

INTERWAR NATIONALISM, 1922–38

The First World War formally ended with the signing of the Treaty of Versailles, along with the ancillary Treaties of St. Germain, Trianon, Neuilly, and Sevres. This was at the time "the most far-reaching and comprehensive settlement ever effected in any international dispute" (Lloyd George 1938, 1, 17). The Allies promoted the protection of smaller and weaker nations and declared the right of nations to self-determination. States that had emerged from the ruins of empires were recognized, and the League of Nations was established to oversee the implementation of agreements and to regulate conflicts. However, the Ukrainians, a people of some forty million, who had struggled in 1917–20 to create an independent Ukrainian People's Republic (UNR), found themselves under foreign rule and divided between four separate states. Central and Eastern Ukraine was under Moscow's control, Galicia and Western Volhynia became part of Poland, Northern Bukovyna was incorporated into Romania, and Transcarpathia was incorporated into Czechoslovakia. By far the largest population outside Soviet borders was in Galicia and other parts of Poland, where there were some five to six million Ukrainians, although unofficial estimates sometimes put the figure at seven million.

Many émigrés had fled Soviet rule at the end of the struggle for independence. Around 35,000 found themselves in Poland. About 27,000 were military personnel who had fought for independence, some 20,000 of whom had been interned in camps until 1922 (Portnov 2008, 62, 86). Denied the right to live in Galicia (the territory officially known as Eastern Galicia before the First World War), many moved farther west.[1] An estimated 50,000 Ukrainian émigrés eventually settled in Czechoslovakia, where President Masaryk's government provided them with support. Prague and Poděbrady became the acknowledged centers of émigré life. However, there were also large communities in Vienna,

Paris, Berlin, Warsaw, Belgrade, and Sophia. The total number of Ukrainian émigrés throughout Central and Western Europe has been estimated at 100,000 (Mandryk 2006, 91).

Like their compatriots in Western Ukraine as a whole (Galicia, Volhynia, Bukovyna, and Transcarpathia), the émigrés held grievances against the Entente Powers, Poland, and the Soviet regime. The Entente had supported the Poles and General Denikin's White Army and had denied help to the Ukrainians (including medical aid during the typhoid epidemic). The Polish army of General Haller, which had been trained and equipped by the French, had been used against Ukrainian forces.[2] In postwar years, Poland failed to honor the guarantees it had given Western Powers in the Minorities Treaty of 28 June 1919, when, after signing the Versailles Treaty, it received authorization to occupy Galicia. Its incorporation of Galicia was officially declared at the Treaty of Riga on 18 March 1921. Britain, France, Italy, Japan, and the United States endorsed this arrangement at the Conference of Ambassadors two years later on 15 March 1923. Poland was allowed to introduce a civilian administration on the understanding that it would grant autonomy to the territory and would respect the rights of racial, linguistic, and religious minorities. This, however, did not occur. Ukrainians were denied self-rule, the Galician Sejm (parliament) was closed, and even the territory's name was changed to Małopolska Wschodnia (Eastern Little Poland). The government removed Ukrainian departments at Lviv University and announced that only Polish veterans would be allowed to enroll as students, in this way denying access to Ukrainians who had not fought for Poland during the war. The number of reading rooms operated by the Prosvita (Enlightenment) society dropped from 2,879 in 1914 to only 843 in 1925 (Magocsi 2010, 631). Ukrainians were excluded from government jobs in education, railways, the post, law courts, and taxation offices. As a result, thousands of people who had held administrative positions remained jobless. A law passed on 31 July 1924 stipulated that the term "Ukrainian" could not be used in administration, courts, and schools, but was to be replaced with "Rusyn." Although the total number of schools in Ukrainian areas rose, most were forced to become bilingual (Polish-Ukrainian) and to use Polish as their primary language. The number of unilingual Ukrainian schools in Galicia fell from 3,600 in 1918 to only 450 in 1939 (Portnov 2008, 38). Analogous policies were adopted in Bukovyna by the Romanian government. Although before World War I, under Austrian rule, the territory had enjoyed a high degree of autonomy, the Romanian state imposed martial law (which remained in force until 1928), shut down all Ukrainian cultural societies and newspapers, and Romanianized the school and court systems. The situation for Ukrainians was best in Czechoslovakia, where the population of Transcarpathia (officially known as Subcarpathian Rus) had voluntarily joined the new Czechoslovak Republic in May 1919 and received a guarantee of self-government.[3]

After the war, in 1920–21, Polish concentration camps held over one hundred thousand people. In many cases prisoners were denied food and medical attention. Some starved; others died of disease or committed suicide. The interned included not only soldiers and army officers but also university professors, priests, lawyers, and doctors who had supported the national movement. The Red Cross and some Polish newspapers, such as the socialist *Robotnik* (Worker), protested the appalling conditions. Treatment of internees and the abuse of the civilian population were documented in publications like Osyp Megas's *Tragediia Halytskoi Ukrainy* (Tragedy of Galician Ukraine, 1920) and *Krivava knyha* (Bloody Book, 2 vols., 1919, 1921), a collection of documents produced by the Western Ukrainian People's Republic. These texts became part of a powerful victimization discourse. Among the interned were Jews and members of other nationalities who were sympathetic to Ukrainian independence, and Jews figured among the witnesses who described the murders and abuse. The following passage is an example from *Krivava knyha*: "Even worse were conditions in the prisoner-of-war camp in Pikulychi near Przemyszl, where there were over 20,000 Ukrainian prisoners-of-war and internees. They sleep on the bare earth, typhoid spreads in terrifying way, killing dozens (twenty to eighty) every day. No one is fed anything but soup made from rotten vegetables. The Pikulychi villagers are unable to bear looking at this deprivation and mistreatment, but cannot help because the guards do not allow anyone to approach. On 25 August 1919 during a transfer of the internees to a camp in Zasiania the peasants who wanted to give them some bread along the way were beaten by Polish legionnaires" (*Krivava knyha* 1919, 56). Megas concludes: "Initially the Poles in Eastern Galicia and other occupied Ukrainian lands behaved as though they were in some African country, whose population needed destroying so that they could have a territory for colonization" (Megas 1920, 31). The Ukrainian population of Galicia boycotted the Polish election of 1922 and protested to Western powers over its mistreatment.

Almost a third of the new Polish state's population was made up of minorities. Galician Ukrainians constituting the largest of these. Émigrés from Eastern Ukraine had come to Poland with the exiled UNR government. Symon Petliura, the leader of its armed forces, had in 1920 negotiated an alliance with General Piłsudski, following which his army fought alongside the Poles against the bolsheviks. The subsequent internment of these allied Ukrainian soldiers was viewed as an example of Poland's perfidy. When on 15 March 1923 the Conference of Ambassadors formally ended hopes of a Western Ukrainian state,

Petliura was condemned by many countrymen for having signed the Warsaw agreement in which he had traded claims to Galicia in return for Polish help in the war against the bolsheviks. At the Conference of Ambassadors the Polish government used this agreement to obtain a favorable territorial decision.

When Józef Piłsudski came to power in 1926, he made overtures to Petliura and the exiled UNR government, raising hopes for a Polish-Ukrainian rapprochement. Some leading Polish politicians saw the UNR as Poland's main ally in the Promethean movement, a strategy to unite émigré populations in a struggle against Moscow. However, Petliura was assassinated by a Soviet agent less than two weeks after Piłsudski's coup, and the Soviet Union made strenuous and largely successful efforts to turn the trial of the assassin, Solomon Schwartzbard, into an indictment of the independence movement by blaming Petliura for the pogroms of 1919.[4] On 23 April 1935, two and a half weeks before Piłsudski's death, a new constitution was introduced and the Polish government became more authoritarian. The president's powers were strengthened, while those of the Sejm and Senate were limited. The Endeks (National Democrats; Polish: Endecja) refused to recognize Galician Ukrainians as a nation, insisting instead on their full and immediate assimilation. Many branches of the Ukrainian Prosvita (Enlightenment) society were closed at this time, particularly in Volhynia and Polissia, and efforts were made to prevent the Prosvita and the Ridna shkola (Native School) movements from developing outside Galicia (Wysocki 2003, 40). Books and newspapers were banned from entering territories that the regime had marked for rapid Polonization, such as the Lemko region. The Endeks held that the population there was "Rusyn" or "Ruthenian." The use of these terms, which had identified Ukrainians under the Habsburg monarchy, implied that the population was an entirely different ethnocultural group from Ukrainians living across the border in the Soviet Republic. In order to weaken the Ukrainian movement, only Russian priests were provided, even when the local people identified themselves as Ukrainian and demanded their own clergy. The Polish Roman Catholic Church persuaded Pope Pius XI not to use the term "Ukrainian" in dealing with this population, which it claimed constituted part of Poland's "borderland" and was accordingly subject to colonization A similar policy was applied to the northern regions populated by Ukrainians: Posiannia, Chełm (Kholm), and Podlachia (Pidliashia). Here any contact with the national movement in Galicia was treated as a police matter. Mass arrests of the Ukrainian intelligentsia were conducted in 1922, 1930, 1934, and 1939. A concentration camp was built in Bereza Kartuza in 1934, largely to hold Ukrainian Nationalists, although it also contained communists and common criminals.

A number of scholars have challenged or complicated this victimization discourse by demonstrating that Polish society provided some democratic norms and possibilities for self-realization.[5] Legal Ukrainian political parties existed, the largest of which, UNDO (Ukrainian National Democratic Association), was created in 1925. It contested the elections in 1928, 1930, 1935, and 1938 and elected representatives to the parliament (Sejm) and Senate. Newspapers such as *Dilo* (UNDO's unofficial organ) maintained a dialogue with Polish politicians and intellectuals. Some Polish authorities were sympathetic toward Ukrainian aspirations for an independent state (as long as it did not include any part of interwar Poland), viewing such a state as a buffer against Moscow. Politicians like Tadeusz Holówko and Henryk Józewski, who from 1928 to 1938 was the governor of Volhynia, supported making concessions to Ukrainians so as to develop among them a state-based patriotism. However, in spite of the successes of this policy in Volhynia, where, for example, Józewski was able to Ukrainianize the Orthodox Church, they were unable to shift the weight of public opinion, which was dominated by the Endeks. The latter considered any concession to Ukrainians a sign of weakness and moved quickly to undermine Józewski's policies after the death of Piłsudski. In 1937–39 the state accelerated the Polonization of Galicia and Volhynia and tried to stifle all dissent. Polish lawyers were given preference, Ukrainians were removed from jobs in the transportation sector, and Polish settlement was encouraged along the Przemyśl-Lviv-Ternopil line. Approximately two hundred thousand Poles, many of them army veterans, moved into the villages of Eastern Galician and Volhynia. In Chełm and Podlachia, uniformed Polish police supervised the leveling of 189 Orthodox churches and the transfer of 149 to Roman Catholicism. Out of a total of 389 in 1914, only 51 remained by the end of the 1930s (Kubiiovych 1975, 30). Threatened with deportation or the loss of their land, Orthodox Ukrainians converted to Roman Catholicism and changed their nationality.

An attempt was made to depoliticize the population by dividing it into ethnic subgroups and stimulating regional patriotisms that were linked to a Polish identity. This policy, which constituted a form of tribalization, was applied to various groups, including the Lemkos, Boikos, and Hutsuls. In the Lemko region, state schools were told to provide instruction in the Lemko vernacular, and a separate Greek Catholic Lemko Apostolic Administration was created (Magocsi 2010, 638). Many graduates of teaching seminaries were unable to find jobs, because teachers were government employees and Warsaw was suspicious of educated, nationally conscious Ukrainians. There were quotas in the army for ranks and jobs. Ukrainians, for example, were entirely excluded from the air force, armored regiments, police, sea artillery, and specialized forces (Potocki 2003, 206, 227).

Overall, however, these government policies were counterproductive and have frequently been described as blunders. They exacerbated tensions, spread disillusionment with democratic procedures, and radicalized a large part of the population. While imprisoned in Lviv during the Soviet occupation of 1939–41, one Pole told his Ukrainian fellow prisoner: "we wanted to swallow you, that's a fact; but your thick bones got stuck in our throats; we choked to death, that's also a fact. The most important thing here is our mistake, due to the self-deception we practiced in order to convince ourselves that you had not yet risen from a submissive ethnos to the level of a modern nation. No one fully recognized the dynamic of the Ukrainian national movement" (Shkvarko 1947, 96). Although at points the Polish government offered various minority rights (which it then frequently revoked), the basic problem was that Ukrainians did not consider themselves a minority but a separate nation who had "reached a stage of equality with Poles" under prewar Austrian rule and had then fought for independence. They therefore refused to accept "the status of a minority in their own homeland" (Magocsi 2010, 630).

In 1920 former officers of the Ukrainian army created the UVO (Ukrainska Viiskova Orhanizatsia—Ukrainian Military Organization), which challenged Polish rule by conducting acts of sabotage, burning property belonging to Polish landowners and colonists, and conducting expropriations (notably bank robberies) and political assassinations. In 1922 there were twenty assassinations of Polish police and military personnel, but the most notorious act was the murder of Sydir Tverdokhlib, a Ukrainian writer and leader of the Ukrainian Agricultural Party, which had refused to join the election boycott. Following these events the government arrested twenty thousand Ukrainians, including almost all active members of the UVO (Smolii 2002, 558). Olha Basarab (maiden name Levytska), a member of the underground UVO, was tortured and murdered by Polish police on 9 February 1924. Although the authorities claimed that she hanged herself in her cell, this version of events was not accepted by the population, which was aware of other such "suicides" under interrogation. She had worked for the embassies of the Ukrainian People's Republic (UNR) in Finland and Austria in 1918–23, and had traveled between Germany, Denmark, Sweden, and Norway, before returning in 1923 to Galicia (Diadiuk 2011, 53). Protocols of her arrest and interrogation indicate that she was murdered (ibid., 53–58). Her burial was done quickly at state expense, and the funeral was not announced, a fact that led to mass protests in which Union of Ukrainian Women (Soiuz Ukrainok) took the lead (ibid., 58–59). The autopsy was initially conducted by the police with no outside representatives (ibid., 63). A later autopsy indicated severe beatings and torture (ibid., 67–68).

In these years anti-Polish sabotage and uprisings were also the work of communists (G. Motyka 2006b, 37–38). The UVO's sabotage was called off in the autumn of 1922, when it became clear that a popular uprising would not occur. At this time, and at least until 1923, the UVO formally recognized the leadership of Yevhen Petrushevych, who had been head of the Western Ukrainian People's Republic government and who was now living in exile in Vienna. However, shortly afterward, Petrushevych turned to the Soviet Union for support and the UVO began to act independently. In the years 1927–29 the organization conducted several expropriations, bombings, and assassinations. These were organized in significant degree in order to challenge the political parties who were contesting elections. The UVO refused to accept the leadership of parliamentarians in the Sejm. According to Zynovii Knysh, the organization felt that parliamentary representation "could be useful" as an aspect of the national liberation struggle, but had to "subordinate itself to a national leadership, act as one of its branches, and not take the place of a national leadership" (Knysh 1967, 68). The UVO, of course, saw itself as this leadership. Its aim was to expose what it considered to be the violent colonizing nature of Polish rule in Ukrainian territories. It did, however, give support to the election campaigns of individual figures like Dmytro Paliiv, who had been in the leadership of UVO before he was given a seat on the Central Committee of UNDO in 1925. Friendly relations continued to exist between many leaders in both the legal and underground sectors of Ukrainian political life, relations that had been formed in student days and during military service in the Ukrainian armed forces (ibid. 192).

These terrorist acts often led to arrests, convictions, and executions, but they were effective political propaganda and attracted young people to the organization. Stepan Kasiian, in one of the more candid and self-critical memoirs written by a member of the OUN, has described the mood of young people in the 1920s: "We saw how [. . .] the communists were gaining ground. We felt that the people instinctively desired some determined, stronger means of conducting the struggle. And although we were young and at that time lacked political experience, we thought that the legal work accomplished so far in the cultural, economic and political fields was insufficient" (Kasiian 1967, 8). At a congress held in Vienna in 1929, the UVO fused with a number of clandestine student organizations to create the Organization of Ukrainian Nationalists (OUN). Arsons and robberies, which were encouraged by the organization and committed by student youth, swept through Galicia in the first half of 1930.[6] The Polish government, applying the principle of collective responsibility, responded in the second part of the year with a wave of repression known as the Pacification campaign. Thousands were severely beaten (reports put the number of dead at seven), and much property was ruined. According to official sources, 450 villages were surrounded either by the police or army, told to pay contributions, and then destroyed when the money was not produced. Often the fact that someone subscribed to a Ukrainian newspaper or sent their child to a Ukrainian school was the pretext for violence (Smolii 2002, 550). Yuliian Holovinsky, the OUN leader in Galicia, was murdered, and many institutions were closed down, including cooperatives, Prosvita branches, the scouting organization Plast, and the sporting organizations Luh and Sokil. Ukrainian political groups, including the OUN, tried to bring these events to the attention of the international community. Oleksander Shulhin, who represented the exiled UNR government in Paris, and Ukrainian members of the Sejm like Milena Rudnytska protested to the League of Nations. However, on 30 January 1932, the Council of the League of Nations concluded that Poland did not conduct "any policy of persecution against the Ukrainians," in this way disposing of the complaints (Budurowycz 1983, 488).

The Sanacja regime, as the leadership of Poland in the years 1926–39 was popularly known (from the Latin *sanatio,* or "healing"), was created by Piłsudski's armed coup of May 1926. It restricted civil rights and parliamentary procedures and tried to establish a strong executive. Pro-Ukrainian politicians like Tadeusz Holówko made attempts to negotiate resolutions to the conflict with Ukrainians, but the drift was toward repression and forced assimilation. On 13 September 1934, the Polish foreign minister Józef Beck informed the League that his government would not cooperate with international bodies in the supervision of minorities until a uniform scheme was adopted by all countries, and in the following year Poland formally renounced all guarantees it had given to minorities.[7] After Piłsudski's death the government aimed at a complete socioeconomic transformation of its southeastern regions through colonization, restrictions on the development of non-Polish groups, and the creation of artificial divisions among different Ukrainian populations. This period also saw the growth of official anti-semitism. The Endeks demanded the distribution of Jewish-owned land to Poles and threatened the Jewish population with deportation. Restrictions on ritual slaughter by Jewish butchers was introduced in 1936. Separate ghetto-benches were installed for Jews in university auditoriums and parks, and discrimination was practiced in employment.

Throughout the interwar years Ukrainians showed a remarkable tenacity in maintaining their historical identity and opposing the government's attempts to de-nationalize them. They insisted on their status as a separate people with territorial and political ambitions. From around 1933 increasing numbers of young people were drawn to conspiratorial forms of organization and terrorism. Trials of the OUN's members provided the organization with continuous publicity. In the 1930s, 16 were executed and 121 received sentences of over ten years for terrorist activity or membership in the organization. However, the government had miscalculated: the growth of national consciousness and solidarity was a far wider phenomenon than it thought. Many individuals who disagreed with the OUN's methods and ideology were, nonetheless, committed to the struggle for national rights. Repression often only strengthened support for militant action.

Interwar nationalism was also a response to events in Soviet Ukraine. The Ukrainian Soviet Socialist Republic had been created in 1923 as a concession to national aspirations. For a decade it conducted a policy of Ukrainianization, one that most observers saw as an attempt to fill a nominally independent republic with real Ukrainian cultural content. Already at its creation the republic had been forced to cede to Moscow control of foreign policy, the army, transport, foreign trade, industry, and finance, leaving it—formally at least—with agriculture, justice, education, and public health. Nonetheless, its cultural achievements in the 1920s were indisputable and widely applauded. In spite of its "socialist" terminology, the republic appeared to have placed national cultural development on the agenda. What is now known as the Cultural Renaissance attracted many Ukrainians from abroad. About fifty to sixty thousand Galician Ukrainians and exiles emigrated (or returned) from Poland to take part in the cultural reconstruction. They were joined by some prominent émigrés who had served in the government or military of the UNR. By returning to Kharkiv and Kyiv, these figures effectively legitimized the Soviet Republic as a Ukrainian state. Among them were Mykhailo Hrushevsky, the head of the Central Rada government in 1917, Andrii Nikovsky, a former minister of foreign affairs, and Yurii Tiutiunnyk, a legendary military leader. However, positive assessments of the Soviet Republic were voiced abroad much less frequently after 1933, when Ukrainianization was curtailed and news spread of mass arrests, show trials, and the Holodomor (Great Famine). These events fueled the OUN's militant and intransigent brand of nationalism.

It is important to recognize that in the interwar period, the OUN's ideology was not a majority creed in Western Ukraine or the emigration. Most Ukrainians held democratic views. Parties from across the political spectrum participated in vigorous press debates in spite of the censorship (which in Galicia meant that newspapers were often printed with blank pages to indicate suppressed articles). All political currents desired Ukraine's independence, or at least (as in the case of the UNDO) Galicia's autonomy. Ukrainian communists in the Communist Party of Western Ukraine (CPWU) also sought independence, which they envisaged in terms of Western Ukraine's annexation by the Soviet Ukrainian

Republic. As Snyder has indicated, by using the national and land question to attract Ukrainians to revolution, the CPWU's propagandists, who were mostly Ukrainians and Jews, became articulators of Ukrainian nationalism (Snyder 2010b, 82). Volodymyr Martynets, a leading ideologist of the OUN, wrote that this generation came out of what he called the Sturm und Drang period of the early 1920s: "It was a time when I, a nationalist, could for several weeks (on my own) give talks in the communist student Hromada (Collective), arguing the absurdity and unreality of communist concepts. But is this, in fact, so strange when one considers that these communists fought for Ukrainian post-secondary schools in Lviv alongside others in the common anti-Polish front?" (Martynets 1949, 20). Even though individuals later joined different groups, Martynets felt that they were all bound by the same experience of war and prisoner-of-war camps, and they often found a common language more quickly than "like-minded" party members. In the minds of many observers, what primarily distinguished the OUN from other political currents was its advocacy of militant revolutionary struggle and its uncompromising demand that all lands with majority Ukrainian populations should form a state independent of both Moscow and Warsaw. If convinced by the organization's "maximalist" tactics and strategy, young people often quickly accepted the OUN's ideology of single-party rule and implacable hostility to all opposition, which was analogous to the communist commitment to a "dictatorship of the proletariat" and an overthrow of bourgeois society.

As Ukrainian society mobilized itself in response to government repression, cultural life in Galicia showed strong signs of vitality. One observer described it as "a state within a state" (Shlemkevych 1956, 73). By 1936 the Prosvita society had recovered from the repression of the early 1920s. It boasted 3,071 libraries and reading halls, 377 theatre groups, 1,086 choirs, 124 orchestras, 122 women's organizations, and 275,324 members (Kosyk 1993, 35). In response to the government's closing of Ukrainian schools, the Ridna Shkola movement raised community funds to create private schools. By the end of the 1930s it had 605 kindergartens and 33 elementary, 12 secondary, and 11 professional schools (ibid., 34). In 1937–38, 59 percent of Ukrainian gymnasia (high schools), teacher-training colleges, and technical schools, which represented 40 percent of Ukrainian students at those levels, were run privately (Magocsi 2010, 637). The Underground Ukrainian University, which existed in the years 1921–25, provided a network of courses in a variety of disciplines, including philosophy, law, and medicine. Fifty departments with more than two thousand students were supported by professors based in Czechoslovakia (in the Ukrainian Free University and the Academy of Economics), by Lviv's Shevchenko Scientific

Society, and by hundreds of Ukrainian students at universities and polytechnical institutes in Vienna and other European cities. The Polish police disrupted classes, confiscated books and materials, and arrested professors and students. However, the desire for university education in Ukrainian was strong. Already in the early 1900s, mass student demonstrations in Lviv had demanded the creation of a Ukrainian university. The Austrian government was forced to expand the number of departments that taught in Ukrainian and, on the eve of the war, agreed to create a Ukrainian university.

Self-organization led in the early 1920s to the establishment in Lviv of a self-financed Ukrainian hospital, one that became both a teaching and treatment center. By 1938 it served forty-one thousand patients (68.8 percent were Ukrainians, 22 percent Poles, 9.2 percent Jews, Germans, or other nationalities). Community mobilization also generated the publication of many newspapers and books, the organization of banks, agricultural and trading cooperatives, and the spread of professional organizations and youth groups. These last continued to exist illegally after they were banned, forming in this way part of the semi-conspiratorial culture that developed throughout Galicia.

The national democratic movement condemned the OUN's authoritarian ideology and terrorist tactics. The UNDO's newspaper *Dilo* was the most vocal opponent, but censure also came from periodicals like the Catholic *Nedilia* (Sunday), *Nova zoria* (New Star), *Meta* (Goal), the relatively moderate *Ukrainski visti* (Ukrainian News), *My* (We), *Nazustrich* (Welcome) and *Shliakh natsii* (The Nation's Path), the pro-labour *Hromadskyi holos* (Community Voice), and the pro-Soviet *Novi shliakhy* (New Paths). Alternative views of the relationship between nation and state were voiced. A Christian humanist perspective that stressed respect for religious tolerance and democratic norms was presented, for example, in Havryil Kostelnyk's *Hranytsi demokratyzmu* (Limits of Democratism, 1919). In his opinion, Europe's greatest historical transformation had been accomplished by Christianity, which had turned societies away from paganism, had spread respect for the individual and equal treatment before the law, and had stimulated democratization. This continuing spiritual revolution required the support of Christian churches. The social democrat Volodymyr Starosolsky wrote *Teoriia natsii* (Theory of the Nation, 1922), which distinguished between two kinds of society—the community (*spilnota*) and the association or union (*spilka*). The first represented instinctive or elemental will, while the second represented rational or conscious will, although in practice the two were rarely entirely separate because, argued the author, the psychological-emotional and logical-rational always intersected in the lives of individuals and communities. Nations and national mythologies, he argued, are not the products of abstract logic alone but also "of practical, social and psychological necessities, whose laws in social reality are far stronger and more fruitful than the laws of formal logic" (Starosolskyi 1922, 70). To consider rational thought as the only force governing human conduct would be to miss an essential feature in human development: "the rational is mixed with the irrational, thinking with feelings and drives, logic with psychology, especially with group psychology, conscious-ness with elemental will. Similarly the struggle of peoples for state power occurs not only under the direction of rational thought, but also together with and under the direction of elemental psychic processes." He identified the two main social drives as democracy "in the sphere consciousness" and nation "in the sphere of elemental will" (ibid., 71–72).

Democrats criticized authoritarianism in all its forms, pointing out that bolshevism and fascism had common traits: adherents to both believed in the ultimate triumph of violence and dictatorship and treated the mass of the popu-lation with contempt. In 1932 Vasyl Koroliv-Staryi, a writer and lecturer in the Ukrainian Academy of Economics in Czechoslovakia, who had earlier worked in the UNR mission in Prague, wrote a pamphlet under the pseudonym M. Petryshyn, in which he commented:

> In an oppressed people all classes and all parties are by force of circumstance national, or, if you like, "nationalist" in tenor. This is a revolutionary, progres-sive nationalism, because it struggles for a people's freedom, against oppressors. Therefore the name OUN—"Nationalists"—is inappropriate and unjustified in the Ukrainian reality, since there is no independent political grouping that does not have as its goal the struggle for Ukraine's national independence, for national liberation. In countries that have independent states "nationalist" is used by parties that want to oppress and conquer other peoples. This character-izes the Polish "national democracy" that is ready to swallow Ukrainians, and the same goal was set by the "Russian nationalists" before the 1917 revolution. (Petryshyn 1932, 7)

He criticized the OUN for demanding exclusive and dictatorial powers, for its violent tactics, and its stress on "the irrational will." Terror, he argued, was not a sign of an organization's strength, but of its weakness. It isolated a group and prevented open and full engagement with the broad population. The need for conspiracy and secrecy inevitably led to degeneration and sectarianism. Moreover, it was wrong to spread contempt for organizational work in the economic and cultural spheres, because this turned people away from the hard work of building a community and nation and impelled them instead toward romantic daydreaming. By being drawn into terror, many young people both wasted the opportunity of receiving an education and suffered a stunting of their moral instincts (ibid., 17). Even before Hitler came to power, this commentator warned against placing faith in Western right-wing parties and governments, which would only use the Ukrainian national movement for their own ends (ibid., 30, 34). He concluded: "Our 'Nationalists' speak fine words about the nation being above classes and parties, but their actions contradict this. They place their party's interests above those of the nation. They do not take into account the real interests and desires of the Ukrainian people, but dream only of their future dictatorship and how to advertise themselves in the contemporary world" (ibid., 36). It has been reported that for a long time, members of the OUN tried without success to discover the identity of the pamphlet's author (Zięba 2010, 637–38).

In 1932 a botched "expropriation" conducted at the post office in Horodok by OUN members caused the death of one policeman and the wounding of two others. A member of the raiding party was killed; another shot himself after being wounded. Two students, Dmytro Danylyshyn and Vasyl Bilas, were tried and executed. The death sentence of a third, Mariian Zhurakivsky, was commuted to fifteen years imprisonment. A fourth accused, Zenon Kossak, received seven years. Local Ukrainians had called the police and captured the robbers. As he was being bound, Danylyshyn said, "You will never see a Ukraine if this is the way you fight for it" (Cherevatenko 1994, 374; Mirchuk 1968, 308). Bilas and Danylyshyn behaved courageously at the trial, making it clear that they were patriots. The defense lawyers (Starosolsky, Stepan Shukhevych, Lev Hankevych) spoke eloquently and were given widespread publicity. Starosolsky compared Ukrainian nationalism to liberation movements in Finland, Latvia, Brittany, Ireland, and Catalonia (Mirchuk 1968, 312). The event shocked Galicians into the realization that the OUN was becoming a mass movement. Although public opinion was mostly appalled by the raid, the trial was an effective propaganda tool for the organization. Rudnytska reported: "We have not had a trial like this in over twelve years, and no event has shaken our nation so deeply, found such a resonance among the broad masses, and united, at least for a short time, all citizens in a single feeling, as has the death of Danylyshyn and Bilas. The moral strength of two boys of limited education, their faith in an idea, their simply unbelievable behavior, have made not only them [. . .] emerge as bright heroes but cast a similar light on the organization to which they belonged" (quoted in Onatskyi 1984, 19). *Dilo*, the Catholic *Meta*, and other papers condemned the Horodok raid. Yevhen Konovalets, the OUN's leader who was then living in Geneva, while praising the behavior of Bilas and Danylyshyn at the trial, censured the action's organizers. An internal review took place, and the leader of the Homeland Executive was relieved of his duties (Mirchuk 1968, 322).

Condemnation was even stronger when the violence was turned against Ukrainian society. The OUN paper *Nash klych* (Our Call), which appeared briefly in Lviv before being banned by Polish authorities, created a scandal when it failed to censure students who boycotted the conference and parades of a Catholic organization called Ukrainian Youth for Christ (Ukrainska Molod Khrystovi). The parades were held in the first week of May, on the nineteen hundredth anniversary of Christ's death. On 5 May 1933, *Dilo* reported that the boycotters had thrown stones and jeered participants ("Zhertvy" 1933). One outraged writer charged the Nationalists with placing the nation above God and warned that not all means of struggle were justifiable and ethical (Konrad 1933). When it became clear that public opinion was massively on the side of the Church, the boycott was dropped.[8] The OUN also disrupted the commemoration of Ivan Franko, which was held at the writer's grave. It stoned the young girls who participated as members of the sporting organization Luh. The justification offered was that Luh and its head, Roman Dashkevych, cooperated with government authorities: the organization wore uniforms similar to those of Polish youth, marched behind the Polish flag, and appeared alongside Polish youth at official state events (Orshan 1938a, 26; Pankivskyi 1983, 139–40). Celebrations of the sporting organization Sokil were also disrupted because, it was charged, its leaders ignored the bidding of the OUN and hired the orchestra of the Lviv streetcar workers, which was composed almost entirely of Poles (Pankivskyi 1983, 140).

Andrei Sheptytsky, the metropolitan of the Ukrainian Greek Catholic Church, condemned the killing of Ivan Babii, the respected director of a Ukrainian gymnasium (high school) in Lviv, who had prevented his students from distributing Nationalist leaflets. After first being severely beaten as a warning, Babii was murdered on 25 July 1934, on Stepan Bandera's order. Babii had been an officer in the Ukrainian Galician Army. The metropolitan had appointed him to leadership of Lviv's Catholic Action group, and he had helped organize the Youth for Christ festival. A student assassin shot Babii in the back several times, then, after failing to escape, turned the gun on himself. Before dying in the hospital he admitted that he had acted on the organization's orders (ibid.). Sheptytsky called the killing "an act of common banditry" and stated that every parent cursed "leaders who drew youth into the dead end of crime" (Smolii 2002, 567–68). He warned that an amoral patriotism driven by bloodthirst, anger, and hatred was blind and constituted a dangerous threat to real patriotism, since it could at any moment rebound against its own people: "If you wish to treacherously kill those who oppose your work, you will have to kill all professors and teachers who work for Ukrainian youth, all parents and mothers of Ukrainian children, all guardians and leaders of educational institutions, all political and civic activists" (Sheptytskyi 2009, 177–78). Bandera claimed that Babii by his actions had worked against the revolutionary underground (Mirchuk 1968, 369).

The OUN's relationship to the Church was troubled. John Armstrong was no doubt correct when he stated that within the émigré leadership there remained "strong elements of liberal and democratic, as well as Christian, principles, even when the participants in the movement verbally rejected them" (Armstrong 1963, 23). Andrii Melnyk, who took over the OUN's leadership after Konovalets's assassination in 1938, had in the years 1933–38 headed the Catholic Association of Ukrainian Youth (known as Orly—"Eagles") and had strong clerical sympathies. He was held in high regard by church leaders like the Archbishop of Lviv, Ivan Buchko. Monsignor Avgustyn Voloshyn, the priest who headed the government of Carpatho-Ukraine in 1938–39, praised Melnyk as a cultured European with an ideology founded on Christianity, and he contrasted him with many Nationalists who placed the nation above God (Interview for *Nastup*, 21 December 1940; quoted in Armstrong 1963, 38). However, the Catholic political parties and civic-religious organizations spoke out against the OUN and conflict with the Church lasted throughout the interwar years. Catholic writers denounced the OUN's ideology as an attempt to sacralize politics and create a political religion. The Catholic camp rejected integral nationalism, and especially Dontsovism, as "incompatible with Christian ethics" (Behen, Zaitsev, and Stefaniv 2011, 317). The Homeland Executive of the OUN (its Galician leadership) in turn accused the Catholic parties, along with other opponents, of acting as police informers or of potentially becoming informers "as a result of their political convictions" (ibid., 314).

In the 1930s the Nationalists payed attention to church-state relations in Italy. Yevhen Onatsky, the OUN's representative in Rome, had good contacts with the Ukrainian Catholic hierarchy and Vatican. He informed Konovalets throughout the thirties of the modus vivendi that had been established between the Roman Catholic Church and Mussolini's government. He reported, for example, on the agreement reached on 3 September 1931, according to which the Church obliged itself to refrain from social and political work, to use the Italian flag in its activities, and to allow members of its Catholic Action organization to be members of the Fascist Party (Onatskyi 1981, 191). However, the younger generation in Galicia was more anticlerical than the émigré leadership. Bishop Hryhorii Khomyshyn of Stanyslaviv (Stanislawów) was particularly disliked. He was considered a *khrun* (sellout or collaborator) for supporting the Latinization of the Ukrainian Greek Catholic Church and the celibacy of the priesthood. The bishop saw no contradiction between remaining loyal to the Polish state and conducting a struggle for Ukrainian rights. He obtained permission to hang the banned Ukrainian flag next to the Polish one on 11 November, Polish independence day, as a sign of support for the Poles, and argued that the Ukrainian population should adopt "a loyal attitude towards the state in which we live," and so give the Poles "no reason to oppress and persecute us" (Budurowycz 1983, 490). In a pastoral letter of April 1931, he wrote: "Not the Council of Ambassadors, but God's Providence has placed us, a part of the Ukrainian people, under the rule of the Polish state and we must submit to this arrangement. [. . .] Even if the state oppresses and persecutes us, we must always and everywhere express our loyalty" (Cherchenko 2007, 505–6). He criticized the lobbying campaign mounted in Western Europe by the Nationalists in the wake of Pacification, arguing that the goal of international censure had not been achieved, and instead of "looking reality in the face" and assimilating the required lesson, "the Nationalist press continues to hypnotize the nation and keep it in the dark" (Khomyshyn 1933; quoted in Zięba 2010, 689). Onatsky wrote that the bishop described the Nationalists as "Satan's children" (Onatskyi 1984, 36). Khomyshyn was a particular target because of his active involvement in politics. In 1932 he was instrumental in the creation of the Ukrainska Katolytska Narodna Partiia (Ukrainian Catholic People's Party), which was later renamed the Ukrainska Narodna Obnova (Ukrainian Popular Revival) and whose organs were *Nova zoria* (New Star) and *Pravda* (Truth). *Nova zoria*'s editor from 1928 was Osyp Nazaruk, who carried on a spirited polemic with Dontsov and integral nationalism.[9] One recent researcher has summed up the Church's attitude as follows: "We can affirm that the Catholic camp found Ukrainian integral nationalism deeply unacceptable, especially in its Dontsovian version, which proclaimed the superiority of action over thought and a particular morality that was incompatible with Christian ethics. The greatest alarm among representatives of the Church was caused by the tendency to transform nationalism into a secular religion that threatened to marginalize or engulf traditional Christianity" (Stefaniv 2011, 317).

The UVO and OUN also attacked Orthodox Church leaders whom they considered pro-government. In 1923, as a high school student in Kamenets, Ulas Smachuk was selected and prepared for the assassination of Dionysius, the Ukrainian Orthodox Church's metropolitan bishop of Warsaw and Volhynia, who had agreed to participate in celebrating the Polish constitution. Samchuk pulled back from the killing, and later described the experience in his postwar novel *Iunist Vasylia Sheremety* (The Youth of Vasyl Sheremeta, 1946–47).

On the other hand, some Nationalists found the mystical elements in religiosity attractive. Writing in *Rozbudova natsii* (Development of Nation) in 1932, Yevhen Liakhovych stated, "the historical goals of the state always demand religious ecstasy." He argued that "national feelings have all the characteristics of religious feelings" and that it was the church's duty to "fill itself with national content and to recognize national perfection as one element of eternal perfection" (Liakhovych 1932, 280–81). Other Nationalists appeared to place the struggle for a state above the Church, Christianity, and God. Dmytro Myron (pseudonym Maksym Orlyk) was drawn to the idea of the Church as a militant, fanatical, crusading power, and saw the value of Christianity in the fact that it had united the nation and formed the national soul. He wrote in 1940 that a rebirth of the national spirit should go hand in hand with a renewal of Christianity: "Simultaneously with the name of Christ the child has to be taught the great sacred name of Ukraine. Simultaneously with the cross it should receive the national flag and trident. Why should the Ukrainian child sooner and better know the names of Abraham, Isaac or Moses than those of such Ukrainian rulers as Volodymyr the Great, Princess Olha, Khmelnytsky or those Cossacks who fought and died on fields and in galleys for 'the faith of their fathers'?" (Myron 2009, 189). These more-radical views expressing suspicion of the Church's universal, supra-national status were particularly evident after 1938, when the shift toward a Dontsovian spirit became pronounced among the OUN's Galician leaders.

From the mid-1930s what the UNDO member Kost Pankivsky later called a "hysterical" nationalism began to win over Galician youth. The new cadres differed from the disciplined soldiers who had founded the OUN. A subtle but inexorable transformation was occurring as youth was drawn to integral nationalism:

> Most were sick of the cold realism of "old style" politicians who moreover were branded as failures and defeatists. The organization offered this youth a unifying "cause" that was interesting and useful. People who thirsted for action were drawn into "campaigns"—against participation in elections to the Polish Sejm, against communists, against Polish landowners, etc. Young people who had nothing constructive to do, could express themselves in the conviction that they were doing really patriotic work, fighting enemies, including their own turncoats and sell-outs. [. . .] On the quiet Galician land, in the ranks of the OUN a new type of fanatical professional revolutionary was born; blindly obedient to the leadership, dedicated even unto death, believing only in the nation and revolution, his slogan became "Nation above all!" (Pankivskyi 1983, 138)

Although most democrats were appalled by the violent acts and authoritarian views, some were not unsympathetic to the existence of a terrorist wing in the national liberation movement. Volodymyr Kuzmovych, a member of UNDO and former member of UVO, spoke of the need to "correlate legal and illegal work, so that they support one another" (Onatskyi 1981, 75). Roman Smal-Stotsky, who was viewed by Nationalists as a lackey of the Poles, is said to have commented: "If our underground did not exist, it would have to be created" (Kedryn-Rudnytsky 1976, 351). The reason for such opinions is not hard to find. Even such public expressions of national identity as raising the Ukrainian flag or singing patriotic songs were greeted with state violence. Possession of literature was cause for arrest. A student caught with the Decalogue (the "Ten Declarations" of a Nationalist) could be thrown out of school and sent to jail (Luciuk and Carynnyk 1990, 61). At the international level, promises given first to the Western democracies and then to the "democratic" Ukrainian opposition in Poland had not been kept, while the tragedy of the Holodomor, the Great Famine of 1932–33 in Soviet Ukraine that took several million lives, had been largely ignored in the West. As a result, some parliamentarians were prepared to give tacit support to stronger measures in order to attract the attention of Western opinion. They tried to coordinate a politics that operated on parallel tracks: one legal, the other illegal. Supporters of such combined tactics were perhaps "merely waiting for an international configuration that would permit them to realize their aspirations to nationhood," but Polish authorities frequently regarded all Ukrainians as potential terrorists and irredentists (who, like the Italian nationalist movement of the nineteenth century, wanted to consolidate all territories in which they were a majority into an independent state) and therefore dismissed "all attempts to reach an accommodation as insincere and opportunistic" (Budurowycz 1983, 484). In the mid-1930s, as Ukrainian public opinion expressed increasing frustration with a pro-Polish, pro-democratic orientation, dissatisfaction with the legal or "organic" work of the UNDO and the UNR increased. An agreement had been reached in 1935 by the UNDO with the Polish government. It went by the name "Normalization." Ukrainians were offered nineteen seats in both houses of parliament (the Sejm and the Senate), an amnesty for political prisoners, and some financing of economic organizations. The OUN's press characterized this as a move by career politicians to protect their jobs and privileges. When the Polish government refused the candidacies of Dmytro Levytsky and Milena Rudnytska, the women's organization Soiuz Ukrainok (Union of Women) broke with the UNDO and joined the election boycott. Moreover, the UNDO was prevented from campaigning outside Galicia. Its activists in Volhynia were kept under police surveillance, arrested, and imprisoned. In an attempt to quarantine Volhynia, the activity of the educational society Prosvita was suspended in 1932 and Ukrainian cooperatives in Volhynia were closed or amalgamated with Polish ones (Sycz 1999, 27–29; Snyder 2005, 69). Disappointment with the Normalization agreement immediately led to a split in the UNDO.

On the other hand, however, a number of former members of the UVO broke with the OUN in order to conduct legal political work. Dmytro Paliiv worked for the UNDO in the years 1925–33. He edited the newspapers *Batkivshchyna* (Fatherland, 1934–39) and *Ukrainski visti* (Ukrainian News, 1935–39), and wrote for *Novyi chas* (New Time) and other periodicals that were owned by Ivan Tyktor's publishing company, the largest and most successful in Western Ukraine. Along with two other former members of the UVO, Volodymyr Tselevych and Liubomyr Makarushka, he belonged to the so-called "opposition group" within UNDO. After being expelled from the UNDO, Paliiv created his own party, the Front Nationalnoi Iednosti (Front of National Unity), which was a radical nationalist competitor of the OUN, although it was committed to open debate.[10] Zenon Pelensky also quit the OUN in 1934 to edited the UNDO's organ *Svoboda* (Freedom).

The communist press also supported terrorism—by its own party. It described the Polish regime as "fascist" and Ukrainians who tried to deal with it—including Petliura, the UNR, and the UNDO—as agents of Polish fascism. The Soviet press in 1923 defined *Literaturno-naukovyi vistnyk* (Literary-Scientific Herald) as "fascist," but in the late 1920s made a distinction between the views of its editor Dontsov, who encouraged "a spontaneous brutality" and "willpower" by promoting voluntarism, and those of Italian fascism, which used state power to create an imperialist mentality. Dontsov's ideas, explained the journal, were a reaction to the pro-Polish stance of Ukrainian politicians and to Poland's inability to deal with the national question (G. Motyka 2006b, 73). In 1929 the Soviet view was that the Communist Party of Western Ukraine (CPWU) was leading the national liberation struggle against both Polish and homegrown "fascisms" and that the OUN was merely surfing a wave of legitimate revolutionary anger. In 1929 an article in the Kharkiv journal *Bilshovyk Ukrainy* (Bolshevik of Ukraine) called for educating the masses "in a spirit of proletarian nationalism" (Bratkivskyi 1929, 84). Soviet commentators claimed that the arsons throughout Poland were the work of revolutionary communists. One observer wryly suggested that in reality perhaps as many as half the fires were lit by the estate owners themselves in order to collect government insurance, while responsibility for the other half could be divided evenly between the OUN and the communists (Petryshyn 1932, 22).[11]

In the 1920s Moscow used the popular Ukrainianization policy to interfere in Polish affairs. It played the Piedmont card—the idea that Soviet Ukraine was the best option around which to build the future unified Ukrainian state. However, by the end of the twenties a change had occurred. Firstly, the CPWU, which operated as an autonomous section of the Communist Party of Poland, sharply criticized the Soviet Ukraine's national policy. It was particularly angered by the removal in 1927 of Oleksandr Shumsky, who had been in charge of Ukrainianization. Moreover, although Shumsky's Galician supporters were purged from the CPWU in 1928, the Ukrainians who remained continued to challenge Soviet policy. Secondly, in 1933 the Kremlin backtracked on its position that Russian chauvinism was the greatest threat—something it had held since the Twelfth Congress of the Russian Communist Party (bolshevik) in 1923. It now decided that non-Russian nationalism posed the greatest threat. At this point the Piedmont principle abruptly turned against Moscow: observers began to see Western Ukraine as the territory around which the drive for independence could be consolidated. As a result, communist support began to dwindle among Ukrainians, although the CPWU remained a significant factor, particularly in Volhynia, into which the OUN did not penetrate until the late 1930s and where 70 percent of the population was Ukrainian. As a result, the CPWU became the radical alternative, presenting itself, for example, as a defender of the Ukrainian character of the Orthodox Church and opposing the forced conversions to Roman Catholicism (Snyder 2005, 167).

Western powers also played a role in the radicalization of nationalism. The Entente had brokered the postwar treaties but had made no attempt to restrain Poland in the latter's treatment of its Ukrainian minority. President Woodrow Wilson had proclaimed a policy of national self-determination. However, so had Lenin. Most Ukrainians considered these proclamations deceitful. In 1922 an official of the British foreign office in London wrote: "More harm would in the end be done by unnecessary interference than, even at the risk of a little local suffering, to allow those minorities to settle down under their present masters. [. . .] So long as these people imagine that their grievances can be aired before the League of Nations they will refuse to settle down and the present effervescence will continue indefinitely" (Mazower 1999, 55). Although the League was able to refer cases of abuse to the Permanent Court of International Justice in The Hague, it rarely did so. On the contrary, not only did it fail to champion minorities but it prevented them from appealing directly to the court. Neither the French nor the British were perturbed by the state repression. Weimar Germany lobbied for more intervention because of its concern with the millions of ethnic Germans throughout Eastern Europe, but these efforts were mostly dismissed as attempts to revise the postwar settlement (ibid.) The USSR was allowed to join the League of Nations in 1934 in spite of its trampling of political and religious freedoms and its denial of the Great Famine (Holodomor). Antony Eden, the British foreign minister at the time, reassured questioners that the USSR had agreed to fulfill all its responsibilities as a member of the League. He also refused to countenance any action when Poland officially informed the League that it would not honor its guarantees concerning minorities (Onatskyi 1989, 344).

Some sympathetic Western commentators described the Ukrainian issue as Poland's "Irish Question." Ukrainians, they pointed out, had a different religion from the Roman Catholic Poles and constituted a majority in the rural population of Galicia. Lviv was compared to an "intensely Polish Belfast set down in a Ukrainian Munster and coveted by the Sinn Fein" (Kirkconnell 1939, 85), and the outlawed OUN was compared to the Irish Republican Army. Ireland's example was also invoked by Ukrainians. A booklet by M. Hryhorovych entitled *Iak Irlandia zdobula sobi voliu* (How Ireland Gained Its Freedom, 1924) described the road to Home Rule. Martynets wrote that the OUN was influenced by Russian, Irish, and Polish terrorism. He indicated that in the prewar years Piłsudski had himself conducted expropriations and was lauded for this in the interwar Polish press, a fact that Nationalists raised when their own members were put on trial. They maintained that they had never called the Poles "bandits" for conducting expropriations, and rejected this description of themselves (Martynets 1949, 66, 76).

The main press organs of the OUN were the journals *Surma* (Bugle) and *Rozbudova natsii* (Development of Nation), which began appearing in the late 1920s in Berlin and Prague respectively. *Ukrainske slovo* (Ukrainian Word, 1933–40) appeared in Paris, *Proboiem* (Breakthrough, 1933–44) was published in Prague, and *Samostiina dumka* (Independent Thought, 1931–37) in Romanian-ruled Chernivtsi. In Galicia the Lviv newspaper *Holos* (Voice, 1938–39) was influential. It replaced *Holos natsii*, (Nation's Voice, 1936–37) and was edited by Bohdan Kravtsiv. The journals *Literaturno-naukovyi vistnyk* (Literary-Scientific Herald, 1922–32) and its successor *Vistnyk* (Herald, 1933–39) were both edited by Dontsov. Although neither was a party organ, Dontsov's influence was crucial in turning Western Ukrainian youth toward a cultish form of nationalism, one that the Catholic journalist Osyp Nazaruk warned in 1927 would "transform men into beasts" (Budurowycz 1983, 483).

The OUN's leadership in Galicia, the so-called Homeland Executive (Kraiova ekzekutyva), was formally subordinated to Yevhen Konovalets and the émigré leadership of the OUN, but in fact worked independently. It was made up of young people, often students, who developed their own underground network and tactics of mass mobilization. They organized boycotts of the Polish state monopolies of alcohol and tobacco. One of the most successful mobilizations was the "School Action" of 1933–34. Ninety thousand leaflets and five thousand brochures were distributed encouraging students to speak only Ukrainian, remove Polish symbols, and display the banned Ukrainian flag. During church services celebrating Rosalia (Zeleni sviata, a festival commemorating the dead that is held fifty days after Easter), leaflets were handed out honoring those who had died in the battles of Makivka and Lysonia. The first was the site at which Ukrainian Sich Riflemen had won a famous victory against the Russian army in 1915, and the second was the field on which the same Riflemen had fought the Russian army in 1916 and on which the Ukrainian Galician Army had fought the Poles in 1919. Some commemorations became demonstrations of national strength that turned violent. Twenty thousand visited Makivka on one occasion. Two communists who protested the commemoration were killed, and in the local town the windows of others were smashed (Mirchuk 1968, 452). The OUN's leadership in Galicia encouraged a cult of the fallen soldier, which included processions to cemeteries, church services, and the erection of symbolic graves to those who had given their lives in the struggle for independence. These graves were often destroyed by the police but would invariably be restored the following day. Through such mobilizations the organization hoped to develop a strategy of "permanent revolution" that would radicalize the entire population. Mass actions were most prominent during 1933–35, when Stepan Bandera took over leadership of the Homeland Executive. He also extended the use of terrorism, in particular the assassination of Ukrainians who were considered Sovietophiles, or who opposed the OUN. Sometimes the decision to assassinate was taken without informing the émigré leadership or even the rest of the Executive. Konovalets, for example, confided to Kedryn that he was shocked by the assassination on 27 September 1931 of Tadeusz Holówko, the Polish politician who had promoted the policy of Prometheanism and had sought a modus vivendi with Ukrainians (Kedryn 1976, 227). There is some doubt whether this act was intended by the OUN, since it reflected badly on the organization and undermined the campaign against Pacification. Polish intelligence concluded that it was the work of Soviet agents who had probably penetrated the OUN (Snyder 2005, 76–77).[12] Other high-profile assassinations included that of Aleksei Mailov, an official in the Soviet consulate in Lviv, who was killed in 1933 in retaliation for the Great Famine, and that of Bronisław Pieracki, the Polish minister of the interior, who was killed in 1934 in retaliation for the Pacification campaign.

The émigré leadership differed temperamentally from the young students in the Galician membership. The émigrés worked more openly than the highly conspiratorial underground in Galicia, and were more attuned to the importance of diplomacy and debate. Even as they scoffed at the ineffectiveness of legal parties, they worked with them. Konovalets, for instance, met with eleven Ukrainian parliamentarians from the Polish Sejm who visited Berlin and Geneva in 1928 and facilitated their contact with German authorities. The extensive publicity exposing the Pacification campaign resulted from a joint effort by various groups.[13] The lobbying at the League of Nations by Milena Rudnytska from the UNDO and Oleksandr Shulhin from the UNR office in Paris was supplemented by the OUN's *Na vichnu hanbu Polshchi* (To Poland's Eternal Shame, 1931), a collection of documents, photographs, and eyewitness accounts, and the articles its press bureaus placed in Western newspapers. In 1930–31 over seven hundred memoranda protesting Polish policies were sent to the League (which, according to postwar treaties, was supposed to oversee Poland's treatment of Ukrainians) and to other international agencies.[14] In the 1920s, according to Martynets, no one from the UNDO questioned the need for the UVO's existence, and in the 1930s, even while criticizing the OUN, some members of the UNDO worked with it (Martynets 1949, 297). Rudnytska met Konovalets on her trips to Western Europe, and her meeting with Mussolini in 1933 was arranged by Yevhen Onatsky, the OUN's representative in Rome. During the interview, she discussed the possibility of support for the Ukrainian cause at international forums and state grants for Nationalist youth to study at Italian colleges (Onatskyi 1984, 66, 76–79).[15] However, soon afterward, when Mussolini signed a letter of cooperation with the USSR, Rudnytska wrote him an angry letter (Cherchenko 2007, 514). Two other members of the UNDO, Dmytro Paliiv and Ivan Kedryn, acted as the party's liaison with Konovalets. Kedryn was even invited to attend part of the OUN's founding congress in 1929, where he argued for the importance of legal political work (Muravsky 2006, 326).

Konovalets accepted the need for a party in the "legal sector" and did not absolutize violence, as the UVO's popular literature pointed out (*U.V.O.* 1929, 15). The argument was that acts of a "primitive state of nature" had been forced upon the UVO and reflected "the mood of the entire people." It would seem that with its own state, apparatus, money, army, and police, Poland "should conduct the struggle with an internal enemy using legal means, as indicated by its own laws" (ibid., 29). Instead, it practiced mass detainment, long-term imprisonment without trial, and prisoner abuse. Konovalets originally conceived of the OUN as a legal umbrella organization for which the UVO would be the "military wing." According to Motyl, during the interwar period at least sixty-three assassinations or attempted assassinations took place in Galicia and Volhynia, although the real figure could have been higher since some remained unreported. Over two-thirds of these killings were the work of the OUN. Eleven targeted prominent Poles and Ukrainians, while the rest targeted Ukrainians who were considered collaborators. The total victim count was thirty-six Ukrainians (only one of whom was a communist), twenty-five Poles, one Russian and one Jew (Motyl 1985, 50).

In a letter to Onatsky written on 17 June 1932, Konovalets described how he envisioned revolution:

> We still have not even clarified what our national revolution should look like, what its content should be, its methods and its goals. A national revolution, in my opinion, is a wider concept than sabotage, terrorist acts, even mass unrest, or uprisings. All these are merely means, which should not be immediately rejected and eliminated from our program, but simultaneously we must realize that all this, even when taken together, still does not exhaust the concept of national revolution as a movement that ought to make not only a fundamental change in [political] reality but also in the psychology of our whole people. A national revolution should not aim merely at gaining for the Ukrainian people a state that collapses the following day, but should already in the preparatory stage change the psychic structure of Ukrainian citizenry, allowing it to participate in preparing this revolution. (Quoted in Onatskyi 1981, 423)

He spoke of the national revolution as a "system" that could defend the Ukrainian state against dangers, and indicated that the key to success was winning a large majority of people over to the cause.

In 1930 an attempt was made to forge a relationship with the UNDO and other parliamentary parties—one that would allow the OUN to support Ukrainian candidates (Boidunyk 1974, 375–76; Mirchuk 1968, 247–48).

A number of commentators have pointed out that in the early 1930s the organization never satisfactorily resolved the contradiction between legal work and terrorism, or between mass organization and conspiratorial work (Boidunyk 1974, 374; Pelensky 1974, 520; Onatskyi 1974, 680). Kedryn and Pelensky argued that the OUN should adopt a two-track politics: it should develop a large, legal mass party and a small underground group for "military" action. They viewed the merger of the two as a tragic mistake. Onatsky too, in his correspondence with Konovalets, argued that a large, legal organization and a small, paramilitary one (which could be disowned when dealing with public opinion) required this. "We," he wrote in 1931, "have done the opposite: we have made a large illegal organization and disown everything legal." As a result, he argued, both legal and illegal work were hamstrung (Onatskyi 1981, 406).

The broader society was as impatient with the ineffectiveness of political parties as Nationalist youth. Osyp Nazaruk, who had served in the UNR government, commented in 1924 that future scholars would find it easier to count "all the political parties of the numerous Italian states and statelets in the Cinquecenta" than to list the Ukrainian parties of this period (Nazaruk 1924, 1). He felt that "endless unnecessary negotiations and meetings" distracted social attention from the most important tasks, and that many parties were ineffective and poorly equipped theoretically (ibid., 14, 18). This discontent was exploited by the Homeland Executive. However, this group was much more radical than mainstream Ukrainian society and more impatient than the émigré leadership. The young members of the Homeland Executive had not fought in the independence struggle, had not supported the UNR or tried to raise the Ukrainian question through contacts with international bodies, governments, and foreign presses. They were opposed to negotiating with legal parties in Galicia, whom they termed "opportunists" and "appeasers," and they romanticized terrorism in the spirit of nineteenth-century radicals. Effectively they made the organization into an expanded version of the UVO terrorist underground (Smolii 2002, 5). During an exchange between Konovalets and Bandera in 1933 at an OUN conference in Berlin, the leader explained that assassinations were only legitimate in self-defense against a state that used terror with impunity, a line that *Surma* had argued since 1929. The recent actions of the Galician leadership, he felt, could not be justified before the wider public. Moreover, the ensuing widespread arrests had damaged the organization's capability (Vretsona 1974, 476). Konovalets also explained the importance of contacts with parliamentarians. He stated that the revolutionary struggle was many-faceted and that every devoted Ukrainian could find a place within it; the work of those who did not belong to the organization should not be devalued, because the underground depended in large measure on the success of these "opportunists." He pointed out that members of the Ukrainian socialist parties, such as the social democrats Volodymyr Starosolsky and Lev Hankevych, acted as defense lawyers for accused Nationalists, and the very building in which the conference was taking place belonged to Dmytro Levytsky, the leader of the opposition group within the UNDO (ibid., 478–79). These admonitions were not heeded. Even the economic successes of the cooperative movement were seen by some "principled" radicals as forms of collaboration (Pelensky 1974, 512). The trend was toward ever-greater extremism, the cutting of ties with non-Nationalists, and the branding of "demosocialism" (democracy and socialism) as the source of all evil.

In justifying terror, the people around Bandera in the Galician leadership expressed much more rigid, fanatical views. They tended to define any criticism of their own methods as a betrayal of the nation. In 1936 during his trial, Bandera declared: "We believe that it is every Ukrainians's duty to subordinate his personal affairs and his whole life to the interests and good of the nation. When someone voluntarily and consciously cooperates with the enemy in fighting the Ukrainian liberation movement—and with physical means at that, we believe that such a crime of national treason requires the death sentence" (Mirchuk 1968, 408; quoted in Motyl 1985, 50–51). The interests of the party were, of course, equated with those of the liberation movement and nation.

Decisions to assassinate prominent figures were taken by a small group within the Homeland Executive, mostly by Bandera, Mykola Lebed, and Roman Shukhevych. After Pieracki was killed, mass arrests effectively paralyzed the organization. Bandera was one of twelve leaders put on trial in Warsaw in 1935–36. Three were sentenced to death (later commuted to life imprisonment), while the others received prison sentences of between seven and fifteen years. Bandera and Lebed responded to their death sentences with the words "Glory to Ukraine!" The accused used the trial to denounce the Pacification campaign and Polonization. On 15 December 1935, a Polish journalist commented in the newspaper *Wiadomości Literackie* (Literary News) on the change in public perceptions wrought by the trial:

> Those individuals killed from a desire to serve their people's cause. We do not think that the means served their people's cause. Only now are they successfully serving the cause: three quarters of the Polish press, which for seventeen years refused to recognize the word "Ukrainian," has over the last three weeks learned the word and will not forget it. [. . .] For seventeen years we were constantly told that the spread, even through violence, of the Polish language in the borderlands was equivalent to spreading Polishness, a love of Poland. And here are these individuals who know the Polish language but do not want to speak it. Their hatred of the Polish state, of the Polish minister, publicist and policeman has extended to the Polish language. We were taught that all "Ukraine" was an artificial creation that would disappear with the last traces of the Austrian state that invented it. This "Ukraine" has now erupted with violence against us more strongly than in those old, troubled times. (As quoted in Mirchuk 1968, 397–98)

In the next three years, under Lev Rebet's leadership, the OUN stopped the assassinations and concentrated on rebuilding its network. However, the taste for violence had spread and some individuals refused to subordinate themselves.

They were executed by the organization (Smolii 2002, 569). The "expropriation" of state property was ended after the disastrous Horodok raid of 1932. Anti-Jewish actions, such as the burning of Jewish-owned taverns, were also forbidden by the émigré leadership. However, as had occurred when an order went out to end the burning of Polish property, these actions continued to occur locally. The Polish press insinuated that the anti-alcohol campaign that had been initiated at that time was an expression of antisemitism (Mirchuk 1968, 335). Although the émigré leadership tried to limit the use of terrorism, it was often unwilling or unable to intervene (Boidunyk 1974, 372). The real issue, as Kedryn has written, was that the émigrés had lost control of the organization in Western Ukraine, where the message often became "whoever is not with us is against us" (Kedryn 1976, 162). Konovalets suggested as much in 1932 when he wrote to Onatsky: "In reality we have not until now led this youth; we gave them a certain impulse, and they have begun to think deeper than we did ourselves" (Onatskyi 1974, 688). Maksym Gon has pointed out that there were different tendencies within the OUN and that rank-and-file members sometimes disobeyed instructions from their leaders (Gon 2010b, 262). The UVO in the 1920s and then the OUN did not appear particularly interested in the Jewish minority, which did not become prominent in its propaganda until the late 1930s. Like much of the Ukrainian community, they denounced Jewish parliamentarians for signing an accord with the Polish majority in 1925, and expressed fears that Jews were acting as economic exploiters or supporters of Polish colonizing policies. At the same time, like the mainstream community, the Nationalists showed considerable respect for Zionism, which in many ways mirrored their own movement. However, economic competition between Ukrainian and Jews led to increasing tensions in the second half of the thirties. According to one source, in 1936–37 there were 416 acts of destruction of Jewish property in Western Ukraine, including broken windows and arson (ibid., 266). It is unclear to what extent these acts were the work of Ukrainians or how deeply the leadership of the OUN was involved. In any case, the democratic nationalist press vigorously condemned them, while the OUN, by remaining silent, gave the impression of condoning them (ibid., 266–67).

As will be seen, a stronger anti-Jewish line emerged on the eve of the Second World War, both in the émigré and Galician leaderships, although a number of individuals resisted it. In the field of creative literature, the seven major Nationalist figures avoided voicing antisemitic views. However, these could be found in some plays written by local playwrights, where they took the form of political and economic grievances: the charge that in the past Jews had opposed the independence struggle, that Jewish tavern-keepers were exploiting the population, and that Jewish-owned businesses were opposed to the spread of cooperatives.[16] Admiration for Hitler and more-explicit expressions of antisemitism were voiced on the pages of *Vistnyk* by Dontsov and other writers. Already in 1936 one of the editor's opponents complained: "How many little Mussolinis and little Hitlers have been spawned by the reading of Dontsov!" (Levynskyi 1936, 28).

The rejection of parliamentary democracy was a matter of principle for the Homeland Executive, which had assimilated the message—consistently preached by the émigré leadership for over a decade—that endless discussions and weak leadership had in 1917–20 distracted society from the urgent military task. Martynets had argued in 1928 for the need to end the chaos and anarchy of political parties. He spoke of creating "knights of the nationalist absurd," a new kind of Ukrainian who would "liberate the nation from centuries-long slavery" (Martynets 1928, 237). The phrase was taken from a drama written in 1924 by the Soviet Ukrainian author Borys Antonenko-Davydovych, in which the protagonist complains: "our misfortune is that everyone, whether friendly or unfriendly toward us, becomes our enemy as soon as the cursed Ukrainian question is broached. To others we are mammoths, prehistoric dinosaurs, some sort of historical joke carried into the twentieth century. We, our past, our future do not exist for them; we are only 'an invention, something absurd, nonsensical.' The tragedy of our struggle lies in the fact that we are one of the stateless nations, that in addition to social liberation we also desire removal of the chains of national oppression. In our social struggle we find collaborators and comrades among Russian revolutionary circles, but in the national struggle we stand alone." A second protagonist responds mockingly: "Knights of the absurd, defenders of an operatic dream long ago written off by history" (Antonenko-Davydovych 1924, 9). To young Nationalists the phrase came to signify a fanatical idealism. Some went further and agreed with Dontsov that not only parliamentary democracy should be rejected but also the ideals of altruism, humanism, and international solidarity, that these were merely a rhetorical screen used to dupe the naive, and that in fact behind them operated the real mechanisms of power politics. Ironically, this position accorded with the Marxist idea that bourgeois ideology masked class and state violence.

As will be seen, the OUN's ideological attitude toward fascism and Nazism evolved throughout the 1930s and 1940s. Even though they were sympathetic to Mussolini's Italy, which had spoken out against the Soviet Union, internal documents indicate that the émigré leaders did not accept the fascist label. Aware of the danger that Hitler's idea of a *Drang nach Osten* held for Ukraine, they were even more apprehensive about Nazi intentions. At the Berlin conference of 1933 Konovalets spoke against contacts with Germany (Boidunyk 1974, 477).

When Germany signed its pact with Poland on 26 January 1934, it broke off formal links with the OUN and handed over to Polish police several members of the organization, including Mykola Lebed, who was a suspect in Pieracki's assassination. Konovalets considered relocating his headquarters from Geneva to Sweden or Portugal in order to distance himself from Germany. Eventually in 1936, when it appeared that the Swiss government would deny him long-term residency, he moved from Geneva to Rome. However, he also sent Yevhen Liakhovych to establish contacts in Britain in the hope of countering the perception that the OUN was pro-German, and prepared to visit Britain in 1935 and again in 1938. These plans were scuttled by circumstances. Liakhovych claims to have told the Japanese ambassador to Germany, whom he met in Paris, that Nazism represented Germany's psychological reaction to defeat, that the doctrine was brutally contemptuous toward other peoples, and that his organization hoped that a German-Soviet conflict would result in Ukraine's liberation (Liakhovych 1974, 912, 922). Kordiuk has also stated that Konovalets was never a supporter of Hitler but was prepared to take help from a variety of sources. Foreign support came from several governments, including the Lithuanian, which provided funding, documents, diplomatic help, and contacts (Kosyk 1993, 40; Kordiuk 1974, 970). In 1931 the Canadian poet Onufrii Ivakh (Honore Ewach) wrote, "Vstavai, Lytvo, vstavai!" (Arise, Lithuania, arise!), a call for Lithuania to take up arms against Poland in joint action with Ukraine, as in ancient times. A protest against the Pacification campaign, the poem was broadcast in Ukrainian on Lithuanian radio. Konovalets wrote Ivakh a personal letter of thanks. However, most of the organization's funds were raised from supporters in Europe and North America.

The organization had contacts among younger officers in the German military intelligence (the Abwehr) who were more inclined than older commanders or the ministry of foreign affairs to believe that the Ukrainian masses desired independence (Kamenetskyi 1974, 855). Some of these contacts had been maintained through Alfred Bizants, Rickard Jary, and Roman Sushko, former officers in the Austro-Hungarian army who had also served in the Ukrainian forces. Konovalets himself had, of course, been an officer in the Austro-Hungarian army before his internment in a Russian prisoner-of-war camp from 1915 to 1918. Although the Polish, British, and French presses tried to link the OUN to funding from Nazi Germany in the years 1933–37, they produced no evidence (Kosyk 1993, 40, 45). The intelligence services of Weimar Germany had provided the UVO with funding in the years 1922–28. At this time the UVO supplied Germany, Latvia, and England with information. However, the organization paid a price for this: in 1927 thirty-six members were tried in Kraków for spying and stealing state secrets, while dozens more were arrested. Konovalets was accused of sacrificing his people for German interests. Anxious to avoid being seen as a fomentor of revolution in Poland, Germany curtailed its funding and ended all forms of cooperation. Konovalets moved the OUN's headquarters from Berlin to Geneva in 1929 and completely quit the German city on 2 March 1930 (Kosyk 2009, 66). Although Golczewski states that the OUN's contacts with German intelligence were never completely lost, documents suggest that they were in fact effectively severed in the years 1933–37 (Golczewski 2010, 681). It is true that a representative of German counterintelligence met Konovalets and Jary in December 1932, at which time a verbal agreement was made to restore cooperation (TsDAVO, f. 4331, op. 1, spr. 2, ark. 2; and f. 57, op. 4, spr. 338, ark. 86). However, when Hitler came to power in the following year, this agreement was ignored. An internal Nazi-era memo explains that the OUN's anti-German position was due to the fact that "several close collaborators" of Konovalets had Jewish wives—a reference to Jary, Mykola Stsiborsky, and General Mykola Kapustiansky (Kosyk 2009, 47). It has even been suggested that, in protest at the German-Polish agreement that was signed on 26 January 1934, the OUN may have tried to assassinate both Pieracki and Goebbels on the occasion of the latter's visit to Warsaw in that year. The bomb thrown though the window smashed the glass but failed to detonate (*Sobor na krovi*).

The German-Polish pact involved joint activity against communist organizations and the OUN. Hitler made several attempts to draw Poland into a military alliance against the Soviet Union. Herman Goering traveled to Warsaw in 1935 to propose a joint campaign to Marshall Piłsudski, and during one of his hunting trips in Poland offered Ukraine to the Poles (Budurowycz 1983, 494). Earlier, Arthur Rosenberg in *Die Zukunft einer deutschen Aussenpolitik* (A Future German Foreign Policy, 1927) had spoken of supporting the national movements in the Soviet Union and toyed with the idea of creating a large Ukrainian state under German hegemony. However, in 1933 his office also discussed the possibility of Poland absorbing both Lithuania and Soviet Ukraine, and in 1934–35 it considered Poland's expansion to the Black Sea (Kosyk 1993, 41; Potocki 2003, 109). Even in the first months of 1939 the Third Reich was still trying to attract Poland to an anti-Soviet military campaign by suggesting, among other things, that Poland's "excessive" Ukrainian population could be resettled on the Soviet Ukrainian territories that had been depopulated by the Great Famine and deportations (Potocki 2003, 200). The Nationalist leadership was therefore understandably suspicious of German designs. The Lviv newspaper *Holos*, edited by Kravtsiv, wrote on 10 January 1937: "We must turn our attention to the phenomenon of growing Germanophile sympathies among us.

We are not opposed, as long as this is not taken to excess. The problem is that many are of the opinion that Germany will give us Ukraine. This and similar theories have to be combated by Ukrainian thought. Ukraine cannot become a colony of Germany."

Throughout the 1930s Soviet propaganda worked hard to link the OUN to fascism, Nazism, the Gestapo, and German funding. This strategy was developed during the trials of "nationalists" in Soviet Ukraine in the years 1929–34. Several supposed secret organizations were uncovered, all of which had been fabricated by the secret police. This became the pretext for the arrest of over thirty thousand people who represented the intellectual elite and professional classes. At this time the GPU agent Pavel (Pavlo) Sudoplatov was sent to infiltrate the OUN leadership abroad. He eventually assassinated Konovalets in Rotterdam on 23 May 1938. In his memoirs Sudoplatov states that in 1935 the OUN sent him to a "Nazi party school in Leipzig for three months." He informs that Konovalets met Hitler twice and was the only member of the organization who had "direct access to Hitler and Goering" (Sudoplatov 1995, 14, 13, 106). Volodymyr Kosyk has demonstrated that all of this was invented. Sudoplatov was in Germany only in 1936, from the end of January to the beginning of April. The OUN had its own school for military training, at which there probably was an instructor from the Abwehr. The OUN sought to provide its members with military skills, and had maintained contacts with individuals in the Abwehr since the 1920s, when the German agency had provided firearms, facilities, and instructors for military training. However, Sudoplatov's claim that he met Erwin von Lahausen of the Abwehr is false. The latter worked for Austrian intelligence and was only recruited to the Abwehr by Admiral Canaris in January 1939, after Austria had been annexed (ibid., 49). Nor could Sudoplatov have met Konovalets in some of the places mentioned (ibid., 54). On the basis of the memoirs and letters of the OUN's leadership (written for an internal investigation into the assassination), Kosyk has recreated the sequence of events and has shown inaccuracies in Sudoplatov's account and in Soviet propaganda. It should also be recalled that prior to 1933, Germany and the Soviet Union cooperated secretly and extensively on rebuilding and developing their military capabilities.

By the late 1930s fascist governments had come to power in Italy, Germany, and Spain, and an authoritarian dictatorship had been installed in Portugal. In Central and Eastern Europe, all the countries that had been formed out of the collapse of the prewar empires as parliamentary democracies had also become dictatorships. The exception was Czechoslovakia, which maintained a liberal democracy and the rule of law. The OUN's views were aligned with this drift to the right. The organization attempted to take advantage of anti-communist alliances, while remaining wary of Germany's interest in eastern expansion. When Konovalets was assassinated, a power struggle took place within the OUN. At the same time, rapid developments were occurring in the international arena. The Munich Agreement of 1938 and Hitler's annexation of the Sudetenland suddenly brought the Ukrainian question to international attention, and a shift took place in the organization's politics and ideology.

2

THE WAR AND POSTWAR YEARS, 1939–56

The Munich Agreement of 29 September 1938 forced Czechoslovakia to recognize the autonomy of Carpatho-Ukraine. A Ukrainophile administration headed by Monsignor Avgustyn Voloshyn (Augustin Volosin), a Catholic priest, was installed on 26 November.[1] This event, along with Hitler's statements supporting the self-determination of nations, increased pro-German sympathies among Nationalists, many of whom moved to the autonomous territory, which they now viewed as the embryo of an independent state. Some Nationalist newspapers expressed faith in Hitler's protection. The Canadian *Novyi shliakh* (New Pathway), for example, stated on 12 October 1938 that Germany would not allow Hungary to overrun the territory. From 29 September 1939 the OUN made radio broadcasts from Vienna, in which it argued that the creation of Carpatho-Ukraine was a prelude to the establishment of a united Ukrainian state stretching all the way to the Kuban.[2] Some among both Ukrainian and Western observers argued that Ukraine's abundant natural resources would tempt Hitler to drive out the bolsheviks and make a deal with the Nationalists concerning a future state.

The international press understood the importance of Ukraine to Hitler's strategy, and many Western commentators suggested that Carpatho-Ukraine was a step toward the creation of a "Greater Ukraine." Moreover, Western powers were not displeased to see Germany turn its attention eastward. They were aware that Carpatho-Ukraine had been discussed in German circles in November 1938. Two researchers had been assigned by the German foreign office to analyze the issue and had recommended turning the territory into a Piedmont and rallying-point for Ukrainian national consciousness, "a mecca of Ukrainianism." By allowing a strong program of publishing and education to develop, they felt that Germany would create an intelligentsia favorably disposed toward itself (Zlepko 1994, 252). Some British and French diplomats were convinced that a large Ukrainian state was part of Hitler's long-term planning (ibid., 254, 263; Kentii 2005, 143). The agitation for an independent Ukraine was interpreted as an initial step toward the Soviet Union's dismemberment. In late 1938 this appears to have been the view of Neville Chamberlain and the British embassy in Germany (Kentii 2005, 143). On the other hand, the existence of Carpatho-Ukraine, let alone the possibility of a "Greater" Ukraine brought a strong reaction from Poland, Romania, and the USSR. Ironically, in November 1938 Hitler had already dismissed both the idea of Carpatho-Ukraine as a Piedmont and the concept of a larger Ukrainian state. Working with a selected group of advisers, he was preparing Czechoslovakia's complete destabilization. Excluded from this group were Alfred Rosenberg, his specialist on East European affairs, and Admiral Canaris, the head of the Abwehr—the two figures who were well disposed toward the idea of creating a large Ukrainian state.

Poland argued that an autonomous or independent Ukrainian political entity, however small, would activate Ukrainian populations elsewhere to join this state and destabilize the region. Warsaw was concerned that hundreds of Ukrainians were illegally crossing borders to join the Carpathian Sich, the militia that the OUN had organized in Carpatho-Ukraine. The Nationalists were staging numerous mass demonstrations throughout Galicia in support of Carpatho-Ukraine's independence. Poland meanwhile organized a sabotage force called Łom (Cudgel) which cooperated with Hungary in rupturing the territory's telecommunications infrastructure and attacking border guards and police. Groups of "revolutionaries," each eighty-strong, were sent into the country, where they destroyed a railway bridge, twelve road bridges, a reservoir, a central telephone exchange, and twenty-seven telephone lines. Twenty-seven people were killed, fifteen injured, and twenty-five taken prisoner (Potocki 2003, 193–94). On 12 March 1939, when Hitler decided to occupy Czechoslovakia, he informed the Hungarian ambassador in Berlin that Germany agreed to that country swallowing Carpatho-Ukraine, adding that he had never been bound to the political projects of the Ukrainians (Kentii 2005, 144). As the German leader entered Prague, Hungary occupied Carpatho-Ukraine, a move supported by Poland. The territory issued a declaration of independence on 14 March, which its Sejm ratified on the following day. Conflicts broke out when the Czech army refused to release arms to the Sich, which by then had grown to over ten thousand. Some weapons were seized and the Sich fought the invading Hungarians during 15–18 March. It has been estimated that a hundred men died in combat, but that as many as five thousand were captured and executed by Hungarian and Polish forces (ibid., 145; Smolii 2002, 554). It now became clear that Hitler's support for self-determination applied to the Sudeten Germans and the Slovaks, who were allowed to form a state, but that he viewed Ukrainian Nationalists merely as a potentially useful in destabilizing the region, but dispensable when this purpose had been served. At the time many Ukrainians failed to realize this. Yevhen Stakhiv recalls that on 22 January 1939, the day on which the 1918 declaration of independence was commemorated in Khust, the capital of Carpatho-Ukraine, some in the large crowd naively sang: "We'll get help from Uncle Hitler and Father Voloshyn to fight the Czechs" (Stakhiv, Ie. 1995, 56). According to eyewitnesses, even the relatively well-informed Ulas Samchuk was convinced that Germany would help to build a Carpatho-Ukrainian state and that this "was only the beginning!" (Birchak 1940, 6).

Diplomatic correspondence indicates that Voloshyn's government tried to avoid bloodshed and retain whatever political and cultural autonomy it could (Pahiria 2009, 49–70; Mandryk 2009, 22–85). The émigré leadership of the OUN appears to have issued orders for its members to leave Carpatho-Ukraine, evidently realizing that Germany would not support the tiny state (Mirchuk 1968, 549–50). However, political realism was not the strong suit of those who dreamed of independence. Young men from Galicia and other territories disobeyed these orders and organized resistance. An indication of the venture's quixotic nature can be gauged from an article written in the aftermath of events by Oleh Olzhych, who headed the OUN's effort in the territory. He indicates that the militia had been equipped almost exclusively with money from the Ukrainian emigration. Ten rifles had been received from the Czech Guard, and the Sich had acquired "in secret from various sources 200 revolvers, mainly calibre 6.35, and three machine guns with a small amount of ammunition" (Kandyba 1939, 41). Although the Sich had experienced military instructors and enthusiastic recruits in almost every village, in the end only about two thousand men could be armed. After this experience, the Nationalists became even more concerned with developing their own military. Samchuk later recalled that during the diplomatic crisis that preceded the invasion, even a car and chauffeur could not be found in Khust to transport a minister to the Czech capital for talks. First a vehicle and then a driver had to be sent from Prague (Tarnavskyi 1995, 72–74). Nonetheless, the state's brief existence and its declaration of independence resonated throughout Europe, serving notice of the Ukrainian desire for statehood.

There was another important consequence to these events. The younger generation within the OUN felt that the émigré leadership had betrayed the principle of relying on one's own forces and had failed to provide Transcarpathia with the required support. The émigrés may have calculated that by not antagonizing

Germany they could count on the later creation of an independent Galicia (Mirchuk 1968, 551, 560, 585). The Germans made efforts to persuade them that the concession to Hungary was inevitable but did not signal a resignation from the larger goal (G. Motyka 2006b, 68). However, this was not good enough for the OUN's Galician leadership, which demanded that a national liberation struggle be conducted throughout all Ukrainian lands. Melnyk and the émigré leadership saw such a strategy as doomed to failure and too costly in human lives. They followed a more cautious line, placing their hope in opportunities that would be provided by the unfolding international conflict. The disagreement contributed to a split in the organization, which would be formalized a year later in February 1940.

Street fights had already broken out in Lviv. Mirchuk reports that on 2 November 1938, at a meeting of five thousand Polish students from Lviv University, it was resolved to ban Ukrainians from attending the university and to remove Ukrainian signs in the city. Students began destroying and robbing Ukrainian shops and institutions. Roman Shukhevych played a leadership role in organizing a defense, in which Ukrainian workers participated. The pogromists, some of whom lost their lives, were beaten back. A pitched battle outside the Prosvita building on Market Square lasted several hours, and fighting between Poles and Ukrainians continued for several weeks with the pogromists taking advantage of police protection by day to destroy property, and Ukrainians taking revenge at night. The defense was a violent one. According to Mirchuk, a group of roughnecks was sent into the Polish crowd, where they "operated" with knives, stabbing people in the back. This, he writes, quickly put an end to aggression by the city's rabble (Mirchuk 1968, 475–76). The episode demonstrates that tempers were running high, and also that Ukrainian students and workers were able, under the OUN's leadership, to organize an effective response to aggression.

The immediate reaction to the crushing of Carpatho-Ukraine was anger. On 18 June 1939, the OUN organ in Paris, *Ukrainske slovo* (Ukrainian Word) wrote: "We never nurtured the idea of obtaining something from Hitler, that well-known predator. He is a representative of the 'higher' German race, a sworn enemy of the Slavic races [. . .] And we expect even less from our neighbours, our 'good Slavic brothers.'" After Hitler and Stalin had together dismembered Poland, it wrote on 24 September: "the Germans have no intention of creating an independent Ukrainian state" but are only interested in "Ukrainian territory, Ukrainian coal and steel, Ukrainian wheat, and Ukraine as a German colony" (quoted in Kosyk 1993, 69, 76). However, in the summer of 1939, Germany appears to have convinced the émigré leadership that a war with Poland would lead to the creation of a Western Ukrainian state. Wilhelm Canaris, the head the Abwehr, agreed to create a force of 250 men with Roman Sushko as its commander. Completed on 21 August 1939, it was to be used in the invasion of Poland. The young Ukrainians who were being trained by the Germans believed that their role would be to organize the initial police force for a new Ukrainian administration (Knysh 1959, 99–100). Melnyk even instructed Stsiborsky in the weeks before the 1 September invasion to prepare a constitution for this state. However, when confronted by members of the Homeland Executive, the émigrés admitted that they had received no guarantees from Germany (Mirchuk 1968, 585; *Orhanizatsiia* 1955, 133–34). The OUN's strategy was to take advantage of what it sensed were different scenarios within the German administration in order to push the option of a Galician state. As one participant put it, "we could see that there was a struggle over us in German circles" (Knysh 1959, 100, 112).

Nonetheless, this period saw greater cooperation with Nazi Germany on the part of the OUN, and, as will be argued in chapter 4, an ideological shift. The apogee of the OUN's totalitarian phase, according to Zaitsev, occurred in the autumn of 1939 with the appearance of the "Outline of a Project of the Main Laws (Constitution) of the Ukrainian State." The first article of this document stated: "Ukraine is a sovereign, authoritarian, totalitarian state consisting of occupational estates and bearing the name 'Ukrainian State'" (Zaitsev 2011, 211, and 2013b, 21). Additional evidence for this is provided by the OUN's broadcasts from Vienna and Bratislava, which continued throughout 1939, even after the collapse of the Carpatho-Ukrainian state, and ceased only on 22 September, three weeks after the invasion of Poland. These broadcasts continued to laud Germany and demonstrated a shift to stronger anti-Jewish rhetoric.

Early in 1939 Poland was still discussing with Germany the possibility of joint military action against the Soviet Union. Joachim von Ribbentrop traveled to Warsaw for discussions with the Polish foreign minister, during which he raised the possibility of Poland gaining control of Right Bank Ukraine up to Kyiv and access to the Black Sea (Zlepko 1994, 264, 267; Kosyk 1993, 64). In March and April of 1939, the Poles arrested twenty thousand Ukrainians. Many OUN members were caught up in this sweep and were only freed in September, when Germany and the Soviet Union invaded the country.

In May 1939 German-Polish relations deteriorated rapidly as Hitler demanded that Danzig (Gdańsk) be ceded to Germany. He complained of Polish atrocities against Germans in the city and concentrated troops on the border. During this crisis, on 8 May 1939, Yaroslav Stetsko, a leading figure in the Homeland Executive, published an antisemitic article in the Canadian *Novyi shliakh* under the pseudonym Zynovii Karbovych. It signaled the adoption of a fiercely anti-Jewish tone:

In the past they were orendars [leaseholders] of landowners' estates and tavern-keepers who not infrequently held the keys to churches; as stewards of the Poles they exploited the people. Now in similar manner they have come out against the Ukrainian people's liberation struggle, in aid of Moscow, bolshevism and its satellites. The entire leadership and organizational apparatus of the "Communist Party of Western Ukraine" are composed of Jews. [. . .] As agents of the GPU, spies and numerous commissars, Jews and Russians in Eastern Ukraine are together destroying Ukrainian liberation fighters. Jewry is helping Moscow's bolshevism and, on the other side [of the border] the rest of Ukraine's enemies. It has captured trade in its hands and lives on Ukrainian lands practicing deceit, exploitation, serving Ukraine's enemies. It is a nation of profiteers, materialists, egoists, that demoralizes and undermines the peoples of the world, a nation without a heroics of life, without a great idea inspiring devotion, a nation that knows only personal gain and the pleasure of satisfying its lowest instincts, and wants to undermine the heroic culture of others. [. . .] The main struggle is against Moscow and bolshevism; it is against Jews only to the extent that they help the enemies of the Ukrainian nation and try to exploit and undermine the Ukrainian people. (Karbovych 1939)

The article's timing suggests that it was produced with an eye to pleasing the Nazis during the Danzig conflict. Stetsko's "Zhyttiepys" (Autobiography), which appears to have been written in 1941 shortly after his arrest by the Germans, has also been frequently quoted to demonstrate his antisemitic and pro-German stance. The most offensive sections read as follows:

I consider Marxism to be a product of the Jewish mind, which, however, has been applied in the Muscovite prison of peoples by the Muscovite-Asiatic people with the assistance of Jews. Moscow and Jewry are Ukraine's greatest enemies and bearers of corruptive Bolshevik international ideas.

Although I consider Moscow, which in fact held Ukraine in captivity, and not *Jewry*, to be the *main* and *decisive* enemy, I nonetheless fully appreciate the undeniably harmful and hostile role of the Jews, who are helping Moscow to enslave Ukraine. I therefore support the destruction of the Jews and the expedience of bringing German methods of exterminating Jewry to Ukraine, barring their assimilation and the like. (Berkhoff and Carynnyk 1999, 170–71; italics in the original)

Although the authors who published this document have no doubts concerning its authenticity, Taras Hunczak has argued that it does not accord with other statements made by the OUN-B leaders to German authorities at this time. Viatrovych has indicated that the document has been accorded great attention by those who wish to describe the organization as fully compliant with Nazi policy toward the Jews (Hunczak 2001; Viatrovych 2006, 9–10).

Antisemitism had, of course, long been present in broad layers of Galician Ukrainian society. A publication of the Ukrainian Popular Revival (Ukrainska Narodna Obnova), the Catholic party formed in Galicia in 1930, wrote (misleadingly) that Jews had been the strongest opponents of the Ukrainian liberation struggle in 1917–18 and charged them with helping "the Moscow bolsheviks" to subdue contemporary Ukraine (*Prohrama* ca. 1938, 268–69).[3] This kind of antisemitism was based not on racial beliefs but on the perception of political and economic antagonisms. However, racial prejudice was present. It can be found, for example, in Rostyslav Yendyk's *Antropologichni prykmety ukrainskoho narodu* (Anthropological Features of the Ukrainian People, 1934) and in the articles he wrote for *Peremoha*, the organ of the Front of National Unity (Zaitsev, 2013a, 360–61). Once the linking of Jews and bolshevism—a topos, of course, of Nazi propaganda—was activated and openly employed, it began to assume a biological-essentialist tone, as the above quotation from Stetsko suggests. The tone of this quotation was far fiercer than any previous statement by an OUN leader and reflected the shift to the aggressive form of antisemitism that had spread throughout Europe. At this time the Polish government declared that it must get rid of at least 2.5 million of the over 3 million Jews living within its borders. In 1937 its foreign minister, Józef Beck, suggested forcibly relocating the country's 3 million Jews to Madagascar. Shortly before, the French colonial minister, Marius Moutet, had spoken of sending his own country's Jews there, or to other French colonies. Poland instituted discrimination against Jews. In the years 1937–39 it passed laws that restricted the mobility of Jews, excluded them from professions, and discriminated against their religious practices. This was also the moment at which Mussolini's Italy took a racist turn. Until 1938 the fascist government had not shown any interest in the biological and genocidal variety of racism that characterized Nazism.[4] However, after 5 September 1938, when King Victor Emmanuel II, Benito Mussolini, and Giuseppe Bottai signed the Race Declaration, discussions of Aryanism, racial purity, and "Jewish cosmopolitanism" began to spread.

Although in August 1939 Admiral Canaris had prepared both factions of the OUN for the possibility of an anti-Polish uprising, the signing on 23 August of the German-Soviet pact precluded extensive use of Ukrainian forces. When Germany invaded on 1 September, the Soviet Union delayed its advance from the east. Hitler instructed Canaris to activate plans for a Ukrainian uprising in Galicia. On 15 September a telegram was delivered to Moscow informing that if Soviet forces did not enter the territory "conditions may be created for the formation of new states" in the region (Kentii 2005, 158). This has been seen as a reference to the creation of a Western Ukrainian state. Two days later the Soviet army invaded. The OUN did, in fact, play a role in the collapse of the Polish state by inciting uprisings that disarmed the Polish police and military. So did the communists. In some places the two even forged a "tactical" cooperation. However, the legion trained by the Germans and headed by Roman Sushko, saw little action. After the Soviets invaded, it was quickly removed and demobilized (G. Motyka 2006b, 72).

Although, by denying them broader rights, the interwar Polish state is generally seen to have wasted the opportunity to win greater cooperation from Ukrainians, when the war with Germany broke out the UNDO called on the Ukrainian population to refrain from violence and reaffirmed the belief that an understanding between Ukrainians and Poles was a historical necessity. Declarations of loyalty were made by Ukrainian representatives in both the Sejm and Senate. Paliiv's Front of National Unity (Front Natsionalnoi Iednosti), proposed to serve in the country's defense in exchange for Galician autonomy, while the UNR's representative Roman Smal-Stotsky proposed the creation of two Ukrainian brigades that would fight against both Germany and the Soviet Union. The Greek Catholic Church called for neutrality. The Polish Army of just under a million men contained between 106,314 and 111,910 Ukrainians, of whom 7,834 lost their lives in the conflict. Twice as many were wounded (G. Motyka 2006b, 68). Polish sources state that the population of Eastern Galicia remained basically loyal to the Polish government throughout the invasion (ibid., 73).

The idea that Germany would establish a Ukrainian state had been persistently reported in the Western press from the beginning of the Munich crisis. In 1939, Watson Kirkconnell wrote that Hitler would create such a state if he moved on Kyiv: "Under a strong military and police regime like the U.S.S.R., there is no other possibility of a Ukrainian national movement gathering head; and many Ukrainian patriots, while cynical as to any real sympathy on Hitler's part, have been ready to accept his aid, in the belief that after a generation or less the German control would weaken and Ukrainian liberty would grow progressively more real in the Ukrainian state" (Kirkconnell 1939, 74). In January 1939, both G. W. Simpson and Wasyl Swystun gave Canadian radio addresses, in which they distinguished fascism from nationalism. Simpson noted: "Ukrainian nationalism existed long before the rise of Hitler to power and it will continue long after the shade of Hitler has joined the ghostly procession of those dictators who have violently run their course across a single page of history. It is a conjunction of coincidence in international affairs which at the present time links Hitler's ambitions for power with Ukrainian aspirations for national independence. Such a situation is by no means unusual or novel" (Simpson 1939, 5). Swystun also stressed that there had been a strong independence movement long before anyone had heard of Hitler. Isolation from Western democracies made the movement grasp at German promises of assistance. After the Munich Agreement, "the whole of Eastern Europe" had been handed over to Hitler as his sphere of influence and Ukrainians were not in a position to antagonize him. They believed that any change in Eastern Europe had to be for the better: "In such a change the principle of democracy would not be involved, as in the eyes of the Ukrainians the respective regimes of Russia, Poland and Rumania are not democratic, but dictatorial or totalitarian, though a lip service may be paid by them to democracy" (Swystun 1939, 13). Swystun did not consider Germany's annexation of Soviet Ukraine a possibility, because it would mean first "gobbling up" Hungary, Poland, and Romania, something that went against Nazi racial theories and would create "enormous problems" for Germany (ibid., 14).

In accord with the secret clauses of the Hitler-Stalin agreement, the Soviet Union invaded Finland on 30 November. In the spring of 1940 it demanded Bukovyna and Bessarabia from Romania (their Ukrainian populations were around 302,000 and 461,000 respectively) and began massing troops on the border. It invaded Estonia, Latvia, and Lithuania in June. When in the same month Hitler defeated France, virtually all the European continent found itself under authoritarian or totalitarian rule. Many observers became convinced that democracies had shown themselves to be politically and militarily impotent in the face of systems like fascism and bolshevism.

Pravda printed birthday greetings to Stalin from Hitler and von Ribbentrop on 23 December 1939. The Soviet public was told of the great German-Soviet friendship in newsreels and newspapers that pictured a smiling Stalin shaking hands with von Ribbentrop. The swastika and the hammer-and-sickle were shown fluttering side by side in Moscow, and Molotov explained that fascism was, after all, "a matter of taste." Stalin greeting his fellow-dictator with fervent words about their "friendship sealed in blood" (V. Kravchenko 1946, 333). Aggressive right-wing groups appeared throughout Europe, each mixing its own cocktail of nationalism, Christianity, leadership cults, antisemitism, and anti-communism. Some of these groups were fascist. Others, according to Griffin, can best be described as para-fascist, since they reacted to genuine fascism as a threat, even when they expressed a willingness to seek its cooperation and support (Griffin 1991, 122).

The Hitler-Stalin pact abruptly ended the dream of an independent Galicia, less than six months after the collapse of Carpatho-Ukraine. Under Soviet rule Galicia experienced mass arrests and deportation in the hundreds of thousands. Initially, the majority of victims were Poles, because the regime decided to first exterminate the Polish intelligentsia. Meanwhile, in February 1940 the OUN split into two factions. The older generation continued to support the OUN-M (named after Andrii Melnyk, who had succeeded Konovalets as leader), while the younger membership based in Galicia adhered to the OUN-B (named after Stepan Bandera).[5] The leaders of this latter faction had escaped or were released from Polish prisons in September 1939, and were among the twenty to thirty thousand Ukrainian refugees who made their way to German-controlled territory.

Although it was now allied to the Soviet Union, Germany tolerated the OUN, which posed no threat and provided useful information about Soviet-controlled territory. Germany once again made efforts to repair relations with the Nationalists. The Abwehr dealt primarily with the OUN-B, which allowed some of its people to cooperate with the Germans in exposing Soviet intelligence agents. Although all anti-Soviet propaganda ceased in the twenty-two months after the signing of the so-called Molotov-Ribbentrop Pact, both factions of the OUN expected a German-Soviet conflict to break out, and hoped in the wake of this conflict to establish a Ukrainian state. In 1941 the Abwehr trained several hundred Ukrainian troops, as it had done in 1939, but this time for a possible war against the Soviet Union.

The OUN's émigré leadership continued to put out feelers to other powers. In 1939 it proposed to the French that a Ukrainian force be created that would fight against the Soviet Union in Finland or the Black Sea region. In 1940 Melnyk reportedly traveled to England to look for support and even offered a change in the organization's political stance (Kentii 2005, 166, 163). Germany, however, was the only player that expressed an interest in the organization. When the question of a political orientation was discussed at a conference of the OUN-B held in Kraków in February 1940, Ivan Mitrynga's group suggested the slogan "Together with the Poles, French and peoples of the USSR—for a free Europe without Hitler and Stalin." Bandera's circle stated that the search for "friends" (allied peoples) was over, and that "Ukraine's place was in the new Europe" (ibid., 180). This line prevailed. Kentii informs that 30 percent of the agents sent into the Soviet Union by Germany on the eve of the war were Ukrainians; 52.4 percent were Poles (ibid., 186).

Nonetheless, the Nationalist attitude toward Germany remained ambiguous. While believing, or appearing to believe, in common German-Ukrainian interests, the OUN-B expressed a determination not to be Hitler's marionette. The ambivalence was nourished by various fantastic schemes in circulation at the time, including the idea that a vast state stretching from the Carpathians to the Caucasus would be established (G. Motyka 2006b, 79). Mykhailo Kolodzinsky, who met his death in 1939 as the commander of Carpatho-Ukraine's Sich, wrote that Ukraine's borders should stretch to the Volga and Caspian Sea. This territory, he argued, constituted one geopolitical whole that Ukraine was destined to link with Europe politically, economically, and culturally (Kolodzinskyi 1957, 27, 31). Germany, it was felt, could never establish control over such a vast area. This, the OUN reasoned, provided it with a chance to establish its rule locally in the wake of the military advance and a national revolution, thus confronting the Germans with a fait accompli.

The invasion of the Soviet Union by Germany and its allies—dubbed Operation Barbarossa—began on 22 June 1941. On 30 June, as soon as leaders of the OUN-B arrived in Lviv, they read a declaration of independence. It expressed readiness "to act in concert with the National Socialist Greater Germany, which under Adolph Hitler is creating a new order in Europe and the world, and is helping the Ukrainian people free themselves from Moscow's occupation" (Serhiichuk 1996, 239). The Germans reacted by immediately arresting the organization's leaders. Bandera, Stetsko, and others were transported to Berlin. They refused to rescind the declaration or to curtail their activities, insisting that they were speaking in the name of the Ukrainian people, who desired independence. The OUN-B's leaders stated that cooperation with Germany in the struggle against bolshevism depended on the establishment of a Ukrainian state. Romania, which feared the creation of such a political entity, had suggested in July 1941, that "a future Ukrainian state" should be small, because a forty-million-strong nation would exert pressure on it and other countries (Kosyk 1993, 132). However, the key decision had already been taken on 16 July 1941, when Hitler chose to divide Ukraine between the General Government (Generalgouvernement) and the Reich Commissariat Ukraine (Reichkommissariat Ukraine). Romania, as a military ally, was rewarded with Bukovyna and a part of southwestern Ukraine that included Odesa, a territory it renamed Transnistria. Hitler insisted that Ukrainians would not be allowed even a puppet government or the right to bear arms.

Both factions of the OUN protested this partitioning of Ukraine. They did not reconcile themselves to the fact that there would be no Ukrainian government, and in defiance of German orders continued to agitate for independence, to build networks, and to publish newspapers and leaflets. Members of the OUN encouraged the immediate establishment of local administrations and militias (and of course tried to place its sympathizers in leading positions). However, the wave of self-organizing was not the work of the OUN alone. People took the initiative to revive civic life locally at every level. One observer has written: "No one who lived and worked in Galicia at the time waited for permission from the Germans; we took over the institutions in which we worked, out of personal initiative and desire, for the benefit of the Ukrainian

state, the one that 'had to' arise on our lands after the bolshevik retreat"
(Tarnavsky 1995, 135). Both factions of the OUN had sent hundreds of agitators
and organizers (the so-called expeditionary groups, or *pokhidni hrupy*) into the
country in the wake of the German advance.[6] Wherever they could, they
supported and developed not only local governments and militias, but presses,
schools, and church life, all the while conducting clandestine propaganda for
independence. The initial, military German administration sometimes turned
a blind eye to these efforts. In the first weeks of the war the OUN-B cooperated
with the German forces by creating diversionary actions in the Soviet rear and
destroying Soviet partisans. It also freed prisoners from NKVD jails (Kentii
2005, 212). However, the Germans soon dismantled or brought under its control
any administration that the Nationalists had established, and set about curtailing
all political activities. By 6 August 1941, any hopes for the creation of a Ukrainian
state had been dashed. The Germans banned all political agitation, Ukrainian
flags and insignia, and the singing of the national anthem. As the Gestapo
arrived and a civil administration was established, the full brutality of Nazi
plans, which included the mass execution of Jews, became clear. The OUN-B
warned its members of possible arrests. By the end of August it had recognized
that there was to be no role for a Ukrainian state in Hitler's "new Europe" and
that a conflict with the Nazis was inevitable (ibid., 247, 255).

On 5 September the Germans began mass arrests of OUN-B members and of
the expeditionary groups. About fifteen hundred people were imprisoned (ibid.,
257). In Lviv the Gestapo registered all known Nationalists over a period of
several days and then conducted sweeping arrests on 15 September. In the years
1941–43 an estimated 80 percent of the OUN-B leadership was jailed or killed
(Torzecki 1993, 247). As occurred after the invasion of Poland, the Germans
removed from the front and disarmed the Ukrainian troops they had trained.[7]
Bandera himself was initially kept under house arrest in Berlin, while Stetsko
was allowed the freedom of the city's streets until August. Following a final
unsuccessful attempt on 12 September to get them to retract the declaration of
independence, both were transferred to Sachsenhausen concentration camp,
where they spent the war together with over a dozen other leaders of the organization. Ivan Gabrusevych died there in 1944. From 1941–44 Rebet and
Lenkavsky were imprisoned in Auschwitz, where two of Bandera's brothers were
killed by Polish prisoners. The third was killed in Ukraine. Bandera's father was
executed by Soviet authorities, and his sisters were sent to Siberia.

On 9 November instructions were issued to German forces to watch
all members of the OUN-B and arrest them if they attempted to conduct political activity. On 25 November 1941, after receiving information from captured

documents and its own agents that an armed uprising was being planned, the security police in the Reichskommissariat Ukraine (Kyiv, Dnipropetrovsk, Mykolaiv, Rivne, Zhytomyr, Vinnytsia regions) was ordered to arrest and summarily execute members of the faction (Kosyk 1993, 193). Convinced that the organization could not be trusted, the Germans decided in mid-January 1942 that the only path was "to completely destroy this movement" (ibid., 221).

The OUN's association with the Germans caused irreparable damage to the organization's image, especially in Eastern Ukraine—a fact that the expeditionary forces reported. In the autumn of 1941 the organization began the shift to an anti-Nazi, anti-German line. In September it issued instructions that anyone who cooperated with the Gestapo would be considered a traitor and executed (ibid., 256). The Melnyk faction at this time continued to work more openly and to reassure the Germans of its loyalty. In later years Bandera's supporters claimed that the OUN-M's strategy had been to "earn" a Ukrainian state by serving the Germans. In fact, however, leaders of the Bandera faction also continued to hope throughout July and August that Germans policy toward them would change (Kentii 2005, 233–35). This ambivalence in the face of German behavior severely compromised the Nationalist cause; many observers came to view the call for independence as simply a request for a German satellite state.

In spite of the ban on public meetings and demonstrations, the Melnyk faction organized a commemoration at Bazar on 21 November 1941. On the same day in 1921 at this location near Zhytomyr, 359 captured soldiers of the Ukrainian National Army, who had been on a raid into Soviet-controlled territory, were executed after they refused to join the bolsheviks. They died singing the national anthem. Around forty thousand people arrived for the commemoration, astonishing German authorities who were in many cases convinced that years of Soviet rule had extinguished all national feeling in this part of Ukraine. A total of 720 organizers and participants were arrested. Most were shot or hanged. In December the Germans shut down the journal *Litavry* (Kettledrums) and the newspaper *Ukrainske slovo* (Ukrainian Word), two publications started in Kyiv by the Melnyk faction. Some who worked on the paper were immediately shot. The replacement, *Nove ukrainske slovo* (New Ukrainian Word), was often formed from people who were more amenable, and hostile to the Nationalists. The Germans knew that the OUN-M controlled the Ukrainian National Council in Kyiv, the Union of Writers, and some other bodies. On 3 January 1942 the security forces expressed concern that the Melnyk faction could not be trusted, and on 9 February all members of the OUN-M who had not gone underground were arrested. Olena Teliha, Ivan Rohach, Ivan Irliavsky (real name Roshko), Mykola Chyrsky, and Yaroslav Orshan (real name Orest Chemerynsky) were among those who were shot a few days later in Babyn Yar (Babi Yar). Oleh Olzhych calculated that a total of 4,756 members of the OUN-M were killed in the years 1941–44, 621 of them in Babyn Yar (Zhulynsky 2007, 16; G. Motyka 2006b, 94). Members of the OUN-M had been instructed to conduct propaganda wherever possible in officially allowed publications. They were told that the idea of independence could be promoted indirectly by, for example, describing national struggles for freedom, fighting wars against Poland and Muscovy, even by printing German statements that outlined the goal of reducing Ukraine to a breadbasket, in this way discrediting Nazi policy (Stasiuk 2006, 30–31).

   In the first weeks of the war, the conduct of the OUN-B had been shaped by instructions it had issued to members shortly after its Second Congress, which was held in Kraków in April 1941. These instructions, which had probably been circulated in May, took the form of a document entitled "The OUN's Struggle and Activity in the War." These instructions stressed the importance of orga- nizing rapidly, declaring "Ukrainian rule in every village, in every town, in the army, everywhere and to everyone" (TsDAVO, f. 3833, op. 2, spr. 1, ark. 21). In this way the organization hoped to compel the Germans to deal with an admin- istration of their creation, preempting any other plans. According to the instruc- tions, the Germans were to be told that Stepan Bandera's OUN had taken power and his administration was "prepared to enter friendly relations with allied armies for the common struggle against Moscow and for cooperation." If the Germans refused to recognize this local rule, members were instructed to "announce that those appointed by the OUN could not transfer their rule because only the OUN's leadership could relieve them of their duties" (ibid., ark. 23). Members were to develop their own forces, bearing in mind the impor- tance of having a strong military, so that "two armies, the Ukrainian and German" could arrange a pact in the struggle against Moscow (ibid.). Wherever possible, members were to meet "the arriving allies in an organized manner, bearing weapons" (ibid., ark. 27). The instructions envisaged these events occurring in the context of a popular uprising, during which Russian POWs would be handed over to the Germans, and political commissars and known communists would be killed. It stated: "In a time of chaos and confusion one may allow oneself to liquidate undesirable Polish, Russian, and Jewish activists, especially those who sympathize with bolshevik Russian imperialism" (ibid., ark. 32). It was made clear that in this initial period the organization aimed at establishing a political- military dictatorship whose rule "had to be terrible for its opponents" (ibid., ark. 38). Nationalities were divided into two groups: those favorably disposed toward

Ukrainians, who were the formerly oppressed nations, and those unfavorably disposed, who were the Russians, Poles, and Jews. The first group was to be given equal rights with Ukrainians. The second was to be destroyed if it defended the Soviet regime. Russians and Poles were to be removed from government positions. Jews were to be isolated. If it was necessary to leave a Jew in the administration, he was to be supervised by a member of the militia "and liquidated for the smallest fault" (ibid., ark. 38). Judging from the slogans provided for use among Red Army personnel, the second group could expect no mercy, especially in areas where Ukrainians were a majority. These slogans included: "Stalinist and Jewish commissars are the first enemies of the people!" "Marxism is a Jewish invention!" "The Russian-Jewish commune is an enemy of the people!" (ibid., ark. 77). There is no doubt that this kind of agitation either created or contributed to the mob violence against Jews in the first months of the war. The same instructions also defined the Melnyk faction as "saboteurs," and called upon members to set up revolutionary tribunals to deal with enemies. Such tribunals often became pretexts for lynchings (Cherevatenko 1994, 392; Kentii 2005, 216). Dozens of Melnyk supporters were among those who were killed at this time. Two leaders of the OUN-M, Omelian Senyk-Hrybivsky and Mykola Stsiborsky, were assassinated by a member of the Bandera faction on 30 August 1941, although the circumstances are unclear (the assassin may have been a Soviet agent). Teliha and Olzhych immediately denounced the OUN-B for these killings.[8]

In this context it is worth recalling the warnings issued by Onatsky and Stsiborsky seven years earlier. They had warned that an uncompromising attitude toward foreign colonizers did not mean the propagation of slogans like "Death to communists!" and "Smash the Komsomol members!" This would be foolish, they argued, because it would cause people to "unite against us and behind Moscow simply from an instinct of self-preservation" (Onatskyi 1989, 99). The indiscriminate condemnations and violence indeed turned many potential allies against both factions of the organization.

The instructions make it clear that the OUN-B planned to organize an administration and militia independently of the Germans, expecting that the latter would recognize the inevitability of establishing a Ukrainian state in some form. Great emphasis is placed on a mass uprising (*zryv*) which would convince the Germans that the organization had a powerful following. The revolution is described as a moral force impelling people to self-organization and the construction of a completely new life. The ideal is "not to live in the old, familiar way, but to eagerly strain forward, to create the new" (TsDAVO, f. 3833, op. 2, spr. 1, ark. 26). The focus on inspiring people meant that slogans could not be "small," because only a "great, fanatical idea will throw people into battle" (ibid., ark. 16). The organization is referred to as the avant-garde of the uprising and the state-building drive. The instructions end with a number of songs and poems appropriate to the creation of a fervent, enthusiastic mood.

Reality, of course, proved to be rather different from the fantasy projected by the instructions. Disenchantment came quickly. A memorandum from 22 July 1941, exactly a month after the outbreak of war, pointed out that Poles and other nationalities were often being placed in positions of power by the occupation forces, while Ukrainian activists were being denounced to the police and arrested. The militia that the OUN attempted to set up was in most places forbidden to bear arms or make arrests (TsDAVO, f. 3833, op. 1, spr. 15, ark. 1; Serhiichuk 1996, 256–62). The Germans soon disbanded it, removed known Nationalists and set up their own police. In many regions the OUN encouraged its members to join this police force in order to obtain weapons and prepare for taking power. The Germans tried to prevent them from doing so, a fact noted in Soviet documents (TsDAHO, f. 1, op. 22, spr. 75, ark. 11). The non-German members of this police force were collectively known as the Schutzmannschaft, or simply Schuma, and were made up of various nationalities.[9] They were used by the Germans not only for guard duty, as firemen, and for general police duties, but also to arrest and in some cases to shoot the Jewish population (Pohl 2010, 39, 55).

The Nazis planned to settle conquered territories with ethnic Germans. By securing fertile land and food supplies from Ukraine, they hoped to make a German-dominated Europe economically self-sufficient. All Jews were to be killed; thirty million civilians in the cities were to be starved; and the growth of non-German populations was to be suppressed. Hitler argued against educating Ukrainians, providing them with inoculations, or improving their living conditions (Lower 2005, 27). Hans Koch, the man appointed to head the civil administration in Ukraine, insisted that Ukrainians were to be treated as slaves and not allowed an education beyond the third grade. By the end of 1941 they were banned from all secondary education (Petrenko 2004, 56).

Early in 1942 the Ukrainian population had turned from passive to active opposition. Anti-German leaflets appeared calling on people not to surrender weapons but to join the underground (Serhiichuk 1996, 24; Sokhah and Potichnyi 2002, 30–31). By May 1942 the underground press was describing communists and Nazis both as enemies of Ukraine who were trying to enslave the people. Soviet sources confirm that the Germans understood the danger posed by the OUN and moved to liquidate it; they even indicated that agitators, singers, actors, and musicians were being arrested (TsDAHO, f. 1, op. 22, spr. 75, ark. 8). In the spring of 1942 OUN-B forces began to resist and sabotage the work of the German administration, and by the summer they were carrying out the first armed clashes with German forces (Kentii 2005, 283, 297). These actions were often spontaneous, the result of widespread resistance to the capture and transportation of people to Germany for forced labor. On 30 June 1942, one year after the proclamation of independence in Lviv, an underground leaflet described the arrests, imprisonments, and bloodshed under the "new liberators" and stated that Ukrainians were ready to fight for independence but not for the "new Europe" (TSDAVO, f. 3833, op. 2, spr. 3, ark. 30).

Although at the Kraków Congress of April 1941 the OUN-B had envisioned itself as ruling a totalitarian Ukraine (the instructions issued in the following month affirmed a monoparty state as the goal), at the Third Congress, which took place in August 1943, the organization officially rejected both communism and fascism. From that moment it maintained an "anti-imperialist" line. Soviet sources report that during negotiations conducted on 31 October 1943 the OUN and the Ukrainian Insurgent Army (UPA) informed them that they were fighting the imperialism of both Berlin and Moscow (TsDAHO, f. 62, op. 1, spr. 253, ark. 20–22; repr. in Sokhah and Potichnyi 2002, 104–6). By this time not only had German behavior enraged the entire population but it was abundantly clear that Eastern Ukrainians were overwhelmingly opposed to dictatorship in any form. Moreover, it had become apparent that the Third Reich could lose the war.

The issue of the OUN's complicity in the pogrom of Jews during the first days of the war has been the subject of recent research. The actions were prepared and incited by the Germans, but members of the militia participated (Himka 2011b, 218–20; Pohl 2010, 39, 54; Dean 1996, 173–74; Kruglov 2010, 274; Statiev 2010, 85). If one accepts that the OUN planned and organized some of these actions, a plausible explanation for this might be sought in the organization's desire to show the Germans that its members possessed the ruthlessness and determination required to create a Ukrainian state. The idea of passing the ruthlessness "test" had been instilled in this generation, not least by the writings of Dontsov and the literature of *Vistnyk*. However, in April at the Kraków Congress the organization had opposed pogroms, arguing that they diverted attention from the real source of evil, which was the regime in Moscow. Some have suggested that the OUN-B might have revised this policy on the eve of the German-Soviet war (Himka 2011b, 240). A number of questions remain unanswered. In the case of the Lviv pogrom, for example, the Germans took the city on 30 June, at which time thousands of political prisoners murdered by the NKVD were discovered in the prisons. The violence took place on the following day and was then promptly stopped. It remains unclear how the militia was gathered on the first day of the invasion, what interaction took place with the

Germans, and what chain of command operated. It has been claimed that the OUN "orchestrated" the pogroms (Himka 2012, 430). Whether this was the case or whether the more likely scenario is that some members of the organization were present during the violence and encouraged it has not yet been demonstrated. Various interpretations of the photographic evidence have been presented and used to construct differing scenarios (see Riabenko 2012). Scholars have noted that pogroms did not occur in the first weeks of occupation on territories that had been under Soviet rule before 1939, even when German and Romanian soldiers tried to provoke them. Dieter Pohl has suggested that an explanation for this might be found in the role played by the OUN in inciting pogroms, both in Galicia and Volhynia (Pohl 2010, 54). However, Yaroslav Hrytsak has offered another explanation. The wave of pogroms that took place in Western Ukraine, Latvia, Lithuania, and Estonia occurred on territories that had been occupied by Soviet troops in 1939–40 and had been subjected to rapid and ruthless "Sovietization." This experience made the population more vulnerable to German incitements to violence (Hrytsak 2004, 163). Researchers have reported that in some areas the OUN gained initial control and prevented not only violence against Jews but looting and general disorder (Viatrovych 2006, 59–61). Whatever the case, the organization's propaganda at this time constantly reinforced the message that Jews had frequently been supporters and collaborators of the "Muscovite-bolshevik" regime. There were reports in the German-censored Ukrainian press that the prison massacres discovered in the wake of the Soviet retreat were the work of the NKVD and of a conflated Jewish-bolshevik enemy (Himka 2013, 383, 386).

The OUN's involvement with the militia and police requires further research. Kost Pankivsky, who headed the Ukrainian Homeland Committee (Ukrainsky Kraiovy Komitet) in Lviv in 1941 and 1942, has written that organizing the militia was no easy task. The force had to be improvised, since Ukrainians had been prevented from serving in the Polish police and often in the army. It was subordinated to its own officers and to "every German in uniform" (Pankivskyi 1983, 401). Local Ukrainians wanted to see their people in the militia because they felt this would provide some measure of protection from arbitrary violence, but the German administration also used the force in anti-Jewish operations. The Germans at first executed male Jews who were members of the intelligentsia, acts that might initially be interpreted as wartime excesses. But by August and September, when the transfer from military to civilian administration had occurred, all Jews were being executed, including women and children. At this point the German Gendarmerie units had arrived, the provisional militias were replaced by the Schutzmannschaft (police) force, and efforts were made to remove all Nationalists (Dean 1996, 178). In subsequent months, Himmler's Security Service generally provided the firing squads, but the rounding up and escorting of Jews was done with the support of local police units. Individual policemen also participated in the search for and execution of Jews who had gone into hiding. Martin Dean writes: "The willingness to carry out such actions can be seen in the numerous descriptions from a wide variety of sources depicting local policemen acting on their own initiative in accordance with the general policy" (Dean 2000, 101). Gerhard Paul has estimated that between thirty thousand and forty thousand Ukrainians took part in the Nazi-organized murder of Jews (Paul 2002, 219).

Under occupation, each individual had to make personal decisions and choices. To the charge of collaboration Pankivsky replied in his memoirs that the entire people could not go into the underground. To continue living their lives they required some contact with the occupying power and someone to represent them. Before the war he himself had been a member of the UNDO, and he remained an enemy of the OUN. He writes in his memoirs that he saw his wartime task as easing the burden of occupation whenever possible—by trying to feed the hungry; freeing Soviet POWs; helping refugees; supporting the Red Cross, schools, and cultural life; and intervening with the authorities on behalf of various groups, including Jews and Poles.

Bandera's faction tried to set up a body called the Ukrainian State Government (Ukrainske Derzhavne Pravlinnia), which was to serve temporarily as the public face of the proclaimed independent Ukraine. Surviving minutes from a meeting on 19 July 1941 indicate that a discussion of the German treatment of Jews took place.[10] Some individuals opposed Nazi racial policies, while others supported ghettoizing Jews or sending them to smaller cities. Stepan Lenkavsky spoke of using "all methods" in destroying Jews (TsDAVO, f. 3833, op. 1, spr. 10.1, ark. 1–3). It is not clear whether he was referring to physical liquidation or deportations, but his words were nonetheless chilling (G. Motyka 2006b, 98–99). Frightening unsigned leaflets were produced at this time addressed to "Ukrainian Peasants!" and "Ukrainian Workers!" (TsDAHO, f. 1, op. 23, spr. 931, ark. 121–121b and 164–164b). They painted a picture of Russian bolsheviks, the NKVD, and Jews as exploiters of the common people. The second leaflet described the Jews as follows: "They live in bright, comfortable apartments, eat the best food, wear better dresses, furs. They work at easier jobs. Their working day is shorter, their hours are not set, their wages are the highest, they are well-fed and spoiled. The entire system of production, trade, the direction of industry and institutes are in the hands of Jews and bolsheviks. Ukrainians are labourers in the factories, mines, cleaners, sweepers, and railway conductors. Jews and bolsheviks betray us, condemn us, execute and destroy us" (ibid.).

There has been much recent debate over what most scholars today describe as the "ethnic-cleansing" campaign unleashed by the OUN-B in 1943 against the Polish population of Volhynia. Its origins are not entirely clear, but it was probably conceived as a preemptive strike against any attempt to reestablish a Polish state on this territory after the war. The Polish underground had planned to demonstrate its presence by fighting alongside Soviet forces as they retook Volhynia and Eastern Galicia, in this way bolstering Polish claims to a reintegration of these territories into a postwar Poland. Conservative estimates put the number of Poles killed in the fighting at 40,000–70,000, although the figure of 100,000 is also used. The number of Ukrainians killed is estimated at 15,000–20,000.[11] The conflict's deeper roots lay in interwar attempts to Polonize the population and in a long struggle for the control of land in this region.[12] A significant immediate factor was the refusal of Polish politicians to countenance the loss of Volhynia or Galicia in any postwar order. Their reluctance to retreat from the idea that Ukrainians in these areas should become Poles undermined attempts at Ukrainian-Polish cooperation. Once the killings began, they created an uncontrollable cycle of reprisals and counterreprisals.

There were many calls by community leaders to stop the violence, and contemporary historians have condemned the targeting of civilian populations as inexcusable (Iliushyn 2009, 23, 30–32). Ihor Iliushyn, the most authoritative Ukrainian historian on this subject, states that the armed groups were at first under the OUN-B's command: "the anti-Polish attacks began under its orders." Subsequently, "these groups acted according to their own scenarios" (ibid., 237). In the lawless situation the rural population often organized its own assaults. He argues that only an initial impetus was required, after which the civilian population, "perhaps with the support of a few armed members of the UPA, acted independently" (ibid.). Iliushyn is inclined to believe that the order came from Dmytro Kliachkivsky (pseudonym Klym Savura), the leader of the OUN-B in this region (designated as the northwestern) (ibid., 242–43, 251). It is unclear whether permission to unleash the violence had been granted at the Third Conference of the OUN-B, which was held in Kraków in February 1943. In all likelihood the Volhynian leadership took the decision without the agreement of its superiors in Lviv.[13] Volodymyr Viatrovych, a vigorous defender of the OUN-B, is of the same opinion. He argues that the evidence points to Kliachkivsky initiating the action as the regional UPA commander, and going against the desires of the central OUN leadership (Viatrovych 2011, 72, 75–76). Berkhoff informs that the archives of Ukraine's former KGB "are said to hold documents that point at Kliachkivsky as the instigator, but outside researchers have not gained access to them" (Berkhoff 2004, 98). Whatever the case, observers have suggested that the burden of responsibility for the Volhynian tragedy lies with the OUN-B leadership and the Ukrainian population that predominated in this area, in the same way as the responsibility for the ethnic cleansing of Ukrainians west of the Curzon line (in the Chełm, Podlachie, Nadsianie, and Lemko regions) lies with the majority Polish population (Iliushyn 2009, 22). Yaroslav Dashkevych has written: "the Ukrainian terror of 1942–44 against the Polish population of Western Ukraine, even after attempts to justify it by invoking the idea of revenge for Polish injustices, German and Russian provocations, collaboration by the Armia Krajowa [the Polish underground army] with communist Russia, etc., still deserves a severe and unqualified condemnation" (Dashkevych 1993, 130–31).

There is today a large and still-burgeoning body of literature on the Polish-Ukrainian conflict and the tragic events in Volhynia in particular.[14] The debate has resonated throughout both countries and led to parliamentary resolutions and joint initiatives to study the issue. The reporting of atrocities has generated much heated commentary, as has the definition of the event as a genocide.[15] Much opprobrium has been directed at the OUN's secret service, the SB (Sluzhba Bezpeky), which is known to have killed many innocent families, both Polish and Ukrainian, and "inspired terror in civilians of all ethnicities" (Berkhoff 2004, 289).[16] There is now a strong scholarly consensus that the OUN was largely responsible for the campaign, but there is less agreement about the events that initiated it.[17] One of the most respected Ukrainian historians, Yaroslav Hrytsak, has argued that a document ordering the action will probably never be found because the instructions may well have been oral. He is convinced, nonetheless, that the instructions were given. Mykola Lebid confided several times to his closest circle that there was an OUN-B order to begin the anti-Polish action, and a field commander has confirmed this (Hrytsak 2004, 104). The UPA leadership itself was split concerning the wisdom of beginning such a mass action. "Probably, the decision was taken by a section of the leadership, which wanted to secure its positions in the newly-created Army, and in particular to squeeze out Mykola Lebed from the leadership. In any case, it appears that the anti-Polish action became an important factor in the creation of the UPA, its 'baptism by blood.' According to the norms of international law this was a war crime; from the military-political point of view it was completely senseless; after all, the decisive role in the ethnic cleansing of Poles from Volhynia and Galicia was played not by the UPA's actions but by Stalin's decisions and his agreement with his allies at Yalta" (ibid.).

Polish-Ukrainian relations deteriorated still further in the immediate postwar years. Much bad blood was created when in 1947 the Polish government deported over 150,000 Ukrainians from its southeastern regions in the so-called Vistula

Operation—an action that has been viewed by many as an act of revenge for the Volhynian attacks (Iliushyn 2009, 56). Both Ukrainians and Poles, in attempting to justify these actions, have often employed the charge of collective responsibility.

It should be recalled that the German invasion of 1941 was preceded by twenty-one months of Soviet occupation. The Soviet administration depicted Poles in the worst possible light. Half a million were imprisoned or deported from what had until 1939 been Poland's eastern territories. Seventy thousand were expelled from Volhynia, a figure that represented 20 percent of the region's Polish population (Snyder 2003a, 204). When the Germans invaded, they organized a genocide of the Volhynian Jews. Some perpetrators of the 1943 attacks on Poles had been trained in this genocide (ibid., 198–99). It is clear, therefore, that even before the Polish-Ukrainian conflict of 1943 erupted in Volhynia, the population had become accustomed to waves of "ethnic cleansing" in the form of mass arrests and deportations. Moreover, the Volhynian fighting was preceded by a Polish-Ukrainian conflict in the Chełm and Podlachia areas in 1942–43, in which around four hundred members of the Ukrainian community were murdered and an estimated three thousand to four thousand fighters on either side lost their lives (Kentii 2005, 172, 175). Tensions between the two national groups were exploited by the Germans. For example, Ukrainians in the Generalgouvernement were used against the majority Polish population, while Poles in Volhynia, which was part of the Reichskommissariat Ukraine, were used against the majority Ukrainian population. Sometimes, when one group had been forced out of the police, it was replaced by another, which then conducted acts of reprisal (Serhiichuk 1996, 30; Viatrovych 2011, 78–79). The earlier killings in Chełm and Podlachia, and the mass violence and deportations by successive German and Soviet administrations contributed to the population's brutalization.

Viatrovych has argued that the Ukrainian underground produced no material in which the anti-Polish war was presented as a success, victory, or commencement of a national revolution (Viatrovych 2011, 99). In fact, the available materials describe the action as a failure, a debilitating war between two populations that should have been allied in the struggle against Germans and the Soviets both. In one of its longest statements on the Volhynian massacres, the OUN-B wrote in July 1943:

> The Gestapo unleashed a terror against the Ukrainian population with the help of police detachments, which were composed mainly of Poles and to which armed groups of Polish civilians soon began to attach themselves. Responding to this terror, in a situation of anarchy provoked by the Gestapo,

some local Ukrainian elements spontaneously joined the vengeful counter-action, and, organizing themselves into armed bands, began killing the Polish population. The terror against the local Ukrainian and Polish populations took on horrible, repulsive forms, pogroms against old people, women and children. Armed Polish bands organized by the Germans, surrounded Ukrainian villages, killing entire populations, robbing them of goods and burning them. Parts of the Ukrainian population, driven to despair, did the same to the Poles. The behaviour of the Germans was a provocation. There is evidence that the Gestapo tried by all means possible to create a situation that neither the Ukrainians nor the Poles would be able to control. There were, for example, cases where Germans who were present at pogroms of the Ukrainian population allowed some victims to escape from a surrounded village, saying that they could do nothing because it was the work of "Poles." The purpose of such provocative behavior by the Germans was to encourage further pogroms by the Ukrainian masses against the Poles. (Ibid., 221)

This and similar documents were, however, produced after the Ukrainian-Polish "war within a war" had already been launched and its consequences had become evident. Roman Shukhevych, who replaced Mykola Lebed on 13 April 1943 as the new leader of the OUN-B in Ukraine, began to follow the Kliachkivsky line (Dziobak 1995, 44–45). Even though the OUN-B leadership sometimes did not control the behavior of local forces, a fact to which Soviet documents bear witness, there is now ample evidence that the organization guided many of these actions. Moreover, when Kliachkivsky gave the order on 15 August 1943 that all lands of former Polish colonists were to be transferred to ownership by Ukrainian peasants, this provided strong additional stimulus for peasant attacks on the Polish population (Kowalewski 1993, 196; quoted in Hud 2006, 341). The OUN's secret police, the SB, also shot members of rival Ukrainian organizations, hundreds of UPA members whom it wrongly suspected of disloyalty, and Ukrainian peasants whom it accused of various transgression (Berkhoff 2004, 297).

There are reports of the UPA making attempts to aid the Jewish population in Volhynia by providing or selling false papers and finding places of refuge (Petrenko 1997, 172–74; Lower 2005, 182–83). A number of Jews served in the UPA as doctors, and some individuals, such as Natalia Shukhevych, the wife of the UPA leader Roman Shukhevych, hid Jews (Fishbein 2009). However, there are many more reports of Jews being killed by the insurgents, or Jewish doctors being executed as the Red Army retook territory (Berkhoff 2004, 263–64; Snyder 2010b, 101; Golczewski 2010b, 143; Breitman et al. 2005, 250). Jewish memoirs, such as Moshe Maltz's account of life in the Sokal region, paint a sombre and frightening picture of violence against Jews, some of it perpetrated by Ukrainian policemen and some by partisans who are identified as supporters of Stepan Bandera (Maltz 1993). John-Paul Himka has written, "many Jewish testimonies, taken in different places, in different languages, and over a space of sixty years tell the same basic story: that UPA killed Jews at the same time as they killed Poles and that in the winter of 1943–1944, as the Red Army approached Volhynia, UPA lured survivors out of hiding in the forests, enrolled them in labor camps, and killed them" (Himka 2010, 94). Although horrified by the murder of Jews, most local people, fearing for their own lives, remained silent and watched the genocide unfold. Moreover, as Berkhoff has noted, "the Communist party underground and the Organization of Ukrainian Nationalists, the two political groups that claimed to represent the population, never opposed specifically the mass murder of the Jews, not even in words" (Berkhoff 2004, 310). In the late 1940s, during the final desperate phase of the struggle, the UPA used coercive methods of gathering supplies and sometimes unleashed indiscriminate violence against "collaborators." Among the latter it counted locals who had been forced to join collective farms and whom it sometimes killed. By the time the insurgents reevaluated and ended this policy, they had alienated a large part of the population (See Kudelya 2011).

In Eastern Ukraine members of different nationalities were absorbed into the OUN's underground, which found support, as Shankovsky has noted, in large industrial cities of the south among workers, many of whom had witnessed the collectivization, deportations, and Holodomor. They had often moved to the cities to escape these horrors. The Nationalists found support among Russians in the Donbas, Greeks in Mariupol, Moldavians and Tatars in the south (Shankovsky 1958, 12, 19). The expeditionary forces had been instructed, when working in areas with mixed populations to "leave the political ghetto" and draw in minorities. Shankovsky writes that the Nationalists soon became convinced that "the idea of a sovereign Ukrainian state in which minorities had equal rights with Ukrainians could appeal to and be accepted by Russians, especially those who had been born and raised in Ukraine among the Ukrainian people and who considered Ukraine their homeland" (ibid., 20–21). Reports of the expeditionary groups from southern and eastern regions confirm this observation (Serhiichuk 1996, 304, 334). When the UPA began to fight the Germans and the Red Army both, it absorbed into its ranks former soldiers from both forces, including Uzbeks, Georgians, Azerbaidzhanis, Tatars, and Russians. The underground also protected and hid priests and supported the Christian churches, which under Soviet rule found themselves in the catacombs once more. Church and religious matters, admits Shankovsky, "had not been very popular among Western Ukrainian Nationalists in the thirties" (Shankovsky

1958, 36). Now, however, the need to defend religious communities contributed to a rethinking of ideology. The uncompromising opposition of church communities to Soviet rule made them natural allies of the OUN. In 1949 Bandera even suggested linking the organization's ideology to the Christian faith. The leadership of the underground in Ukraine responded that it viewed religious conviction as a personal matter for each individual to decide. While defending religious freedom and offering support to the persecuted Ukrainian Catholic and Ukrainian Autocephalous Orthodox Churches, in particular, it refused to use the churches as political instruments in the way that Soviet rule used the Russian Orthodox Church (Serhiichuk 2009, vol. 2, 241, 416).

When the war against Hitler ended, many Nationalists found themselves in the Displaced Persons (DP) camps of Austria and Germany, living among some two hundred thousand expatriates. Here, the OUN-B was split between hardliners who continued to subscribe to *vozhdism*, or the "leader cult," and democrats. Bandera tried to reassert control of the organization by conducting a retrenchment that involved reviving authoritarian principles. According to Yevhen Stakhiv, a leader of the OUN who had worked in Eastern Ukraine, Bandera surrounded himself with people who had spent years in prison and whose basic political ideas had evolved little since 1934. They agreed with Dontsov's insistence on strong dictatorial rule and a leader cult (Stakhiv, Ie. 1995, 218–20). In contrast, individuals who had worked in the underground, particularly in Central and Eastern Ukraine, disagreed profoundly with this politics, arguing that it betrayed the principles articulated at the Third Congress (ibid., 221).

In July 1944 the Ukrainian Insurgent Army (UPA) established a body that was to represent its government in the underground. The UHVR (Ukrainian Supreme Liberation Council) was to speak for all individuals and parties fighting for independence. Although at the end of the Second World War perhaps half the UPA's membership belonged to the OUN, both the UPA and the UHVR were conceived as supraparty bodies (Serhiichuk 2009, vol. 1, 600, 604). Several members of the UHVR, including Mykola Lebed, Ivan Hrynokh, Vasyl Okhrymovych, and Emelian Logush, were sent abroad to establish its Western Representation—a public face in the emigration. By 1946 this Western Representation of the UHVR, which included a range of political parties (only the OUN-M refused to join), was in profound disagreement with Bandera's organization over the issue of democratization and the Third Congress.

A political opposition crystallized within the OUN-B. It argued for the observance of democratic principles both within the organization and in any future independent state, and attacked the retrograde concept of *vozhdism*. The leaders of this democratic opposition were Lev and Daria Rebet, Zinovii

Martiuk, and Vasyl Okhrymovych. It constituted a majority within the UHVR's Western Representation, which was the official voice of the underground in Ukraine. By 1948 the opposition had succeeded in winning over many supporters. Stanley Frolick, who left the OUN-B in 1952, confirms this analysis: "I wrote a letter to Bandera in which I said that I saw no need for a conspiratorial network in Canada. Make the organization open and let anyone who agrees with its principles join it. Bandera replied that we would not be able to control an open organization. I asked him what difference that made. Uniformity of thought could not be imposed. If people agreed with us, they should be welcomed. If they changed their minds, they should be free to leave the organization" (Luciuk and Carynnyk 1990, 155). Some leaders in the Bandera faction appear to have regarded the public positions of the UPA and UHVR as mere gestures meant for Western consumption, a necessary pretence. They spoke of the need to remain faithful "in reality" to prewar principles (G. Motyka 2006b, 135).

The writings sent from the underground in Ukraine in the late 1940s and early 1950s were often written by Roman Shukhevych, Osyp Diakiv (pseudonym Hornovy), and Petro Fedun (pseudonym Poltava). They affirmed the anti-totalitarian, anticolonial and anti-imperial positions of the UPA and the Homeland UHVR and dismissed Dontsov's views (Serhiichuk 2009, vol. 2, 355, 373). Diakiv wrote in 1950: "As for Dontsov, his writings contain no serious critique, but only abuse, a dishonest twisting of facts, speculation and base insinuations" (ibid., 374). Although some questioned the authenticity of this correspondence, the democratizers within the OUN were convinced that Ukraine's population opposed elitism, national chauvinism, and dictatorship; they argued that "German fascism could not be replaced with Ukrainian" (ibid., 243). Shankovsky made the same point in summarizing the experience of the expeditionary forces. He argued that the people of Dnieper Ukraine "rejected all monoparty systems, and declared themselves decisively for a democratic state and a parliamentary system in which different parties could express themselves." Some ideas held by OUN members from Western Ukraine, he said, "were simply loathsome to these masses, especially anything to do with the so-called theory of voluntaristic nationalism, the amoralism of an initiative-taking minority, Machiavellianism, exclusiveness, and thirst for power" (Shankovsky 1958, 21). In fact the change had been coming since September 1942, when the first issue of the OUN-B's wartime journal *Ideia i chyn* (Idea and Deed, 1942–46) appeared. Ten issues were published over the next four years. They denounced both Nazi and Soviet rule, and aligned the UPA with other national liberation movements within the USSR.

In 1948 the UHVR's Western Representation formally broke with the Bandera faction (Stakhiv, Ie. 2005, 250–51). An internal struggle continued within the latter until 1956, when the opposition established its own party, the OUN-Z (for *Zakordonom*, meaning "Abroad"), under the leadership of Lev Rebet and Zenon Matla. This group contended that the OUN-B was still wedded to the totalitarian program of 1941 and viewed democratic slogans only as a tactical maneuver. According to Krychevsky, Bandera thought there should be one program—the organization's basic credo—for members and supporters, and another for "external" use (Krychevskyi 1962, 26–27). The democrats explicitly rejected Dontsov's promulgation of amorality in politics and his equation of strength with ruthlessness, arguing instead that real strength lay in moral values (ibid., 41). Bandera, they stated, had allowed Dontsov to attack not only the democratic opposition but also the propagandists working for the underground in Ukraine (ibid., 41, 90).[18]

The positions argued by these propagandists of the UPA and UHVR were far removed from the authoritarianism of the prewar OUN. Fedun (pseudonym Poltava) had been drafted into the Red Army, where he spent time in Eastern Ukraine. After being taken prisoner at the beginning of the German-Soviet war, he escaped the fate of the three million POWs whom the Germans starved to death. It is likely that he was freed through the efforts of Volodymyr Kubijovyč (Kubiiovych), the Ukrainian Central Committee and the Ukrainian Red Cross, who managed to rescue thirty thousand prisoners. On the OUN's instructions, Diakiv (pseudonym Hornovy) joined the Komsomol in 1940 and narrowly escaped imprisonment by the Soviets in 1941. Both men had a good knowledge of Soviet ideology and reality, and Fedun in particular knew Eastern Ukraine. They joined the UPA's propaganda team in 1944, were promoted to the Homeland UHVR's secretariat, and were killed by Soviet special operations troops in 1951 and 1950, respectively. Neither had any time for Dontsov's ideas. Both downplayed the use of emotional rhetoric, and avoided the symbolism of traumatic military episodes like the Battle of Kruty. Instead, they focused on social justice, democracy, the rights of nations, and opposition to all imperialisms. They were clearly opposed to a monoparty system and for parliamentary democracy. This was of course part of a larger trend in postwar Europe, which saw a turn away from right-wing parties and ideologies. Moreover, the OUN-B and UPA should be considered separate entities, although some commentators have questioned attempts to make this distinction (Rudling 2011, 23). Yaroslav Hrytsak contests attempts by historians sympathetic to the OUN-B to "monopolize" the history of UPA, which, toward the end of the Second World War, drew in many young people, who joined for various reasons and held various views. Often they simply wanted to avoid mobilization into the Soviet army, which for Western Ukrainian youth meant a death sentence, since they were frequently used as cannon fodder (Hrytsak 2004, 106).

Rivalry between the three branches of the OUN continued in emigration. Fighters from the underground UPA who escaped to the West sometimes joined Bandera's organization. In 1948 Bandera's OUN began working with British intelligence, while the Western Representation of the UHVR and the OUN-M cooperated with American intelligence services (Hałagida 2005, 62). After 1948 intensive efforts were made to contact the UPA leadership in Ukraine, whom all sides felt was the ultimate arbiter in any émigré disputes. Recent research has shown that the couriers sent by Bandera's faction all went through Leonid Lapinsky (Leon Lapiński), who was known by the code name "Zenon." A member of the OUN-B since 1941 and its leading figure in Eastern Poland (in Chełm and Podlachia), after 1947 he began working for the Polish and Soviet secret services. He controlled all the organization's channels both within Poland and from Poland into Ukraine. The organization's contacts were therefore compromised; all its couriers were captured or shot.

The Western Representation of the UHVR used other channels and was more successful in contacting the underground in Ukraine. Letters from the underground leadership and writings of the UPA's chief propagandists favored their ideological stance. When in October 1949 the leadership of the underground in Ukraine sent a letter "to the whole Ukrainian emigration," it explained that the people's struggle was against imperialism and totalitarianism, and for the universal ideals of humanity: freedom for the individual and for peoples, the slogan that had been carried since the first issue of *Ideia i chyn*. The letter was signed by twenty-two individuals in the leadership of the UHVR, the UPA, and the OUN ("Zvernennia Voiuiuchoi Ukrainy" 1984, 32–33). It urged that all propaganda focus on political and personal liberation. Therefore the OUN in Ukraine, and to a large degree in emigration, had come full circle since the first congress of 1929: having jettisoned authoritarianism, it had now embraced the democratic nationalism it had once deplored.

IDEOLOGY

3

DMYTRO DONTSOV

Although never a member of the OUN, Dmytro Dontsov exerted an important influence on its ideology. In fact, many OUN members felt that his ideas defined their generation. He saw the nation in psychological and spiritual terms as "the will to act" and a "program of social action," as Tomasz Stryjek has pointed out, and he is particularly interesting because of his attempt to formulate a new ethical doctrine (Stryjek 2000, 111). In the early 1920s he called for a fundamental transformation of Ukrainian intellectual and spiritual life and indicated the key role that literature should play in bringing about this metamorphosis. He himself wrote in a powerful, acerbic style and delivered many well-attended lectures in Lviv, Stanislaviv, Kolomyia, Przemyśl, Lutsk, Vienna, Kraków, Warsaw, and other cities. The Warsaw lectures to the Ukrainian student group, for example, always drew hundreds of listeners in spite of the admission charge (Portnov 2008, 143).

Dontsov's father was a merchant and landowner who moved from Russia's Voronezh region to Melitopol in Ukraine's south. His mother, whose name was Frantsiska, had an Italian grandmother, and her stepfather had been a German colonist. After Dmytro finished the gymnasium in Tsarskoe Selo near St. Petersburg, he attended the universities at St. Petersburg and Vienna, and then completed a law degree at Lviv University. He began writing for German, Swiss, Russian, and Ukrainian newspapers in 1917, and in 1918 served as press secretary to Hetman Pavlo Skoropadsky's government. From 1919 he worked in the Ukrainian Press Bureau in Berne, Switzerland, before moving to Lviv to edit *Literaturno-naukovyi vistnyk,* a position for which he was recommended by Konovalets, who was on the journal's initial editorial board and provided some of the early financing.[1] The UVO leader was, however, unable to fund a second journal that Dontsov tried to launch, *Zahrava* (Crimson Sky, 1923–24), which was conceived as the organ of a new political party on the radical right. The editor always blamed Konovalets for the failure of this venture.[2]

Dontsov was sensitive to the charge that he was a typical Russian intellectual who had first embraced Marxist socialism and then radical nationalism, both with the same fervent, almost mystical faith. Volodymyr Doroshenko made a similar comment on 13 September 1931, in a letter to Malaniuk, who forwarded it to Dontsov. The latter responded: "I was born in Tavriia, where I spent my first seventeen years, in a land that can be called our America, an ethnographic mixture of Ukrainians, Poles, Jews, Bulgarians, Germans, Greeks, Turks, and Russians. [. . .] Russian influences could only come from Jewish friends in the secondary school [*realna shkola*]." He insisted that his strongest influences had come from reading Western literature and Ukrainian writers like Oleksa Storozhenko and Mykola Hohol (Nikolai Gogol) (BN, Mf. 82671, 115). However, there is evidence that social Darwinism had early become a substitute for religious faith. In a brochure entitled *Shkola a relihiia* (School and Religion, 1910) he argued that "the dismal teachings of Christianity and its priests" had far too much influence and should be removed from schools. Darwin, whom he called "this British genius," was hated by the church more than any other figure because he had "decisively turned the old Christian worldview upside down" (Dontsov 1910, 11). In a vehement style that was soon to become familiar to readers, he argued that religion was characterized by "an ethics of submission, slavish endurance, non-resistance to evil, love of the enemy, and other asinine virtues, an ethics that sees the highest virtue in the denial of everything earthly, in an asceticism that teaches misfortune and belief in heavenly rewards" (ibid., 22). In the spirit of Nietzsche, he argued that religion was to be replaced by an ideology of force.

In the 1920s and 1930s Dontsov preached the need for a new kind of patriotism. During a talk in Stanislaviv (Polish Stanisławów, now Ivano-Frankivsk) in 1925 he commented: "Someone said that among the great nations the Englishman loves his native lands like a woman whom he must conquer, the Frenchman like a lover whom he wishes to serve, the German like an aging mother for whom he must care. The Ukrainian is not mentioned, but I believe he loves his native lands like an old nanny who must worry about him (not he about her), and on whose breast he can place his hypersensitive, lachrymose heart. [. . .]This same lachrymose heart and hypersensitive humanitarianism made our generation into principled pacifists" (BN, Mf. 80370, 659). Dontsov blamed socialist ideas for the loss of statehood in 1917–20; he promoted voluntarism in place of rationalism, and an initiative-taking minority of "new people" in place of the democratic majority. Two books brought him fame, *Pidstavy nashoi polityky* (Foundations of

Our Politics, 1921) and *Natsionalizm* (Nationalism, 1926), but his influence was exerted through the editorship of *Literaturno-naukovyi vistnyk* (1922–32) and *Vistnyk* (1933 39). The first enlisted a large number of collaborators, while the second drew on a much smaller group.

Pidstavy nashoi polityky can claim to have changed the thinking of a generation. All leading Nationalist intellectuals, a generation looking for answers to the UNR's defeat, were weaned on it. The text depicted the conflict between Europe (to which Ukraine belonged) and Russia as a clash of civilizations. The author argued that Western societies thrive because they nurture social dynamism, allow conflict and the free play of forces, recognize the role of great individuals and the primacy of law and logic (Dontsov 1921, 20). This structured, organized social order is the polar opposite of the monochrome, repressed Russian society, in which the state takes all decisions and demands obedience. The more-developed Western societies allow "logic and well-defined procedures" to dominate. In politics this means "the institution of parliament, the principle of majority rule and persuasion of an opponent" (ibid., 23). Western self-government is contrasted with Russian absolutism, both tsarist and bolshevik: "In politics the Russian [*moskovskyi*] genius rises indignantly against all well-defined forms, through which the will of the people must be expressed. Therefore it rejects parliaments and the whole principle of representation, the division into a society that governs and one that is governed, appealing instead to the obscure, illogical popular voice that can be grasped intuitively (the dictatorship of the lumpenproletariat, government pogroms)" (ibid., 34). Russian society is portrayed as profoundly hostile to European liberalism. In every aspect of life—cultural, political, or religious— Dontsov extols Western individualism and parliamentary democracy and castigates the Russian idea of freedom as a descent to the lowest common denominator, which represents the destruction of individual initiative. The Russian mind, he argues, worships the ignorant, resentful, and impoverished masses. Ukraine must align itself with European republicanism and parliamentary democracy.

Although the contrast with the writer's later views is striking, there are continuities. One is the demand that Ukrainians develop an amoral "national egoism" that is focused on action. A second is the animosity toward Russians, which is related to his anti-Jewishness: in prewar years he had condemned anti-semitism; after 1920 he complained that Jews were extraordinarily active both in the press and theater in voicing pro-Russian opinions. Consistent too is his European orientation, even though the idea of what constituted Europe's greatness came to be reinterpreted. In this first book, Britain and France are treated favorably as Russia's greatest antagonists. Ukraine's cultural traditions are viewed as deeply occidental, Germano-Latin, and respectful of the individual, legal norms, the constitution, and private ownership. These traditions uphold "the principle of democracy as it is understood in the West" (ibid., 109). The social ideal is not an atomized mass, but a community of well-organized social groups who advance their interests within a structured political system. Such a system strengthens society and produces strong individuals, not a slavelike equality. Within four years the rhetoric had changed. Dontsov dropped all positive references to parliamentary democracy and revised his attitude toward history and the people.

As concerns culture, *Pidstavy* argues against European nihilism, to which he consigned bolshevism, Wagner's "musical demagoguery," Hungarian futurist art, the communist Henri Barbusse, and the pacifist Romain Rolland (both of whom later turned out to be great admirers of Stalin and the Soviet Union). He soon omitted Wagner (Hitler's favorite composer) from the list of baneful influences. If his diary entitled *Rik 1918, Kyiv* (The Year 1918, Kyiv) is to be taken at face value (it was only published in 1952), already while working in the press bureau of Skoropadsky's German-backed government he felt a strong aversion to "lachrymose" cultural products, such as the music of the composer Kyrylo Stetsenko. He complains in the diary that the composer had turned Lesia Ukrainka's despairing pain into "sweet Little Russian sentiment" (Dontsov 2002, 49). In prewar Vienna Dontsov found "anaemia, impotence, fatigue, an escape from great traditions into the personal, into easy enjoyment and peace"—all symptoms of the slow expiry of "great-power aspirations and energy" that foreshadowed the empire's political death. Austrian literature, art, and music had displayed the signs: a lack of "bright colours, great problems, the hot pulse of blood." The examples he gives are Arthur Schnitzler's elegant but decadent eroticism, Richard Strauss's music, and the "chaos" in Wagner's works (ibid., 128–29).

In *Natsionalizm* Dontsov began to exalt will over intellect, action over contemplation, instinct over logic, and aggression over pacifism. The book's entire tone breathes the spiteful resentment of Dostoevsky's Underground Man. Some of the argumentation and phrasing echo the words of this character from *Notes from the Underground*, especially the need to dominate others and the rejection of generally accepted truths, such as "the laws of Nature" and the fact that "two plus two equals four." Dontsov scoffs at the "eternal" laws and history's "iron necessity," which Western intellectuals have invoked to subdue oppressed nations and discourage them from struggle. The typical Ukrainian "Provencale" (a term of abuse that carries the connotation of a lukewarm, purely cultural or regional loyalty) has been mesmerized by "stable" relations and "evolutionary" laws (Dontsov 1926, 22). In place of timid rationalism, which accepts the status quo and the need for slow, incremental progress, he offers blind faith, overpowering desire, and irrational will. He knows that the idea of a nation having its own will and desires has been dismissed by "rationalists" as metaphysics, but counters: "Species that are healthy place no limits on the willful instinct. For them affirmation of the right to life, of the *genus*'s continuity carries an axiomatic character; it is primary. They [healthy species] elevate the nation's eternal, nonrational [Dontsov uses the word "arational"] right to life above everything temporary, phenomenal, ephemeral, rational—above the life of a given individual, the blood and death of thousands, the wellbeing of a given generation, abstract mental calculations, 'universal' ethics, and intellectually elaborated concepts of good and evil" (ibid., 29).

In this overtly authoritarian phase Dontsov attacks liberalism, democracy, humaneness, and pacifism, which, in his view, affirm the primacy of the individual over the collective and state. He, on the contrary, affirms the rights of the state over the individual. He supports the cult of the soldier who has sacrificed his life for future generations, of "the great idea." He laments the lack of patriotic books that show not only war's tragedy but also its glamour and excitement: "The great crusades of chosen people have led to the creation of mighty monuments to human genius, such as the British Empire, the Europeanization of Africa, the cultivation of India" (ibid., 33–34). He also admires the settlement of the American West, the Russian conquest of Siberia, and the Ukrainian "liberation of the Steppe from nomads." There is an "eternal urge among strong races to extend the boundaries of their dominions" (ibid., 36–37). The writings of a pacifist, skeptic, and ironist like Anatole France are treated with contempt, and the lower classes who fail to understand the national imperative are looked upon with disdain. These last have "a basic aversion to the great organizing collective, which demands sacrifices in the name of its enduring interests, and places burdens on the individual, the people, and separate classes" (ibid., 42). To be sure, the masses do have their local patriotism, but this is insufficient for a developed nation. The national will in these masses has not progressed beyond an early, primitive, and naive love of the native land. This kind of will cannot understand the importance of aggression and power "without which no nation can emerge from its provincial diapers" (ibid., 68).

The support for passionate, frenzied, and ecstatic forms of expression signals another change. Dontsov began at this time to teach the attractions of chaos, uncertainty, and "the abyss" (ibid., 115). He was attracted not to the cognitive but the viscerally and emotionally affective, to forms of expression, which, as Dominick LaCapra has indicated, "often seem to be traumatic writing or post-traumatic writing in closest proximity to trauma" (LaCapra 2001, 23). Some of his own writings have been described as "séances of hatred" (Stryjek 2002, 169).

Dontsov stressed the role of rhetoric and performativity and embraced hyperbole. A writer or a critic, in his view, was to be guided by subjective enthusiasm, not facts. He wrote in 1927: "There are no facts in the world; only a movement and will that governs them. There are human passions that instigate events and people" (Dontsov 1927, 273). He himself wrote, "in a trance-like state," as he admitted in a letter to his wife written on 26 August 1937 (TsDAVO, f. 3849, op. 1, spr. 17, ark. 116). The ability to sweep readers up in the flow of his own thoughts and emotions was part of his success as a journalist. Shevelov has attested that Dontsov seemed to exert a hypnotic power over individuals and entire circles (Shevelov 2001, vol. 2, 107).

Dontsov's literary preferences were for temperamental, strong-willed authors. He argued that Ukrainian literature was conventional in both sentiment and form, and had for decades cultivated moods of sadness and pity. Among exceptions to this rule were Shevchenko, Storozhenko, Lesia Ukrainka, and Mykola Khvylovy. The country required a new, daring writing that embraced myths and legends of struggle, and focused on the individual's conflict with surroundings. Unfortunately, the relationship of Ukrainian writers to the material world was "usually passive, almost photographic," full of "entirely intellectual" observations and long lucid expositions. It was necessary to learn from modernist experimentation: "The smudged silhouettes and darknesses of Rembrandt, the arbitrary treatment of material, its ruthless incorporation, the clearing of a free path for the unbridled creative Ego—all this is viewed by us as 'futurism' and not literature. We always talk about everything with a vulgarizer's clarity and a photographer's exactness" (Dontsov 1926, 127). In place of an aesthetics of harmony, balance, and classical restraint, Dontsov called in *Natsionalizm* for an expressionist probing of the irrational in the human soul and extolled "blind dynamism"—the mysterious creative principle that is allied not to the conscious mind but to instincts and irrational forces (ibid., 161).

Dontsov was fascinated by futurism and expressionism. He was drawn to their artistic potential for violence and their disrespect for past forms. Literature and art, like politics, should, he felt, build the collective philosophy of a nation on "the will to life, without sanctions, without justifications, without motivation" (ibid., 165). The literary hero should express this willfulness by imposing himself on the environment or by rejecting it. On no account should his will be broken; he must not bend, but must perish rather than accept a foreign power over himself. Dontsov advises developing an instinctive desire for conquest, expansion, and struggle—signs, for him, of a healthy organism. Such an instinctive desire is based in physiology, "in the same way as a dog reacts to the sight of a cat, or an antisemite to the sight of a Jew" (ibid., 167).

His journalistic talent was recognized by opponents. Stepan Smal-Stotsky called him the only Ukrainian publicist of European rank. Yevhen Malaniuk described him as a phenomenon (Kentii 2005, 64). Even Shevelov admitted to being fascinated by his ideas and slogans in the years 1943–46 (Shevelov 2001, vol. 2, 107). Dontsov created an emotionally driven argument, one that has been described as convincing through pathos (Ilnytskyi 1999 9). He had a gift for personifying virtues and vices: his "Don Quixote" or "Provencale," for example, became instantly recognizable ideological avatars that could be invoked at different times. However, as a critic he had enormous limitations: he refused to countenance alternative perspectives, made crassly reductive judgments, and lacked interest in technical artistry. His focus was almost exclusively on the fanatical individual. In fact, Shevelov described the entire *Vistnyk* group as autistic: they spoke only to themselves and gave the impression of being slightly deaf (Shevelov 2001, vol. 2 108).

In the 1920s Dontsov invoked the authority of Nietzsche, Sorel, Spengler, Spencer, and Barrès to reject quietism and complacent faith in progress. Like the Italian futurists, he glorified struggle, sport, and war and celebrated not the pursuit of clarity but the need to bend material to the artist's will. Futurism exhibited the desired qualities of dynamism, conflict, and movement. Expressionism and romanticism were admired for portraying the individual in revolt against established norms and peaceful ideals. Sorel was praised for appreciating the "barbaric philosophy of myth" as an element in political revolution. These prescriptions constituted a reactionary form of modernism, one that rejected naturalism, photographic realism, and classicism (which he defined as *kalos kagathos*: the beautiful and the good). When Dontsov spoke of tradition, he glorified only elements from the past that accepted violence and compulsion in the name of change. Tradition was for him "the armour that defends the collective from enemy attacks" (Dontsov 1967, 11). He insisted that Ukrainians had to choose their traditions, to select their own legends, to learn how to love and hate. In 1923 in the essay "Pro 'Molodykh'" (On "The Young") he made a long statement on his preferences in literature and art:

> The revolution that has dethroned the saints of positivism has replaced them with intuitivism in philosophy (Bergson) and expressionism in art and literature (in poetry it was first called "symbolism"). The new worldview has broken irrevocably with everything old. This was a revolt in the name of everything elemental, subconscious in the human soul. Feeling took the place of reason, the personal "I want" took the place of laws, mysticism took the place of phenomena. At the source of everything there appeared a will that knew no compromises, or more correctly its protoform—an obscure

drive. Once more the world appeared as the play of turbulent, blindly raging forces, as a chaos in which nothing is but everything is just becoming. The individual "Ego," its autonomous creativity, and its untiring activism became values in themselves, independent of aims and content. Ethical pathos and "amorality," *fas* and *nefas*, the delight of the creator and the malice of the destroyer all became mixed up in the cult of the naked force and power that hates everything sickly or condemned to die, and that is the sole guarantor of victory in our epoch of lost illusions, unparalleled boredom, and war of all against all. (Dontsov 1923, 268)

The best writing, in his view, portrayed heroes who were focused on "abstract" goals, that is to say distant ones beyond the ken of ordinary people. He suggested that Christopher Columbus and the conquistadors provided appropriate subjects, as did the apocalypse, the final battle, the fight to the finish by martyrs for a cause. This kind of literature represented the occidental Faustian spirit. Since in the mid-1920s he was still orientated toward Britain and America as examples of successful civilizations, his *Natsionalizm* includes odes to their imperial greatness: one passage is devoted to the British Empire and one to American idealism and its conquering spirit (Dontsov 1926, 212–13, 217–18). In both passages he insists that only the strong survive. Ukrainians must therefore choose between developing an aggressive, expansionist civilization (following their own "abstract" ideal) or succumbing to the ideal of another civilization.

Dontsov preferred a *littérature engagée* that dramatized the play of opposites. His mind worked by constantly juxtaposing: friend versus foe, West versus Russia, elite versus mass, aristocrat versus plebeian, predator versus grass-eater, active versus passive. The tone is always categorical.[3] He is prepared to express admiration for communist, nationalist, or fascist literature of the 1920s if they exhibit a spiritual dynamism and striving. Even some Kyiv and Kharkiv writers of the twenties are admired, because "blood," he says, "spurted from both" (Dontsov 1925, 335). By the same token, the Kyiv neoclassicists of this decade were criticized for "lacking faith in passion" (ibid., 325).

However, the most controversial shift in Dontsov's views concerned the justification of violence. It was framed in Sorelian terms as support for legends capable of stimulating revolution by inflaming the popular imagination, but Dontsov also sanctioned violence against one's own people. By the late 1920s he was openly aligning his political and aesthetic views with fascism. In 1928 he praised Italy's fascist movement and its desire to cut links with the past. Like the prewar Polish Socialist Party, Italian fascism represented "dreamers" able to envision a future and prepared to "grasp life by the throat" (Dontsov 1928, 84). The world, he argued, was imagined and created by strong personalities. His introduction to Mykhailo Ostroverkha's book on Mussolini, published by the *Vistnyk* library in 1934, lauded the dictator's concept of creative "leadership" over the amorphous mass, his idea of "social punitiveness and order" (Ostroverkha 1934, 4). The book is a political hagiography that highlights the importance of war for forging national unity. Mussolini is described as sympathetic toward Ukrainian independence. He is quoted (from an issue of *Il Popolo d'Italia* on 6 September 1919) as saying: "Threatened by the greed of other peoples, exhausted by panrussianism, lacking weapons, means, isolated, under the skeptical gaze of all Europe, the Ukrainian people liberated its land from bolshevik infection and won back its capital. Free nations have been moved by the power of these battles, although their governments pretend not to see the strivings of this people. The Ukrainians are not only defending themselves, but all Europe" (ibid., 56). Ostroverkha concludes that Mussolini "supported our cause with complete enthusiasm" (ibid.). In *Patriotyzm* (Patriotism, 1936) Dontsov wrote admiringly of Japan's transformation within two generations, and of fascist Italy, which "had changed beyond recognition the entire nature of its people, the whole moral and spiritual face of a nation that until then had been lazy, feeble, beggarly, locked into its peninsula" (Dontsov 1936a, 40). A fascist-inspired spiritual and psychological transformation had elevated Italians from the level of a plebeian people to that of a master nation. Neither Ostroverkha nor Dontsov were members of the OUN, but both did much to popularize fascism. Ostroverkha's *Nova imperiia* (New Empire, 1938) has been described as the strongest apologia for Italian fascism "that ever came from the pen of a Ukrainian" (Zaitsev 2012).

Although Dontsov had already expressed his support for fascism in 1923, by the mid-1930s this support had become almost unconditional (Golczewski 2010a, 573; Motyl 1980, 113–14). In an article entitled "Poputchykam" (To Fellow Travelers, 1935) he wrote triumphantly that fascism in opposing communism and liberalism had produced "a new vital, contemporary ideology" (Dontsov 1935b, 915). His publishing house issued Rostyslav Yendyk's book on Hitler, which described the Führer as representing the whole German nation, inspiring mystical adoration in his people, defeating Marxism and social democracy, and reducing the influence of Jews (Iendyk 1935, 59). Yendyk praised the unification of the German people around the principles of blood and soil and the strong personality that represented "the nation's crown," rejecting parliamentary "cretins" and intriguers (ibid., 8). Readers were told that the broad masses had to be conquered through "the fiery word, not the chatter of literary aesthetes and salon heroes" (ibid., 34). Publications like these spurred the social democrat Volodymyr Levynsky to write that Dontsov did more than anyone else to popularize Mussolini, Hitler, and other strong men (Levynskyi 1936, 28).

Dontsov's views were challenged. In 1922 Isaak Mazepa, a social democrat who had served in the UNR government, indicated the mechanistic argumentation of *Pidstavy*: an abstract, predetermined idea is first presented and then supported with countless unreferenced quotations, which are often misquotations. He detected Dontsov's admiration for firm government and challenged his interpretation of Cossack rule, pointing out that previous historians like Kostomarov had an entirely different opinion of Cossackdom. They had emphasized its antidespotic, freedom loving, and anarchic instincts (Mazepa 1922, 60). Behind Dontsov's yearning for strictness, the reviewer saw a secret desire for autocratic rule and quoted the words: "I am not a principled opponent of the monarchic form of political order and would be pleased if this form (in the guise of a national monarchy) were to appear in our history" (Dontsov 1921, 200). Dontsov, said Mazepa, was not favorably disposed to society's democratization or to a politically active mass population, but was focused on a strong ruling class. The review concluded: "If in contemporary conditions one could create a state based on Dontsov's ideas, it could only be a police state in which the popular masses serve mutely as material for the experiments of various 'brilliant cynics'" (Mazepa 1922, 60).

Social democrats like Mazepa and socialist revolutionaries like Mykyta Shapoval (Sribliansky) concurred that Ukraine's key problem in 1917–20 lay in its predominantly peasant social structure and poorly developed professional and urban classes. "The cities in Ukraine," argued Shapoval, "were in large measure not Ukrainian" (M. Shapoval 1923, 7), a viewpoint he later developed in his *Velyka revoliutsiia* (The Great Revolution, 1928). Dontsov, on the other hand, saw the problem as psychological, and found the solution in voluntarism. His views initially came out of the conservatism that spread in the early 1920s. Its most respected champion was Viacheslav Lypynsky, who pointed out the importance of a state-building elite. The democrats and socialists, he lamented, had in the revolutionary years embraced a concept of nation too closely identified with language, ethnicity, and peasantry. They had often turned away "the gentry" (*pany*) or people of foreign origin (like Lypynsky himself, who was of Polish background) because of ideological prejudices. He also found appeals to material interests insufficient and lamented the lack of a national idealism nurtured on edifying legends that could inspire unity. In his *Lysty do brativ khliborobiv* (Letters to My Fellow Farmers), he wrote that Ukraine needed to bring together its three sons: the farmer, the member of the intelligentsia, and the worker. These sons, who often belonged respectively to the conservative, democratic, and bolshevik camps, lacked a clear unifying vision. They needed to see themselves as citizens of one state. Lypynsky had also worked in Skoropadsky's government, and Dontsov shared his conservative precepts. However, Dontsov lacked the measured, rational, and lucid tone that characterized Lypynsky. Moreover, rather than unity, Dontsov sought division; in place of compromise, he praised fanaticism. His writings shifted the debate from an analysis of social forces to the importance of desire.

Authoritarian politics went against the Galician habits of patient community building and stolid resistance. Mykola Shlemkevych, who wrote under the pseudonym M. Ivaneiko and was close to Dontsov in the 1930s, argued after the war that the latter's "anarchizing idealism" represented a departure from the culture of realism, in particular from the calm, modest, reasonable self-limitation and the talent for self-organization that had always been the Galician karma (Shlemkevych 1956, 156). Under Dontsov's influence the OUN had come out with the idea that "not truth, morality and logic are important, but power, strong actions and the will; it was not knowledge that counted, but strong desire" (ibid., 92). This anarchic strain, stimulated by the temptations of amorality and cruelty, had begun to spread in a youth that had never experienced "statehood as a moral institution and moral value" (ibid., 97). The doctrine of moral relativism had, in Shlemkevych's view, become widespread. It was evident in the Soviet Union, where everything was defined as either useful or harmful to the class struggle, and in the authoritarian right-wing regimes, which trampled treaty obligation and ignored human rights, enforcing the belief that politics was, in essence, the cynical use of violence.

When Dontsov broke with Skoropadsky's supporters in 1926, he criticized Lypynsky, whom the OUN leaders held in the highest regard as a theorist of conservativism. Lypynsky responded with an exasperated letter to the New Jersey newspaper *Svoboda* (Freedom) on 12 May 1926. He complained of misrepresentation, and mailed a copy of his letter to Dontsov, whom the newspaper had quoted:

> In issue 94 of your newspaper dated 23 April of this year you wrote that I "agitate for dropping the goal of independence and for voluntarily recognizing Ukraine's place in the Russian empire."
>
> I know you Ukrainian intelligentsia snakes too well to be surprised by these lies, to have any desire to answer them, or to engage in polemics with you. Keep lying. The more your lies besmirch the Ukrainian name, which you yourselves represent, the more your baseness will drive away all honest Ukrainians, and the sooner the branch on which you sit will fall, and you boors will die, blinded by your own spite. (BN, Mf. 83984, 108)

Dontsov wrote to Lypynsky on 15 May 1926 of his "extreme concern" with the latter's mental health and offered to put him in touch with "all our known psychiatrists" in order to find him a place in a Vienna or Lviv asylum (BN, Mf 82671, 78).

Many readers found Dontsov's contemptuous, bravura tone attractive. Lypa, for example, wrote of Dontsov's "fine, audacious articles" whose "implacable militancy" was the most important thing (TsDAVO, f. 4465, op. 1, spr. 577, ark. 6). However, others warned that the tone was damaging the capacity for careful, reasoned thought, and decried Dontsov's tendency to distort an opponent's position into unrecognizable form so as to dismiss it. The strongest analyses along these lines came from Sviatoslav Dolengo (real name Andrii Kryzhanivsky) in 1938 and later from Sherekh (Shevelov), who in 1948 demonstrated how Dontsov manipulated quotations, often to produce a meaning opposite to what the original text had intended (Sherekh 1948, 11–12). This, of course, was part of Dontsov's strategy. As Omelchuk has written, it did not matter what the text said, because the critic's job was to create the desired text, to shape attitudes to his or her own subjective, culture-creating or myth-making intentions (Omelchuk 2011, 24–25).

The primary competition for Dontsov and the Nationalists in the battle for Galician hearts and minds were the liberal and democrats grouped around the UNDO party and the Lviv newspaper *Dilo* (Work). The periodical condemned terrorism, Dontsov's writings, and the rise of authoritarianism. On 3 January 1933, M. Tvorylo asked: "Why the sympathy for a 'strong hand'?" He offered the following explanation: "The main reason is that we live among undemocratic states and slogans. Willy-nilly we submit to overly strong foreign influences, and become infected by dubious pseudo-democrats, who are especially plentiful among our neighbours." Democracy, he offered, tries to regulate relations between individuals and national groups, but authoritarianism grows wherever a middle class is lacking or weak and the possibility for social advancement is unavailable. Vasyl Mudry, the newspaper's editor and a member of the Sejm, spoke out against Dontsov at an UNDO congress on 24–25 December 1928. He complained that the critic was "grafting elements of anarchy onto the souls of his supporters," teaching young people to paralyze national life and even to physically destroy those who opposed "nationalist" romanticism. The speech was printed in booklet form. Vladimir Kysilevsky, a Canadian who ran the Ukrainian Bureau in London, met Mudry on 13 January 1933 during a visit to Lviv. He reported in his diary that the editor spoke "about the irresponsibility of Nationalist youth, about the creation in Galicia of something akin to the Irish 'gunman' who is beginning to terrorize the Ukrainian community" (LAC 10). The Polish police had informed Mudry of a planned assassination in revenge for his article condemning the Horodok raid. He felt compelled to apply for permission to carry a revolver.[4]

The former UVO leader Volodymyr Tselevych wrote a series of articles in 1933 condemning the use of terror against one's own people, arguing that "nationalism has never anywhere used these methods of struggle" (Tselevych 1933a). The belief that ends justify means had caused a crisis among youth, and he warned that "amorality has a tendency to spread from one sphere of human life to all others." Dontsov's *Natsionalizm*, he wrote, had poisoned minds. Youth read the book without analyzing it (Tselevych 1933b).

Terrorism was becoming a threat to journalists and writers. Ivan Kedryn, an editor of *Dilo*, who maintained contact with Konovalets, later commented that among the many uneducated hotheads recruited to the OUN were numerous provocateurs and agents. One student came and hit Mudry in the face. Another was sent to do the same to Kedryn but turned back in front of the editor's office. Student youth issued "death sentences" to community leaders, including the director of Prosvita. It is not clear whether these were just bad jokes or part of a plan later paralyzed by saner heads in the underground (Kedryn 1976, 145). In some cases, as has been seen, the threats were carried out.

When the *Kurier Lwowski* (Lviv Courier), an organ of the Polish Endeks associated *Dilo* with the Nationalists, the paper replied that this was an attempt to throw responsibility for the OUN's actions onto the whole community, to make all Ukrainians pay for acts of terrorism. The root problem, it countered, lay in Poland's laws and nationality policy, which provided the soil for terrorism to grow. *Kurier*, in contrast, was convinced that the terrorists would "never be satisfied," and that "all gains would be used to strengthen their organization, which would demand more without lowering its aggressiveness." *Dilo* answered on 3 November 1933 that this was a convenient view that enabled *Kurier* to dismiss a priori the right of Ukrainians to a legal, evolutionary struggle within the Polish state. The OUN, said *Dilo*, did not "hang in the stratosphere," but came out of specific national and sociopolitical circumstances, which were turning youth into material for the OUN. As these motivating sources dried up, so would the revolutionary work ("Iaku garantiiu" 1933).

Any outspoken or defiant Ukrainian was widely identified at this time as pro-German and nationalist, both in Poland and the Soviet Union. Although support for independence could not be equated with support for the views of the OUN or Dontsov, society in the 1930s was affected by an attitudinal change that blurred the distinction between democratic and authoritarian nationalism. This was evident in creative literature, which encouraged Ukrainians to admire heroic figures, take pride in their identity, and assert themselves. The trend represented both an acceptance of modernizing change and recognition that Ukrainians needed to grasp control of this process. The moderate *Shliakh natsii*

(Paths of the Nation) wrote: "A firm reality forces upon us new forms of organized life whether we desire them or not; and the main problem is the question: will we hold out psychologically in this new era, will we be able to pour our own Ukrainian national content into new forms of organized life that are being imposed upon us from outside. That depends, in my view, on the nation's development and the moral strength of each individual Ukrainian" (Hnatyshak 1936, 23–24).

However, Dontsov's support for the nonrational (Dontsov's term is "arational") and cult of dictators set him apart not only from liberals and democrats, but also from many in the OUN. His *Natsionalizm* was debated among Lviv's students for months (Martynets 1949, 286). Some readers rejected his amorality, arguing instead for an ethical politics based on love of nation. While recognizing Dontsov as their "spiritual father" and his *Natsionalizm* as their "gospel," they recoiled from the cult of negativity, the promotion of motiveless self-assertion, and the disdain for Ukrainian history (D. Rebet 1974, 174, 492). However, many readers were inspired by the invitation to exercise their will and to despise passivity or cowardice. It is clear that Dontsov's undermining of all rationality and destruction of traditional morality made the idolatry of nation more difficult to resist. There were those who found it attractive and who welcomed the call to use unscrupulous methods in pursuit of political goals. The critic spread a special tone that was fanatical, driven by ecstatic faith, attracted to danger, and determined to exert willpower.

Some of his most celebrated essays throw light on this "abstract" fanaticism. In "Poetka ukrainskoho risordzhymento (Lesia Ukrainka)" (Poet of the Ukrainian Risorgimento—Lesia Ukrainka), which appeared in the opening two issues of *Literaturno-naukovyi vistnyk* and served as a manifesto of sorts, he suggests that her greatness lies in her ability to "infect" readers with a tone. He praises her cult of energy and movement, and her contempt for halfheartedness. The key to her style, he writes, lies in not giving the content of emotions, but merely suggesting their nature and intensity. She reproduces the logic of dreams without actually giving "the Sphinx" a name. In another article on Ukrainka—this one produced on the eve of the Second World War—he describes her as rejecting "the general human morality of peace and love for one's neighbour" as the "religion of slaves" (Dontsov 1938b, 140–42). Readers could only speculate on how such an attitude should be translated into concrete political action.

By the late 1930s Dontsov had traveled a considerable ideological distance from his prewar days. In 1909 he had written articles (under the pseudonym Dmytro Chornii) for the social democratic *Pratsia* (Work) in which he denounced an "all-Ukrainian" orientation as obstructing the class differentiation of Ukrainian workers. He called for entering the "all-Ukrainian" concert playing the "proletarian drum" (*Pratsia* 1 and 2 [1909]; quoted in Levynskyi 1936, 16–17). Although Olena Pchilka became one of his literary heroines in the thirties, in the prewar years he continually attacked *Ridnyi krai* (Native Land), the journal she edited, and "right-wing Ukrainianism" for its "antisemitism, religious fog and nationalist demagoguery" (Levynskyi 1936, 34–35). Levynsky makes the point that, like many self-styled rule-breakers, Dontsov was in some ways deeply conformist. Even when in 1913 he espoused separation from Russia, he had in mind not Ukraine's sovereignty, but its attachment to Austria (ibid., 21). His admiration of strong states and military prowess was, many felt, related to his desire to serve a strong ruler and to his lack of faith in the Ukrainian masses. Throughout the interwar period he avoided any criticism of Poland's internal policies or treatment of minorities. He only complained in 1934 that the Polish government had retreated from a policy of "cultural messianism" with respect to Russia, that it had dropped the idea of subjugating the East and had taken a defensive position vis-à-vis the Soviet Union (Stryjek 2000, 148). Stryjek maintains that Dontsov favored a "cordon sanitaire" with Russia and supported a strong Poland, Romania, and Hungary. This, in the scholar's view, explains the fact that Dontsov downplayed any Polish-Ukrainian conflict and always cast Russia, and not Poland, as the main enemy (ibid., 129).

The psychological attraction exerted by authoritarianism has been commented upon by Arthur Koestler. A self-transcendent drive, in his opinion, allows individuals to imagine themselves as part of a large social entity. However, a perversion of this self-transcendent drive enables people to subordinate themselves to a hierarchy and deny personal responsibility for their actions. Self-transcendence is often driven by a dread of isolation and a flight from inner chaos. Submerging oneself in a cause sanctions fanaticism and the suppression of individual conscience (Koestler 1976, 187–88). In the interwar period many prominent individuals admired and excused both communist and fascist dictatorships, arguing that they were a viable alternative to the unworkable democratic process. Lenin in a speech on 26 June 1920 said: "Freedom is a bourgeois notion [. . .]What Russia wants is an iron Government of a few determined men, and that she happily has got." He added: "Grumbling is as bad as treason, and will be as sharply punished" (quoted in "The Crisis of Democracy" 1931, 519).

In the later 1930s, as the democratic parties appeared increasingly compromised, authoritarianism began to fascinate Galician society. Independent publishers, such as Desheva Knyzhka (Inexpensive Book), produced political brochures that were widely read, including some authored by Dontsov. This unaligned, Lviv-based press helped to create an admiration for strong political leaders and dictators. In 1938 it published popular booklets on Hannibal, Napoleon, Gengis-Khan, Ataturk, De Valera, Bolivar, and Hitler. Earlier booklets had carried attacks on Ukrainian radicals and socialists and supported the Falangists, monarchists, and Carlists in the Spanish Civil War. Strong sympathies were voiced for the Catalans and Basques, who in their struggle for independence had mistakenly, it was said, put their faith in socialism and communism. The booklet on Hitler was particularly uncritical, failing either to mention his attitude toward eastern expansion or to distance itself from antisemitism. It concentrated instead on lauding the German leader's successes in unifying the nation and expanding the state. The Desheva Knyzhka firm also initiated the Lviv periodicals *Samoosvitnyk* (Self-educator), *Antybolshevyk* (Antibolshevik), and *Iuni druzi* (Young Friends). These made the firm enormously popular and influential, but it was boycotted by the OUN for refusing to subordinate its publication program to the organization's requirements (Mirchuk 1968, 480).

Galician fiction of the 1930s often portrayed the individual in desperate circumstances and produced in the reader a sense of urgency and a conviction that violence was required. Protagonists attempted to break with the past and to act heroically. Impatient with small deeds and practical measures, they searched for the one great, defining act. This literature explored the emotions of anger, hatred, exultation, and ecstasy. Dontsov's own writings represent a politically extreme version of this trend. Among his unpublished works written under the pseudonym Basavriuk is a short dramatic sketch entitled "Habemus Papam." It describes the selection of a new Ukrainian *Führer* (the German word is used). The chosen one rises, gives the fascist salute, and addresses the assembled crowd on the need for strict social hierarchy and one-party rule. When someone in the ecstatic mass cries out "Heil, Hitler!" he says: "I would not go so far. I caution our importers, who search for examples abroad when these can so easily be found under our noses." The *Führer* says: "We are democrats [. . .]but respect the authoritarian principle of natural leadership" (BN, Mf. 80370, 779–84).

In the early 1920s, Dontsov's attacks on democracy had still been muted. He insisted, for example, that Britain and America paid lip service to democracy, but in fact the governments of these countries fully controlled the masses. His enthusiasm for fascism, which came largely from reading French writers and studying the example of Italy, had literary and "aesthetic" origins (Omelchuk 2011, 220–23). Nonetheless, despite postwar denials (expressed in 1966, for example, in his introduction to the third edition of *Natsionalizm*), he placed great hopes in fascism, and by the 1930s he had become a confirmed opponent of parliamentary democracy. In his *Dukh nashoi davnyny* (Spirit of Our Past, 1943) he blamed the democratization of Europe, "which has taken enormous steps over the last hundred years," for destroying the old wisdom of rule by "the best people" (Dontsov 1951, 130).

Moreover, although he had begun using elements of racist theory after Hitler came to power, these became especially prominent on the eve of the German-Soviet war. In 1942 Dontsov scoffed at people who used the phrase "zoological nationalism." According to them, he wrote, "zoological nationalism applies to everyone who, for example, is not dragged into a united front with world Jewry for the struggle against Hitlerism " (Dontsov 1942; quoted in Weiner 2001, 241). *Dukh nashoi davnyny* links literature to race. The racially inferior Ostian type, it argues, is "unfortunately" widespread in Ukraine and has certain aesthetic tastes. This type prefers a chaotic form and dislikes "everything clearly defined, contoured, bright, pronounced in literature, in politics, in philosophy, in daily life" (Dontsov 1951, 222). In contrast to what he had written in the 1920s, the author here advocates a literature that expresses clear dogmas, rules, and axioms. These should "inflame the masses with faith," as he put it in 1938 (Dontsov 1967, 129). The message should remain simple, coherent, focusing on a leader and rule by an elite group. At this point he abandoned futurism and expressionism in favor of disciplined "classical" forms. His views on literature had therefore also gone through a considerable evolution. The constants were a belief in radical change, a spirit of intolerance, an emphasis (since *Natsionalizm*) on the importance of the irrational in human conduct, and promotion of the negative sublime that encouraged an overstepping of ethical boundaries. LaCapra has suggested that appeals to the sublime may represent "a secular displacement of the sacred in the form of a radically transcendent, inaccessible, unrepresentable other (including the alterity of radical evil)" (LaCapra 2001, 93). It has been argued that the Nazi sublime, which involved "the ability to perpetrate and endure scenes of unheard-of devastation and horror," was a factor in shaping the ideology and behavior of fanatically committed leaders (ibid., 93–94).

Dontsov was already in 1933 a firm admirer of Hitler himself, a fact that is clear from his correspondence with Iurii Klen, who was then living in Germany and writing for *Vistnyk*. Dontsov indicated in his first letter from 28 July 1933 that *Vistnyk* was equally opposed to bolshevism, conservatism, and clericalism, and that he considered himself an outsider in Galician political life. On 22 March 1934 he wrote that the barricades separated the "old, humane, beautiful-souled, feeble, Jewish-Masonic, Socialist, Russophile [*moskvofilskyi*] world with all the prejudices of democratic and mechanical progress," from "our side," which was "the world of Mussolini and Hitler, the world of creative (and brutal) individuality, the world of work and dedication, hostile to those who made politics and literature into a business, to scoundrels, careerists and cowards who searched everywhere for compromises" (TsDALIM, f. 1361, op. 1, spr. 535, ark. 11). He was flattered when Klen suggested that in Ukraine he could become a Goebbels, responding on 24 September 1936: "What you say is true; I could be a Goebbels. But there is no Hitler. No, the problem is not that there is no Hitler, but that there are no Hitlerites, and it is unclear whether they will appear, because without them [there can be no] Hitler" (ibid., ark. 25). In 1938 *Vistnyk* openly celebrated Hitler's imperial expansion in Eastern Europe, commenting that the path "from Europe to the East is the path of giants, the one taken by Alexander, Napoleon, and England—it has also been taken by the Third German Reich" (Dontsov 1938b, 734). Dontsov attributed the German leader's success to the fact that he had "impregnated his people with the explosive, dynamic force of the idea that he carried within himself" (ibid., 736) and that "in contemporary Europe (besides Italy) there was only one dynamic force that was taking the path of giants, the one followed by Charles XII, Napoleon, and the Kaiser's army" (ibid., 738). Ukrainians should learn from the Germans that one could liberate oneself from "superstitions." Among these he placed a sense of racial inferiority, and a belief that "the world's conscience," justice, outdated agreements, natural boundaries, protectors, or European solidarity were of crucial importance. There was only one fact that counted through the ages—"force, the moral force of an idea" (ibid., 739). He spoke enthusiastically of how the Nuremburg rallies had been described: "the music, songs, exalted words repeated by hundreds of thousands, a patriotic liturgy broadcast from loud-speakers, a forest of flags in flaming red colours, 140 projectors, a crowd of 200,000 that piously sang Deutschland, Deutschland, über alles!" (ibid., 735).

In May 1939 Dontsov wrote another apotheosis of Hitler and Nazism, in which he quoted repeatedly from *Mein Kampf* and the writings of Alfred Rosenberg, and denounced Jewish influences in politics and art. Only two lines at the end of the article express a reservation: "It is unclear what road the new Germany will take in the future. It is an open question whether on this new path which is taking it into Central and Eastern Europe it will find an idea that will speak as convincingly to this Europe as it does to itself (the idea of German Lebensraum is not such an idea)" (Dontsov 1939b, 342). In the preceding issue he had declared: "The independence to which Dnieper Ukraine aspires is the same as that enjoyed by France, Germany, England. All other forms of this independence are a fraud" (Dontsov 1939a, 302). These articles indicate that the Vistnykites became willing participants in their own subjugation to the "new gods" (Omelchuk 2011, 22). Olesia Omelchuk points out that Dontsov knew of Hitler's plans concerning Eastern Europe but chose to ignore them in favor of his own doctrine of enthusiasm; doubts were sacrificed "on the altar of a desired, aestheticized reality—one created by his own imagination" (ibid.). Stryjek considers that Dontsov's engagement with Germany and Hitler went beyond a reasoned analysis or admiration of political success. It was deeply emotional and expressed itself in descriptions of Hitler as "the real Messiah" and of Hitlerites as "militant Medieval barons encased in steel" (Stryjek 2000, 146–47).

Dontsov contributed to the spread of Nazism's biological racism by stressing his admiration for Hitler and by classifying people as superior or inferior according to inherited and immutable traits. Moreover, he aligned his antisemitism with Nazism. In an article from 1937 he lamented the fact that the Ukrainian leadership had not whipped up antisemitism during the 1917–20 revolution in the way the Nazis were doing, and in 1939 he repeated Hitler's claims that international Jewry was a subversive force politically and a degenerative one in literature and the arts.[5] After the war he continued to argue that Judaism emphasized the physiological and sensual rather than the immaterial, and that New and Old Testaments represented, respectively, the "Aryan" and "Semitic." Christianity in his view was closer to the religions of Greece and Rome than to that of Moses (Dontsov 1957, 10, 14). There was no recoil from violence in these later writings, nor any reflections in old age on the sacredness of human life—only a renewed call to imitate the violence of the crusades and the fanaticism of conquerors.

Rostyslav Yendyk, one of Dontsov's most faithful followers and a contributor to *Vistnyk* developed the focus on blood and its purity. His works include the book *Antropologichni prykmety ukrainskoho narodu* (Anthropological Features of the Ukrainian People, 1934) and the short story collection *Rehit Ariadnyka* (Roaring Laughter of Ariadnyk, 1937). The first book purports to be a study of different racial types. It claims that psychological and cultural features are dependent on racial origins: "phenomena of a psychic and physical character are two different expressions of the same foundation" (Iendyk 1934, 105). It suggests that some races are inferior: "They lack the physiological antibodies that would defend them from new diseases, the mental energy to find work and bread in the conditions imposed on them. The cold embrace of death is their only end" (ibid., 37). Jews are assigned to the "Oriental type," while Ukrainians are classified as closer to the "Nordic" type dominant in Europe. A great deal of space is devoted to the description of physical appearances, including scull formations, eyes, and hair. Amusingly, photographs of some well-known personalities are included as illustrations. Dmytro Paliiv's portrait is presented as "primarily Nordic but with an Armenoid addition," while a picture of Sviatoslav Hordynsky, whom Yendyk disliked, is presented as an example of "the Laponoid type" with "a faint addition of the Nordic." The book describes the Laponoid as dominant in Russia. A caricature of "a bolshevik agitator" serves as the illustration for "the Oriental type" (ibid., 37, 41, 46). His postwar *Vstup do rasovoi budovy Ukrainy* (Introduction to the Racial Structure of Ukrainians, 1949) presents his understanding of racial stereotypes, one based largely on now discredited nineteenth- and early twentieth-century writings. It argues that the Nordic race has been responsible for most civilizational achievements over the last three thousand years and is present in the leadership of European nations, including the Ukrainian (Iendyk 1949, 247–48, 286). Yendyk states that Jews are harmful to other peoples not only from the "genetic" but also from the "cultural" point of view. He provides figures for their overrepresentation in certain professions and in bolshevik commissariats, but gives no sources for this information (ibid., 407–9).

Zaitsev has defined Dontsov as "an ideologist of protofascism" (Zaitsev 2013a, 235). Dontsov's contemporaries also viewed him as the initiator of a fascist spirit in Ukrainian life. When a Society of Fascist Studies (Tovarystvo Fashyzoznavstva) was created in Paris in the 1930s, it sent him its statutes, one of which stated: "Fascism as a worldview completely corresponds to certain historical traditions and to contemporary Ukrainian ideational currents whose initiator and propagator was D. Dontsov" (BN, Mf. 82671, 412). However, as will be seen, in the thirties most of the OUN's leadership resisted Dontsov's extremism. Since the organization was focused on the task of developing a mass movement, Dontsov's favorite notion of a people divided into knights and fellahs (Egyptian peasants) undermined its attempts to mobilize and recruit. Its goal was an independent state, whereas Dontsov's agitation focused on the idea of spiritual metamorphosis.

In the postwar years Dontsov's legacy was strongly condemned, especially by the émigré writers in Germany who were grouped around MUR (Artistic Ukrainian Movement). Some in the Banderite camp were openly critical. Petro Mirchuk called him "a medieval pope of the Inquisition" who damned anyone who did not accept his views (Mirchuk 1969). When Dontsov objected to the publication of essays by Diakiv-Hornovy, the UPA publicist who died fighting in the underground, Mirchuk wrote that the struggle was not against the Russian people, but for an independent state, and called Dontsov's "zoological" hatred of Russians as unacceptable to the Ukrainian people (ibid.). In an attempt to exorcise Dontsov's ghost, Mykhailo Sosnovsky, a leader of the OUN-B in Canada, published a study in 1974 urging rejection of Dontsov's voluntaristic, antidemocratic views and especially the idea that an "initiatory minority" must subordinate all groups to itself by using "creative force" (Sosnovsky 1991, 128). However, Yaroslav Stetsko, the leader of the OUN-B, refused to go along with this. He wrote in 1967: "A time will come when our writers and those of other countries will assess Dontsov as one of the greatest guiding lights of Western political thought, [a man] with the visions of a political prophet" (Stetsko 1967, 34). Stetsko denied both Dontsov's orientation to Nazism and his racism, but praised his glorification of fanatical faith and willpower In the 1990s some critics have attempted to rehabilitate Dontsov, claiming that all interwar literature was dominated by *Vistnyk* (Bahan 2009, 22, 28).

Prominent Ukrainian intellectuals have reacted negatively to Dontsov's views and style. After reading his pamphlet *Culture of Primitivism* (Kultura prymityvizmu) Mykola Zerov, the leading literary critic in Soviet Ukraine during the 1920s penned a note stating that Dontsov's method was simple: he accepted the caricatures in Dostoevsky's *Besy* (Devils) as reality, as though they illustrated the political life of Russia (TsDALIM, f. 28, op. 1, spr. 66). The historian Mykhailo Antonovych, who lectured at the Universities of Breslau and Vienna, tried to explain Dontsov's success to the literary scholar Volodymyr Miiakovsky, who had recently come from Ukraine and soon emigrated to the United States: "His brilliant articles, normally studded with numerous quotations from European thinkers, gave the impression of depth, erudition; they thrilled and fascinated the ordinary public [. . .], the more so since what he proposed seemed such an effective break with the past, something completely new (TsDAHO, f. 269, op. 2, spr. 33, ark. 110). However, writes Antonovych, by the mid-1930s the intellectually shallow Dontsov was repeating himself: "Deeper and more thoughtful natures were no longer satisfied with his brilliant phrases, his firework-like quotations, and began to turn away from *Vistnyk*. Moreover, at this time Dontsov's negative qualities became prominent: an inclination to gangster journalism, dirty tactics such as publishing private letters, and a sort of hysterical, abusive tone, aptly noted by Dolengo, which demonstrated his main fault: lack of a positive program, the dominance of pure negation" (ibid.).

The OUN-B's refusal to disavow Dontsov or its own totalitarian past continued to dog the organization in emigration and made many observers question the organization's commitment to democratic norms and practices. This image of Ukrainian nationalism as driven by a totalitarian fantasy has persisted. Although in some cases the image reflects a reality, in most cases those who admire the "Banderites" rarely have the OUN's authoritarian doctrine of the 1930s in mind, but focus instead on the organization's commitment to national liberation. Nonetheless, in contemporary discourse the legacy of authoritarianism and intolerance produce a negative and debilitating image of the OUN, one that is exploited, as it was in Soviet times, to discredit wider and entirely laudable Ukrainian political campaigns and causes.

Griffin has described fascism as promising "to inaugurate an exciting new world in place of the senescent, played-out one that existed before, to put

government in the hands of outstanding personalities instead of non-entities"
(Griffin 2007, 39). In his view, this kind of attitude is more than a political viewpoint, but also represents an alternative modernism (ibid., 47). It sees the modern
world as ushered in through a violent mass revolution led by a fascist party.
Dontsov subscribed to such a view. He envisioned a ruling caste of warriors
governing a reinvigorated society. Since in this scenario general disorder could
break out at any time, the caste's power has to be institutionalized and legitimized. The body politic lacks cohesion, is unable to shape and articulate itself,
and therefore the caste must provide it with the required identity narrative.
Should the narrative alone prove insufficient, the caste must dominate through
violence. This scheme leaves no place for concepts like justice, respect for the
law, or protection of the weak. These contradict the idea that constant war represents humanity's normal condition, and that it is "natural" for the strong to
enslave the weak. Dontsov's ruling caste and ignorant herd are, in fact, comple-
mentary. Since human beings are naturally base and weak, the need to impose
oneself on another can also be seen as "natural." It stems from the view that the
superior individual has a greater propensity for self-assertion. Dontsov's modernized caste system is a fantasy in which a feudal lord governs an abject population, humanity forms part of an amoral universe in which the fittest rule, and
chaos is the norm. As Stryjek has emphasized, Dontsov's thinking was governed
by the conviction that hierarchical relations and caste systems were the foundation of all human relations and any societal order (Stryjek 2000, 153–54, 190). In
the end, this uncompromising faith divided him from almost every political
party and rival publication, and it caused him to break with anyone who criticized his views, including, as will be seen, sympathizers of the OUN and writers
who contributed to *Vistnyk*. He remained proud of his isolation and convinced
that his opinions were consistency and correctness. In 1938, for example, in
"Mizh molotom a kovadlom" (Between Hammer and Anvil), he spoke contemp-
tuously of all currents and publications, even of his critics on the radical right,
claiming that he had been the first to formulate the ideas of modern nationalism, and that these ideas had only later been picked up by the fascist and Nazi
press. He refused to compromise with the majority, which, he claimed, had
formed a united front against him. On the eve of the Second World War he
wrote that *Vistnyk* stood alone: "Our world is not their world; their world is not
ours. The world of those groups is destined for political death. It will be crushed
between the hammer and anvil of our terrible reality. True, this is still their time.
The night is still dark. The hyenas are howling. But I do not envy them the
moment when the night ends and the day dawns!" (Dontsov 1938a, 386).

4

THE ORGANIZATION OF UKRAINIAN NATIONALISTS

The OUN's first émigré leaders were mostly army officers who had fought for Ukraine's independence in the Ukrainian Galician Army and the armies of the Ukrainian People's Republic (UNR). A key group came from the Sich Riflemen (*Sichovi striltsi*), a unit of the UNR forces that had served with great distinction. In the 1930s the OUN's key ideologists became Volodymyr Martynets, who lived in Berlin and Paris, Dmytro Andriievsky in Brussels, Mykola Stsiborsky in Paris and Vienna, Yevhen Onatsky in Rome, and Oleh Olzhych, the youngest member of this group, who lived in Prague, Warsaw, and Berlin. *Surma* (1927–33) and *Rozbudova natsii* (1928–34) were the flagship journals. The latter was created to prepare readers for the organization's founding congress of 1929 and was described by Martynets as a "laboratory" for testing ideas. Aware that friend and foe alike would scrutinize them, ideological or programmatic articles were first distributed for commentary to all members of the émigré leadership. Problematic passages were removed and saved for discussion at the congress. The editors took the position that in an official organ "each word" should be a "completely formulated thought, even a dogma" (Martynets 1949, 282–83). Although this might have been possible in cases where there was general agreement on a topic, the practice soon proved unworkable. Martynets points out that their ideas evolved; he later disagreed, for example, with some of his own statements published in what he jokingly described as the "Nationalist Talmud" (ibid., 294). Controversial articles appeared with an editorial disclaimer. Moreover, as the organization was still only being created when the journal began to appear, attempts were made to attract individuals who belonged to different groups and parties. The journal, for example, published Ivan Kedryn (real name Rudnytsky), a national democrat (he was a leading member of the UNDO) and friend of Konovalets. The émigré leadership in any case was suspicious of universal theories, finished programs, and doctrines. Its first concern was to establish general principles that would serve as guides to action.

The tone of internal debates was set by Konovalets, who was an effective mediator and refused to impose his views, preferring ideas to arise from discussion and practical activity. In private correspondence he stressed the importance of critical opinions and sometimes provoked discussion when he sensed that there was too much unanimity on a topic. Lengthy discussion took place over the Decalogue (Ten Declarations of the Ukrainian Nationalist). Originally authored by Stepan Lenkavsky and published in 1929 as an insert to *Surma*, it went through several changes before its final form was agreed upon in 1933.[1] The OUN's program of education, the Twelve Character Traits of the Ukrainian Nationalist, and the Nationalist's Forty-Four Rules of Conduct went through a similar process before acceptance (Wysocki 2003, 178–79; Mirchuk 1968, 126–29). A network of newspapers and bulletins broadcast the organization's political agitation. The journals *Samostiina dumka* and *Proboiem* devoted much of their space to creative literature. Martynets was editor in chief of *Surma* and *Rozbudova natsii*; Olzhych together with Sylvester Nykorovych edited *Samostiina dumka*, which appeared in Chernivtsi. The leading figures consulted with the Konovalets, who lived in Geneva until 1935 and then in Rome. Andrii Melnyk commanded the paramilitary UVO in Galicia until his arrest by the Polish police. Released in 1928 after serving five years in prison, in the years 1933–38 he worked in Lviv as head of the Catholic Association of Ukrainian Youth. Following Konovalets's assassination he moved to Rome to assume the organization's leadership, and in 1940 he transferred the organization's headquarters to Berlin.

Although the OUN's main social base was Galicia, its views were developed in émigré centers, the largest and most active of which were Prague and Poděbrady. With moral and material support from the Masaryk government, this community ran a university, a pedagogical institute, an art college, an academy of economics, a high school, and other institutions. It issued many publications. The OUN had to defend its views within the broader political and cultural discourse. It is no small irony that the Nationalist leaders, who were universally appreciative of the benefits of life in democratic Czechoslovakia, began in the late 1920s to argue that the Western commitment to humanism and internationalism was hypocritical—a mere veneer for each country's national egoism—and to attack socialism, democracy, and liberalism. The European democracies were described not only as mired in a deep economic and political crisis, but morally bankrupt. Ukrainians were enjoined to develop their own forces, relying on a spirit of solidarity and self-sacrifice. The OUN's stated aim was to instill in youth an "intensified" nationalism that provided "a sense of dignity and honour, a sense of the Nation's own 'ego'" (B-k 1936).

The symbolic embodiment of feckless Western demoliberalism (from "democracy" and "liberalism") was the decadent writer and artist. He was also ridiculed in the communist press. For example, the pro-Soviet *Novi shliakhy* (New Paths) published in Lviv wrote in 1930: "The contemporary decadent has removed himself from the whole world, from its reality, from all unusually complicated and profound social transformations. [. . .] The contemporary intellectual decadent is soft-bodied, lazy, cautious, helpless, and impotent even in the simplest of life's questions" ("V dobi" 1930, 93). Because authoritarian nationalists of all brands, including the OUN, saw the interwar crisis as fundamentally psychological and spiritual, they focused on the intelligentsia's defeatism, on its undisciplined "nature" and the sentimental, pacifist attitudes that had made the previous generation reluctant to even raise an army. A *Vistnyk* publication in 1937 professed the need to learn from bolshevism in this regard: "The spirit of aggression is the spirit of the great game. It does not desire certainties, only possibilities. Therefore a heroic people is displeased to see dying made into something touching and sensitive. We do not need an apotheosis of dying but an apotheosis of the person who dares to oppose fate, who feels stronger than it" (Temliak 1937, 14). Young people were urged to learn the rigors of combat, to obey, like young soldiers, not the commandment "Thou shall not kill," but the command "Thou shall kill" (ibid., 16).

Articles in *Vistnyk* (many of which were written by Dontsov, some under pseudonyms such as Basavriuk) urged this attitudinal change. In fact, Dontsov was adamant that he alone had introduced "the *Vistnyk* doctrine" and was responsible for the sea change in public feelings. He described it in terms of a stark choice between pacifism and violence, between the world that existed prior to the publication of his *Natsionalizm* in 1926 and the one that arose afterward. However, although Dontsov's writings were influential, neither he nor *Vistnyk* represented the OUN, and the editor's relationship with the organization was far from smooth. Dmytro Andriievsky and Yevhen Onatsky were the only OUN leaders who contributed to the journal (publishing a few articles in the years 1923–26). Andriievsky corresponded with the editor in 1927, mailing him various publications from Brussels, among them the Soviet Ukrainian journal *Vaplite*. A civil engineer who had studied in Kharkiv and St. Petersburg before completing Ghent University in 1920, during the struggle for independence Andriievsky had served as secretary of the UNR's diplomatic mission in Switzerland, and in the interwar years he ran the Ukrainian Press Bureau in Brussels. On 15 June 1927 he wrote to Dontsov: "I cannot understand how it came about that you are not with

us and that there can be rumours about fundamental differences between yourself and us. [. . .] The situation is even more paradoxical because every layman
can see our obvious genetic link to you, to the ideas you have publicized. You
deny us, at least in your letters to me, but nonetheless you will be held responsible
for our appearance in the world" (BN, Mf. 82673, 76). This overture was a move
to engage the critic, an attempt to draw him closer to the organization and give
him some direction. In the same year Martynets made a trip to Galicia to meet
Dontsov and propose a collaboration. Later Stsiborsky and Konovalets met him.
The editor ignored all advances and openly criticized the émigrés, a fact that was
noted during the OUN's founding congress in Vienna (Muravsky 2006, 65).
Dontsov described Ukrainian politicians as lacking the fanatical spirit and unable
to make the radical break that fascists had accomplished. Even the OUN, he felt,
was unable to reject "the old authorities" (Mandryk 2006, 239). Yevhen Onatsky,
who challenged Dontsov's blanket dismissal of all past Ukrainian leaders came in
for particular ridicule (Dontsov 1935a and 1935b). Within the organization
Andriievsky was a strong critic of the *Vistnyk* editor. Already in 1928, in a letter to
Konovalets from August 28, he described Dontsov as proposing "maximalist,
absurd precepts," and argued forcefully against the editor's line of conducting a
"war against everyone" (Cherchenko 2007, 98, 101). In 1933, in a speech delivered
to members of the organization, Andriievsky described the editor as "organically
incapable of living with people, either in private or public life" (Cherchenko
2010, 321). Andriievsky complained that Galician youth were beginning to brand
anyone who did not think in Dontsovian terms as a sellout or opportunist (ibid.)
Recognizing Dontsov's influence as a journalist, and the dangers posed by his
irascible and intemperate nature, Konovalets persisted in attempts to steer him
(ibid., 10–11). These attempts were not successful. In 1933, speaking of Dontsov as
an ideologist, Andriievsky called him an "epochal phenomenon" but "dangerous"
(ibid., 380). In 1934 an exasperated Stsiborsky wrote to Martynets calling Dontsov
a "swindler, panic-monger, and morally spineless speculator" (TsDAVO, f. 3833,
op. 3, spr. 1, ark. 171). The issue was Dontsov's extremism: his insistence on a
complete break with all past ways of thinking, and his outspoken support for
fascism and Nazism. The editor demanded that the OUN embrace the new ruthless attitude represented by fascism. When Onatsky polemicized with Dontsov
over this issue, the latter branded him a halfhearted radical, an apologist for
socialist ideas, and a member of the generation responsible for the failed revolution of 1917–20 (Dontsov 1935b, 920).

The disagreement with the OUN concerning rule by an aristocratic caste
was a long-standing one. Dontsov spoke uncompromisingly and constantly of an
orden—a chosen order or elite who were called upon to rule. Stsiborsky countered

this by emphasizing the need for constant contact with the common people and for action in concert with the population (Stsiborskyi 1935, 64–65). Clearly, Dontsov's contempt for the "common herd" was incompatible with the leadership's desire to build a mass organization and launch a popular revolution.

Another issue was the approach to violence. Although the OUN maintained that the struggle for independence required this, it recognized that physical aggression against opponents and use of murder as a political weapon needed strict control. The lead article of the November–December 1933 issue of *Rozbudova natsii* drew on Sorel's argument that the working class should move out of the parliamentary arena and use revolutionary violence in the social struggle. "Our circumstances," it argued, "demand the greatest firmness, determination, and élan" (Inzh. D. 1933, 253). However, continued the author (who may have been Andriievsky), "violence is a double-edged sword and hides as many dangers as it does advantages. The use of violence can as soon reduce a society to anarchy as restore it to health. To achieve the second and not the first, violence should be ethical. It should arise from a sense of responsibility, dignity, awareness" (ibid.). The author provided the example of Irish revolutionaries, who, it was said, were "full of dedication and the ethical attitude that is so required for achieving great acts" (ibid.). There could be no place for "unmotivated" or "villainous" actions by individuals who "do not deserve to play the role of national avengers" (ibid.). Onatsky, in an indirect answer to Dontsov, also stressed devotion to the collective cause and insisted that this and not an antisocial and self-serving individualism should guide the Nationalist (Onatskyi 1933, 164–65).

Resentment of the *Vistnyk* editor's relatively comfortable position no doubt also played a role. After 1922, because he avoided criticizing Poland, Dontsov was able to live and publish in Lviv and Warsaw without fear of censorship.[2] The OUN's publications, on the other hand, were frequently banned and its members imprisoned. Dontsov avoided the consequences of his call to embrace extremism, whereas the OUN had to weigh the practical consequences of every act. This, coupled with the fact that anyone who criticized Dontsov was immediately treated by the latter as a political and personal enemy, irritated several émigré leaders.

However, the editor had fanatical admirers within the OUN, especially in the Homeland Executive, which was pushing for an extension of terrorism. In 1928 Stepan Lenkavsky wrote enthusiastically that Dontsov had introduced new notes: "recklessness and fanaticism," the "amoral nature" of political struggle, of its divorce from "a sentimental sense of justice toward others" (Lenkavskyi 1928, 275). Lenkavsky admired the concepts of dynamism and energism, and the idea that "the will is the basis of life and ethics" (ibid., 276).

After the war, Martynets listed the organization's disagreements with the editor of *Vistnyk*. He mentioned the mystical faith in irrational will and action for its own sake, something that Dontsov called the "ecstatic dance" (Dontsov 1934b, 581). The émigré OUN had been schooled in soldierly discipline and focused action. Mysticism, irrationalism, like the idea of an aristocratic caste, were not part of their way of thinking or operating. The leadership resisted Dontsov's desire for a complete break with traditional ethics, especially the suggestion that all forms of action are permissible in service to the cause. Martynets summarized the argument this way: "Not the cult of elemental force, but the organizing potential, not social chaos but the principle of order, an emphasis on national unity and solidarity, on developing a sense of national dignity, pride, patriotism and the cult of fanatical self-sacrifice with the goal of creating spiritual independence" (Martynets 1949, 158). The surrender to hatred and intolerance turned away potential allies, and the cult of negation undermined the values of unity, solidarity, and self-respect, eroding the "positive" patriotic message. Since one of the organization's aims was to "overcome the slave in our souls" and "instill self-respect and daring" it bristled at the national self-flagellation in which Dontsov appeared to engage (ibid., 160).

Perhaps the crucial issue was the tension between the émigré leadership's stress on organization and Dontsov's obsession with voluntarism. Martynets argued that the critic never had to deal with practical organizational tasks. Since his call for "new people" who would be amoral, intolerant, and violent was never attached to any organizational project or political plan, how, asks Martynets, were his readers to apply his ideas?

> Should they join an underground organization, or the latest legal one? Or both? Or neither, but do something else? Should they struggle against the occupier by taking up arms, or only verbally (with speeches in a hostile parliament), or with the pen (articles in the press), or some other way? And against which occupier? Against all, or only against Moscow? Or against all of them except Poland? And what should they struggle for? A nationalist Ukraine? Fine! But how exactly was this nationalist Ukraine to look? What were to be its borders? What was to be its state order? Its socio-economic order? What were to be its external political alliances? How was it to be won? By external intervention? By internal revolution? Or by both? (ibid., 47)

Martynets complained that Dontsov's attacks on history and tradition, which continued "for years on end," spread a negativity (ibid., 228). In a 1926 review of *Natsionalizm*, he had drawn attention to the editor's cult of amorality and lack of edifying images. He did so again in a brochure entitled *Zabronzovuimo nashe mynule!* (Let Us Bronze Our Past! 1937), in which he called upon writers to devote more attention to national victories and less to defeats: "Only bright images from our past and contemporary times, only heroes and great charac-ters, only great acts and passions are educational tools" (Martynets 1937, 23). He concluded: "Let us not create black myths but instead bronze our past!" (ibid., 32). Excessive criticism, he said, is as counterproductive for nations, as it is for children, because it creates an inferiority complex. If you repeatedly tell a child that it is "an ignoramus and good-for-nothing, never praise it, but instead criti-cize its every good act, you will raise an ignoramus and a good-for-nothing" (ibid., 23). The brochure also called for more humor in Ukrainian life and suggested facetiously that the Ukrainian Free University in Prague should establish a department of humor (ibid., 10).

Dontsov took these comments personally. When Konovalets informed him that his answer to the "bronzers" had made a bad impression, the critic responded testily that the OUN leader underestimated "the denseness of our general public":

> Did, for example, Onatsky's campaign against me make a bad impression? It was an unpleasant one with a clearly denunciatory character. Did Kosach's article in *Ukrainske slovo*, in which he attacked *Vistnyk*, make a bad impres-sion? And anyway, who began this? If I had ignored the brochure of the "bronzers" it would have meant negating everything that I had written until then and continue to write. How could I do that? And would it not have sur-prised people to see support being offered to those (Iu[rii] L[ypa] and others) waging a determined campaign here against *Vistnyk?* It seems that they are always allowed to criticize me and *Vistnyk*, to make astonishing charges in articles and letters, without anyone uttering a sound. [. . .] Our relations are so strained that I have a great desire to leave this Botokudia [the name of an African tribe that Dontsov used as a synonym for "backwater"]. The more so because the people remain silent and various scoundrels from the "responsi-ble" press speak in its name. I am sick of fighting all those idiots in *Nova zoria* [New Star], *Hromadskyi holos, Dilo, Ukrainski visti* [Ukrainian News] and so on. Maybe a "Führer" is exactly what this land needs? (UCEC, Konovalets archive 307/18 16, Dontsov letter to Konovalets, 28 April 1938)

Unlike Dontsov, the OUN attempted to develop a critique of fascism. In 1929 the editors of *Rozbudova natsii* prefaced an article on fascism with the following note: "We underline the inappropriateness of the term 'fascist' which opponents have used to describe Ukrainian Nationalism. Fascism is the move-ment of a people with a state; it is a current born out of a social underpinning that has struggled for power in its own state. Ukrainian Nationalism is a national-liberation movement, whose purpose is the struggle to win a state, to which it has to lead the broadest masses of the Ukrainian people. Therefore Ukrainian Nationalism cannot be identified with Italian fascism, or even closely compared to it. With even greater reason Ukrainian Nationalism cannot be compared to other socially and politically reactionary currents among other state peoples that are similarly called fascist" (Mytsiuk 1929, 262). The author viewed the "fascist" label as a tool of hostile propaganda. From the early 1920s, Soviet publications had used the term to denounce almost anyone critical of the USSR. In the 1930s liberal social democrats in Germany were termed "social fascists." Even Trotsky, Zinoviev, and the old bolsheviks were called fascists. Numerous fictitious groups dreamed up by the GPU and NKVD were also declared "fascist spies." The term's misuse spread an inadequate understanding of political reality and perhaps even made "fascism" appear more acceptable to some who saw the ridiculousness of the charges and for whom the term (like the ubiquitous "kulak") came to signify little more than an opponent of the regime.

In 1933 a number of articles appeared in both *Rozbudova natsii* and *Samostiina dumka* in response to charges in the Galician press that the OUN was a copy of national socialism. The journals refused the identification with both fascism and national socialism. A popular booklet published by *Rozbudova natsii* in 1933 made the point that Ukrainian nationalism existed long before Italian fascism came upon the scene and evolved independently. The two phenomena were "entirely different and not connected" (Anon. 1933, 42). Ukrainian nationalism should sooner be viewed in connection with the national liberation movements of the Irish, Latvians, Lithuanians, Finns, Poles, and Czechs (ibid., 42, 70, 85). Its task was to get the people to recognize their political and spiritual enslavement and to prepare them for a mass uprising. Not all Ukrainians could be members of an underground organization, but all should be involved in the great struggle for self-liberation "as far as their strength and possibilities allowed" (ibid., 109). The most pertinent model was provided by Poland. The two leaders of the Polish national movement, Józef Piłsudski and Roman Dmowski, were invoked as examples to be emulated. It was argued that their intransigence and focus on military success had won Allied support in 1917–19 and paved the way to Polish independence (*"Realna"* 1933, 113–14, 116–17).

The most authoritative statements belonged to Mykola Stsiborsky and Yevhen Onatsky. Stsiborsky's *Natsiokratiia* (Nationocracy, 1935) defined fascism as "first and foremost an ideational and spiritual reaction to the contemporary condition created by democracy, socialism, and communism." In his view political democracy had become "saturated with rationalism, cosmopolitanism, and unnatural international doctrines," and had gradually lost "the spiritual and national basis for its existence" (Stsiborskyi 1935, 50). Fascism, by contrast, recognized the spiritual, the power of will and idea, and was replacing the chaos of "demoliberalism" with hierarchy, rule by an elite, and social discipline. A former officer in the UNR army, Stsiborsky had been interned in a Polish camp in 1920–22. He completed a degree in engineering and economics at the Ukrainian Academy of Economics in Czechoslovakia before moving to Paris in 1930. Many viewed him as the OUN's main ideologist and articulator of the "party line." Later, in 1941 he and Omelian Senyk would organize the Melnyk faction's expeditionary groups. It is interesting, therefore, that within the organization Stsiborsky was known as a strong critic of both Italian fascism and German national socialism. Yevhen Liakhovych (pseudonym Okei), wrote: "I cannot understand why he [Stsiborsky] has such a hatred, and a principled hatred, of fascism or Hitlerism. This is after all an elemental force which today has swept the world, and we are precisely the [political] current that should correspond to that elemental force. Of course we should not blindly ape others, because we have different tasks and live under completely different conditions, but in principle we should not reject this elemental force" (Onatskyi 1989, 106–7). Stsiborsky outlined his position in two works published on the eve of the Soviet-German war. They describe the desire to control and market Ukraine's grain as the driving force behind foreign imperialism in Ukraine—whether Polish, Russian, or German. The first two installed a parasitic landowning class to extract the grain. The Germans attempted something similar in 1918, when they appointed Hetman Skoropadsky. This period is described by Stsiborsky as "the darkest and most tragic page of our recent history," a time of brutal requisitioning that discredited the idea of Ukrainian statehood among the broad masses (Stsiborskyi 1939, 17). It should be recalled that Dmytro Dontsov served in the Skoropadsky administration, and that Konovalets and Petliura had organized the popular uprising that toppled this regime, which was supported by the big landowner-capitalists whom Stsiborsky identified as "the agrarian aristocracy" (ibid., 35–36). The alternative to foreign exploitation, he argued, was a national policy that would, in the interests of all citizens, support the individual farmer as well as collective forms of organization—a platform elaborated in his *Zemelne pytannia* (The Agrarian Question, 1939). Such a policy would prevent a foreign ruling class from extracting a surplus from the peasantry. The foreign element would be mercilessly "uprooted from the nation's social organism" (ibid., 54, 85). This message was aimed primarily at the imperial and colonizing ambitions of Russia and Poland. The desire of Polish nationalists to regain Right-Bank Ukraine was well known; it was, he argued, inscribed in the Warsaw agreement that Petliura had reluctantly signed with Piłsudski (ibid., 57; Sciborsky 1940, 26–29). However, it took little imagination to also see Germany in the role of such an exploiter. The reference to German policies of 1918 was clear enough, but Stsiborsky spelled it out in his *Ukraine and Russia* (1940). He wrote here that Ukraine did not intend to become the object of foreign intrigues but would instead pursue its own independent life, acting as a barrier between "two great imperialisms," in this way protecting Europe "from Russian encroachment" (Sciborsky 1940, 92). He makes it clear that the favorable disposition toward Germany was tactical and based on the latter's anti-Russian orientation: "Had this anti-Russian front been initiated, not by Germany, Italy and Japan, but by England, France and the United States, Ukrainian nationalists would have supported these countries since they were then, as they are now, ready to fight Moscow to the end despite the fact that it is now a 'friend' of Berlin" (ibid., 85). He argued that Ukrainians had in a similar way taken advantage of the situation created in 1938 when they had been allowed to create the Carpatho-Ukrainian state, and he expressed the conviction that had French, English, or American leaders been in the same situation, they would have acted similarly: "The necessity of obtaining German support does not mean that the Ukrainians were or are Germanophiles" (ibid., 86). This line was maintained by the émigré leadership during 1939–40, a time when they made overtures to Western democratic powers (Stasiuk 2006, 154–56). These overtures were rebuffed, and, as has been observed, the years 1938–41 brought a political and ideological shift toward Berlin. There were dissenters. As already indicated, in 1941 the group around Mitrynga proposed maintaining a consistent anti-imperialism, which was encapsulated in the slogan: "Together with the people of Poland, France, and the peoples of the USSR—for a free Europe without Hitler or Stalin" (ibid., 158). This was rejected by the OUN-B, which envisioned Ukraine within the "new Europe."

Yevhen Onatsky wrote extensively on Italian fascism, and within the émigré leadership he was perhaps its greatest champion. Born in the Eastern Ukrainian town of Hlukhiv, he entered Kyiv University in 1914 and in 1917 became one of the youngest members of the Central Rada. In 1919 he served in the UNR's diplomatic mission in Rome and then settled in the city, where he worked as a journalist, contributing to Italian and Ukrainian periodicals in Europe and North America. He taught Ukrainian in Naples at the Higher Eastern Institute from 1936 to 1940 and at the University of Rome from 1940 to 1943. His scholarly publications include numerous works on ethnography, the *Mala Ukrainska Entsyklopediia* (Concise Ukrainian Encyclopedia, 1957–67), and a Ukrainian-Italian dictionary. In addition he translated many works from Latin, Italian, French, and English into Ukrainian, and from Ukrainian into Italian.[3] Asked by

Konovalets to join the OUN in 1930, he became an invaluable correspondent, reporting regularly on Italian developments. The four published volumes of his diary, which span the years 1930–34, are a primary source for the study of the OUN in this period. They record his discussions with the émigré leadership on questions of ideology and tactics, and his contacts with Italian politicians, scholars, and writers. Arrested by the Gestapo in October 1943, he spent over a year in prison. In 1947 he emigrated to Argentina. Like the rest of the émigré leadership, Onatsky liked Italy as a country, which reminded him in many ways of Ukraine. An admirer of Mussolini's political successes, he nonetheless made it clear that an enormous gulf separated Italian fascism and Ukrainian Nationalism despite their similarities, which included a hierarchical organization, faith in a cause, and an emphasis on the young generation. He argued in 1928 that unlike Italians, Ukrainians lacked a state and, as a result, their primary task was state-creation (Onatskyi 1928, 95).

This argument was used by the editors of *Rozbudova natsii* in 1929. When Zenon Pelensky, a leading member of the OUN at the time, was asked to outline some of the benefits to Italy of limiting freedoms and censoring the press, he refused the assignment and informed Onatsky on 16 January 1930, that in his opinion the Ukrainian and Italian situations were completely different. Pelensky argued that the Nationalists must oppose fascist methods in Galicia, because censorship was being used by the Polish regime as a weapon, and the OUN would benefit from freedom of speech, press, and political activity: "the fascist weapons are in the hands of our enemies, who could use my article—and similar ones—against us" (Onatskyi 1954, 43–44). At the time, he was editor of the Przemyśl newspaper *Ukrainskyi holos*, the OUN's first legal organ in Poland. Because its issues were frequently confiscated, the paper eventually closed down. In 1934 he left the OUN and joined UNDO to become editor of its official organ *Svoboda* (Freedom).

As Pelensky's reply indicates, the distancing from Italian fascism was partly a question of managing the organization's public appearance. Andriievsky stated this explicitly. In a letter to Onatsky from 5 November 1930, he urged caution in revealing ties to Italy's government: "we ought not publicly express our links with fascism, but use them to keep in check other states [. . .] Also we have to consider that our closeness to fascism might turn people in Eastern Ukraine away from us" (Onatskyi 1954, 428). However, the "links" with Rome were extremely limited. Onatsky was merely a talented journalist who was trying, largely unsuccessfully, to interest the Italian government in the Ukrainian question. The orientation toward Italy was, of course, itself "tactical" and dictated by considerations of Realpolitik. Since serious opposition to the Treaty of Versailles came only from those states that had ended up on the losing side in the First World War—Hungary, Austria, Bulgaria, Turkey, Greece, Germany, and Italy—the OUN explored the possibility of an alignment with them. Onatsky argued that Ukraine had been shut out of all Europe's postwar conventions, and Italy appeared to be the only state working against the existing "pseudo-liberal" and "pseudo-democratic" order. In 1930 he recorded in his diary that its corporate state (which claimed to fuse the interests of capital, technology, and labor) was a significant achievement, but expressed doubts about fascism as a "method" or ideology (ibid., 200, 245). He quoted approvingly from *Antieuropa*, the organ of the young Italian fascists, which wrote that "their" fascism was revolutionary because it was the movement of a nation still finding its place in the world, whereas other fascisms were conservative because they represented nations that had already "arrived" and were trying to maintain the status quo (ibid., 245). Onatsky thought at the time that fascism had transformed Italy into "one of the most modern and cultured states," while bolshevism, despite professing the most modern and progressive slogans, "had thrown its state into Medieval barbarism" (ibid., 248). He was impressed with the solidarity and sense of renewed national energy that he observed in Italy, and because of this his assessment of Italian fascism remained positive throughout the 1930s.

As for the application of terror, in 1930 Onatsky drew attention to Schwartzbard's assassination of Symon Petliura, commenting that this was an example "that we can take from the Jews" (ibid., 529). However, although he dismissed the idea of nonresistance to evil, he was far removed from any cult of ruthlessness, which he described as "characteristic of small-minded spirits and cowards" (Ontaskyi 1989, 5). His politics underlined an individual's responsibility for their words and actions, civic courage, and devotion to the cause of liberation. Like all leaders of the émigré OUN, he criticized personal egoism and underlined the need for self-education, self-control, and discipline. Onatsky expressed violent opposition to the assassination of Babii in 1934 and threatened to resign from the organization. He was mollified when he learned that this action had been the decision of the Homeland Executive and not of the émigré leadership, and that *Ukrainske slovo* (Ukrainian Word), the OUN newspaper in Paris, had condemned it (ibid. 263–68).

The ideological debate over Nazism began when Hitler came to power. The correspondence of the OUN leaders reveals that they had carefully avoided contact with the Nazis, even though in order to discredit Konovalets the Polish press had spread the rumor that he met Hitler in 1931 (Cherchenko 2007, 327, 360, 441). *Rozbudova natsii* pointed out that both racism and terrorism contradicted the teachings of Christianity and for this reason Catholic Church leaders were hostile to Hitlerism (Sh. 1933, 33). In 1934, along with other Italian commentators, Onatsky called Hitler's policy of sterilizing the sick, mentally defective, and criminals an attack on human freedom and pointed out that Beethoven, the son of an "alcoholic and degenerate," would never have been born under such a policy (Onatskyi 1989, 11). His most outspoken criticism of Hitler came in 1934 in an article called "Kult uspikhu" (Cult of Success, 1934). Konovalets warned him that these articles were known to the Nazi leadership (ibid., 373). In 1938, the Germans described them as exhibiting "hatred" toward Nazism and constituting part of Konovalets's anti-German campaign in the years that followed Hitler's accession to power (Kosyk 1993, 52, 467). When in 1943 Onatsky was imprisoned by the Gestapo and accused of conducting anti-Nazi policies, he feared that these articles would lead to his execution (Onatskyi 1949, 106).

"Kult uspikhu" draws a clear distinction between Italian fascism and German national socialism. The first is presented as much more pragmatic and less obsessed with destroying the past, the second as dogmatic. Nazi ideas of racial purity, with their policies of ostracism and racial cleansing are described as irrational, absurd, anti-Christian, and a direct threat to Ukrainians. The German theory of racism divides nations into the "successful" and "unsuccessful," denying any possibility of change. It views force as the only condition for success and therefore rejects broad-mindedness or compassion. The Nazis think that a higher race cannot be governed by the rules of morality and the sense of honor that are common currency among other peoples, because the "morality of masters" cannot be the "morality of slaves." However, he says, history shows that force alone is insufficient for success; its misuse produces powerful resistance in a weaker opponent and leads to the latter's unexpected victory. Not a single people has reconciled itself to German subjugation; each has preferred death to submission; and each has found in itself the required strength of spirit, because no despot is strong enough to break the will of a nation that refuses to submit. Onatsky quotes from Hitler's *Mein Kampf* to show that Nazi racial theory views the German people as "the embodiment of the highest humanity on earth" and treats all other races as inferior. Ukrainians, says Onatsky, can grasp the way national socialism regards them from Hitler's comment that oppressed people are "of lower value from the racial point of view" and that the Nazi movement champions the German people and cannot advocate on behalf of others (Onatzkyi 1934, 721–22). The following words are quoted from *Mein Kampf* to demonstrate Hitler's plans for Ukraine: "When we today speak about new territories in Europe, we must think in the first place about Russia and the states subordinated to her" (ibid., 722). Nazi doctrine, including the idea of Germans being a "chosen people," warns Onatsky, is "completely foreign" to Ukrainians (ibid., 723, 726). As a warning against German intentions, the émigré leadership translated all the passages in *Mein Kampf* that were considered relevant to Ukraine, added a commentary, and mailed the package to various members (Knysh 1959, vol. 1, 96). *Mein Kampf* was in any case freely available in Lviv's bookstores for those interested in reading it (Pankivskyi 1983, 440).

Hitler's racial theories are also ridiculed in Onatsky's diary entry from 23 April 1934. He points out that the Catholic Church had made an arrangement with Italian fascism, which allowed it to celebrate the same saints and the same religion, whereas the national socialists were creating their own "North-German religion" with its own morality (Onatskyi 1989, 130). In the entry for 13 June of the same year, he repeats the point that Nazi racism threatens not only Jews but also Ukrainians, and informs that he has mailed articles on this topic to the North American newspapers *Svoboda* (Freedom) and *Novyi shliakh* (New Path) (ibid., 191–92).

Earlier, on 2 February 1933, he had written to Bishop Ivan Buchko: "the Italian clergy all sing paeans to Italian fascism and do not find that it contradicts the spirit of Christianity, or Catholicism, but on the contrary that it is very helpful to it" (Onatskyi 1984, 40–41). On the other hand, he writes, the same clergy rejects racism and eugenics and is hostile toward German national socialism. "On this point," wrote Onatsky, "our Ukrainian Nationalists also stand against national socialism. We will never be racists, although we (not myself!) are being prodded toward racism by the antisemitism that is so understandable in our conditions." On 14 October 1933, he wrote admiringly that fascism had succeeded in creating "a great psychological unity of the Italian nation," in which no importance was assigned to race. It differed entirely from Nazism in its attitude toward Jewry: "For the German racists even the most patriotic and socially useful German who has a Jewish wife, or even grandmother, poisons the German race and therefore has to be excluded from it, but Italian fascists judge every Italian not by origins but by behavior" (ibid., 411). On 12 August 1933 he reported a talk by a former officer in the Sich Riflemen by the name of Khomiak, who had six days previously escaped from Soviet Ukraine. The officer affirmed that the identification of Jewry with communism and the Cheka was incorrect. Although there were many Jews in these institutions of power, they had often been sent from outside Ukraine. The attitude of Jews toward Moscow and communism was negative, particularly after the New Economic Policy, which had allowed a degree of free enterprise and a limited market economy, was ended. Onatsky records in his diary: "From 1929 their support of Ukraine and its national interests has been growing. Among Jews, especially in the Komsomol (Communist

Youth Organization), there are many who identify themselves as Ukrainians and are captivated by national attitudes. They are actively engaged in work along these [pro-Ukrainian] lines." In Khomiak's opinion, violent attitudes toward Jews, if they were to appear in Ukraine, would be unjustifiable and would harm the national cause. He predicted that the overwhelming mass of Jewry would support the Ukrainian movement at the decisive moment and stated that there were "even now, telling symptoms of this" (ibid., 334). The Ukrainianization policy had made such startling progress that the communist authorities had become alarmed and were determined to reverse it. Russian and Russified workers could be overheard commenting: "what Ukrainianization has accomplished in a few years cannot now be destroyed even over decades" (ibid., 331). The officer calculated that 70 percent of Communist Party and Komsomol members were "nationally attuned" [meaning pro-Ukrainian] (ibid.). In short, Onatsky at this time pointed out that fascism and Nazism were at odds over racism and antisemitism, even if they agreed on the need to oppose bolshevism, liberalism, and the Versailles treaty that had created the borders of postwar Europe.

Onatsky's views on the value of tradition, the harmfulness of antisemitism, and the ridiculousness of dividing all humanity into plebeians and aristocrats were attacked by Dontsov. In correspondence with Konovalets and Martynets in July 1935, Onatsky affirmed his readiness to take on the *Vistnyk* editor, because a conflict, in his view, was inevitable. He would argue openly, using his real name. The organization, he said, could indicate, if it wished, that he was expressing his own opinions. If the organization really wished to educate the masses, it had to stem the flood of harmful Dontsovian influence (NTSh., Onatsky, BIF 2, 214, 226). Konovalets agreed that *Vistnyk*'s division of people into two castes, plebeians and aristocrats, had produced a generation of arrogant young men who were capable only of criticizing others: "Our movement is for the people's rights [*narodopravstvo*], even if in the form of a temporary dictatorship, but when one takes a look at Dontsovism, it has nothing in common with people's rights; it rejects these and elicits in youth a contempt for the popular masses. We must demand in youth a love for those popular masses, because only through our love for them will we be able to arouse love and enthusiasm in those same popular masses" (ibid., 226). When this response to Dontsov was not printed, Onatsky threatened once more to resign. Konovalets prevailed upon him not to do so, citing Dontsov's popularity with readers and the fact that *Samostiina dumka*, if it printed the response, would have to close down (ibid., 280). Although Martynets and Olzhych supported Onatsky, other editors did not. Martynets informed Onatsky that Mykhailo Mukhin, who worked for

Rozbudova natsii, was fiercely pro-*Vistnyk* and called all Dontsov's detractors "swine" [*khamy*] (ibid., 213).

The issue of antisemitism was discussed by the OUN in connection with the revolution of 1917–20, the future independent state, and Nazism. Stsiborsky wrote an article for *Rozbudova natsii* in 1930 entitled "Ukrainskyi natsionalizm i zhydivstvo" (Ukrainian Nationalism and the Jewry). After rehearsing many complaints about the insularity of Jews, their part in the economic exploitation, and political subjection of Ukrainians in the past, the article concludes with a warning not to think that all Jews supported the bolsheviks. During the revolution, the Jewish masses, it states, remained indifferent or opposed to bolshevism, which destroyed their economic and religious life; bolshevik policy went against their interests and psychology. It is true, he reminds readers, that Jews were initially indifferent to the Ukrainian political struggle, which they understood poorly, but so were the Ukrainian masses and so was much of the intelligentsia. It was only after the 1919 pogroms that the Jewish attitude toward the Ukrainian revolution became negative. The violence against ordinary civilians severely damaged Ukrainian-Jewish relations, and world Jewry's turn against Ukrainians was a blow to the latter's state aspirations. On the other hand, there were no pogroms in Western Ukraine, where order prevailed in Ukrainian army ranks, and the relationship with Jews was consequently much better. Stsiborsky emphasized the importance of persuading Jews that a future Ukrainian state would hold "no dangers for them," and that social and economic conditions would be better for them in this state:

> It is imperative to clearly indicate to Jewry that our movement for statehood sees no grounds for or benefit in limiting the legal status of Jews in Ukraine. On the contrary, the goals of the state will be to give Jews a situation of equal rights and the possibility of expressing themselves in all socio-political, cultural, and other activities. This will bring about the quick disappearance of Jewish isolation. As for the fear that equal rights for Jews might harm the state, one should bear in mind that Jews are not a minority in Ukraine with *subjective* reasons to fundamentally oppose our independence. On the contrary, favourable conditions of existence, participation, along with others in the whirlpool of state-social activity—all this will create a feeling in the Jewish masses not only of loyalty but also, in time, of state patriotism. The patriotism of Jews in states where they enjoy conditions of equality with other citizens indicates that this is not a fantasy. (Stsiborskyi 1930, 272)

Nazi racial theory was also dismissed by Martynets. Writing in 1936–37, he pointed out that Italian and German nationalisms had emerged from opposite principles: the first viewed the nation as a spiritual reality; the second as a biological one. Like Onatsky, he warned that the Nazis relegated not only Jews but also Ukrainians to the lower races, and provided examples of Germans refusing contact with Ukrainians, whom they considered racially worthless. In any case, there is no pure Ukrainian race, he insisted, just as there are no pure races anywhere (Martynets 1937b, 96). Ukrainians are not a blood group but a group created by a shared past. Thinking in terms of "higher" or "leading" races is fruitless and futile; circumstances change, and what a particular group lacks at any given time can be learned from another group. Jews, he wrote, do not provide the best example for emulation because, with the exception of Disraeli, they have not demonstrated state-building abilities; instead they have shown an excessive commitment to internationalism. But in any case, he says, state-building skills have nothing to do with race. Jews, like all other nations, should be encouraged to use their talents for the benefit of the future Ukrainian state. One of the greatest mistakes in the independence struggle of 1917–20 was the rejection of talented, committed individuals who wanted to serve the cause, on the grounds that they were "non-Ukrainians" (ibid., 60, 107). He stresses that the assimilation of foreigners should be encouraged and that numerous prominent Ukrainians were descended from different nations and races, including leading ideologists of nationalism like Dontsov, Mykola Mikhnovsky (who came from Tatar stock), and Viacheslav Lypynsky, and writers like Lesia Ukrainka (who had Italian and Serbian ancestors) and Ivan Franko (whose forebears were German) (ibid., 126–32). Martynets indicates that the current leadership of the OUN contains individuals of Polish, Czech-German, Polish-Russian-Moldavian, German, Tatar, and Russian origins, and comments ironically that only two are "pureblooded" Ukrainians. Among the UVO leaders, two have Polish origins, one Czech-German, one German, and only one is a "racially pure" Ukrainian (ibid., 127). His list of prominent figures of foreign origin includes Bohdan Khmelnytsky and Ivan Mazepa, and the contemporary writers Mykola Khvylovy, Maksym Rylsky, Yurii Klen, and Yurii Lypa. The point, of course, is that discussions about race are senseless, because race and nation are entirely different things. The important issue for Nationalists is to develop a strong nation. In 1952, when he provided an explanation of the OUN's program, Zynovii Knysh wrote that only Ukrainians, not foreigners, could be members of the organization. However, this did not mean that one had to be born of Ukrainian parents. Although based upon people of Ukrainian blood and background, "the concept of Ukrainian national identification is not limited by this, but includes everyone who accepts Ukrainian culture and nationality as their own, is ready to work and struggle for them" (Knysh 1952, 81).

The OUN's brand of authoritarian nationalism was not a monolith. Many of its adherents came out of the experience of the UNR and the Western Ukrainian People's Republic (ZUNR), whose policies toward minorities—and Jews in particular—were progressive. However, antisemitism, defined as an attempt to systematize anti-Jewish grievances, had strong roots in Ukrainian society. As already noted, it generally focused on political and economic grievances (the charge that Jews failed to support Ukrainians in their struggle for independence or hindered the development of a Ukrainian business and trading class). In Galicia, contemporary conflicts with the Jewish community arose over the latter's perceived pro-Polish politics. Unlike Ukrainians, Jews did not boycott the elections of 1922, nor did they refuse to recognize the legitimacy of the Polish state. Maksym Gon has argued that the Schwartzbard trial of 1926 and the famine of 1933 were important turning points; after each of them, Ukrainian-Jewish relations deteriorated (Gon 2010b, 257, 259).

The first issues of *Rozbudova natsii* that appeared in 1928–29 on several occasions mentioned Jewish support for Soviet rule and described urban life in Ukraine as dominated by Russians and Jews (Bokush 1929, 85). Stsiborsky's article of 1930 appears to have been written to counteract this rhetoric. Mytsiuk's long work on Jews in the economy of Ukraine, which was serialized in *Rozbudova natsii* in 1931–32, also made the point that historically Jews had in most cases sided with Ukraine's oppressor. Moreover, it suggested that Jews played a key role in Russian culture and communism. The motives for cultural or political conversion, the writer insinuated, were personal gain:

> Jewry augmented the Russians; augmenting the Ukrainians is for the time being unprofitable. Jewry reached deep into Russian culture, which began to lose its Great Russian character and was accused of not being national. [. . .] Jewry saturated Russian society and became an influential factor in oppositionist and revolutionary currents. Some say frankly that it "drove them" [. . .]. It began to dominate the periodical press. Some say that it "governed" or "controlled the Russian press," adding that the periodical press is so important because whoever controls the press largely controls the mind of the reader, the thinking person who governs human life. (Mytsiuk 1932, 129)

These collected articles by Mytsiuk were published in book form as *Agraryzatsiia zhydivstva Ukrainy* (Agrarianization of the Jews of Ukraine, 1933). One letter to the editor in *Rozbudova natsii* complained that the articles were trying the patience of readers: "Firstly, they create the impression that RN like some pogromist organ is deliberately targeting the Jews and is arguing that the problem of Jewry is the most important one for the Ukrainian Nation. How otherwise can one interpret the fact that RN has devoted to it over a dozen pages in every issue for years on end. Secondly, people are fed up of reading about Jews for two entire years. Do a survey of your readers and you will see that not more than ten read these articles. So, for whom is RN writing?" ("Iz lystiv" 1932, 317).

Another letter complained that Jews sided with the oppressor nation in Ukraine, "whether Poles, Russians, or Germans," and regretted the absence of a "national-Ukrainian Jew," the analogous figure to the patriotic German or English Jew. This writer pointed out that Ukrainians knew too little about the life of Jews outside Ukraine. He insisted on an end to "all that political mysticism, all those cock-and-bull stories about the covert power and underground mafia of international Jewry, about 'the seven wise men of Zion' who sit somewhere manipulating world developments, controlling hidden organized forces, who are omnipresent, who know and decide everything" (Mylianych 1929, 271). He supported Herzl's idea of Jewish emigration to Palestine and a Jewish state, believing that this would eventually lead to the establishment of normal, friendly relations, between Jews and others (ibid., 272).

Neither the racially based antisemitism of the Nazis, nor the religious anti-semitism with roots in Christian discourse were major factors in the OUN's ideology. A greater source of social tension with Jews stemmed from the growth in the 1930s of the cooperative movement, Ukrainian businesses, and commu-nity organizations. The temperance campaign directed against the Polish monopoly on alcohol was seen by many as anti-Jewish because it penalized Jewish tavern keepers. Sometimes Jewish parliamentarians were blamed for allying themselves with Polish interests and not supporting Ukrainians. Because some Jews were visible in the Soviet leadership, Jews as a whole were some-times blamed for the collectivization and the famine of 1932–33, along with the mass arrests and deportations that destroyed millions of lives. But the key role in the intensification of antisemitism was played by events in Germany and throughout Europe. The issue of quotas for Jewish students attending Polish universities had been debated since the 1920s, and, as mentioned earlier, in 1936 pressure from Polish extremist groups led to the installation of "ghetto benches" for Jewish students in Lviv University. In 1937 the Polish foreign minister Józef Beck suggested forcibly relocating the country's three million Jews to Madagascar. It should be recalled that the French colonial minister Marius Moutet considered sending his country's Jews to the French colonies. and in 1938 Italian fascism took its antisemitic turn.

The animosity toward Jews, which had until then often been expressed in the form of insinuations, in the years 1937–39 took on a fiercer tone in the writings of Nationalist leaders and in the OUN's broadcasts from Vienna and

Bratislava. These were permitted by the Germans during the existence of Carpatho-Ukraine (November 1938–March 1939).[4] When the organization began broadcasting from Vienna in 1938, it used formulaic phrases such as "Moscow-Jewish riff-raff" with regularity.[5] In 1938 Martynets also published his "Zhydivska problema v Ukraini" (Jewish Problem in Ukraine) in which he spoke about isolating Jews from Ukrainians in a future independent state.

A debate regarding Jewish-Ukrainian relations was taking place within the émigré organization. Mykola Nitskevych, an ideologist of the OUN and its main organizer in Bulgaria, wrote a letter to Konovalets from Sofia in May 1938, shortly before the latter's assassination (which occurred on 23 May).[6] It is worth quoting at length:

> I consider the question of our relations with Jewry a question of principle. I am not a Judeophile, but at the same time I refuse to be a Judeophobe — not only because Judeophobia runs against all our interests, negatively affects the psychology of our people and confuses our cards in international agitation for the idea of Ukraine's liberation. Ukrainian Judeophobia, like Judeophobia in general, spreads because from somewhere the conviction has arisen that Jews are enormously powerful, that they are a complete monolith, and chiefly that there exists a world Jewish center that strives to conquer the world. I cannot accept this as an axiom, because I know that the Jews are divided, as are we sinners, into countless ideological tendencies and political groupings. I think that you are aware that even in the bosom of Zionism there are several warring tendencies. [. . .] The existence of "the Elders of Zion" is a fairy tale dreamed up by a Moscow professor, not without the obvious interference of the Union of Russian People, to provide fodder for the bishops of the Black Hundreds and to explain the steadily ebbing strength of Moscow's empire. I understand that for some the protocols of "the E. Z." are a very convenient card, and whoever finds it useful can play it, but for us, it is a knife in the back of our revolution [. . .] Everyone, who has even a passing acquaintance with Russian "culture" is aware that bolshevism's origins are Russian and stretch back to the first Europeanizing experiment that placed European top-hats on Asiatic heads. One has to be blind and deaf not to see bolshevism as part of a whole continuous chorus line in Russian literature and Russian imperial brutality.
>
> When one views bolshevism in this way — the only possible way — one has to recognize that the Jews simply played no role. They attached themselves to the bolshevik revolution in the same way as they did to European capitalism. (UCEC, Konovalets archive 307/18 10, M. Nitskevych letter to Konovalets, 9 May 1938)

Nitskevych complains in this letter that antisemitic articles in the Nationalist press involuntarily help the Russians to paint themselves as innocents and to shift blame for their own antisemitism onto others. "Their most convenient scape-goats, were, are, and will continue to be the Jews," he writes, and concludes: "I simply cannot understand how our Nationalist press can say that the Jewish popu-lation in Eastern Ukraine is becoming Ukrainian, that the Jews have evidently changed their view concerning Ukrainian statehood, and then simultaneously print clearly antisemitic articles, that are, if I may say so, completely unnecessary and harmful to us (ibid.).

The Munich Conference of the "Four Powers" (Germany, Britain, France, and Italy), which took place on 20–21 September 1938, ceded the Sudetenland to Germany, thereby recognizing the right to self-determination of small peoples and the possibility of border changes. The move signaled for many the end of the League of Nations and of a Europe governed by the Versailles treaty. Antisemitic policies in Germany also led to a large Jewish emigration. On 8 November 1938, Onatsky wrote an article for the Canadian *Novyi shliakh* in which he described the effect of the new race laws in Italy, which had been proclaimed on 1–2 September 1938. The decrees were aimed primarily at recent Jewish refugees, but even those who had come earlier and had been granted Italian citizenship were expected to leave: "The Italian press underlines that this is not a question of religion, but of race, blood [. . .]. Native Jews are seen as a foreign body, as not assimilating, and as retaining their own psychology, mentality, and world view, which brings them closer to international Jewry and Italian Jews, rather than to the Italian nation" (Onatskyi 1938). On 2 September the Council of Ministers issued a decree removing Jewish professors as of 11 October. "No one," writes Onatsky, "was prepared for this. Where are Jews to go? France is closed to them and *Le Temps* has offered a racist explanation why: 'the influx of an excessively different and often unsuccessful element.' England has begun to close its door to them in response to fears of jobs being taken away from a population already suffering large unemployment, as the *Daily Express* pointed out on 2 September. New Zealand, Australia, the Scandinavian countries, Argentina, Uruguay, and Brazil have also closed their doors." Onatsky expresses fears that a Jewish terri-tory, which would become a Polish-Romanian protectorate, is being considered in Galicia and Bukovyna. "If," he writes, "this proposal really exists" (it had apparently been floated in two British newspapers) "it must be rejected as one more insult to the Ukrainian nation" (ibid.). Onatsky was not unsympathetic to the situation of the Jews but made it clear that Jewish emigration to the "already overpopulated" lands of Western Ukraine was undesirable and that the problem created in Europe could not be solved in this way.

It might be recalled in this context that in the 1920s Mussolini had been widely viewed as pro-Jewish. In 1928 a reporter from the *Canadian Jewish Chronicle* held an exclusive interview with the Italian leader. After introducing him as "the most interviewed and described political figure in the world today," the reporter quoted the dictator on the tolerant attitude of Italians toward racial minorities. Jews are described as "having participated fully and with distinction in the political, artistic, and scientific spheres of our national life for many, many years." The reporter detected sympathy for the Zionist movement and the picture of a Palestine that would soon "receive its builders" and ended the article by informing readers that "there was something so utterly unconventional about his demeanour, so free of pose that I was completely won by him. I became convinced that Italian Jewry has nothing to fear from Fascism or the moulder of the new Italy" (Straus 1928).

In 1936 the fascist government of Mussolini's Italy had stated: "From the earliest times the Italians have been a mixture of races, and successive invasions have added so many strains to their blood that there is no danger of a racial theory of Italian nationality. In physical characteristics they differ widely, from the tall, red-haired types found in Lombardy and Venetia and Celts of Romagna, to the Mediterranean type prevailing in the South" (Schneider 1936, 2; quoted in Connor 1994, 218). Two years later, after forming an alliance with Hitler, the government felt obliged to convince the people of their consanguinity and to diminish Italy's ethnic heterogeneity by outlawing local vernaculars and emphasizing a common Italian ancestry. The so-called Manifesto of Racist Scientists promulgated throughout Italy in 1938 read: "If Italians differ from Frenchmen, Germans, Turks, Greeks, etc., this is not just because they possess a different language and different history, but because their racial development is different [. . .] A pure 'Italian' race is already in existence. This pronouncement [rests] on the very pure blood tie that unites present-day Italians [. . .] This ancient purity of blood is the Italian nation's greatest title of nobility" (Delzell 1970, 193–94; quoted in Connor 1994, 199).

On 8 November 1938 Yevhen Onatsky published an article in *Novyi shliakh* on the new racist policies in Italy. Jews, he indicated, were in a tragic situation because after expulsion from one country they were being denied entry by almost every European state, and even by a country like Canada, which had enormous territories available for settlement.

Konovalets, as former commander of the Sich Riflemen during the revolutionary wars, was aware of how anti-Jewish pogroms had damaged the Ukrainian cause and how the UNR government had tried to fight them.[7] Moreover, he witnessed the manner in which Schwartzbard's trial had been used by the

Kremlin to smear the entire national movement as antisemitic. After Konovalets's death, however, as the organization drew closer to Germany, anti-Jewish statements multiplied, particularly among the OUN's Galician activists. *Holos* (Voice), the organization's newspaper in Lviv, published articles that saw Jewish influence behind the international criticism of Germany. As has been observed, on the eve of the German-Soviet war, a fierce anti-Jewish line was disseminated by the OUN-B in its instructions of May 1941. This rhetoric linked Jews to bolshevism by, for example, characterizing agitation for a better future under communism as "lies of Jewish deceivers," calling Marxism "a Jewish invention," and denouncing the "Russian-Jewish commune" (TsDAVO, f. 3833, op. 1, spr. 69, ark. 3). The same phraseology was used in articles published by Nationalists in the first months of the German-Soviet war.

Yaroslav Orshan (real name Orest Chemerynsky), who headed the émigré leadership's press bureau in Berlin from 1935 to 1940, wrote a pamphlet in 1938 entitled *Doba natsionalizmu* (The Age of Nationalism). It presented the OUN's view of Nazi ideology. After discussing the origins of Nazi racial theory, Orshan delivers the verdict that "as a scientific theory, it does not stand up to criticism, but to the Germans themselves it has become a full-fledged science" (Orshan 1938b, 11–12). Ukrainians, he writes, have to develop their own ideology; they must meet the Nazi challenge "head-to-head," and show that they are a European nation. The new ideology has to link the present to its premodern ethnic roots and to elaborate myths, such as those of a strong leader and a national mission. This mission, Orshan suggests, lies in "the creation of a new life on the border of two worlds" (ibid., 15). The brochure makes it clear that, although the racial aspects of Nazi ideology should be rejected, the idea of an intensified, myth-laden national life is to be welcomed. The population has to be taught the spirit of self-sacrifice for the nation's benefit in preparation for revolution. In this sense, he says, Nationalism resembles Italian fascism and German national socialism: "Ukrainian Nationalism uses the term 'nationalism' in the same way as German and Italian nationalisms use the terms 'national socialism' and 'fascism.' [. . .] Nationalisms— fascism, national socialism, Ukrainian Nationalism and so on—are the various national expressions of one spirit, which is marching against the same opponents (demoliberals on one side and communist bolshevism on the other) and taking the path of revolutionary struggle for the highest development of their respective nations" (ibid., 29). However, the pamphlet argues, Ukrainian Nationalism is singular in that it is primarily driven by the idea of liberation from a foreign yoke.

In a second pamphlet from the same year entitled *De stoimo?* (Where Do We Stand?), Orshan argues strenuously—and tortuously—that any "occupier" must be forced to "retreat in the face of Ukrainian life" (Orshan 1938a, 10). The primary goal, he says, is destruction of the Soviet Union and creation of an independent state. Achieving this goal requires giving strategic support to the fascist camp. This coded language signaled that the organization would be a potential partner in any eastern advance but would resist becoming a tool of Germany. He wrote: "Such a politics can only be conducted by an organization that stands firmly on Ukrainian ground and is capable of acting *there* as a *partner* to foreign forces, but not a prospective agent 'waiting for a war'" (ibid., 31).

Stsiborsky's articles from the years 1939–40 take a similar position. Between 1937 and 1941 this kind of maneuvering characterized the organization's ideology. It represented a dance of acquiescence and resistance, an attempt to demonstrate to the Germans that the Nationalists could be partners in war, but only on their own terms. Accordingly, the organization attempted to outline its affinities with German national socialism, while simultaneously indicating its disagreements. It is useful to bear in mind Armstrong's distinction between avowed and real attitudes. He has argued that the degree to which the organization really regarded concepts like plutocracy, cosmopolitanism, liberalism, democracy, or antisemitism as subversive of the national ideal is questionable. A fanatical hard core certainly accepted them, but the antisemitic rhetoric largely disappeared after 1942 and the shift to a "democratic" platform occurred in the following year. As with a number of reactionary movements in Western and Eastern Europe, cooperation with the Germans was tactical, a move considered necessary to overcome domestic enemies. The focus on independence, however, was constant and unwavering (Armstrong 1968, 406, 409).

Yurii Sherekh (the pseudonym of Yurii or George Shevelov) has offered an argument that is worth recalling in this context. According to him, a legitimate liberationist nationalism had become confused with an illegitimate, exterminatory nationalism. Mainly this was due to the influence of the gifted and charismatic Dontsov:

> [T]he spokesman for the idea of extreme nationalism became the only popular ideologist of nationalism, even though his excesses were alien to and far removed from the great majority of the Ukrainian people. While accepting to a degree D. Dontsov's ideological leadership, it [the people] in fact continued to bring to the movement—its liberation movement—a nationalism with a content that was "moderate," "humanistic," "democratic," "Christian," or however else one wishes to label it. D. Dontsov was undeniably the ideological leader, the main publicist and the flag-bearer of the Ukrainian liberation movement for fifteen years, but the paradox is that this movement, even in slightly wider circles, never accepted a single one of those excesses to which Dontsov was ready to drive it. (Sherekh 1948, 15)

If one accepts this line of reasoning, the spike in aggressive attitudes toward minorities between 1937 and 1941, one that was inscribed in the OUN-B's instructions of May, 1941, can be seen as evidence that the leadership circles in the Bandera wing of the organization at this time accepted an ideological turn that was both pro-Nazi and Dontsovian. What would have occurred if Germany had installed a puppet regime? Zaitsev, who considers the Croatian Ustashe movement analogous to the OUN, has written: "The independent Croatian State of 1941–45 is a revealing model of what a Ukrainian state under the Third Reich might have become. Its experience shows that in such conditions Ustashism becomes transformed into 'full-fledged' fascism" (Zaitsev 2011, 220). Zaitsev's conclusion is that the OUN can be described as proto-fascist. However, it "differed from fascism typologically" and as the integral nationalism of a stateless nation can be classified, rather, as "a variety of Ustashism" (Zaitsev 2013b, 29).

The least known ideologist of Nationalism, and one of the most interesting, is Yuliian Vassyian. During the founding congress of 1929, his writings provided the movement with a philosophical underpinning. A former member of the Sich Riflemen Regiment commanded by Konovalets, after release from Polish internment he organized the Ukrainian Underground University and then himself completed Charles University in Prague with a degree in philosophy. Arrested in 1931 in Poland, he was sentenced to four years imprisonment for attending the OUN's founding congress and was then imprisoned again in 1939. In 1944 he was arrested by the Gestapo and spent a year in a concentration camp. Vassyian wrote numerous philosophical essays, relatively few of which have been published. A man of deep convictions and a spellbinding teacher (as fellow prisoners have attested) he never achieved wider recognition. In 1953 he died in Chicago, where he survived by working as a cleaner and dishwasher.

Vassyian, an admirer of Edmund Husserl, had read widely in German phenomenology. Three essays written in prison in 1934 were later published as *Odynytsia i suspilnist* (The Individual and Society, 1957). Two more essay collections appeared in 1958 and 1972–74. His philosophy strove to break down the dichotomous worldview that he associated with Western rationalism and liberalism—one that rigidly separated the subjective and objective, isolating the individual from the collective. Like Heidegger he was concerned with the totality of human culture and the theme of destiny. Although conducted at a high level of abstraction, his work is accessible to the general reader through a discussion of myths. He makes use, for example, of the mythical figures of Prometheus, the phoenix, the biblical serpent, and the knight who defends his country. He also examines the importance of the artist's role in creating new ways of thinking and feeling. One of his books is devoted to the writer Vasyl

Stefanyk, whom Vassyian admired for breaking through to an understanding of deeper layers in the human psyche.

Five of Vassyian's political essays were published in *Rozbudova natsii* in 1929–30. One of these, "Ideolohichni osnovy ukrainskoho natsionalizmu" (Ideological Foundations of Ukrainian Nationalism, 1928), was also delivered at the OUN's founding congress. In it Vassyian describes the social instinct as an integral part of human nature but dismisses both collectivism and individualism in their radical forms. He argues that an excessive focus on the past means frozen contemplation of what has been, while an "extreme futurism" leads to rejection of the entire previous sociopolitical order in a futile attempt to begin human history anew. Both traditionalism and futurism lack the form-creating force; the first is merely a reflex, while the second lacks organic links with social life and strives to create a living unity from atomized fragments. Vassyian calls instead for the past to be active in creating the future. The human individual, history's decisive factor, simultaneously embodies the past and employs his or her sovereign will to create new values. Individuals who are aware of themselves as subjects or sovereign forces leave an imprint on the malleable material of their surroundings. Nations too can assert themselves in this way. The Ukrainian movement for self-assertion is not simply a reaction to external pressure, namely to oppression, but is "an organic-creative movement" with all the signs of "autonomous will" (Vassyian 1929, 69). Nothing in reality stands in the way of the nation playing a world historical role, "except perhaps inner weakness" (ibid.). The role of Nationalism, therefore, is to create a worldview that helps its people achieve concrete tasks, and the best artistic expression of such a worldview lies in the creation of forms that have the greatest internal tension and dynamism. Such forms are created through addition and synthesis, not through elimination and negation.

These views resemble those of the Italian philosopher Giovanni Gentile, who first elaborated his philosophical system in 1916 and later served as minister of education in Mussolini's administration. He called his new ethical system "actualism." In his view actions impregnated with ethical self-awareness resolve the tension between the subjective and objective, mind and body, inner and outer reality. His views, according to Griffin, were mediated through the Florentine prewar periodical *La Voce*, which was founded in 1908 and to which some of Italy's brightest intellectual stars contributed. This periodical fought "a vociferous campaign for a comprehensive reawakening of the nation through the forces of culture conceived in a way that melded aesthetic, cultural, social, and political visions of renewal to a point where they were indistinguishable" (Griffin 2007, 192). Vassyian's thought, like Gentile's, provides a rationale for an interventionist approach to history by stressing the concept of continuous self-creation and history making. For Vassyian, abstract thought became a way of managing the terror of Cronos, or the passage of time that destroys all. What Griffin says of Gentile is also applicable to Vassyian: "In a period of acute historical crisis he harnessed his academic specialism to the subliminal drive to achieve spiritual transcendence, spending his whole life translating the primordial *topoi* of mytho-poeia into the linguistic register of modern philosophy" (ibid., 194).

The idea of the active subject was meant as a challenge to much contemporary Marxist theorizing, which focused on human consciousness as a passive reflector of economic realities. In 1926 in Soviet Kharkiv, the rebellious Mykola Khvylovy wrote his essay series "Apolohety pysaryzmu" (Apologists of Scribbling). In the famous thirteenth chapter he challenged this "vulgar Marxist" determinism by insisting on the active human element in history. In his banned pamphlet "Ukraina chy Malorosiia?" (Ukraine or Little Russia?, 1926) he stressed that the drive for independence was unstoppable and historically progressive: "If any nation [. . .] over the centuries demonstrates the will to manifest itself, its organism as a state entity, then all attempts in one way or another to hold back such a natural process block the formation of class forces on the one hand, and, on the other, introduce an element of chaos into the general historical process at work in the world" (Khvylovy 1986, 227). Although phrased in Marxist terminology, this was the same argument for human agency and national will that Vassyian developed.

Some of Vassyian's most provocative and stimulating essays survived in unpublished notes and were printed in the 1958 collection *Suspilno-politychni narysy* (Sociopolitical Essays). One describes the origins of the peace-loving agricultural way of life and its impact on his people's pacifist psychology. Another is a meditation on the power of Christian faith and its influence on Western civilization. He interprets Christ's life as an ideal, a call to love and future perfectability directed toward a contemporary world ruled by hatred. It also interprets Ukrainian culture as internally multityped (*mnohotypova*). Like Western civilization it professes universal values and the ideal of peace, but like the same Western models it also finds its religious ideals in conflict with the rules of history, which demand an implacable struggle for existence. Religion's role is to struggle with nihilism in face of the fact that every individual is aware of his or her eventual death. A third outlines some of the great issues in Ukrainian historiography that still require research: the unexplained puzzle of Kyivan Rus's fall, the symbiosis of the Varangian and local, the Ukrainian element in the early Eastern Slavic language, and the difference between Byzantine spirituality and Moscow's Orthodox religiosity. A fourth essay calls for a serious analysis of Shevchenko, who had not produced criticism worthy of his stature. Vassyian's style captivated the émigré writer Hanna Cherin, who described it as "metaphoric, passionate, electrifying and crafted in writerly fashion" (Cherin 1974, 13).

The nonconformism and originality of Vassyian's insights suggest that his remaining notes need editing and publishing. His essays rival those of Malaniuk and Lypa in their importance for understanding Nationalism, especially in the awareness they demonstrate of dialectical processes and contradictory trends at work within culture. In his view, different aesthetic strategies and various mythologizations of the past (pre-Christian, Kyivan Rus, Cossackdom, the Revolution of 1917–20, regional) have interacted over time to forge the modern Ukrainian identity. He envisages the new nation emerging from a synthesis between global processes of change, on the one hand, and the human need for rootedness and a metaphysical life on the other. Vassyian's work inspired other Nationalists. It identified key problems in Ukrainian culture and indicated where synthetic studies were still required. But above all Vassyian underlined the active creation of a new Ukrainian individual and nation, a task in which the artist and intellectual had to play an enormous role.

A Soviet-educated intellectual, Yurii Boiko (real name Blokhyn), played a leading role in reshaping the OUN-M's views in wartime and postwar years. He came from Mykolaiv in Eastern Ukraine. After he was arrested in 1929 and accused of membership in the SVU (Spilka Vyzvolennia Ukrainy—League for the Liberation of Ukraine), an organization fabricated by the GPU, he spent six months in prison. He was released and was eventually able to complete Odesa University. He then moved to Kharkiv in an attempt to hide the traces of his previous arrest, and began contributing literary criticism to scholarly journals. During the war he joined the Melnyk wing of the OUN and worked for its Kharkiv newspaper *Nova Ukraina*. In 1945 he moved to Munich, where he became one of the organization's leading members. Together with Vassyian he was tasked with revising its ideology, and until 1964 remained its official spokesman on ideological questions. He lectured in Munich at both the Ukrainian Free University and the Ludwig Maximilian University.

Boiko's writings are an indicator of the shift in postwar Nationalist ideology. In 1946–47 he published two articles in response to the publication *MUR*. Entitled "Kudy idemo? (Where Are We Going?) and "Odevertyi lyst do Iuriia Shrekha" (An Open Letter to Yurii Sherekh), they challenge the view that politically engaged literature is by nature inferior (Boiko points to the example of Polish romanticism) and that pursuit of formal complexity is the sole criterion of literary excellence. He is committed to the educational and inspirational role of the arts but readily admits that Dontsov played a negative role in promoting a certain kind of literature and in popularizing inhumane ideas and totalitarian regimes.

Boiko's most important codification of the revised Nationalist doctrine can be found in *Osnovy ukrainskoho natsionalizmu* (Foundations of Ukrainian Nationalism, 1951). He begins by admitting that "not everything" written about the Nationalist worldview has stood the test of time, and therefore the time has come to winnow out the essential and unchanging (Boiko 1951b, 5). Boiko's major move is to disassociate Nationalism from both fascism and Dontsov. At the core of fascism, he writes, lies a contempt for the masses and an underestimation of the creative role played by ordinary people in the historical process. In a similar vein he argues that Dontsov saw people only as blind tools whose sole purpose was in realizing an idea, and that the OUN members who had fallen under Dontsov's influence tried to create obedient pawns—"mechanical little soldiers," as he put it (ibid., 35). Boiko quotes Lenkavsky: "From the standpoint of the new ethics the human individual is not some sort of absolute value that cannot be violated, is not an existing fact with its separate world, with small joys and sorrows that must be respected. The human individual is a momentary potential force, the sum of countless possibilities, possibilities for the realization of the idea. Only the idea, which (alone!) defines the direction of the will, has an absolute value" (Lenkavskyi 1928, 275). This, says Boiko, is the Dontsovian "formula."

Boiko then elaborates his second major objection to Dontsov. Dontsov's negativism attracted the more primitive minds. He never researched any topic in depth, and showed no interest in historicism. His impressionistic style represented the "how I see it" approach of a dilettante. Under his influence many Western Ukrainians grasped confidently at superficial answers to sociopolitical questions and substituted mythmaking for careful thought (ibid., 43). Boiko drew a distinction between this approach and the tone of *Rozbudova natsii*, or Olzhych's careful historical and anthropological studies of myth.

Osnovy draws heavily on Vassyian's writings to demonstrate the individual's importance in Nationalist thought. Already in 1929 Vassyian had argued that the foundation of any nation's development lay in the spiritual enrichment and growth of the individual. Boiko quotes the following lines: "A nation's spiritual-cultural richness and the socio-political differentiation of its internal life are normal phenomena in historical development" (Vassyian 1929, 67). It is logical, therefore, saya Boiko, that one should respect different points of view within the national community; they all constitute part of the same process that leads to greater self-awareness. Valuing another's opinion without submitting to it slavishly should be the ideal in human conduct (ibid., 92). This new emphasis on the individual conscience was of course symptomatic of ideological changes that were taking place within the OUN-M and other branches of the organized nationalist movement.

A second brochure published in the same year, *Na holovni magistrali* (On the Main Roads), stresses the links between nationalism, faith, and religion. Boiko sees "irrational" religious conviction as analogous to national commitment. He draws heavily on the sermons of Metropolitan Vasyl Lypkivsky, the metropolitan of the Ukrainian Autocephalous Orthodox Church, who in interwar years was kept under house arrest and was then executed in the Great Terror. Boiko aligns the religious with the national community. He also aligns Eastern Ukraine with the OUN's brand of nationalism. He argues, for example, that the writers Hryhorii Kosynka, Mykola Khvylovy, Oleksa Vlyzko, and other leading figures in Soviet literature of the 1920s and 1930s were sympathetic toward the OUN's ideas. Boiko's intention in this brochure was, no doubt, to rescue the ideology of prewar OUN by associating it with wider currents of thought. He was also keen to demonstrate the strength of national feeling in Eastern Ukraine. However, by aligning all expressions of nationalism with the prewar OUN, he blurred important distinctions. Moreover, he appeared to confirm the GPU's claim that conspiracies in Soviet Ukraine were inspired by the OUN. In the years 1929–34 tens of thousands in the Ukrainian intelligentsia were arrested, sentenced, executed, or exiled for membership in a string of bogus underground organizations that had all been dreamed up by the secret police. As one of the thirty thousand people who had been arrested in connection with the SVU trial of 1930, he knew well that in his own case at least the charges were false, but the temptation to link dissent among leading intellectuals with an organized political organization was strong. Boiko even claims in this work that Mykola Skrypnyk, the leading figure in the Communist Party (bolshevik) of Ukraine who headed the powerful Ukrainianization Ministry, was arrested in 1933 because behind his back stood Ukrainian nationalists, "who were even organizationally linked into the OUN network, as is evident from Soviet police-party sources and from information in L[ieutenant] Ie[vhen] Konovalets's circle" (Boiko 1951a, 98). There is no evidence for this. Even though there was plenty of seditious thinking in these circles, no organizational links to the émigré OUN have been confirmed; research into secret-police files and interrogations demonstrates that the existence of any such links is highly unlikely. This has not prevented some émigré commentators from making claims that the SVU and other organizations were, as the GPU declared, part of the OUN's underground, thus appropriating the fairy tale created by the secret police and then extracted from prisoners under torture. In making his case, Boiko may simply have followed the party line, or he may have succumbed to a form of wish-fulfillment.

It is significant that despite defending the individual conscience and voice, these pamphlets of the early 1950s continued to use the prewar terms "demoliberalism" and "demoliberal-rationalist" when describing opponents of the OUN. At this time the organization positioned itself as a radical, revolutionary project within a national community that, it recognized, held predominantly liberal-democratic views. The "Leninist" concept of the party as an organizational weapon placed an emphasis on authoritarian structures in political life. This concept was in conflict with the idea of national emancipation as an extension of social equality, individual freedom, and justice. The clash was especially evident in the treatment by Dontsov and Lenkavsky of people as mere potential for the seizure of power, rather than values in themselves. Such a view of human beings as subjects for radical social engineering had already been rejected by the OUN during the war. It appeared even more anomalous in the context of Western Europe, where over the centuries the definition of citizenship had slowly expanded, and where the achievement of civil, political, and social rights was celebrated as contributing to the individual's liberation.

Boiko attempted to deal with this contradiction. He retained the prewar focus on the "organic" nature of national communities, each with its own distinct identity and historical development, and insisted on the priority of winning independence. But he retreated from the prewar emphasis on a nation's unique destiny or mission, and his writings do not insist on the primacy of the collective over the individual. Despite his rhetorical dismissal of "demoliberalism," Boiko aligns his party and national liberation movements in general with the struggle for human rights and freedoms.

Perhaps most significant is the new tone, which is reasoned, mannerly, and avoids emotional cliché. It appeals to a universal sense of justice and fairness. Boiko is at pains to show that in the 1920s and 1930s this tone was already present in *Rozbudova natsii*, the OUN's main theoretical journal. Its ideologists, he writes, took "everything that was positive" in Dontsov and developed it while applying a different "method" from the publicist: "Not just feeling, but also often scrupulous analysis. Responsibility for every word uttered. A marked tendency toward professionalism" (ibid., 44). In this manner Boiko's revisionism attempts to maintain ideological links to the organization's past while charting a new course.

MYTH

5

NATIONALIST LITERATURE BETWEEN
MYTH AND MODERNISM

Interwar Ukrainian literature produced outside the Soviet Union had several centers. A "Prague School" grouped émigré writers, some of whom had lived in the city only briefly. It included Yurii Daragan, Oksana Liaturynska, Nataliia Livytska-Kholodna, Oleksa Stefanovych, Halyna Mazurenko, Iryna Narizhna, Andrii Harasevych, Ivan Kolos, Natalena Koroleva, and Yevhen Malaniuk. There are disagreements concerning whether a school existed in any formal sense. Malaniuk, for example, denied this.[1] There were two groups in Warsaw, one around Yurii Lypa and another around the journal *My* (We). In Lviv, Catholic writers were grouped around the journal *Dzvony* (Bells), a Bohemian circle formed around the group Dvanadtsiat (The Twelve), and around various independent periodicals. The journal *Vistnyk* had a core group of five writers, none of whom lived in the city: Yevhen Malaniuk, Oleh Olzhych (real name Kandyba), Olena Teliha, Leonid Mosendz, and Yurii Klen (Osvald Burghardt). Two other prominent figures, Yurii Lypa and Ulas Samchuk, are normally added to this list because they published for a while in the journal. These seven writers also published in the OUN's periodicals. As a group they best represent in literature the authoritarian brand of nationalism, one that is most closely associated with the integral nationalism of the OUN.

Among the seven writers whom the public identified with the journal and are considered Nationalist writers, Malaniuk was the greatest poetic star. A richly endowed, compelling poet and essayist, he made his reputation in the early 1920s. However, he stood aloof from organized political life. One critic has written that throughout his life Malaniuk tried to avoid "becoming a tribune, being directly involved in political life, hitching himself to someone's wagon."

Temperamentally incapable of a severe, voluntaristic life, he appeared to be "a light version of the bohemian type, something along the lines of the Parisian intellectual from the Latin Quarter" (Boichuk 2009, 691). He was more a product of the wider, less-political Prague School. Sometimes described as the "emperor of iron stanzas," Malaniuk was a useful figurehead for *Vistnyk*. The other six major Nationalist writers are closely linked to the OUN through organizational and personal ties. Malaniuk, Teliha, Olzhych, Mosendz, and Klen contributed to the journal regularly in the 1930s. For a while so did Lypa. Although initially they were all drawn to the editor and appeared to share his views, most were eventually repelled by his behavior. Lypa broke ties with the editor first; Malaniuk grumbled in private but stayed loyal; Mosendz, Klen and Samchuk cut ties with Dontsov during the war.

There were, of course, other notable literary figures who were associated with the OUN's publications, such as Bohdan Kravtsiv, Oles Babii, Maksym Hryva (M. Zahryvny), Mykola Chyrsky (Podoliak), Ivan Irliavsky (Roshko), Andrii Harasevych, Ivan Kolos (Koshan), and Yurii Horlis-Horsky (Horodianyn-Lisovsky). Kravtsiv initially made his reputation as a poet of youthful enthusiasm and a translator of the Song of Songs. His collection *Ostannia osin* (The Last Autumn, 1940) is a civic poetry that calls for self-sacrifice and struggle. But in the interwar years he was best known as the editor of the Galician periodicals *Visti* (1933–34), *Holos natsii* (1936), and *Holos* (1937–38) and the literary journals *Dazhboh* (Sungod, 1932–35) and *Obrii* (Horizon, 1936–37). Babii wrote the poem "Marsh" (March, 1929), which became an anthem of the OUN. In 1932 he was imprisoned for attending the OUN's founding congress.[2] The careers of several writers were cut short. Hryva, who fought in the resistance to bolshevik rule after the Cheka raped his sister and murdered his father and brother, died of tuberculosis in 1931. Chyrsky, who fought in the UNR army, contracted tuberculosis during internment and died of the disease in 1942. At the age of twenty-three, Irliavsky was shot by the Germans in Babyn Yar in 1942. Harasevych died in a mountain-climbing accident in the Alps in 1947. Horlis-Horsky's enormously popular *Kholodnyi Iar* (a place name that literally means Cold Ravine) went through numerous editions after its two volumes appeared in Lviv in 1934 and 1937. A memoir of anti-bolshevik partisan warfare conducted in the Chyhyryn area from 1919 to 1922, the book popularized the idea of armed struggle in the underground.

There were similarities in the sensibilities and interests of Ukrainian writers who published outside the Soviet Union during the interwar period. They were attracted to the dominant mythmaking of the period, in particular the dream of a regenerated society, or palingenesis (from *palin* and *genesis*: born again).

They turned to the distant past in search of what Peter Berger has called a "sacred canopy"—a stable, normative cosmology that could provide meaning and comfort.[3] Premodern culture offered shelter in a world that lacked intrinsic spiritual purpose, a world that, if contemplated without the protective lens of myth, seemed to make "nonsense of all human efforts to create anything of lasting value" (Griffin 2007, 75). The appeal of nationalism, Griffin has suggested, may lie in the human attraction to groups or movements that seem capable of symbolically defeating death and thereby overcoming existential malaise. Nationalism's ideology buffers this kind of death-anxiety: the nation appears to unite all compatriots, to reach far into the past, and extend into the future (ibid., 87). Yet, in spite of the consonances, there were substantial differences not only between the wider circle of interwar writers and those close to the OUN, but also within both groups.

The editor of *Vistnyk* tried to set his journal apart from others. Already in 1928, when the governing board of *Literaturno-naukovyi vistnyk* (which was losing readers and encountering financial problems) reviewed his editorship, he complained that this action was part of a campaign against him by the Soviet consul, the UNDO, the Union of Journalists and Writers, and personal enemies (BN, Mf. 82671, 69, 71). Although the board reappointed him as editor, the journal eventually closed down in 1932 for financial reasons. In the following year Dontsov created *Vistnyk*. Tensions immediately developed with contributors because he rejected works that were not to his taste. In refusing a story by Andrii Kryzhanivsky, he informed the author on 30 January 1930: "Heroes have to want something and aim for something, and not accept the world's blows passively. When heroes do not exert themselves, there is no action. When there is no action, there is no novel, no story" (ibid., 108). Antin Krushelnytsky wrote to Kosach on 10 April 1934, that Malaniuk had called Dontsov "an exploiter of literature" but, because he was intimidated by the editor, had stopped his criticism (TsDAVO, f. 4462, op. 1, spr. 4, ark. 44b). Lypa also voiced disagreement with Dontsov's literary tastes. He informed the editor on 20 March 1929: "unfortunately, I have to state that I look to you for advice concerning my literary work as little as you, for example, look to me concerning your political work" (BN, Mf. 83984, 118).

Both Malaniuk and Lypa were much more sophisticated interpreters of Ukrainian cultural history and Russian imperial mythology than Dontsov, and more attuned to the literary qualities of works. They felt constrained by the editor's imperious rule over *Vistnyk*. In 1929 they created in Warsaw an organization named "Tank," which planned to publish a periodical and almanac that would promote Ukrainian statehood and a literature celebrating the heroic and noble. The group was to include Avenir Kolomyiets, Kosach, Teliha, Mosendz,

Bohdan Lepky, Mykhailo Rudnytsky, Natalia Livytska-Kholodna, Oleksa Stefanovych, Mykola Chyrsky, Bohdan-Ihor Antonych, and Andrii Kryzhanivsky. The publications would allow writers to avoid passing their works through the "prism of Mr. Dontsov," as Kosach admitted to the latter on 1 May 1929 (BN, Mf. 83983, 287–88). A manifesto with articles by Malaniuk and Lypa appeared. Dontsov refused to publish it (Omelchuk 2011, 7). The group created the publishing house Variah (Viking) and the periodical *My* (We). An early editor of the latter, Ivan Dubutsky, wrote to Kosach on 27 June 1933 that the periodical's aim was to group "the artistic elite of the Western lands" (TsDAVO, f. 4462, op. 1, spr. 4, ark. 27). Variah put out the works of Borys Olkhivsky, Livytska-Kholodna, Sviatoslav Hordynsky, Kryzhanivsky, Mosendz, and others. Eleven issues of *My* appeared in the years 1933–39 and published Lepky, Livytska-Kholodna, Hordynsky, Antonych, Olkhivsky, Malaniuk, Lypa, Rudnytsky, Kosach, Iryna Vilde, and Kryzhanivsky. The periodical championed freedom of expression and sophistication of form. The critic Mykhailo Rudnytsky, wrote: "Internationalism and nationalism are two literary daughters of the same consumptive mother: agitation. We know their granny: an accessible literature with a national and social tendentiousness" (Rudnytskyi, "Ievropa i my," *My* 1 (1933), 99; quoted in Ilnytskyi 1995, 113). *My* proclaimed a modernist orientation (the code word was "European") and polemicized with Dontsov. Incensed, the latter successfully pressured several writers, including Malaniuk, Teliha, and Mosendz, to break ties with the competing periodical after the first issues.

Initially *My* saw itself as an alternative literary forum and was not hostile toward *Vistnyk*, but things changed when Kryzhanivsky, who was a strong opponent of Dontsov, took over as editor in 1934, as can be judged from the following letter written to Kosach on 10 April 1934:

> One has to step back from life and create "real" literature. This is something, by the way, that Dontsov does not understand! He wants to create a literature that is "adapted," forgetting that such a literature will always be an "ersatz." This is my conflict with him. By the way, about Dontsov. Did you read his response to my review? Remarkable! Another indication of my old conviction that he is a small, petty figure, with a pure card-sharper's ability to twist the thoughts of opponents. I will, of course, answer him very frankly and very seriously. Dontsov's methods and his style are beginning to be a gangrene on our body. One is really inclined to think that he has been "spiritually numbed" by the tactics and methods of bolshevism.
>
> His frequent attacks on them and continual interest in their (Soviet) life have been fatal. Such things happen. That's why doctors in mental asylums often go insane themselves. However, D's articles bear witness to our time.

Really honourable elements are dying off completely in our life. The stage is being taken over by modernized Ivan Karamazovs dressed up as Hitler. Sometimes he resembles a Petr Verkhovensky from [Dostoevsky's] *Devils*. (TsDAVO, f. 4462, op. 1, spr. 4, ark. 44–44b)

In another letter to Kosach from 28 January 1935, Kryzhanivsky commented: "You write that you are infuriated by Dontsov. Don't be. Dontsov's actions are becoming baser and baser. He walks through the Galician world like a simple snub-nosed Mephistopheles [a reference to the main character in Vynnychenko's novel of that title]. The poor man has forgotten the ancient truth that even 'great people' must recognize their time to die. And here he is galvanizing himself in a Hitlerite manner that is foreign to him" (ibid. 45–45b).[4]

The non-OUN literary periodicals published in Lviv included *Naperedodni* (On the Eve, 1937–38), *Nedilia* (Sunday, 1929–36), and *Nazustrich* (Toward, 1934–38). The last, which was edited by Mykhailo Rudnytsky and Sviatoslav Hordynsky, published Vasyl Sofroniv-Levytsky, Antonych, Vilde, and Kosach. It carried information about Western European developments, including, for example, an interview from Paris with Volodymyr Vynnychenko and a discussion of Archipenko's work. In addition there were various religious periodicals, such as the Catholic *Meta* (1931–39). Catholic writers who belonged to the "Logos" group published in *Postup* (Progress) until 1931 and then in its successor, the widely read *Dzvony* (Bells). There were also publications for women, youth, and the professions.[5] Literary production, in short, was a diverse field, in which supporters of the OUN often published alongside opponents. *Vistnyk* was immediately distinguishable in this field by Dontsov's angry and uncompromising attitude toward almost all other periodical publications.

Another direct challenge to *Vistnyk* was posed by the journal and publishing house *Novi shliakhy* (New Paths, 1928–32) and the periodical *Krytyka* (Criticism) (1933). Both had been organized by Antin Krushelnytsky. The journal *Novi shliakhy* soon developed a Sovietophile orientation. According to some reports it was shut down by the Polish government in 1932 along with all other pro-communist publications, although it has also been suggested that the real reason for closure was the drying up of Soviet funding. Because Stalin did not trust "Western" leftists, he made efforts to draw them into the Soviet Union, where they could be controlled or silenced (Tarnavsky 1995, 16–17). Krushelnytsky was the target of such seduction. He was widely known, well connected, and corresponded with Mykola Skrypnyk and other Soviet writers, including Mykola Khvylovy, Mikhail Semenko, Serhii Yefremov, and Yurii Mezhenko. In 1934 he took the tragic decision to emigrate to Soviet Ukraine, where he intended to contribute to the Ukrainianization process. After a large farewell evening on 15 April, the entire Krushelnytsky family was seen off from Lviv's railway station by a crowd on 8 May 1934. They were all arrested on 7 November. His two sons, Ivan and Taras, who were also writers, were executed in December. The other family members were killed in the Gulag in 1937; Antin died there in 1941. The Krushelnytskys were the most prominent Galician Sovietophiles and implacable critics of both Dontsov and the OUN. All of Galicia could see the falseness of the accusation that they were part of a Nationalist underground and complicit in Kirov's murder. The fate of the family caused a sensation (Krushelnytska 2008, 89, 103). *Dilo* printed the text of the sentence in large type on the front page of its 22 December 1934 issue, with the names of all the writers and the final words: "to be shot."

Initially the publishing house Novi shliakhy included on its governing board figures who represented mainstream Galicia, such as Kost Levytsky, Ilarion Svientsitsky, and Mykhailo Rudnytsky. It published the expressionist poet Antin Pavliuk, the surrealist verse of Vasyl Khmeliuk (who went on to achieve fame as a Parisian artist), and Hordynsky's stunning book covers, which were influenced by expressionist graphic design. Novi shliakhy was linked to the left-leaning Western Ukrainian Artistic Union (ZUMO). Its *Almanakh livoho mystetstva* (Almanac of Left Art, 1931) was edited by Ivan Krushelnytsky (Antin's son) and reproduced avant-garde art, including work by Ukrainians living in Paris or who exhibited in Western capitals. Among these were Mykhailo Andriienko-Nechytailo (Michel Andreenko), Mykola Hlushchenko, Roman Selsky (who founded the "leftist" Artes group), Mykola Butovych, Leonid Perfetsky, and Hordynsky. The Krushelnytskys had themselves lived in Vienna in the 1920s. Antin was fascinated by the art of Edvard Munch, the music of Richard Strauss, the work of Rilke and Hugo von Hoffmanstahl (whose son became a close friend of Ivan Krushelnytsky), and the theatrical ideas of Gordon Craig.

An appreciation of European trends was treated with suspicion by some observers, who in the later 1930s began to argue that modernism was intrinsically internationalist and therefore leftist. Nationalist art, in their view, had to develop out of its own historical traditions. Ivan Krushelnytsky's position, while strongly marked by the "vulgar sociological" Marxist approach (he considered art to be "an auxiliary force in the class struggle"), was nonetheless committed to developing Ukrainian art. Art's content, he wrote, did not make it national; but neither did it become international by ignoring the national question—an attitude he denounced as "national nihilism" (Krushelnytska 2008, 75). *Novi shliakhy* neither preached "art for art's sake" nor ignored the national imagination. A similar kind of leftism also characterized another pro-communist Galician writer, Vasyl Bobynsky, who edited the left-wing journal *Vikna* (Windows). He also moved to Kharkiv in 1930, was arrested, and later executed in a prison camp of the Solovki Islands.

Modernism was prominent in the world of Galician and émigré art. The Lviv-based Association of Independent Ukrainian Artists (ANUM), created in 1930 by Mykhailo Osinchuk and Yaroslava Muzyka, mounted thirteen exhibitions before the outbreak of the Second World War. In 1931 Parisian Ukrainians like Mykhailo Andriienko-Nechytailo, Alexis Gritschenko (Oleksa Hryshchenko), Mykola Hlushchenko, and Vasyl Perebyinis were shown alongside French and Italian modernists and avant-gardists like Gino Severini, Andre Derein, Maurice de Vries, Van Dongen, and Filippo De Pisis. The exhibition of 120 works by forty-one artists led to a discussion in the press of impressionism, expressionism, futurism, cubism, and constructivism. Some critics viewed these trends as leftist. In the years that followed, they argued that modernism was synonymous with individualism, decadence, and internationalism, and that it sought to downplay national forms in art. Mykailo Ostroverkha argued in 1938 that throughout Europe the art of 1920–35 represented "the height of insanity [. . .] an aberration of the brain." He expressed amazement that one could find "any sort of aesthetic" in Amadeo Modigliani, the eyes of whose women expressed "an abyss of hashish, morphine, cocaine—the black, exhausted souls of the dissolute human being." Ostroverkha hoped that "this art of a morphino-perfidious culture would never again return in Europe" (1946, 70).

In 1942, under German occupation, this debate erupted at the Union of Artists in Lviv. A number of speakers attacked abstract art and formalism; others championed Byzantinism. However, the most authoritative voice was that of the art critic Ilarion Svientsitsky. He defended artists who had studied abroad, and pointed out that a work's content and theme did not make it Ukrainian. Art, like music, he said, recognized international canons (P. 1942). Sviatoslav Hordynsky, who was both an accomplished artist and poet, and who had organized ANUM's exhibitions in the 1930s, defended the inclusion of French and Italian modernists. He argued that the exhibitions, monographs, and magazines produced by ANUM in the thirties, and the participation of its members in numerous international exhibitions had aligned Ukrainian art with modernist trends and in this way changed its face.[6]

In fact, many Ukrainian artists were internationally known avant-gardists. Archipenko, Exter, Gritchenko (Hryshchenko), and Andreenko, for example, had made names for themselves in the École de Paris. Eugene Deslaw (Yevhen Slabchenko), a member of the UNR emigration in Prague, moved to Paris in 1922 and played an important role in French avant-garde cinema with works like

La Marche des machines (1928), *Montparnasse* (1929) and *Autour de la Fin du monde* (1930). Marcel Slodki, who came from Lodz in Poland and was of Ukrainian background, was a Dadaist painter who worked in Paris and Berlin. And, of course, in the 1920s some Ukrainian artists who lived the Soviet Union, such as Kazimir Malevych and Volodymyr (Vladimir) Tatlin, gained international fame.

The modernist influence was also inescapable in music and dance. In the 1920s Igor Stravinsky, who had close ties to Ukraine, lived in Paris with his Ukrainian wife. Jazz and cabaret theater were popular throughout the major European cities, and many Ukrainians were active in modern dance. The interwar generation stylized and choreographed folk dances from various regions of Ukraine as a way of incorporating regional diversity into national identity. Although the use of dance as patriotic display dated back to the theater of the 1880s and 1890s, the interwar years transformed choreography by introducing modern dance as an aesthetic form. Isadora Duncan and her sister Elizabeth, who had a studio in Prague, were influences, as was Emil Jaques-Dalcrose in Geneva and Paris, Gertrude Bodenwieser in Vienna, and Mary Wigman in Berlin. Wigman helped to stage the dance spectacles of the 1936 Berlin Olympics that are depicted in Leni Riefenstahl's *Triumph of the Will*. Goebbels canceled the Dance Olympics that Wigman had planned as a parallel event to the games (Griffin 2007, 146). Avant-garde or expressive dance was part of the modernist search for health and was related to the palingenetic myth of societal regeneration. It represented the interwar fascination with the body as an expression of health, harmony, and connection with nature, and was associated with the cult of the body in antiquity.

These trends influenced Ukrainians. Oleksandra Siropolko introduced modern dance into her studio in Prague, where she worked with the painter Halyna Mazepa, blending liberated movements with traditional forms (Pasternakova 1963, 38). Oksana Fedak-Drohomyretska studied with Dalcrose in Geneva, then opened a rhythmic dance school in Lviv. Daria Kravets-Yemets studied with Ruth Sorel in Warsaw and performed in Lviv. Iryna Holubovska worked with Gertrude Bodenwieser, then taught and performed in Western Ukraine.

Related developments were taking place in fashion. The Lviv periodical *Zhinka* (Woman) was a beacon for the new modern woman. It described women who had been successful in literature and the arts, business, fashion, and politics, recommending courses in anatomy, hygiene, geography and history, European cooking, hotel and boardinghouse management, and interior decorating. The fashion-conscious woman could find photographs of the latest styles on display in European capitals. In this way the periodical taught women how to read the female body and construct an ideal that was at once modern, European, and Ukrainian.

Interwar nationalism came out of this atmosphere. Like other modernists, nationalist writers of all camps expressed a dissatisfaction with conventional writing and for most of the interwar period did not distance themselves from innovative currents. Writing in 1929 in *Rozbudova natsii*, H. Kalytskyi praised futurism as "the strongest artistic expression of the new emotional-voluntaristic worldview" (Kalytskyi 1929, 154). Futurism's formal and stylistic experimentation, which had provoked so much protest, was seen as its most useful contribution because it breathed life into the stifling atmosphere of positivistic rationalism (although Soviet Ukrainian futurism was dismissed as derivative and outdated). This critic also found that the writers of *Literaturno-naukovyi vistnyk* had failed to create a modern poetry of pathos and action that pulsated "with the rhythms of contemporary life" (ibid., 162). He urged a modernist writing that would be completely "fused with the Western spirit" and that had made a complete break with populism, realism, and "passive aestheticism" (ibid., 165–66). He praised the prewar modernists Lesia Ukrainka, Mykhailo Kotsiubynsky, Petro Karmansky, and Vasyl Stefanyk, and the Soviet modernists Mykola Khvylovy, Valeriian Pidmohylny, and Hryhorii Kosynka. A similar line was taken by M. Hnatyshak, who wrote in *Rozbudova natsii* in 1930 that Galician theater lagged far behind experiments in the West and in Soviet Ukraine. He warned that it had to learn from modern Western European theater or die (Hnatyshak 1930, 169). Hnatyshak praised Brecht's *Threepenny Opera*, Max Reinhardt's experiments, and the innovations made in modern dance by Dalcrose, Rudolf Lahan, and Mary Wigman, and was particularly enthusiastic about the use of choruses, group dances, and new lighting techniques in stage productions (ibid., 171–72).

It was only in the later 1930s that leading Nationalists, under the influence of antimodernist rhetoric emanating from Hitler's Germany, began to denounce modernism. As will be seen, the OUN's cultural spokesman Olzhych developed antimodernist positions in the years 1938–44. Even so, modernist forms and trends continued to exert an influence. The journal *Samostiina dumka (Independent Thought)*, for example, praised the work of Richard Strauss, the leading contemporary German composer, who cooperated with the Nazi regime. It also carried information on the work of Igor Stravinsky and followed the careers of Soviet composers like Levko Revutsky and Borys Liatoshynsky, as well as the Soviet writers like Mykola Khvylovy, Hryhorii Kosynka, Oleksa Vlyzko, and Yurii Yanovsky. The dialectic at work in Nationalist literature and art was therefore a complex appropriation of some Western or international trends and a rejection of others.

This generation's turn to myth and history was part of a wide-ranging phenomenon that captured much of European modernism. Max Weber famously argued in 1918 that modern times were characterized by rationalization and intellectualization and, above all, by "the disenchantment of the world," and that as a result people were turning to myths as compensation for the dull, oppressive regularities in their lives (Weber 1958, 155). The use of myth in this sense can be seen as a form of storytelling that helps the reader to understand the world and provides rules and precedents for moral action. The myths that drive storytelling convey important information about a society, especially about how it imagines its beginnings and its future. Myths of origin reveal a people's fundamental character, while eschatological myths describe a civilization's end or the fall of an evil power. This kind of mythmaking often acts as a condensed expression of a religious or political faith. As such, it brings meaning and harmony to the lives of people, reassures them that they are part of a greater destiny, and connects them to a morally coherent world.

Modernists summoned visions of a heroic past not out of nostalgic yearning, but as a way of criticizing the present and forging the future. Galicians realized that living in the past was not an option. When their literature postulated a homogeneous tradition, with beliefs and rituals rooted in ancient times, it did so to calm readers who feared the tempo of modernization. However, the driving force behind this literature was a desire to acquire modern reflexes, to respond to rapid change. The past provided examples of superior, stronger people who could act as models for the imagined future.

Although denounced by those who counterpose myth to rationality and enlightened thought, mythmaking should be seen a universal impulse. This was realized by the surrealists and Walter Benjamin, who saw enchantment and mythic images all around them: in advertising, commodities, and collective dreams. After reading Louis Aragon's *Le Paysan de Paris* (Paris Peasant, 1924), Benjamin began to view urban sites as expressions of a modern mythology that had gone unacknowledged. The surrealists taught him that the conscious mind was structured by the unconscious and tried to imitate it, that myth was "the path of the conscious mind, its magic carpet" (Aragon 1970, 103). In the 1920s Benjamin spoke of a "modern mythology" through which people worship their own products and fetishize their cities. He admired some forms of the mythic, such as counterhistories of the oppressed.[7] Because mythological compulsions operate at a subliminal level (in dreams, visions, and delusions), he felt that they needed to be experienced imaginatively through "careful experiential (rather than conceptual) immersion in mythopoeic activities" (Scholem and Adorno 1994, 287). Only then could they be dealt with critically. The power of myth needed to be understood, not denied.

Fascination with myth was strong in Germany during the Weimar Republic of the 1920s, where it became a "category of absolute conceptual and historical primacy" in modernist artistic movements and all cultural and political ideologies (Mali 2008, 140). The mythological in Ukrainian literature arose democratically at this time as a way of affirming political identity. This literature produced its own myths of origin with their symbolic, sacred places, and its myths of greatness with their golden ages. In national mythology, as Anthony Smith has argued, the "homeland" becomes a sacred space, a nation's cradle and the site of its historic memories. Modern versions of old stories reaffirm bonds to the past by repainting landscapes, retelling legends, and revisiting monuments, by drawing on ancient chronicles and sacred stories (such as the lives of saints), and by resurrecting folk heroes (Smith 1988, 1991). Awareness of these bonds endows the national identity with dignity. In Ukrainian literature, some stories, such as those from the *Primary Chronicle* (originally produced in Kyiv around 1113 c.e.), have for centuries provided frameworks for self-definition. In this sense there was nothing remarkable in the fact that interwar writers looked back with nostalgia to the cultural achievements of Kyivan Rus and the Cossack state, or discovered in these times people who were strong in character and committed to the body politic. These writers were exploring links to the past, urging readers to identify with historical leaders and to admire past expressions of group solidarity.

The era of Kyivan Rus was introduced into poetry by Daragan, Liaturynska, and Stefanovych. The Princely Era (the tenth to thirteenth centuries) and Cossackdom was treated in the historical fiction of Volodymyr Birchak, Andrii Chaikovsky, Semen Ordivsky, Viacheslav Budzynovsky, Vasyl Grendzha-Donsky, Natalena Koroleva, Bohdan Lepky, Antin Lototsky, Osyp Nazaruk, Yuliian Opilsky, and Yurii Kosach. Mass uprisings and their relationships to political elites and political change became favorite themes. Birchak's *Volodar Rostyslavych: Istorychna povist z XI-ho viky* (Ruler Rostyslavych: A Historical Novel from the Eleventh Century, 1930) is a tale of internal discord in the face of an invading Hungarian army. When the discord is eliminated, the Ukrainian forces are able to defeat the invaders. The message is that solidarity and courage bring victory. At the end of the decade, Ordivsky published popular novels dealing with the Cossacks. His *Chorna Ihumenia: Istorychna povist z XVII st.* (The Black Abbess: A Historical Novel of the Seventeenth Century, 1939) describes Hetman Ivan Vyhovsky's struggle against Moscow's encroachment upon Cossack rights in the period following Khmelnytsky's death. It depicts the *chern* (common people or rabble) as an anarchic and destructive force motivated by greed, personal gain, and jealousy of Cossack riches and privileges. The *chern*'s communist-sounding rhetoric is only a cover for the desire to plunder. By contrast, the Cossack class understands the struggle for political rights and the need for discipline. Vyhovsky tries to keep his Cossacks in line but is undermined by Pushkar, who whips up the mob. The tsar, who wants to gain the right to appoint Ukraine's rulers and has spread agents throughout Ukraine, pits Pushkar against Vyhovsky. The chief female character is a mysterious black abbess, who tells Pushkar that neither he nor the *chern* know how to build anything, because they have only learned how to destroy. She warns him not to trust Muscovy, which is treacherous and duplicitous—warnings that of course prove prophetic. The final pages reveal that she is the dreaded avenger who has murdered various traitors to the Ukrainian cause. Once married to a Russian, she has learned her lesson, as have many other women who now secretly help Cossacks in need. However, Ordivsky's novels express not so much support for autocratic or authoritarian rule as a fear of disorder. The author, whose real name was Hryhorii Luzhnytsky, was a founding members of Logos, the Lviv-based organization of Ukrainian Catholic writers. After studying in Graal and Prague, he edited the Lviv journal *Postup* (1921–31), which popularized the works of the world's Catholic writers. Ordivsky's craving for a stable social order is at odds with Dontsov's stress on the fanatical spirit. The popular novels of Andrii Chaikovsky are written in a similar vein: they focus on the patriotic virtues of the Zaporozhians. He was a member of UNDO and a prolific writer, who in 1924 became head of the Ukrainian Writers and Journalists in Lviv. Both Ordivsky and Chaikovsky advanced similar reasons for Ukraine's state-building difficulties, whether in the distant past or in 1917–20: divisions within one's own forces, an unpreparedness caused by antimilitaristic tendencies, and the interference of Moscow.

When the Nationalists turned to history and myth, they were often drawn to the apocalyptic. The modernist version of this kind of sensibility was often linked to the sublime, in which beauty is experienced against a background of superhuman chaos, disorder, and desolation, producing in the reader or viewer a feeling of awe or fear. Some works present apocalyptic scenarios that combine terror and decadence with the hope of revival. Nationalist writers gravitated toward the depiction of terrible and tragic events, and attempted to construct powerful mythic structures.

Malaniuk's poetry and essays, for example, construct an influential dualistic myth of Ukraine, which resonated in the interwar period. She is a Hellas of the Steppe or the Christian Maria, a beautiful woman who represents a culture of harmony and grace. But she is simultaneously a whore who has slept with all invaders, an Anti-Maria. The Steppe is both Ukraine's glory and its curse. Lacking natural boundaries, over the centuries this rich land has tempted countless invaders. Ukraine needs to reacquire Roman "iron," to reactivate the state-building gene it once possessed. Yurii Lypa's mythmaking, as Hanna Cherin has pointed out, revolves around a related image: the need to awaken the slumbering Sphinx of the Steppe (Cherin 1974, 13). As will be seen, he celebrates the Hellenic and harmonious in Ukrainian culture.

More than other interwar Galician or émigré writers, the Nationalists infused these modernist myths with notions of innovation and change, often with an aesthetics of rupture. They agreed that the leaders of 1917–20 had failed the nation, yearned for a new leadership that would be hard and competent, and expressed the desire for a rapid march to a regenerated society. They were influenced by Dontsov's call to cultivate a fanatical crusading spirit. Several major works that emerged from this period adopt an apocalyptic, epic tone in an attempt to turn cultural fragments into meaningful elements of a whole. Samchuk's novels, especially his *Maria* (1934–52), and Klen's monumental poem *Popil imperii* (Dust of Empires, 1943–57) are examples. They can be read as modernist attempts to manage disjunction and diversity by providing an overarching unity and a complex vision of history.

The Dontsovian tone affected not only contributors to *Vistnyk* but also those in "unaligned" groups. Ivan Cherniava can serve as an example. He belonged to a Lviv bohemian group called Dvanadtsiat (The Twelve), which was dedicated to producing an innovative literature and changing the nation's temper. Cherniava married a Pole, moved to Warsaw, and worked as a journalist in the Polish press. In 1943 he was murdered near Warsaw by the Nazis. His novels were not publications of the OUN or *Vistnyk*, which considered frivolous The Twelve's taste for light humor, satire, cabaret theater, and translations of French comic dramas. Moreover, the group's leading lights—Bohdan Nyzhankivsky, Zenon Tarnavsky, and Bohdan Tsisyk—published in *My* and a number of Lviv journals, including *Litopys chervonoi kalyny* (Cranberry Chronicle), which was edited by Vasyl Sofroniv-Levytsky. One of their mentors became Mykhailo Rudnytsky, a leading Lviv critic who was despised by Dontsov for his urbane tone and emphasis on aesthetic considerations.

Cherniava's novels, *Na skhodi—my* (In the East—We, 1932) and *Liudy z chornym pidnebinniam* (People with Black Palates, 1935), embrace Dontsov's concept of a radical spiritual change. The first is set in the future and describes Ukraine winning a war against Russia, thereby extending its eastern border to the Caspian Sea. Peace slogans, the reader learns, are peddled only by blind fanatics or cynics; the real world has always been governed by Realpolitik, and it is time that Ukrainians woke up to this fact. The novel purports to tell the hard facts of life, and Krukevych is the spokesman for a new militarism. He informs that "swinishness" has never hurt the reputation of successful individuals or nations, as the

conquests of Caesar, Napoleon, and Suvorov show (Cherniava 1932, 47).
Unfortunately, "six centuries of the knout" have taught Ukrainians to bow their
heads before Moscow's power. It is time to employ some of the same "swinish"
behavior—political deceit and mercilessness—that have been used by other
nations. The novel romanticizes combat and ridicules antiwar novelists like
Remarque. Krukevych, for example, admits that his greatest thrill is viewing
defeated enemies. A woman's role, he feels, is to produce strong, healthy children. Men, on the other hand, should not place the love of women above service
to nation; this would lead to degeneration and desertion from the army. The
"egoism of the people" has to be strengthened until it rivals that of predators from
the East (ibid., 164). In reality, over the centuries "immorality in all its forms" has
steadily augmented as cultures have developed. World literature, the indispens-
able guide to life, shows that individuals with bright spirits and good intentions
are rare exceptions. The book urges that young people not be given the "decadent
books of our old literature" (ibid., 197). The novel is constructed in an action-
packed, fragmentary, cinematographic style, as the narrator puts it, so as to avoid
boring the reader with long descriptions of "every feeling and facial expression"
(ibid., 186). One of the more shocking passages describes a soldier's reaction to
the picture of a young girl who has been killed during the invasion of Russia:

> He picked her up by the shirt.
> "This child, after millions of ours, is the first foreigner. She probably got
> in the way of a soldier, so he kicked her in the head. What's strange about
> that? Of course, we are here to fight soldiers, not children, but when you
> chop wood . . ."
> His laugh was hearty and loud.
> "There were probably several Russian [Moskaliv] in the house, who had
> to be killed, or maybe a good-looking Russian woman [Moskovka] . . ."
> He threw the girl into the house.
> Bilyi stared with bright, frightened eyes.
> "A Russian woman?" he echoed. "What justifies that, when soldier fights
> soldier? . . ."
> "Do you know the parable about life? . . . In the face of death a person
> searches for some honey. And if a good-looking woman appears . . . In the
> eyes of death the thirst for life grows powerful." (Ibid., 81)

This passage presents itself as championing life's bitter realities in contrast to
the sentimental humanism of the "old" literature. Whether one reads it as
preaching fanatical commitment to nation and cold ruthlessness or as discerning
what Joseph Roth called "the whir of the vast machinery which was already beginning to manufacture war" (Roth 1985, 88), the debt to Dontsov is unmistakable.

The chief protagonist of the second novel is Bunio. He breaks with his father and the Galician environment, which he holds in contempt, and decides to devote himself to a new philosophy that celebrates active engagement and the romance of "travel into the unknown" (Cherniava 1935, 74). Love and humanism are presented as mystifications. Leveliuk, like Krukevych in the first book, acts as a kind of political guru to the younger generation. He scoffs at those who speak of higher values and humane feelings, because they have allowed Russians "to murder several million people through hunger, to murder them in full awareness and with a considered plan" (ibid., 79–80). The novel also condemns some forms of modern art—those in particular that concentrate on sexual titillation or pretentious and incomprehensible abstraction. One visitor to an exhibition of contemporary Ukrainian art asks in Polish why none of the pictures deals with the Great Famine of 1932–33. He is informed: "Political events and art are . . . two completely different things" (ibid., 119). In this way the novel criticizes self-indulgent creativity that turns a blind eye to the suffering of millions. Bunio tries to rid himself of the influence of Knut Hamsun, Stefan Zweig, and Nikolai Kuprin, but the whole of Galician society is infected with their preciosity. In Bunio's view Galicia can be compared to a plebeian who suffers from the sickness of "aristocratism." It is a society that has learned to lisp "like a lord," but still has "dirty fingernails and a servile soul." The cultivation it displays is superficial and affected. This is also true of Galician politicians, who have only mastered the art of "signing documents" and "walking on parquet floors" (ibid., 120).

Cherniava's novels were condemned in Lviv's journals. A reviewer in the Catholic *Dzvony* (Bells) called the first novel "a militant nationalist Ukrainian Gospel," and another in the Catholic *Nova zoria* (New Star) commented that the author had drunk from Dontsov's "imperialist energetic" and had been seduced "by the old tempter" (Gabor 2006, 272–73). The OUN's journals also attacked Cherniava. A reviewer in *Samostiinist* (Sovereignty) complained that the author of *Na skhodi—my* knew nothing about Nationalism. Dontsov also disowned the work as "the ideology of a nomad, not the philosophy of a conqueror" (Dontsov [O.V.] 1933). He found the novel unconvincing, called the language of love hackneyed, and described the new people as more concerned with declarations than actions. Later Malaniuk commented that despite its naiveté, Cherniava's work was not without literary merit (Malaniuk 2008, 57; quoted in Omelchuk 2011, 136). Dontsov's disapproval was likely caused partly by Cherniava's affiliation with the Dvanadtsiat group, but the critic may also have sensed a parodic intent. The posterlike futurist style and hallucinogenic scenes of apocalyptic war are so excessive that they make the reader recoil. It is possible that the young writer, in pushing the revolutionary thesis that old ways of thinking had to be opposed, produced a demonic and self-condemning antithesis. Whether Cherniava deliberately aimed at such a cathartic effect is unclear, but Dontsov immediately sensed that this was the novel's effect.

The OUN's official statements underlined an interest in the dominant myth of national renewal or palingenesis. At the founding congress of the OUN in 1929, Makar Kushnir painted a vision of the new society: "Our nation will finally gain control of the cities, those centres of culture and civilization. Moreover, the required intensification of agriculture will at least double our grain production. Then Ukraine will be covered with new railway lines and automobile routes, European buildings of stone will appear everywhere, our cities and villages will entirely change their appearance, electricity will shine and new industrial giants will be raised" (Muravsky 2006, 237). The same vision of a redeemed world appears frequently in its creative literature: a protagonist is transformed by a confrontation with modernity; a personal quest leads to a moment of transcendence; technological achievements change the nation and awaken creativity.

Jeffrey Herf has used the term "reactionary modernism" to describe what he sees as a fundamental duality: the acceptance of renewal, change, technology, and modern forms of organization, on the one hand, and the search for ancient foundations and an allegedly unique past, on the other. In his view, reactionary modernists were irrationalists in that they placed a low value on the role of reason in politics and trusted more to apocalyptic visions of violent civilizational transformations, but were rationalists in their commitment to modernizing society. Nonetheless, he emphasizes that the vision of German nationalism between the wars was "not a backward looking pastoralism but a beautiful new order, a technologically advanced nation" (Herf 1984, 2). Griffin emphasizes that in this modernism, even the term "reactionary" had a futuristic orientation: it expressed "a mission to change society, to inaugurate a new epoch, to start time anew" (Griffin 2007, 244, 62).

It is useful to recall that within mainstream modernism there were strong "reactionary" temptations. Modernism, for example, had its own, far-from-"rational" romance with social Darwinism. Darwin's theory, which had initially challenged biblical dogmas in the name of science, had been used since the late nineteenth century to support the idea that competitiveness was intrinsic to human "nature" and that imperial or national rivalries were inevitable in the struggle for survival. The theory stimulated an interest in instinct, animal energy, and vitality. In the 1930s the fashion spread for vigorous, manly writers. Kipling and Jack London became familiar to Ukrainian readers, as did their Soviet Ukrainian equivalents —

Mykola Khvylovy, Yurii Yanovsky, Oleksa Vlyzko, Mykola Bazhan, Mykola Filiansky, and Arkadii Liubchenko. The initial interest in Italian futurism and German expressionism also fell into this category. These movements had set the tone for militant and radically inclined artists. The OUN admired futurism's cult of war and virility, which was described by Vassyian as "the militarization of the spirit" (Vassyian 1929, 66).

Many in the interwar generation as a whole felt that the contemporary world was losing the elements that were required for a healthy civilization. This anxiety could be traced to the decades that preceded the First World War, at which time concern with degeneracy, decay, and the loss of manly values had spread through political, religious, and literary discourse. The call for a "muscular Christianity" had its counterpart in Max Nordau's "muscular Judaism." His widely read *Degeneration* (1892) cataloged contemporary decadence and ended with the idea of "clubbing to death" the most decadent human specimens as a way of ensuring the survival of the fitter ones. Shortly afterward Nordau adopted Zionism as his palingenetic dream (Griffin 2007, 15?). In the interwar period, the strongman Siegmunt Breitbart gained European fame, becoming "arguably the most visible performer of Jewish masculinity at the time" (Gillerman 2012, 197). He entertained the Central and East European public by demonstrating his strength and by acting the role of Hercules or a Roman centurion. Himself the product of a poor Jewish neighborhood in Łódż, he linked strength to survival, promoted the strongman as an answer to Jewish powerlessness, and became a strong supporter of Zionism. At this time the discourse on eugenics, which was related to social Darwinism, developed both a right-wing and left-wing current. The first voiced concern with the impact of racial decay on the empire's strength, while the second (which included George Bernard Shaw, H. G. Wells, Sidney and Beatrice Webb) framed its argument in terms of improving health, breeding, and social welfare.

The literature of prewar Ukrainian modernism followed this European trend and is known for its concern with degeneracy and decay, but also for its attempt to move away from cultural pessimism toward palingenetic hope. This can be observed in Lesia Ukrainka's dramas, in poems like her "Contra Spem Spero," and in Olha Kobylianska's Nietzschean aristocrats of the spirit. The politics and culture of the UNR period and the struggle for independence were strongly influenced by this mood. In postrevolutionary Soviet Ukraine the same myth of national regeneration found powerful expression in the work of figures like Khvylovy and Yanovsky, who were admired for their messianic faith in a cultural renaissance and their portrayal of strong individuals. Interwar writers—whether pro-Soviet or anti-Soviet—showed little patience with pacifists. The Nationalists, for example, singled out for ridicule Romain Rolland, who was awarded the Nobel Prize for literature in 1915 as an antiwar gesture by the Swedish judges. The seven Nationalist writers who were associated with *Vistnyk* shared modernism's belief in achieving transcendence through cultural, social, and political transformations.

Griffin, who has indicated features shared by modernism and authoritarianism, insists that fascism should be seen as a political variant of modernism:

> This peculiar genus of the revolutionary project for the transformation of society [. . .] could only emerge in the first decades of the twentieth century in a society permeated with modernist metanarratives of cultural renewal which shaped a legion of activities, initiatives, and movements "on the ground." In its varied permutations fascism took it upon itself not just to change the state system, but to purge civilization of decadence, and foster the emergence of a new breed of human beings which it defined in terms not of universal categories but essentially mythic national and racial ones. Its activists set about their task in the iconoclastic spirit of "creative destruction" legitimized not by divine will, reason, the laws of nature, or by socio-economic theory, but by the belief that history itself was at a turning point and could be launched on a new course through human intervention that would redeem a nation and rescue the West from imminent collapse. (Griffin 2007, 6)

The official OUN position balanced between an attraction toward myth and modernism, and the need to educate and inspire revolutionary cadres. Its attitude toward literature and the arts was outlined in a resolution taken at a meeting of the Cultural-Educational Commission held during the founding OUN congress in 1929. It read:

> Ukrainian Nationalism as a complete worldview cannot limit itself merely to a narrow political activity, but must encompass and organize all aspects of the nation's life, including the sphere of culture and art. Basing its ideology on the nation's urge to life and growth Ukr[ainian] Nationalism will support cultural production that awakens a healthy drive toward strength and might, but will struggle against manifestations that weaken or ruin the healthy national organism. Synthesizing in its ideology conservatism and revolutionism, Ukr[ainian] Nationalism will nurture art that is rooted in healthy elements of our past, that draws on the cult and heroism of knighthood and the voluntaristic, creative attitude toward life. Ukr[ainian] Nationalism is attentive to the voice of the native land and nurtures culture as the organic flower of the Ukr[ainian] national soil, while opposing its culture to international, bolshevik culture. On the other hand, it counterposes its art to Muscovite

nihilism and pessimism, turning its attention instead to Wes[tern] Eur[opean] cultures with their cult of optimism, joy of life, and activism. (Muravsky 2006, 162)

Encoded in this proclamation is an ambivalent attitude toward the West and modernism, a view of the nation as an organic entity, an interest in vitality, and a concern with art's purposefulness. Like all prescriptive approaches to art, the Nationalist one eventually led to art's instrumentalization. Already in the mid-1930s some commentators had reached the conclusion that literature's primary goal was the dissemination of martial attitudes. Oksana Kompaniiets's *Lesia Ukrainka* (1936), a popular brochure in the Desheva Knyzhka series, can serve as an example:

> The tasks of every people's literature lies not only in leisure, in escape from the mundane into the realm of the writer's imagination and dreams. The task of every people's literature lies in being that people's educator, in using the word to prepare the way for action, in affecting the emotions just as political programs and slogans affect the mind. Literature is like a loud orchestra, or resounding fanfares that play the march for a military expedition, that make the stirring call "Alarm! Alarm, for we must advance. Alarm, for the enemy is near!" [. . .] Literature, its ideas and its spirit are closely interwoven with a nation's history. However, literature has an especially great and irreplaceable value for a stateless people, which is, obviously, deprived of leaders and oppressed by its prisoner fate; it loses faith in its strength, forgets about its national political mission and gradually begins to renounce its political struggles and lowers itself to the level of a mass lacking political ideals, the will to struggle for its national community's liberty, strength and growth. In such a situation only word masters, writers, national *kobzars* can awaken liberty from sleep, resurrect the fighting spirit by unfolding before the nation the history of its glorious past. (Kompaniiets 1936, 4–6)

According to these precepts, literature's primary purpose was to instill patriotism and militancy. During the Second World War this view was expressed in the propaganda of the OUN-B. A leaflet from October 1941 reads: "we will strive to create a Nationalist culture based not only on a Nationalist form, but above all on the spiritual nature and traditions of the people, on the heroic struggle to create its own national-ethical cultural ideal—one that is indissolubly tied to the whole life of the nation, and that in its essence and forms will constitute a sovereign, self-sufficient Ukrainian spirituality" (TsDAVO, f. 3833, op. 2, spr. 1, ark. 212). Diminished opportunities for self-expression under wartime conditions meant that civic poetry was often favored. A poetry anthology produced in

Prague in 1943 and entitled *Dekliamator ukrainskoi heroichnoi poezii* (Ukrainian Heroic Poetry for Declamation) announced itself as an attempt to embody the "national spirit" through the ages. The editor informed that the heroic poetry in the anthology demanded an appropriate recitation, not the "customary" melodramatic one, but "one that is solemn and elevated" (TsDAVO, f. 4036, op. 1, spr. 23, ark. 2–3).

This, however, was not the full story. Olena Teliha, herself an icon of Nationalism, insisted in her essay "Prapory dukhu" (Banners of the Spirit, 1941) that "Ukrainian Nationalist art was never simply agitation and cannot be this, even if it is now turned against our greatest enemy, Moscow. Our art must not use those cheap, hackneyed stereotypes that are the legacy of Muscovy's intrusiveness. [. . .] It must always remember that even the most brilliant agitational speech delivered in front of the masses has no value as a literary work" (Teliha 2008, 148). The task of art, she argued, was not to educate police chiefs or commissars. This essay was written in Rivne as she assimilated her first impressions of Soviet reality following eighteen years in emigration, and represented her initial reaction to the debased, ritualistic forms of expression she encountered. She observed that the deeply ingrained forms and practices of socialist realism were now evident in obsequious writings in praise of the new masters. The same "religious" liturgy was being employed, the same panegyric code that praised the great Soviet leader, state, party, victorious army, or radiant future. Teliha, Samchuk, and other Nationalist writers repeatedly complained about the mind-numbing effects of such an undemanding form and stereotypical sentiments.

Formal perfection, as Teliha remarked, remained a goal. This is one reason why a turn to neoclassicism appeared in Nationalist writings of the late 1930s. It combined an enthusiasm for form (in particular for the monumental and well constructed) with clarity and conciseness of thought. Poets encased emotion in a tight, disciplined meter. The ornamental or chaotic (now often associated with a negative view of avant-garde experimentation) was rejected in the name of focused, organized effort and a clear message. This label of "classicism" was sometimes applied to the leading poets close to the OUN—Teliha, Olzhych, Klen and Mosendz. Their work was seen as both transgressive and monumental. Although it borrowed its visionary and rule-breaking nature from modernism's energy and drive (especially from futurism's "military" inflections and attacks on bourgeois reality), the new classicism was seen as a rejection of modernism's "anarchic" individualism, its self-indulgent and often-frivolous experimentation. Romantic adventures, dreams of valor and glory were still indulged, but the form was disciplined and orderly, suggesting submission to a great collective project. The formal features of this "classicism" were an increased focus on rhetorical devices (alliteration, parallelism, repetitions), on generalizations that often took the form of aphorisms, on historical allusions and a strong confident voice—one that spoke for the millions and revealed no self-doubt (Rubchak 2009, 703). In lesser writers this tone could degenerate into a civic lyricism full of hackneyed patriotic phrases, but in the work of the main Nationalist writers it echoed the Kyiv neoclassicists of the 1920s, who valued poise, the well-chosen epithet, a strong logical structure, and a powerful flow of thought.

The modernized classicism of the late 1930s may have cultivated nostalgia for the order and splendor of the past, but it looked to the future. In 1934, Mussolini, when asked about the style of his time, is reported to have said that the times of carved columns and Gothic windows had passed: "We now need more light, sun, air, cleanliness. The more rational modernism, the better, as long as it is healthy and beautiful, and satisfies the real needs of life" (Onatskyi 1989, 226). In the late thirties, even as Nationalists distanced themselves rhetorically from the avant-garde and modernism, in practice they often aligned themselves with this aspect of the new "modern" style, as is suggested by the romance with sleek, volumetric, or abstract forms in art, design, and advertising. Pavlo Kovzhun, Robert Lisovsky, Sviatoslav Hordynsky, Edvard Kozak, and Myron Levytsky are among the artists who in the thirties and forties introduced this kind of form, which transformed Ukrainian book design and graphic art. All but the first continued their work in postwar emigration.[8]

The modernist and classical were combined in the art and architecture of both Italian fascism and Nazi Germany, as Griffin, Spotts, and others have observed. Italian architecture allowed visionary modernist architects and designers to blend classical symmetries with glass and steel. In fact, after 1935 it promoted neoclassicism as a form of modernism. Aesthetic modernism was on view in German industrial design and consumer durables, which adopted Bauhaus principles. Walter Gropius and Ludwig Mies van der Rohe, former directors of the Bauhaus, applied for Third Reich patronage. Although Gropius emigrated in 1934, van der Rohe continued working in Germany until 1938, when he left for the United States. He designed skyscrapers in New York and Chicago that have become icons of modernity. Le Corbusier, the third great pioneer of modernist architecture, sympathized with French fascism and worked for the Vichy regime. It has been observed that the symmetrical use of massive blocks of polished stone produced under Nazism evoked not an "Aryan" past but the supposedly "eternal" qualities of smoothness, geometry, and propor-tion that are central features of international modernism (Taylor 1990, 128–43). The interest in neoclassicism in the 1930s must therefore be seen not simply as a rejection of modernism, but as part of the symbiosis of modernity with the "eternal" that lies at the heart of an alternative modernist aesthetics (Griffin 2007, 288).

The turn to classicism was linked to a reaction against the sweetness and sentimentality that had characterized much literature of the prewar symbolists and decadents. Many interwar Ukrainian writers believed that life was ruled by the cruel god of political necessity. In their view a Christian worldview that emphasized love and charity had retreated or died, and its place had been taken by the Nietzschean vision of a society dominated by those individuals who had the strongest psychic and physical powers. This version of the modernist sensibility shaped Nationalist writings.

6

The Myth of Palingenesis

Inspiration for the palingenetic myth came from several sources. One was Nietzsche, who in the final three chapters of *Birth of Tragedy* (1872) produced a defense of myth as a "concentrated image of the world," a "condensation of phenomena." Chastising a world without wonder that has been disintegrated by the "critical-historical spirit," he argues here that without myth every culture loses the "healthy natural power" of its creativity, and "only a horizon defined by myths completes and unifies a whole cultural movement" (Nietzsche 1967, 135). Myths nurture young souls to maturity and provide the state's unwritten laws. Because foreign myths cannot be transplanted without injury, he calls upon Germans to turn away from the formerly dominant French culture and to cultivate their own. Only the elimination of foreign elements will enable the German spirit to renew itself. These ideas, like his celebration of the Dionysian spirit that draws on deep, tumultuous forces, and his desire to smash through the rationalism of modern culture and morality in order to go "beyond good and evil" struck a chord with modernists on the right and left.

Another inspiration was Henri Bergson's celebration of *l'élan vitale* and his ideas of time and becoming. His *Introduction to Metaphysics* (1893) encouraged artists to intuitively combine memories and present impressions and the anticipation of future events into an orchestrated whole. The synthetic consciousness created in this way would hold together the past, present, and future. Some modernists saw the nation's struggles over the centuries as just such a way of synthesizing fragmented personal and historical experience.

Interwar writers, like the nineteenth-century romantics, believed that by reimagining the past they could transform the present. They searched for images that, when revealed, would illuminate and inspire national development. The philosopher Mykola Shlemkevych, who in the 1930s became an

ideologist of the Front of National Unity, and who, using the pseudonym M.
Ivaneiko, edited and contributed to the Front's journal *Peremoha* (Victory,
1933–39), has provided an example of such a discovered image. The vigorous
new superman, he wrote, had made his appearance in Galician literature in the
early twentieth century and had transformed "the nation's passive resistance"
into active engagement (Shlemkevych 1956, 41). The new heroic figure, he
argued, had been portrayed in Mykola Mukhyn's interwar sculptures, particularly in his depiction of *chumaks* (carter-traders):

> Mukhyn's *chumak* is a ruler, a terrifying emperor of the Ukrainian Steppe.
> And we seem to hear his unspoken words . . . So what if for time immemorial
> until now so many foreign hordes have trampled my Steppe? So what if the
> Pechenegs and Polovtsians used to roam here, and the Tatars brought a
> deadly flood? So what if for so long the Crimean horde tore apart the living
> Ukrainian body? So what if the Polish winged hussars flew over it so many
> times? So what if it bent and groaned under the hard boot of tsarist dragoons?
> Already in our living memory terrible German iron monsters have crawled
> over it breathing fire. But where are they now? The horde of bolsheviks will
> disappear in the same way. And I will be left in the Steppe, its first ruler and
> its inheritor. I, with my slow, *chumak* wagon will reach my destination.
> (Ibid., 12)

The accent in this image is on the self-confidence, strength, and endurance
of the national liberation movement throughout the ages. Strength is associated
not with violence but with the idea of slow, organic work that creates conditions
for social and economic development. The assumption is that the population's
strength will continue to augment until it controls its own land and society. The
passage also attributes a powerful sense of identity and solidarity to the people,
who are an organic national body. It should be noted that, like the OUN, the
Front of National Unity espoused integral nationalism, but, unlike the OUN, it
avoided terrorism and instead stressed the importance of "organic" work.

The myth of palingenesis encoded in these texts is in many ways anodyne. It
holds out the promise of future greatness without insisting on revolutionary
upheaval. The two master narratives of social emancipation and national liberation, both of which have a long history in Ukrainian writing, often express the
dream of rebirth in this manner. They depict heroic acts or portray great leaders
without abandoning democratic ideals. The Ukrainian modernism that flour-
ished at the turn of the century embraced such a version of palingenesis, one
that strove for a spiritual-psychological transformation, that often used legendary
settings, and in which the Nietzschean hero's revolt is ultimately meant to

enlighten the masses. A leading critic of this generation, M. Sribliansky (Mykyta Shapoval), encouraged writers to create such edifying myths, which he referred to as powerful ideals and fairy tales (Iakovenko 2006, 62).

Like the Ukrainian romantics who had begun to collect legends, traditions, and folk stories in the 1830s, interwar nationalists imaginatively incorporated regional identities into the nation by publishing the legends of Chełm (Kholm), the Lemko territory, histories of Przemyśl, Belz, and other border towns whose identities were sometimes contested. Patriotic children's stories portrayed self-sacrificing young boys or girls showing attachment to the native land in the spirit of Joan of Arc. The first story of Antin Chekmanovsky's collection *Viky plyvut nad Kyievom* (The Ages Sail Over Kyiv, 1938) describes a poor boy who wishes to fight the invading hordes of Tatars and dedicate his life to defending his people. An image in Kyiv's St. Sophia Cathedral communicates with him and sheds a tear, which immediately turns into a pearl. With the money earned from selling the pearl, the boy is able to outfit himself for war and battles a red knight.

However, the works of Teliha, Malaniuk, Lypa, Samchuk, and Mosendz differ in tone from such stories. When recounting or rewriting legends, they often voice strong impatience and anger and a desire for immediate action. In their works the paradigm of rupture and renewal takes on a messianic coloring. This is also evident in the fervent tone of many essays and articles, which sometimes cross over into a kind of "ecstatic" writing that seeks to stir powerful emotional responses rather than convince through rational argumentation. Ostap Hrytsai, an essayist who contributed to the OUN's periodicals, specialized in such high-flown, inspirational rhetoric. His texts read like poetic prose. The following, written in 1934, recalls the princes of late medieval Kyivan Rus and Galicia-Volhynia:

> Established by glorious rulers as an empire from the Carpathians to the Caucasus, and from the [River] Sian to the Black Sea, a great law-creating power standing guard over its blessed achievements for the good of the world—it found itself at war from the very beginning. At war with the barbarian hordes, in a war of culture against savagery, of religion against paganism, of light against darkness. This was a contest of brilliant Beauty against loathsome, demonic children. Is this not so, Ihor Sviatoslavych, unforgettable knight? You, for whom the trees and flowers of Ukrainian fields bowed their sorrowful heads after you were defeated in the Polovtsian Steppe. Is this not so, Danylo, king of the Galician land, whose ruined tower is still today shrouded in a heavy sadness after the Tatar pogrom, in grieving memory on Kholm's listless plains? Oh, what angry fires even now boil up in my heart

against the barbarian savage! How I would like to take from the thousand-year-old grave mounds the shield of Oleh, the saddle of Sviatoslav, the swords of Monomach and Roman, and throw myself along with the angered lions and lynxes, eagles and bulls at the enemy ranks so as to fight for the Ukrainian land from the light of dawn until evening, from evening until dawn![1] (Hrytsai 1934b, 1)

Hrytsai later distanced himself from Dontsov, claiming that a religious idealism characterized his own work (Vynar 1964). However, this "poetic" style, which became popular in the 1930s, could be interpreted as consonant with Dontsov's call for instilling emotional commitment and fanatical faith. Onatsky considered Hrytsai "almost the only member of the older Galician generation who had accepted the path of Ukrainian Nationalism sincerely" (Onatskyi 1989, 213–14).

Georges Sorel's *Reflections on Violence* (1908) was a strong influence on the Nationalist version of palingenesis. Sorel noted the courage of people who participate in violent upheavals. He suggested that they were inspired by a myth or vision that enabled them to believe in the ultimate triumph of their cause after a great battle. Christians, for example, have cultivated pictures of martyrdom and the apocalypse that were out of all proportion to their actual persecution (Sorel 1969, 184–85). Socialists, he said, should ignore the "bleating herd of moralists" and cultivate proletarian violence, which would not only make the future revolution possible but was perhaps "the only means by which the European nations — at present stupefied by humanitarianism — can recover their former energy" (ibid., 92, 190). He was convinced that a new myth of community was required to generate militant action and bring about a spiritually united society. The Nationalists accepted this shift away from Enlightenment rationality toward antirationality, intuitivism, and mythmaking. In palingenetic myth-making they sought visions that could transform social consciousness. Sorel's work inspired the journal *Peremoha* (Victory), an organ of the Front of National Unity, which competed with the OUN for the hearts and minds of Galician youth. Its first issue of 1936 published an article on Sorel and many quotations from his works. Some of its essays give the impression of shamanic or prophetic speech. One, for example, describes a man skiing high on a mountain. As long as he feels the strange force within him, he is intoxicated with joy, but as soon as he loses his self-confidence, he is gripped by terror and is forced to descend.

As the harbinger of a regenerative revolution; one that promised to overthrow existing governmental institutions, inaugurate a new order, and awaken new creative potential in the individual, modernist mythmaking captured both extremes of the political spectrum. Bolshevism and fascism identified the same enemies: the rationalist Enlightenment, liberal parliamentarianism, and Western democracies. Both movements found a moral value in violence, which, they felt, could transform the individual by tapping into deep, unexplored sources of energy. In this way it could help society escape inhibitions and resolve disorder. Later thinkers have voiced similar opinions. George Bataille admired the fascist aesthetics of violence as a way of challenging liberal democracies and introducing a new collective mythology. André Breton famously celebrated random violence in his *Manifesto of Surrealism* when he wrote: "The simplest surrealist act consists of dashing down the street, pistol in hand, and firing blindly, as fast as you can pull the trigger, into the crowd." In his "Critique of Violence" (1921) Walter Benjamin contrasted "law-preserving" and "lawmaking" violence (Benjamin 1996, 248). The first supposedly represents the bourgeois state's hidden essence, which emerges during times of crisis to crush revolutions, but the second is part of a revolution's mission to sweep away corrupt social institutions and is therefore purifying, mystical, and avenging, like the divine violence of the Last Judgment. Of course, in practice the two kinds of violence are identical. Even the imagery used by those who justify them (purifying, missionary, avenging) is the same. Ukrainian Nationalism also yearned for a violent upsurge, one that promised to eject oppressors and establish independence. Its literature was attracted to the themes of revolt and sacrifice and to rituals that commemorated traumatic loss: the defeats of Kruty, Bazar, the death of Olha Basarab, and the assassination of Petliura.

Palingenetic modernism encouraged the dream of personal freedom and escape from the dead weight of the past. Futurism, for example, often suggested the possibility of a new world with enhanced human mental and physical capacities. Early Ukrainian futurist painters, although less obsessed with the machine or industry than their Italian counterparts, were interested in breakthroughs in perception. David Burliuk's desire for change and experimentation was framed as a rediscovery of powerful primitive energies, while Alexandra Exter linked the transformation of art to a rediscovery of the creative élan and color palette of folk artists. Less drawn to urban scenes, technology, and machinery, these artists were nonetheless fascinated by new ways of seeing and feeling. There is a clue here to why Marinetti's antagonism to ancient buildings and his championing of a mechanized world was resisted. Italian futurism, it was felt, had a strong sense of its own national identity and could therefore afford to reject much of the available past. Ukrainians, on the other hand, were trying to establish their connection to a past long denied by imperial mythmaking. By incorporating this past into a national narrative they were "internalizing" it. This was the logic behind the rejection by Galician writers of what they saw as Soviet futurism's machinelike uniformity and destruction of the national heritage. Dmytro Andriievsky wrote: "Communism is the enemy of nature, fears it, because from it diversity flows into the world. [. . .] To the law of the earth it counterposes the law of the machine" (Andriievskyi 1928, 5).

The racist aspects of Nazi palingenetic mythmaking were generally rejected. Alfred Rosenberg's *Der Mythus des zwanzigsten Jahrhunderts* (Myth of the Twentieth Century, 1930), which along with Hitler's *Mein Kampf* is viewed as the main proclamation of Nazi ideology, focused on blood and primeval biological or mystical impulses. It went against Ukrainian historical tradition, as did his racially motivated antisemitism. An indication of this can be found in attitudes toward the Khazar state, whose rulers adopted Judaism in the ninth century. Mainstream historians like Mykhailo Hrushevsky and Dmytro Bahalii depicted Khazaria (the Khazar state) as playing a positive role in holding back nomadic invaders from the East. So did Dmytro Doroshenko, who in the 1920s praised Khazar rule for allowing the early Ukrainian state to expand and establish itself. The émigré archaeologist Vadym Shcherbakivsky—an important influence on Olzhych—expressed the same view. Khazaria's unfortunate collapse, in his opinion, had forced the ancestors of Ukrainians to abandon the Black Sea littoral (Shcherbakivskyi 1941, 117–18). Attitudes to the large Khazar state by the Caspian Sea have always been a litmus test of racist and antisemitic attitudes; these are marginal in interwar scholarly writings.

Emilio Gentile has argued that modernism and the avant-garde produced palingenetic visions of a new political and artistic culture in which the individual and the nation were seen as expanding in power. Modernist nationalism's principal feature was "the frank acceptance of modern life as an era of irreversible transformations that were affecting society, consciousness, and human sensibility, and that were preparing conditions for the rise of new forms of collective life, a new civilization" (Gentile 1994, 60). Since shaping life through human design was an underlying theme, the engineer came to stand for the human power to make change. In the 1930s "revolutionary" European literature—both fascist and communist—celebrated heroes who reorganize industrial production, discover new products, and the like. By serving as models for the reader, these heroes become engineers of human souls. This kind of literature legitimizes the idea of experimentation and change. At the same time, many of these works show a faith in hierarchy and despotic control. Modernism, in other words, demonstrated that it was "hospitable not only to anarchic individualism but also to authoritarian designs" (Fritzsche 1996, 12).

In Italy, Germany, and the Soviet Union transformational change was often linked to the imperial sublime. Mass pageants created a sense of power, youthfulness, activism, and a spirit of adventure. Their participants were encouraged to see themselves as soldier-workers or parts of a gigantic machine. During the 1930s the Soviet version of this sublime incorporated the history of tsarist conquests and glorified ruthless statesmen. The vision of a regenerated society projected by these rituals suggested that national weakness had been replaced by youth, anarchy and decadence by order and health, mediocrity by great leadership.

Nationalist writers incorporated similar visions of transformed consciousness into their narratives. They too introduced the engineer and visionary planner. However, against the sense of imperial power, their palingenetic myth set the image of imminent, wrenching, empire-destroying change. In an article entitled "The Rebirth of Myth," written in a lyrical, "ecstatic" style, Yu. Volynsky wrote in 1934 of "the wave of resurgent myth" that was rolling through Europe, capturing America and Asia. He saw its classic example in the new fascist Italy, where the strict, mighty beauty of the ancient world was being reborn in contemporary society, and in Germany, where the rebirth of national myth had filled "the many-millioned strivings of society" (Volynsky 1934, 7). However, the author went on to say that all nations, including Latvia, Romania, Hungary, Ireland, Greece, England, France, Poland, Sweden, and Spain were developing their own political myths.

Malaniuk imagined palingenesis as a "fiery downpour" or "bath." In his poetry the country emerges from such a baptism clean, tempered, and clothed in the white robes of renewal. As Yurii Klen observed, this theme of passing through suffering and torture into a new blossoming Eden is a biblical one; it can be found in Ezekiel, Jeremiah, and Isaiah. He quotes Malaniuk's "Zemna Madonna" (Earthly Madonna): "Sooner give us battle, so that the fiery downpour May be a baptism for your land." According to Klen, Malaniuk was indicating here that the struggle would lead eventually to a new renaissance. (Klen 1936, 832–32).

One of the most important example of palingenesis available to the Nationalists was the image of Mussolini's Italy as the Third Rome. The association with ancient Rome suggested the rebirth of a stable and powerful state, one in which all elements maintain their proper functions, serving the common good and voluntarily obeying the ruling elite. This was not necessarily a totalitarian myth; it had also been Cicero's ideal of a republican Rome. The Roman world also provided the ideal of strong bodies and minds. Andriievsky wrote: "Only strong people are able to create out of crisis and difficulties new principles of morality and ethics, as did the ancient Romans or the British citizens of our days, creating the international concepts of Pax Romana and Pax Brittanica, and translating them into life" (Andriievskyi 1928, 81).

In similar fashion Zenon Pelensky compares contemporary New York to Rome:

> Once before in history there has been a similar city to this. Rome. All roads led to it, in the same way as today they lead to New York. Everything flowed to Rome from the East and West, the North and South, to serve Roman lords and conquerors. In exactly the same way all valuables of the so-called Old World today flow to New York and America. All Europe, and not only Europe, is in the situation that Greece found itself two thousand years ago vis-à-vis Caesar's Rome. Still half-barbarian, simple and ruthless, still not dis-integrated by the old cultures of Hellas, Egypt, Syria, and all the countries of the Levant, the ancient Romans looked half in disdain and half in curiosity, and above all with a sense of their own superiority, on all those tsars and kings, philosophers and comedians, artists and pagan priests, money-makers and politicians, slaves and athletes, poets and street arabs, and at everything that the *gentes minors* brought with them to the Sacred City. Thousands of languages mixed in Rome, a mighty current of cultures and people, thou-sands of new gods were allowed their temples. The Romans brought and imported all this not because of some deep inner need, but from a sense of being the victor, of power, and because the Old World believed in those things and valued them. Two thousand years later a similar thing occurred. (Pelenskyi 1928, 6, 229)

Significantly, Pelensky accepts that the world must change, that mechaniza-tion and technology must transform the countryside. He even praises Soviet Ukrainian writers who make this point. His only caution is that technology must not be an end in itself, otherwise growth will be merely quantitative, a faster pace of production that lacks soul and refinement. This is his critique of American civilization. One cannot, however, help feeling in these words a strong admiration for the achievements of the New World. Just as Rome held sway in ancient times, "Today Americans decide what is good for people and useful, what should be raised to an ideal, and what should not" (ibid., 7–8, 296).

Rome also provided examples of literature's edificatory function, of rhetoric as a way of marshaling thought and training the individual for political activity. Roman literature taught glory and the cult of forefathers. The past served as a guide. Cicero wrote: "Ours are the trophies, ours the monuments, ours the triumphs. Those who dedicate their powers to the literary celebration of such events are increasing the fame of the people of Rome itself." He continued: "For literary commemoration is a potent factor in enhancing a country's prestige. And to those who hazard their lives for the sake of glory, such literature is a vigorous incentive, stimulating them to risk fearful perils and perform noble endeavours" (Cicero 1969, 159–60). When in the late 1930s Ukrainian Nationalist writers began to voice dissatisfaction with futurism's "negation of the world of absolute values and absolute norms," they could point to the ancient world as providing examples of the required firm and unchanging foundations (Orest 1948, 7).

Roman culture also fascinated because of the pervasive theme of war, whether for survival or empire building. Its literature had created the conventions of representation that governed the way Romans perceived themselves. One critic has written: "Remembrance of things past—Roman style—revolved around the great figures who invariably enhanced Roman power in a seemingly endless series of wars" (Holkeskamp 2006, 480–81). War was seen as a positive cultural process that developed virtue (*virtus*), while loss of connection to the glorious past caused decline. Sallust in *Bellum Ingurthum* (The Jurgenthine War, 40s b.c.e) and Livy in *Ab Vrbe Condita* (From the Foundation of the City, 20s b.c.e–10s c.e.) attributed military victories to steadfast determination in the collective character. They were reluctant to portray Romans as losers. In Livy even the soldier who has lost the use of his arms attacks his enemy by biting off his nose and ears. The Jewish-Roman historian Josephus in *Jewish War* (70s–80s c.e.) justifies the Roman right to rule the world with reference to superior military virtues.

Rome was the Italian equivalent of the invigorating Faustian spirit and drive, without which, Oswald Spengler argued in his *Decline of the West*, the sun would set on Western civilization. In the 1930s the Roman ideal of masculine vigor and assertiveness became a virtual obsession. Marinetti produced a futurist cookbook (*La Cucina futurista*, 1932), which encouraged Italians to avoid pasta and eat more meat in order to strengthen their masculinity and desire for conquest. Pasta-eating Italians, according to him, were prone to indolence and sluggishness; meat eating would provide an antidote by encouraging activism and aggression. To emphasize his point he even shot a bullet into a plate of spaghetti carbonara. Volodymyr Martynets's essay "Ideolohiia chy biolohiia?" (Ideology or Biology?) which appeared in his *Za zuby i pazuri natsii* (For the Nation's Teeth and Claws, 1937), is an amusing version of this argument. It tries to demonstrate how periods of meat eating have coincided with successful state building among various peoples.

If the English had not become eaters of beefsteaks, the essay informs, it is doubtful they would have founded the most far-flung empire in the world. English cuisine is famous for its large and nutritious dishes: "half-raw beef and lamb, roast beef, steaks, lots of ham, eggs. The English add sharp spices" (Martynets 1937b, 20). Carnivores, says Martynets, are more warlike and expansionist. For much of their existence Germans were famous potato and cabbage eaters; they became an aggressive, meat-eating nation only recently. The loss of Jewish statehood came at a time when Christ called upon people to stop sacrificing animals and instead to practice bloodless sacrifices (bread and wine). This occurred during a period when the socioeconomic life of Jews was undergoing a great change: they had ceased being herders and were becoming grain growers and traders. Embedded in these comments is a disparaging reference to Christianity as a religion of the meek and weak. This faith appeared precisely during the decline of the old Roman Empire. However, although it proposed loving one's neighbor, in the hands of Western Europeans it acquired a warlike character, fueling crusades, religious wars, bloody inquisitions, and inspiring the missionaries who helped to conquer foreign lands (ibid., 34). Comments concerning religion's refusal of violence are more directed against Buddhism and Hinduism. They occur in Martynets's discussion of Japan's former weakness as resulting from the Buddhist prohibition against killing animals. The Japanese, he suggests, "sat immobile on their islands for tens of centuries" until they began eating meat and decided to expand their state. And the greatest "grass-eaters" (*travoidy*) in the world are the Hindus, for whom killing and eating a cow is a mortal sin, and whose ideal is Nirvana.

Martynets contrasts civilizational cuisines, explaining the appearance among Americans of the admired Jack London by the fact that these people grew up eating bison. This diet is juxtaposed with the popularity of *mamalyga*, a corn-meal porridge that was a staple among poorer people of the Carpathian foot-hills. The reader is informed that a foreign doctor had even forbidden his son from eating *mamalyga*, because it was known to stunt brain development and lead to the dulling of intellectual capacities (ibid., 32). Martynets laments the fact that there are "hundreds of thousands or even millions of people" whose daily diet consists of *mamalyga*. He asks: "Is this, perhaps, the reason why our Transcarpathians and Bessarabians are the least developed branch of the Ukrainian people?" (ibid., 32). Diet is also tied to politics in a discussion of Volodymyr Vynnychenko, who had visited Prague in 1937 and presented his theory of concordism, or harmony, which he was developing and which involved vegetarianism. Personal happiness, Vynnychenko urged, depended in large part on avoiding meat, fish, alcohol, and narcotics, including coffee and tea, because these stimulated bloodthirsty, warlike instincts. The visit to Prague by the former prominent leader of the Central Rada and Directory governments of 1917–19 provided Martynets with another opportunity to dismiss Vynnychenko's socialist politics by linking them to pacifism, physical weakness, and degeneracy.

Martynets makes the observation that Ukrainians exhibited a militant nature during the state-building periods of Kyivan Rus and Cossackdom. The Kyiv ecclesiastical elite in 1621 spoke proudly of Hetman Sahaidachny and his Cossacks as the "descendants of Japhet, who in the days of [Prince] Oleh sailed to Constantinople and stormed it." The author quotes documents to show the extent of hunting and fishing, and the quantity of meat consumed in the days of Cossackdom. Unfortunately, he writes, since then Ukrainians have become grain-consumers or "grass-eaters" (*travoidy*). Predominantly rural, they consume far less meat than people in the cities, and as a result are prone to passivity. To make matters worse, they have been exploited and starved, as happened during the Great Famine of 1932–33 in Soviet Ukraine, when all food was exported to Russia and millions died of hunger.

The Ukrainian diet, often inadequate and meatless, has influenced the culture. How otherwise can one explain the fact that Ukrainians "have created the most beautiful art, but also the most sentimental songs, the most sentimental poetry, the most sentimental prose, the most sentimental music, and the most sentimental . . . politics?" (ibid., 35). The myth of a fundamentally passive folk is challenged by certain moments in history, such as the stubborn resistance of partisans in Kholodnyi Yar, a deep, inaccessible ravine south of Kyiv, which has over the centuries hidden outlaws and which in 1919–21 provided a refuge for those who fought against bolshevik rule (ibid., 35). In a postscript Martynets adds a note of caution: meat should not be overfried or overstewed, so as to avoid cancer, the disease of "civilized peoples." One should remember that the Huns and Tatars ate meat raw; the American Indians, who vigorously resisted the expansion of the white race, ate it lightly roasted; while the English, who defeated the Indians and today have a world empire, "eat meat half-raw" (ibid., 47). He concludes by recommending (1) a diet of half-raw meat, and good nourishment; (2) improved hygiene; (3) as little peace as possible (with this goal in mind he suggests the consumption of as much "animal" ideology as possible); (4) a change of occupation (more commerce and industry, to which a half or three-quarters of one's time should be devoted); (5) more optimism and laughter; and (6) a partial transfusion of foreign blood. The last recommendation refers to the assimilation and integration of non-Ukrainians into the political nation.

These reflections, like those in Marinetti's cookbook, were written in a semiserious tone, perhaps as a tongue-in-cheek response to fascist ideology's infatuation with strong and dynamic men. Marinetti's book and the events he organized related to a "futurist kitchen" were themselves gentle parodies of the various parodies of fascism that were circulating. Martynets may, like Marinetti, have hoped to gain greater public attention by using provocative and hilarious tactics, while at the same time affirming the conviction that all culture had to be radically changed. When Martynets read this essay at a conference in Prague in the summer of 1932, the Galicians attending reacted with indignation. Konovalets, on the other hand, was mildly amused. The visitors asked why they had been subjected to such nonsense. Konovalets answered: "Do you really think that everything written is so important? Deeds always speak louder than words. A lot gets written, but to little effect. Martynets is a remarkably industrious and dedicated person, and I greatly respect him for this. You see some things differently, and perhaps with the passage of time you will yet again see them in a different light. Therefore one should be understanding and tolerant" (Kordiuk 1974, 960). Konovalets, who was a good listener, paid attention to an individual's character, as well as to the ideas being presented. He also possessed a wry, ironic sense of humor, which was often self-deprecating (ibid., 962). Martynets's essay, delivered in deadpan style, may have been written to appeal to this sense of the comic. As one of the most entertaining (and ridiculous) Nationalist essays, it deserves a high score for ingenious argumentation and an ability to engage in self-parody. It was connected to a larger discourse. The question of different "tastes" and the role they played in cultures had already been raised earlier in *Rozbudova natsii* in an article that referenced the sociologist Robert Michels and his idea of warring cuisines (Masiukevych 1931, 293). Marinetti's highly entertaining "Manifesto of Futurist Cooking" had appeared in the Turin *Gazzetta del Popolo* on 28 December 1930. It called, among other things, for sculpted dishes, the abolition of the knife and fork, the banning of political discussions and speeches during meals, and the presentation of some dishes not for eating but only for savoring by the eyes and nose.

To explain Martynets's essay one might turn to Homi Bhabha's notion of mimicry, in which he argues that the colonized, in their attempts to mimic the colonizer, inevitably produce something distinctive (Bhabha 1994, 86). Within the Ukrainian context Martynets's performance of fascist bravado and the masculine stereotype produces a parody that undermines notions of militarism and manliness. It does not challenge the perception that Ukrainians are politically disenfranchised and physically vulnerable, but it spoofs exaggerated images of the warrior's physical strength, dominance, and willpower. The essay indicates the presence of ideological slippage and excess, perhaps even a refusal of German masculine stereotypes as peddled by Nazi propaganda. Significantly, it elicited an indignant reaction from the young Galicians who resisted any subversion of the commitment to physical force or anything that disparaged the heroic image of their struggle.

Martynets's repeated comments on integrating non-Ukrainians into the political nation indicate, as he explained in another article, that the OUN thought of national consciousness as "exclusively a matter of ideology, of the spirit, not of biology, and certainly not of physiology, and therefore it is not a question of race, food, occupation, etc." (Martynets 1937b, 163). This implies, of course, that his dissertation on meat eating should be taken with more than one grain of salt. The serious part of his message is in the recipe for psychological change:

> We, the Ukrainian nation, [. . .] need to be strong, because otherwise we will die encircled by those who are stronger. We need to say this openly to ourselves and to look clear-sightedly at the world around us, and at ourselves, particularly at our failings and weaknesses. The German racists are not ashamed of pointing out the failings of their race-nation, and to change it for the better. The Italian fascists do not close their eyes to their nation's weak-nesses, but [strive to] transform this soft, relaxed nation of "macaroni-eaters" into a nation of conquerors. We too should not be ashamed to do this. To hide our heads in the sand would be most inappropriate, because the inabil-ity to see and correct failings and weaknesses contributes to the deepening of our present servile condition. (Ibid., 165)

It is interesting in this context to consider the Marquis de Sade's moral discourse, which is also rooted in a discussion of nourishment. He felt that Neapolitans were incapable of political revolution and lacked political strength because of their daily food. Sade saw vice as depending on the quantity and quality of food consumed. In his view, the weak and those with no political will, eat too simply or too little. It is therefore unsurprising that a minister dreams of starving the population into submission. Bread serves in *L'Histoire de Juliette* as the food of the poor, of dungeons, the underground, and inferior social spaces; it is also associated with the Bible, the transubstantiation of the host, and reli-gious superstition. Meat on the other hand is a sign of corruption and strength (St-Martin 2007, 38).

Another myth that lies hidden behind these Nationalist reflections is the rebirth of the healthy pagan or barbarian. A more anodyne version of this myth portrays the Ukrainian nation as youthful and unspoiled: "Every nation has its natural development and only at a given moment is it capable of creating a real political body. Most nations, like people, can only be taught in their youth. Aging and sick peoples cannot stand reforms. Rebirth among peoples who have *not been consumed* [*nezuzhytykh*] can come through revolution, but when they are used-up, uprisings destroy them; then they need an *overlord* with a 'strong hand,' not a 'liberator.' [. . .] The Ukrainians are a young, healthy and uncon-sumed people" (Nykorovych 1933, 175). A more-alarming version of the myth sees the barbarian as a strong warrior, a disciplined member of the collective, who is prepared to fight for the survival of his nation and state. The neo-pagan sees the world in social Darwinian terms, as a place where the fittest survive and impose their will on others. He therefore accepts the imperative to nurture strength of spirit and body. In 1938 an article called "Fragmenty na temy mystetstva" (Fragments on the Topic of Art) appeared in *Almanakh: Ha sluzhbi natsii* (Almanac: Serving the Nation, 1938) as a contribution to the OUN's discourse on art. The author called for pagan strength and commitment to the national collective, and expressed impatience with an art that elevated the ideals of peace and personal happiness. Art, it was argued, should be dynamic and forceful, full of strong feelings, and not overly intellectual. In words that echo the futurists, it rejected the art of the past: "We are not denying the old opera and ballet their artistic value, and we appreciate everything that has its traditions; however, they should have gone to the museum a long time ago. The new art schools will use them as valuable historical material" (Demo 1938, 101). The author calls for a break with past forms, however painful this may be, and for the creation of a new dynamic art. The guiding image, however, is not the machine, but "the primeval rhythms of nature" (ibid., 102). A breakthrough is urged to the vigorous and healthy feelings of the pagan who saw the world in all its freshness.

Others saw such frank admissions of the beast in man as a challenge to Western civilization, which had been built on both classical and Christian humanism. Christianity had introduced the values of fairness, justice, and love into Western literature and art, thereby transforming these societies. Kirkconnell wrote in 1944: "Man is not merely an animal to be fed, clothed and sheltered from the weather. Neither is man merely an economic organism to be adjusted to industrial development and guaranteed a fair share in the products of an industrial process. He is not just a back to be bent or a belly to be filled. Man is a living soul with a spiritual destiny" (Kirkconnell 1944, 4). Totalitarian solutions fashion societies of robots who are conditioned by mass propaganda to believe in the superiority of their civilizations. He continued:

> In seeking to satisfy man's inborn yearning after communion with God, Nazi racism runs inward to the demon of its own animality; in trying to slake that same thirst, Marx-Leninist atheism turns to the creative achievements of industry, the titanism of man's vast industrial projects.
>
> Both are alike, however, in their use of hatred as the great motive power of their systems. In the case of the Nazis, the hatred is one towards other races, especially the Jews. [...] The Marx-Leninists, on the other hand, preach Klassenhass, class hatred, as the driving power working for the proletarian revolution. They lament the good will and toleration prevalent in

democratic countries and devote much of their propaganda to fanning mal-
odorous flames of envy and ill will wherever they can be found. (Ibid., 7–8)

In the 1940s a number of thinkers dismissed the mythic and heroic without
being able to account for their power to influence the mind. Ernst Cassirer was
unable to acknowledge the fact that Machiavelli accepted the heroic in Livy's
legends and the Roman veneration of the mythic-historic as a way of teaching
courage, fortitude, and comradeship. Machiavelli embraced historical myths
such as that of Romulus who killed his brother Remus, or that of Brutus who
executed his sons because they demonstrated that loyalty to the patria should
prevail over loyalty to a family member (Mali 1999, 153).

Interwar Galician and émigré Ukrainians commented widely on Roman
virtues and Machiavelli. They admired the emphasis on the public sphere and
the political stage and accepted the idea of the world as a clash of irreconcilable
forces. They were convinced of the need for action, the harnessing of the individual to a greater purpose—national independence—and the necessity for
war. A justification for war, if such was required, had already been provided by
medieval moralists. Augustine wrote: "Those men do not break the commandment which forbids killing, who make war by the authority of God's command,
or being in some place of public magistracy, put to death malefactors according
to their laws" (St. Augustine, *Civitas Dei*, I, 20).

The myth of palingenesis therefore expressed itself in numerous versions:
the ancient resident who emerges from the rubble of earthshaking change, the
apocalyptic terror that leads to personal transformation, the epic gaze that
reveals kinship with a distant past, Rome as a great power reborn, masculine
vigor and virility recaptured, primitivism as pagan health rediscovered. Writers
made use of the myth in all these variations.

LITERATURE

7

OLENA TELIHA

Olena Teliha was born in St. Petersburg and educated among the imperial capital's intellectual elite (her godmother was the writer Zinaida Gippius). Her father, Ivan Shovheniv, was a high official in the Ministry of Agriculture. After the fall of tsarism he served in Kyiv as a minister in the UNR government and was forced to emigrate when the bolsheviks established their rule. In 1923 Olena and her mother illegally crossed the Polish border under gunfire to join him. They lived in Poděbrady, where Shovheniv was president of the Ukrainian Academy of Economics. In the 1920s contacts between Russian and Ukrainian émigré circles were often still close. For example, they attended one another's lectures and concerts, and Olena's brother Serhii wrote Russian verse and belonged to Russian literary circles. She, however, began to write in Ukrainian. Samchuk recalls that she described her conversion in the following terms:

> Imagine a great-power, Petersburg, imperial chauvinist who from her earliest years was used to viewing the whole territory east, west, and north of Petersburg as her own private possession. And who could not care less about the living human entities who filled those territories [. . .] I was thunder-struck to learn that my own father, the well-known and distinguished Russian professor Ivan Shovgenov, who for some reason had been renamed Shovheniv, was no less than the president of a school called the Academy of Economics, where teaching took place "in the language" and where portraits of Petliura hung on the walls [. . .] It happened during a great ball [. . .] that had been organized by some charitable committee of Russian monarchists under the patronage of the well-known Karel Kramarz. I was then in the company of brilliant chevaliers; we were sitting at a table and drinking wine. For some reason someone began speaking about our language, bringing up the usual "zaliziaku na puziaku," "dog's language" [. . .] "mordopysnia" [nonsense

words that sound Ukrainian and are amusing to the Russian ear][. . .]
Everyone roared with laughter [. . .] I immediately felt within myself a sharp
sense of protest. My indignation flared. I don't know why. Unable to restrain
myself, I rose, struck the table with my fist and cried indignantly: "You boors!
That dog's language is my language! The language of my father and mother!
From now on I want nothing to do with you!" (Samchuk 2008, 304)

To the amazement of her acquaintances and the entire Academy of
Economics, from that moment Olena spoke only Ukrainian. After her mother's
death her father remarried and moved to Warsaw. In 1931 Olena and her
husband Mykhailo also moved to the city. They lived in poverty; for a while
Olena worked as a dressmaker's model to make money. She disliked her step-
mother and became estranged from her father. She also distanced herself from
UNR circles and gradually fell under the influence of Dontsov, who at one
point lived next door to her in Warsaw. By the end of the decade she had joined
the OUN and in 1941 volunteered to be part of the Melnyk faction's expeditionary force to Kyiv. Here in late 1941 she established the literary journal *Litavry*
and headed the Union of Ukrainian Writers. The German administration hired
numerous individuals who were hostile to Ukrainian separatism. Many were
informers or provocateurs; some were Soviet agents. Teliha made enemies
among Russophiles who objected to her uncompromising views on independence. When she rejected writing that glorified Hitler and the "new Russia"
(often composed in the same style as Soviet dithyrambs to Stalin), she was
denounced to the Gestapo. The following lines by an unnamed author are an
example of such sycophantic verse: "May the earth resound with song, In this
proud soaring time, Hitler's words are among us, Hitler's will is ours" (quoted in
Teliha 2008, 324). After a brief existence *Litavry* and the newspaper *Ukrainske
slovo* were shut down in December, their staff arrested, and all Ukrainian
symbols, including Petliura's portrait, were removed from the editorial office.
Kostiantyn Shtepa was made editor of the new, anti-Ukrainian and antisemitic
Nove Ukrainske Slovo, whose first issue appeared on 14 December. It announced
that "extreme nationalists and bolsheviks" had been purged for attempting to
make the newspaper into their own organ. Teliha refused to work for the new
paper. Although she had an opportunity to leave the city before her arrest, she
refused to do so, replying: "There has to be someone who looks death in the
face and does not retreat" (Zhulynskyi 2007, 16). She and her husband were
killed in Babyn Yar in February 1942.

In the 1930s Teliha was Dontsov's faithful disciple. When in 1937 Lypa
criticized the latter, she responded with an article in *Vistnyk* that praised the
achievements of Italy and Germany, putting these down to the revitalization of

the national spirit that Dontsov demanded. She expressed satisfaction that a bold poetry of "slashing" [*rubannia*] and passionate yearning was once more in vogue (Teliha 1937, 653). The important thing was to dedicate oneself to a goal. This truth had been understood "by people in the nations that are now growing and strengthening before our very eyes: Italy and Germany" (ibid., 649). Strength Through Joy (Kraft durch Freude), she informed readers, was the name of a mass German youth organization, which had been created to improve the lives of ordinary Germans and which was enthusiastically supported by the population.

The organization was indeed popular; it offered holidays abroad for the working classes who would not have been able to afford them otherwise, brought music concerts to factories, and created sports halls. Kraft durch Freude was also the name that Hitler gave the Volkswagen in 1938. The organization's technocratic modernism was also characteristic of two other related organizations, the German Work Front (Deutsche Arbeitsfront) and the Office for the Beauty of Work (Amt für Schönheit der Arbeit). The leader of the former, Robert Ley, tried to apply Taylorist principles. Griffin explains:

> [M]aximum productive efficiency would be delivered by a racially pure workforce enjoying hygienic factory conditions, an equal-opportunity work market and employment rights (for men), regular retraining and continuous education, an extensive welfare and benefits system, a comprehensive scheme of social insurance, pension rights, and an access to health care which combined preventive, alternative, and hi-tech medicine. While slaves went to their excruciating, anonymous deaths, their heroic "Aryan" counterparts would be housed on new estates in green suburbs in dwellings designed to encourage sound principles of social and ecological health. (Griffin 2007, 327)

Teliha's article cited Olzhych as the best example of a poet for whom "struggle and life are synonymous." He was, she wrote, the Ukrainian equivalent of the enthusiastic young generation in Germany and the Alcazar cadets (who in 1936 fought on the nationalist side in the Spanish Civil War) (Teliha 1937, 653). Teliha also named Bohdan Kravtsiv and Serhii Kushnirenko, who contributed poems to *Vistnyk*, as representatives of the brave, ambitious type of individual who was now common "in all the revitalized countries of Europe" but was still not accepted by many as representative of the Ukrainian spirit (ibid., 657). She described Lypa, in contrast, as a poet who belonged to the camp of erotomaniacs and "culture elaborators" [*kombinatory-kulturnyky*], a term that suggests tricky intellectual manipulation. Worst of all, he had tried to elevate "a cult of the grey masses" by praising their "unspoken commitment" to the cause (ibid., 657). Committed masses were a good thing, she commented, but individuals who shape these masses and teach them commitment are even more important. These arguments were, of course, a defense of Dontsov's ideology.

Fiercely loyal to the editor, Teliha cut contacts with her best friend Natalia Livytska-Kholodna when the latter continued working with *My* after this journal's editor, Antin Kryzhanivsky, strongly criticized *Vistnyk*. A maximalist and highly partisan structure of thought and feeling characterizes Teliha's writings. Passionate and spirited, she was quick to denounce compatriots, either for lacking civic courage, as in her essay "Partachi zhyttia" (Life's Spoilers, 1941), or for disagreeing with the OUN's ideology.

Her poetry is most frequently concerned with love and a mood of anticipation, but it also introduces patriotic sentiments and a yearning for great acts of self-sacrifice, as in the lines: " "May God send me the greatest gift: A fiery death—not a cold expiration" (Teliha 2008, 39). She looks forward to the coming of a great storm: "Swing your arm! Spill the wine! Someone shout—let the storm begin" (ibid., 58). One of her civic poems is dedicated to Bilas and Danylyshyn, the two OUN members who were executed in 1932. It ends with the image of "inspired hundreds" who desire "to walk the path on which you were cut down" (ibid., 66). Perhaps her best-known poem is "Povorot" (Return). In it she imagines her future meeting with Ukraine: "We will ford the stormy waters, To take full possession of everything that belongs to us, And to fuse again with our people" (ibid., 30). The lyrical voice speaks for an entire generation that has mythologized the "homeland" from which it had been banished, or which, in some cases, it had never seen. It is a confident voice that attempts to give aphoristic form to patriotic feelings. In this poem Teliha prophetically foresees her reacquaintance with Ukraine as a bittersweet experience: "Everything awaits us: despair and insults, And our native land will be foreign to us" (ibid., 29).

Her poetry exhibits some features of the "classicism" that became popular in the 1930s. Dreams of valor and glory, as in the poetry of Mosendz and Olzhych, are encased in a regular meter and a crafted form, suggesting personal restraint and commitment to a collective project. Various critics have drawn attention to this "classicist" aspect of her work. Shevelov has seen it as an attempt to discipline her own emotions (Shevchuk 2008, 409–10). Derzhavyn has also drawn attention to the formal regularity of her verse and her search for the memorable and elegant turn of phrase. He, however, sees in her verse a suppressed desire for ecstatic feelings, a longing to be transported and transformed in heroic action (Derzhavyn 1950, 2009a). Whatever the interpretation of her work, critics agree that the tension between form and feeling produces a lyrical excitement, that is always poised and dignified, never drunken or orgiastic.

In "Do problem styliu" (On the Problem of Style), an article published on 14 February 1940, in *Krakivski visti* (Kraków News), Teliha offers two images that she feels capture the age: a night filled with blinding lightning, and the red glow of a sunrise. It is a tempestuous and transitional time. Incessant movement prevents contemplation and demands immediate action. Rapidly changing events and impressions have obscured the boundaries between right and wrong. In this situation it is vital to look for guidelines, to discern what is most profound and constant. Only the artist, who can briefly glimpse the past and future in those moments when flashes of lightning illuminate the world, is able to chart the correct path. The style of the age is synthetic. It "gathers scattered facts into one clear line from the past to the future." In the midst of catastrophe, Teliha writes, the reader will search for enduring values and will desire to hear them expressed in a direct, laconic manner. This suggests that she aimed in her poetry to provide a sense of steady conviction during an apocalyptic time. The tension between form and feeling in her work can therefore be read as expressing her attitude toward the political environment.

In her own life Teliha boldly faced the political storm that raged around her and courageously embraced the opportunity for heroic action. Her choice was deliberate, and she appears to have foreseen her own martyrdom. A sense of the sublime haunts her poetry. She communicates a feeling of awe and terror in face of an approaching cataclysm. However, at the same time the measured verse conveys a composed, determined tone of voice. This attitude has been identified as typical of *Vistnyk* writers in the later 1930s: "They were attracted to cultural images and political figures that did not demonstrate weakness in themselves or in front of others; personal feelings were transformed into controlled gestures and meaningful rituals. In other words, passion had to be 'cold,' immovable, strict—the passion of people whom Dontsov counted among the higher race, the spiritual aristocrats, the knights" (Omelchuk 2011, 71). Such a passion was to be distinguished from "exhibitionism," "pornography," and "sentimental hysteria." Its distinguishing feature was what one *Vistnyk* writer called "the new generation's style" and described as "an external coldness that hides behind it passion" (Sternytskyi 1933, 441).

Literary criticism has generally presented Teliha as a woman ready for action. She quickly came to represent the female equivalent of male heroism, an image that was cultivated by the OUN's publications in the years that followed the war. However, a closer look reveals complexities in her writings.

Teliha's literary production was slight—some forty poems and a dozen essays. However, her reputation rests not only on the poetry but also on the poetic persona she created, and on the aura that surrounded her in life and death.

Derzhavyn's articles about her, written in the late 1940s and early 1950s, are prefaced with genuflections. One begins: "There are themes which the writer should approach with unqualified respect, with the deepest Reverence of which the human spirit is capable" (Derzhavyn 2009a, 638). Teliha, he writes, is the embodiment of female heroism, and the early collection of her verse, *Prapory dukha* (1947), should serve as the foundation for a spiritual cult of "our national heroine" (ibid., 639). During the war her poetry and presence were indeed an inspiration to many compatriots. She possessed great personal charm and was aware of the impression she made on others. Samchuk has noted that she took care "to always be in form and to shine," even during times of great hardship (Samchuk 2008, 302). Her impeccable physical appearance and attention to dress contributed to the image of a successful professional woman, a strong character who at the same time radiated a natural femininity. This appearance, like her writings, represented a protest against timidity, mediocrity, and despondency. Not surprisingly, after her death she became a symbol both of the struggle for independence and of the Nationalist approach to life. The "mythologization" of Teliha developed within a discourse concerning womanhood. Derzhavyn compared her to Joan of Arc, Queen Elizabeth I, Charlotte Cordier, and Princess Olha of Kyivan Rus. Dontsov spoke of her as the ideal, strong Ukrainian woman endowed with "manly" virtues. He stressed her desire to transgress boundaries and take risks, her hatred of the mob, the slave, and the servant, and emphasized the fact that she was attuned to the "distant sound of unborn poetry" (Dontsov 1953, 15). In his view she represented the "warrior" psyche and the victory of spirit over matter (ibid., 30). Her opposite was Andromache, the kind of woman who refuses to send her men to war.

Teliha responded to a number of these issues in her article "Iakymy nas prahnete" (How You Desire Us, 1935). In it she complains that male Nationalist writers like Malaniuk and Mosendz can only portray foreign women—Joan of Arcs or a Mary Stewarts—as strong figures. The Ukrainian woman appears in their work as either a slave or a vamp, two literary images that have remained unchanged for decades. Both, in fact, represent the same kind of woman—one who exists as a source of momentary pleasure, to make the male's life comfortable. Malaniuk presented his image of Ukrainian womanhood in the poem "Ukrainski vizantiiski ochi" (Ukrainian Byzantine Eyes, 1929) and in the portrayal of various Madonnas (of the Steppe, the Wild Lands, the Black Hellas). Out of them emerged his dichotomous image of Ukraine as a beautiful woman who is also demonic and immoral. This ambivalent attitude toward a feminized Ukraine is associated with the image of a country that has been weakened because it has for centuries been a buffer zone and is now dominated by political and psychological chaos. Moreover, some of his poems suggest the symbolic murder of this female Ukraine: the feminized culture requires insemination by a Steppe Messiah, which is an act simultaneously of destruction and recreation. In this way Malaniuk's symbolic system hearkens back to the oldest myths, to the idea of culture-creation, the turning of chaos into order (Omelchuk 2009, 751).

However, the immediate impetus behind the appearance of Teliha's article was the publication by Malaniuk of "Zhinocha muzhnist" (Women's Masculinity), in which the author observed disparagingly that Ukrainians were a "feminine nation" (*Nova khata* 1931, no. 12; quoted in Diadiuk 2011, 86). He described gender in modern terms, as a social and cultural construct, but expressed profound anxiety concerning the manner in which gender features were distributed: "When we consider objectively the contrast between the Ukrainian woman and man we have to admit not only the predominance in the basic female Ukrainian type of the element M over F, but something stranger, a kind of mutual transfer of these elements, some tendency in our national nature toward embodying almost the absolute male in female form" (ibid., 13). He continued, "Crudely put, the relationship between M and F in the Ukrainian species gives the impression that men and women are trying to psychologically change places" (ibid.). Malaniuk was convinced that this was not something his nation needed. He suggested that there was something unnatural in such a process, and urged that "the unnaturally attributed elements of M and F in the Ukrainian psyche" had to be "regrouped into their natural proportions to produce a healthy and harmoniously united Nation" (ibid., 14). Clearly, he had a rather "traditional" understanding of male and female roles and was concerned by what he considered to be ambiguity in gendered identity.

In her essay "Iakymy nas prahnete?" Teliha expresses the view that Ukrainian men are indeed profoundly confused concerning the kind of woman they want. Malaniuk's images of the slave and vamp exclude any possibility of respect for women (Teliha 2008, 82–83). A third image, the amazon, represents, in her view, the feminist, an image of woman that she also rejects. This third type, she argues, fails to consider the interests of the family and therefore poses a threat to the nation, which for its survival requires reproduction and continuity from generation to generation. Teliha therefore dismisses all three types. The first, the slave, represents in her opinion the fascist ideal as encapsulated by the four K's (*Kleider, Küche, Kinder, Kirche*). This woman will always remain an Andromache, a devoted mother and wife inevitably focused on life's small collective, the family. She will make daily compromises in order to survive, and will never inspire her children to consider the happiness of the wider collective, the nation. Nor should a woman be the object of brutal and cynical treatment, as suggested by the image of the vamp. Teliha reminds readers that the most masculine writers, among whom she counts Jack London and Kipling, allow their male protagonists to express tenderness and love toward women and in return expect strong, sincere feelings. In another essay she described Olzhych's lyrical heroes as men who do not "refuse the pleasures of life out of fear that these pleasures will hinder them in their struggle. They are always sure of their power and their commitment to the goal" (Teliha 1937, 654).

Teliha therefore suggests that all three dominant male images of women are unsatisfactory and demeaning to women. Her comments can be seen as a critique (in large part a refusal) of the barbarian macho image that was popular in the interwar years. Her rejection of male attitudes may also be related to the disastrous Soviet experience with "sexual revolution." In 1925 an article in a leading Soviet Ukrainian journal, *Zhyttia i revoliutsiia* (Life and Revolution), had referenced Alexandra Kollontai's argument that women should satisfy all their needs by choosing, if required, different men: the need for love could be satisfied with one partner, sex with another, work with a third, and so on. However, it continued, the behavior of youth had assumed "terrible forms." Suicides among deceived girls and infanticides among mothers unable to care for their offspring had multiplied. The "most primitive" approach to sex was being touted as communism. Every young man in the Komsomol asserted the right to satisfy his sexual urge and announced that sexual abstinence was philistinism. A woman who had been selected by a male had to go along with his wishes or be accused of holding bourgeois attitudes. The journal's readers were asked to imagine the trauma suffered by a village girl who succumbed to the "communist ideology" of "a young buck with a Komsomol card." As a result of problems caused by such an attitude, new laws on marriage had been drawn up to protect women. Common-law marriages were recognized, and male partners were expected to assume their responsibilities. Kollontai had called for the creation of a common insurance fund to pay for alimony, because in many cases the male partner was too poor to do so.

Teliha suggests that the ideal woman should display both strength and femininity, that she should be capable of both love and friendship. In Kipling's "William the Conqueror," she says, the woman requires her lover to struggle against hunger in India, but when the danger has passed she finds time for love, laughter, music, dancing, and flowers. This kind of woman will follow her man into the most dangerous enterprises but will never become "an amazon lacking feminine charms" (Teliha 2008, 92). She will be able to transform herself from temporary amazon into a "one hundred percent" woman with the skills to create the home her husband needs. Contemporary amazons, the ubiquitous "men in skirts," will never be a source of inspiration for men, "who need seriousness in action and work, but tenderness and humour during leisure" (ibid., 93). In short, the Ukrainian woman is neither slave, nor vamp, nor amazon: "She wants to be a Woman. A woman who differs from a man and yet is his equal, a faithful ally of men in the struggle for life, and, above all, for the nation" (ibid., 96). Teliha finds examples of this ideal in some works by male writers, in, for example, the strong-willed but fascinating Aglaia of Khvylovy's novel *Valdshnepy* (Woodsnipes) and in Vassa of Hryhorii Epik's novel *Persha vesna* (First Spring). The essay "Iakymy nas prahnete" is Teliha's credo on the question of woman-hood and represents her answer to the imagery produced by several male writers in the Nationalist camp. Her ideal woman combines the quasi-religious idea of readiness for sacrifice with the idea of attractiveness and charm. It is significant that this woman is a strong figure, politically aware, and the male's equal. And it is telling that Teliha cannot name such an admirable figure in Ukrainian litera-ture produced by her contemporaries outside Soviet Ukraine.

After her death, Teliha's image was immediately appropriated by Nationalist writers. Dontsov developed a picture of her as simultaneously steely and femi-nine. The same description occurs in Samchuk: "She knew how to be excep-tionally feminine, almost naïve, very tender, but at the same time [. . .] She was the steel that made sparks fly" (Samchuk 2008, 302). This image represented to a great degree a Nationalist response to the feminist liberationism that was a strong current in interwar Galician and émigré society and which emphasized a woman's right to self-assertion. The most prominent Galician feminist, Milena Rudnytska, was a leader of the UNDO and a member of the Sejm. Her eloquent, courageous, and incisive criticism of the government was impressive and drew a crowd: the owner of the Sejm's restaurant complained that when she spoke, his premises emptied (Kedryn 1976, 194). In the 1930s Rudnytska headed the Union of Ukrainian Women (Soiuz Ukrainok) and in 1934 organized their congress in Stanislaviv (now Ivano-Frankivsk).

The Ukrainian women's movement was powerful, affected all spheres of life, and worked to transform society by overturning patriarchal models of behavior. It contained between forty-five thousand and sixty thousand members and developed a wide network throughout the towns and villages of Galicia (Diadiuk 2011, 92–93). It was a democratic organization that accepted all social classes and members of various political parties. In the 1920s some of its members were communists (contacts with the Communist Party of Western Ukraine date from 1926), but these left after the Union passed an anti-Soviet resolution in the Spring of 1930 (ibid., 130–31). The Union of Ukrainian Women was, moreover, resilient. The Polish government banned it on 6 May 1938 as a threat to the security of the state and shut down its main publications *Zhinka* (Woman) and *Ukrainka* (Ukrainian Woman). In response, the leadership organized the Princess Olha Cohort (Druzhyna Kniahyni Olhy) as a political organization, thus allowing the Union to focus exclusively on cultural and educational work. Both the Union and Cohort supported the idea that women should be themselves and not "satellites" of men, as Rudnytska put it (ibid., 119). Aware that some Western European concepts and slogans would not work in Western Ukraine, the organizations generally avoided using the term "feminist," although this was clearly what they were (ibid., 121–22). Both organizations felt that women should defend the Ukrainian people's rights and aspirations to self-rule. They saw no contradiction in simultaneously defending the dignity and equality of women; the ideas of national liberation and feminism, according to Rudnytska, "hide no contradictory tendencies." On the contrary, she said, "the Ukrainian women's movement aims to express all creative possibilities available to women, and by this very fact strengthens the nation's vitality and energy" (ibid., 126).

Milena Rudnytska, the Union's undisputed leader, defended the rights of Galician Ukrainians at international forums and congresses, using her contacts in the international women's movement to do so. In 1929 she raised the issue of minorities at an international women's congress in Berlin to a warm reception, which was reported in *Rozbudova natsii* ("Kongres" 1929, 249–50). Through her contacts in the women's movement, she was able to intervene at the League of Nations and the Council of Nationalities, where she raised the issues of Pacification in 1930–31 and the Great Famine (Holodomor) in 1933. With Olena Sheparovych she founded and co-edited the newspaper *Zhinka* (Woman), which Kedryn described as "the best periodical in the history of the Ukrainian women's press" (Kedryn 1976, 194).

Such a large, influential organization presented a challenge to the OUN. The latter's ideologists felt discomfort with international feminism and with Rudnytska in particular. Not only was she able to garner enormous Western publicity, but her newspaper *Zhinka* challenged the OUN's glorification of machismo and its hierarchical view of gender roles. It portrayed the liberation of women, their education, and political activism as worthy goals in themselves. This caused a palpable ideological confusion in the OUN. In 1938 one writer in the organization's paper *Holos* called *Zhinka* "an enemy of the Ukrainian nation" (BUTRO 1938). A note of desperation crept into the article when it insisted that international feminism could not provide guidance for Ukrainian women because the latter required a made-in-Galicia leadership. The writer appears to have forgotten that this was precisely what Rudnytska represented. Implicit in this Nationalist criticism was a rejection of female liberationism and self-realization as goals in themselves; they had to be subordinated to the national struggle. However, Nationalists had no wish to go against the vast majority of educated women who were readers of *Zhinka* and who saw no contradiction between supporting women's rights and the struggle for national independence. On the other hand, Teliha's position was acceptable to the OUN leadership. In spite of the amazon comments, it represented a feminist assertion of equality but simultaneously appeared to concede that a woman's needs should be subordinated to those of the male soldier. Above all, it forcefully directed attention toward the overarching goal of national revolution. Teliha did not approve of the self-organizing drive of women, and she offered some support for the ideal of a masculinized culture that leading Nationalists advocated.

Rudnytska, moreover, was a consistent opponent of one-party states and total-itarian movements in any form, whether Nazi, fascist, or bolshevik, and made her views known on the pages of various publications. Teliha responded by criticizing Rudnytska and Ukrainian feminism for supporting "liberalism" and "humane-ness," attitudes that, in Teliha's opinion, weakened the liberation struggle. A number of Nationalists considered the success of Rudnytska's movement, espe-cially its ability to mobilize entirely independently of other political organiza-tions, to be a threat to unity. In consequence, "whenever the Ukrainian feminist movement was mentioned, Teliha, along with several other Vistnykites [. . .] assumed a polemical tone or the position of an observer" (Omelchuk 2011, 198).

It should also be noted that in the 1930s, Teliha closely followed Dontsov's line on supporting Hitler. She made the following comment on the Führer's assassination of Ernst Röhm and the destruction of the SA (Sturmabteilung, the Nazi Party militia) in 1934 during the so-called night of the long knives: "What is strange about this? After all, even Christ had to take a whip to his 'own' race to drive his 'blood brothers' out of the temple." Machiavelli, Mussolini and Hitler, she continued, "were not always merciful and tender in reeducating their 'blood brothers'" (Teliha 1936, 615). Dontsov also defended Hitler's action as inevitable and necessary for the nation's spiritual unity; he referred to the work "of history's Nemesis herself, who had to wrench the fifth wheel off the wagon" (Dontsov 1934a, 140). The killing put an end to any threat to Hitler's power and has been described as "the first mass murder in the Third Reich" (Gellately 2007, 310). It should be noted that the vast majority of Germans accepted what they saw as the sentencing to death of a hundred culprits in order to prevent an armed revolt and that Hitler remained enormously popular with the German public.

The issues of beauty and biology were problems for Nationalists. They raised difficult questions. Was female beauty merely an animalistic attraction, a woman's way of stimulating a male and finding a mate? Should biological determinism be allowed to govern her surrender to passion and procreation? The answer was found in the idea that beauty and sexual attraction were not merely personal pleasures. Their purpose, as Teliha suggests in a number of poems, is to inspire men to political action. Female beauty, in short, should serve the great cause. Just as a work of art cannot be viewed as merely a form, or a fetish, neither can a woman's beauty; it should not merely gratify its possessor or admirer. As a result of this way of thinking, Nationalist literature often sublimated or ignored the sexual drive. This is one reason why Teliha terms Lypa's frank acceptance of sexual pleasure "erotomania." The eroticism in her own work (the yearning for ecstasy and self-sacrifice, the anticipation of joy) is only allowed to exist as a subtext. Sexual energy is transformed into a spiritual force that benefits the nation. Like other "feminist" freedoms, the pursuit of sexual pleasure suggested to Nationalists the specter of unbridled individualism or an apolitical exploration of the world and the body for their own sake. Such freedoms and pursuits could be seen as distractions from the political struggle. The "soft" aesthetics of charm radiating from the pages of *Zhinka* could also be seen as suspect. They challenged the "hard" aesthetics of the sublime (which focused on awe and apocalypse), and appeared to reject the message implicit in Teliha's "steely" character and "classical" verse form.

The extent to which Dontsov's description of Teliha leans upon sexuality as a biological drive, and nature as an amoral force, is therefore surprising. He calls her works "a hymn to instinct" that express an "animal-like sense of joy" and "physical pleasure" (Dontsov 1953, 12, 13). The other women in his pantheon—Lesia Ukrainka and Olha Basarab—are not allowed such biological drives, or even the suggestion of an erotic life. They are constructed as images representing pure will and fanatical devotion to the cause. Teliha is the exception. The explanation may lie in her personal relationship with Dontsov. Their correspondence began in 1928 when she asked his opinion about her verse and thanked him for commenting on her "primitive" rhythms and rhymes. At the time, her poetic interest, as she herself admitted, was in capturing daily life's "countless varied moods and their indefinable, or scarcely definable nuances" (BN, Mf. 83986, 441). When their paths crossed again in the 1930s, the behavior of Teliha and Dontsov resembled that of lovers. On 8 June 1933 Teliha wrote to her confidante Livytska-Kholodna: "Perhaps, the greatest number of arguments and misunderstandings between us have been over Dontsov. But, Natusenka, you cannot imagine how dear he is to me. I can see [. . .] you laughing ('a pathological phenomenon'). Maybe it is 'pathological,' but it is undeniably strong and very sincere. I cannot define what it is: love, adoration, friendship, or infatuation, or none of these, but this feeling is so deep, that you, if you love me, must once and for all reconcile yourself and not treat it lightly, because otherwise I could not be completely open with you" (Teliha 2004, 400).

The following poem in Dontsov's archive appears to be written to Teliha. It is marked "strictly private" and dated 5 May 1933:

The earth resounds under the carriage's wheels
A rain of golden sparks in the warm window
Your image disappears, dissolves
Into half-tones as though in a dream.

About an hour ago
There was this: some sort of fear
At first (will it happen?) and
An alarmed question in the eyes.

Then a sudden frenzy
Flooded our brains,
Carried us in a wild gallop
Like alarmed racing horses
Into the tart and sweet whirlwind . . .

II
The earth resounds under the carriage's wheels
And the memory fades . . . Loathsome fatigue
Again weighs upon me like a nightmare:
Tens of contented moronic eyes

Behind, in front, to the side, opposite —
In the half-light of the stuffy compartment.
The triumphant banality of the mob
Shows its disgusting face.

A fever in the head . . . the devilish laughter of hyenas,
Clamors in the temples (I will face you as is fitting),
The chaos depresses.

III
And here it is.
The platform and that straight figure,
That laughing, child-like, little head,
A hand raised in parting . . . Only a moment

But the chaos is already disappearing.
And I can see the shore again.

And someone's narrow hand
Smoothes my tired brow again . . .

Once more something pulls and draws me
To dive headlong into
Another whirlwind.
Soit benie, ma petite,
Merci, I will come again.[1] (BN, Mf. 80370, 786–7)

This poem is almost certainly an answer to Teliha's "Bez nazvy" (Without a Title), which is dedicated to Dontsov. In it she says: "Not love, not tenderness and not passion, But a heart—an awakened eagle! Drink the splashes, fresh and sparkling, Of unnamed, joyful sources!" It suggests a woman using her charms to restore and reinvigorate a man. Dontsov's poem appears to be the grateful male's acknowledgment that this is precisely what their meetings have accomplished. Both poems link romance, biology, and the warrior's need for revived energy and replenished force.

A second poem in Dontsov's archive, which is dated 25 March 1933, mentions various meeting places: Luxemburg, Lac Leman, Lago di Garda, and the committing of a "dark, spring-time sin!" It contains the lines: "Wherever life's unpredictable fate took me, She appeared with the spring wind! Whatever name they gave Her, She and the spring were always together!"[2] (ibid., 789)

Both of Dontsov's poems construct woman as the inspirer of male desire and the accomplice of nature. The tone of both is brutal and taut; they suggest that lurking beneath beauty's surface lies the attraction to physical passion. Both poems leave little space for personal female agency but do indicate the power of women to inspire. In the first poem Dontsov shows his disdain for the common herd that is incapable of understanding his thoughts and feelings or, perhaps, his sexual morality. He was apparently supremely indifferent toward anyone who censured his extramarital affairs. His links to prerevolutionary modernism and the St. Petersburg milieu out of which he, like Teliha, emerged, are perhaps the unacknowledged source of this culturally transgressive attitude. The Russian symbolists and decadents (among whom Zinaida Gippius—Teliha's godmother—was a prominent figure) were known for experimenting with sexual relations, which they described in their literary works and memoirs. Given Dontsov's views, it makes sense that he would not hide his impulsive libidinal drives or his contempt for social prohibitions. Natalia Livytska-Kholodna thought that the Dontsov-Teliha romance was platonic. Teliha, she said, greatly enjoyed flirting in company and was always animated and cheerful. As a consequence, various rumors constantly circled around her (Boichuk

2009b, 814). However, the poems of 1933, written when they were neighbors in Warsaw, imply that they were lovers. Dontsov appears to have taught Teliha to discipline her emotions and to have drawn her into the "romantic" world of radical nationalism. When asked to become the public face of the OUN in Kyiv, she willingly accepted and allowed herself to be used as a figurehead. After her death Samchuk and Olzhych immediately expressed a sense of guilt for having allowed her to act out the drama of self-sacrifice.

Teliha's relationship with the editor of *Vistnyk*, her writings, correspondence, and life are underresearched aspects of the discourse within interwar nationalism around the issues of femininity, masculinity, biology, and nature. However, her relationship with the women's movement has now been studied. Some commentators within the OUN accused the Union of Ukrainian Women of ruining the family, diminishing population growth, and spreading internationalist and pacifist tendencies (Diadiuk 2011, 127). Others opposed the existence of a separate women's organization and saw feminism as a symptom of a deformed society (ibid., 133–34). However, there were many within the broader society, and the OUN in particular, who looked with respect and admiration at the Union of Ukrainian Woman and Rudnytska in particular. The Union had organized mass protests immediately following the murder of Olha Basarab and Rudnytska had spoken out in defense of Danylyshyn and Bilas. Dmytro Andrievsky admitted that Rudnytska had done more than anyone to publicize the Ukrainian cause abroad (ibid., 138), and in 1933 Konovalets told Onatsky that she stood close to the OUN's positions and had the organization's full support in the propaganda work she was doing in Western Europe (Onatskyi 1984, 43). Onatsky himself described her work in international diplomacy as invaluable (ibid., 139). These comments were made in spite of the fact that she constantly condemned the OUN's tactics. The positive attitude toward her was enhanced when she expressed opposition to the UNDO's "normalization" (accommodation strategy) and was ejected from this organization on 12 November 1935 (ibid., 184).

In the later 1930s she drew close to Dmytro Paliiv and his Front for National Unity. This organization and its periodical *Peremoha* consistently supported her. Moreover, by 1939 the leadership of the Princess Olha Cohort, the political arm of the woman's movement, contained supporters of various political parties. Five were aligned with the UNDO, five-with the OUN, two with the Front for National Unity, and one with the Ukrainian Social Revolutionary Party. These women leaders, nonetheless, worked together to consolidate the organization (ibid., 201).

They were more united than was immediately apparent. A tradition of strong, politically active women developed in Western Ukraine during the interwar period. It had roots in the earlier feminist movement of the 1880s but had been greatly bolstered by the image of women serving in the army, especially in the Ukrainian Riflemen Regiment and the Ukrainian Galician Army (Diadiuk 2011, 47, 69–81). Some, like Olena Stepaniv, became legendary figures. They had taken part in combat and were decorated as officers (ibid., 49). Their achievements were reported not only in the Ukrainian press, but also in German, Italian, Austrian, and other periodicals (ibid., 50). In the debate that took place between the Union of Ukrainian Women and Teliha, it is clear that the two sides shared similar aims and treated each other with great respect. The Union welcomed Teliha's entry into the discussion, called her an intelligent opponent and accomplished writer, but rejected the claim that liberalism or the Union of Ukrainian Women was responsible for Ukraine's political woes. On the contrary, the women's movement saw itself as part of the overall dynamic that was leading to national and personal liberation (ibid., 136).

At this time the Church also condemned the Union of Ukrainian Women in no uncertain terms. Feminism was described as an expression of social degeneracy. Bishop Ivan Buchko of Lviv saw the contemporary press, theater, cinema, and fashion as full of moral degeneracy. Bolstered by the Catholic Action movement initiated by Pius XI in 1922, the Ukrainian Greek Catholic Church insisted that marriage and childrearing were to be seen as a woman's primary vocation, and often described feminism as "pagan" or "radical" (ibid., 143–44). There is no doubt that both Rudnytska and Teliha were united in challenging such "traditionalist" and patriarchal views and were politically much closer than later critical opinion has allowed.

8

LEONID MOSENDZ AND OLEH OLZHYCH

Like Teliha, Mosendz had a conversion experience. He came from Eastern Ukraine and counted Lithuanians and Poles in his background. According to family lore, one ancestor fought the crusaders in 1410 at the battle of Grunwald. Another fought alongside the Poles against Muscovy and was deported to Siberia. Mosendz admitted that until 1918 he had been a Russian patriot. He became a Ukrainian in one month, after reading Hrushevsky's history (Kravtsiv 1960, viii). During the First World War he served in the Russian army on the Romanian front, then joined the Ukrainian army in 1918. He worked as a teacher from 1918 to 1920 near Vinnytsia and participated in the revolutionary brigades that fought bolshevik troops at night (Nabytovych 2001, 29). After reenlisting in the UNR army, he was decommissioned at the end of 1920. Mosendz worked in the UNR's ministry of National Education, the Ukrainian library in Częstochowa, and a law office in Lutsk. He was arrested by the Poles as a member of the Prosvita society in April 1922 and interned in a camp, where he contracted tuberculosis, from which he suffered for the rest of his life. After his release he crossed the border into Czechoslovakia and enrolled in the Ukrainian Academy of Economics in Poděbrady. He qualified in chemistry and oil technology and obtained employment as a chemist in Bratislava, where he married a Slovak. Mosendz translated, wrote for various publications, and mixed with the Prague intelligentsia; he was friendly with Olzhych, Teliha, Olha Rusova (the daughter of Mykhailo Rusov), Livytska-Kholodna, Dmytro Chyzhevsky, and Malaniuk. He tutored children of Ukrainian professors, including Olena Teliha. In the years 1937–39 he found employment as a teacher in Carpatho-Ukraine (Subcarpathian Rus), but spent much of the time treating his tuberculosis. In 1948 he died of the disease in Switzerland.

Mosendz began contributing to *Literaturno-naukovyi vistnyk* in 1927. Like Teliha he was a loyal supporter of Dontsov and defended the latter in 1937 against Lypa's charge of sectarianism. After all, Mosendz argued, "Hitler, Mussolini and Ataturk" all came out of sectarian doctrines (Mosendz 1936a, 728). However, like Klen, he had a change of heart after 1941. His published works include *Zasiv: Povist* (Seeding: A Novel, 1936); two prose collections, *Liudyna pokirna* (A Submissive Person, 1937) and *Vidplata* (Revenge, 1939, republished as *Pomsta*, 1941); the verse collection *Zodiak* (1941); the long poem *Volynskyi rik* (Volhynian Year, 1948); and the novel *Ostannii prorok* (The Last Prophet, 1960).

Whereas poets like Daragan, Liaturynska, Stefanovych, Lypa, and Livytska-Kholodna turned for inspiration to Kyivan Rus, or the Ukrainian baroque, Mosendz searched a range of European classics. His preference for well-wrought poetic forms was part of this generation's alignment with modernity and modernism. It represented a rejection of populism, which had drawn on folk songs and diction. Similarly, his interest in the great books of the past represented a desire to explore new sources in order to enrich the national tradition. His two favorite themes were personal conversion and the curse of emigration.

In the autobiographical *Zasiv*, the protagonist is a strong-willed boy who chooses a Ukrainian identity. Nino's family lives by the Dniester River. His father is descended from Ukrainian and his mother from Polish gentry. The latter still uses the family's old Catholic prayer book, even while attending Orthodox services, and continues to write letters in Polish to her family in Volhynia. A Russian heavily influenced by Ukrainian is spoken in the home, while Ukrainian is used in the marketplace, with the servant, the nanny, or "ordinary people." Like the young Kipling, Nino spends all his time with the local children, grows up speaking their language and identifying with them:

> It is hardly surprising that the child already knows his environment is divided into muzhiks and gentlefolk, and that he and his parents belong to the latter. But "gentlefolk" education only touched the child on the surface, and his parents' teaching only stayed in Nino's head as long as he was indoors. [. . .] Nino played with the boys on the broad courtyard overgrown with grass, or ran with his friends over the surrounding meadows and vineyards, climbed the mulberry trees, the sweet cherry and sour cherry trees, and splashed in the shallow waters of the Derlo.
>
> Nino's friends were children of neighbouring urban folk — those typical descendants of town Cossacks who for centuries competed with the gentry [*shliakhta*] for the rights and liberties of the Ukrainian towns. To this day some families preserve old certificates as keepsakes, and on holidays the

women go to church adorned with several strands of corals and old ducats
that have come down to them from mother to daughter. (Mosendz 1936c, 14)

The child asks "Who are we, grandma?" and receives the answers "We are
Rus." The boy's mother, however, insists that they are not Rus, but Russian, and
that he has to speak Russian and not talk "like the muzhiks" (ibid., 12–13). Nino
is unwilling to switch to Russian, a language in which he cannot express what
he has learned in his environment. His Ukrainian imprinting has much to do
with myths and legends. He learns of the pagan gods Dazhboh and Perun. On
a trip to the market, the driver, Havrylo, describes the Cossack state that was
once boldly defended by its knights against Polish hussars, Tatar horsemen,
Turkish troops, and Muscovites.

The banks of the Dniester contain caves that were carved out by monks to form
a church and monastery. According to legend, a time will come when people will
again have to hide in these cliffs by climbing though one of the holes. Like the
arcades of Paris in Benjamin's imagination, the mysterious site becomes the
entrance to a mythical world in which history and contemporary life intertwine
and illuminate one another. The boy's imagination is captured by the story of this
underground monastery: "Without turning away he caught every word from granny's lips, and he could visualize stern black monks, like the ones he had seen in
Tarlashivsk Monastery. They travelled in a long line through the narrow passages
of the vaults, candles in hand, going deeper and deeper into the earth to escape
the Muslim attacks. He could also see the Turkish horde, an amorphous mass in
red fezes, each of whom looked like the Turkish baker. They were shouting above
the cliff, making a din, waving their swords and wailing with impotent rage at the
monks whom they could not get to in their hiding-place" (ibid., 32).

When his grandfather describes crosses in the cemetery and burial mounds
in the Steppe, the boy is mentally transported to another world. These stories
that have been passed down through the generations describe "everything that
his clan had experienced or witnessed" (ibid., 34). Nino's parents are unmoved
by his enthusiasm for history. His father has muffled the voice of the past within
himself and cannot answer when his son asks why he did not tell him about
Ukraine. When Nino discovers that his uncle was exiled to Siberia for Ukraine,
he rebels against studying the "lord's language." He dreams of escaping to the
church in the white cliff and the monastery in the steep banks of the Dniester:
"Yes! He will escape there! Under the ground, in the long dark passages his
parents will no longer find him and cannot compel him to be one of the gentlefolk or to learn the "gentlefolk" language. Other boys will join him, many boys,
all those who suffer and are persecuted at home in the same way. They will

have sharp swords! Not wooden ones, but real ones! And lances and rifles! They will hide underground until they grow up. Then, strong and numerous, they will come out into the light and conquer the whole world!" (ibid., 60–61). The young generation will allow the people's language to be spoken and will reveal the country's suppressed history and identity.

Nino's development, it is suggested, mirrors what is occurring in the nation's psychology. The book ends with the image of a sower in a ploughed field who walks toward the rising sun, while a boy sleeps in a furrow. The obvious interpretation is that the earth is fertile and, although sown late, the harvest will be a good one: the boy has discovered his heritage late, but his awareness will ripen. An epigraph from the Bible reinforces the message: "The good seed will fall on good soil and bear fruit." *Zasiv* was highly praised for its skillful depiction of a child's psychology, and was awarded the Ukrainian Catholic Union's literary prize.

Mosendz believed strongly in the inspirational power of myths. He was particularly fascinated by the moment in time when a human spirit catches fire. In an essay published in 1936 he interprets Cervantes' hero as captured by a beautiful illusion. Sancho Panza, on the other hand, is content with his mundane existence and devoted to the satisfaction of his stomach. He admires his master's irrational idealism but also fears it. Sancho represents mass man, the throng, whose spirit has spread throughout the world. These people want peace "at any cost," and are ready to forgive in advance all wrongs done to them and those that will be done to their children (Mosendz 1936b, 340). The most perfect expression of this type is the impractical crony, who would like to transform the world into a sleepy consumer paradise. For Don Quixote to emerge from the good-natured lord, says Mosendz, the old man really does have to go out of his mind. When this occurs, everything that the "collective spirit" has told him for fifty years suddenly appears foreign and useless. What accomplishes this miracle of transformation? Where does the spark of individuality come from? Mosendz answers: the desire for immortality. Action is a means to glory; glory is the path to immortality. The epigraph is from Cervantes: "To reach eternal fame and glory." The crucial thing is to discovery the mechanism that awakens the creative impulse, that uncovers the foundation of individuality deep in every person. Mosendz compares Don Quixote's metamorphosis to that of the pastor who became Moses, the premature baby who became Caesar, and the tender girl who became Joan of Arc. The essay was stimulated by Dontsov's article "Sancho v nashii diisnosti" (Sancho in Our Time, 1934), which argued that after Khmelnytsky and Mazepa, the Ukrainian elite had degenerated into Sanchos.

A similar yearning for transformation and desire for heroic action is explored in an essay on Muhammad, who made the Arabs into a world power, and in *Shtain: Ideia i kharakter* (Stein: Idea and Character, 1935). The latter deals with the life of Karl von Stein, who helped to unite the German princedoms in struggle against the French. The stories in Mosendz's collection *Liudyna pokirna* (The Submissive Person, also called *Homo Lenis*) focus on the definitive moment when a protagonist rebels or acts decisively. Each narrative concentrates on one event and builds toward a climax, which usually occurs in the last sentence and represents a sudden reversal or dramatic conclusion. Because of their highly crafted nature, these stories were described as rationalistic products of an exacting struggle for perfection, or of a mind that privileged clarity and "mathematical harmony." However, they were also praised for their originality and power (Nabytovych 2001, 59–60). In his introductory remarks, Mosendz explains how his generation came to the idea of transformation: "Souls nurtured on meditation began slowly to become aware that the only vital principle is Action. Souls nurtured on the principle of defence, the passive principle of all the submissive, began to understand that the guarantee of victory lies in an entirely opposite principle: Attack!" (Mosendz 1937, 7). He indicates that the stories come out of conversations held in Prague's "Completely Free Club," where Ukrainians gathered in the 1920s. The opening story, "Liudyna pokirna," describes the death of Kaler, a railway engineer. Russian soldiers deserting from the front are rolling across Ukraine, protesting against any rule or order (ibid., 15). A frenzied, anarchic crowd demands that the train set off immediately and decides to lynch the engineer, who in their minds represents discipline and organization. The last line is the climax: with a noose around his neck Kaler does not wait for the chest to be knocked from under his feet but kicks his Siberian executioner in the face: "A crunching sound could be heard, blood spattered and the Siberian twisted and fell . . . At the end of the taut rope swung Kaler's body!" (ibid., 20). "Na utvor" (Toward Creation) examines the unwillingness to take risks. An episode from the independence war is described. A mass of prisoners, strong young men, are being tortured by "a few puny chekists." The hundred young men dig a ditch for their own execution: "But throwing themselves all at one time at the guards would probably have been enough. Some would have died! Maybe even half! However, the rest would have escaped! But no! Submissively they put their heads under the chekists' revolvers" (ibid., 94). "Povorot kozaka Maikelia Smailza" (The Return of the Cossack Michael Smiles) describes the transformation of an American, Michael Smiles, who knows from the family Bible that his distant ancestor Mykhailo Smilsky came to Virginia in the seventeenth century and was the son of a captain from

Smila in Cossack Ukraine. When asked whether he feels Ukrainian, a son of the people for whom he is risking his life in the war, Smiles replies negatively. However, it is clear that he is making an effort to understand Ukraine, because he continually asks questions and searches for links to his ancestor's past. The denouement comes unexpectedly. The bolsheviks capture the insurrectionists and offer Smiles a chance to save his life by joining them. He is an American, they say, and has nothing in common with "these Petliurite bandits." Before his execution Smiles slowly and clearly enunciates in Ukrainian: "I am not an American, but a Ukrainian Cossack, Mykhailo Smilsky" (ibid., 142). A return to ancestral roots, the author suggests, can occur even in later generations.

Revenge is the theme of the second collection *Vidplata* (also published as *Pomsta* in 1941). The eponymous opening story describes a dying pope paying back a cardinal for once stealing his lover. He waits for a chamberlain to die and then names the cardinal to the vacant position, in this way forestalling any possibility of the cardinal becoming pope. It is the chamberlain's job to announce the death of a pope, but he himself can never be one. As he expires, the pope recalls the fact that his beloved Speranza was taken from him by a rival in love, mumbling that it was "not long ago." The message to the reader is that revenge is a powerful and lasting motivator.

First published in 1933, the poetic drama *Vichnyi korabel* (Eternal Ship) appeared as a separate book in 1940. It develops another favorite theme: political emigration as a curse. Set in late-sixteenth-century Netherlands after the murder of William of Orange, known as the Silent, it echoes depictions of Brugge (Bruges) in Georges Rodenbach and Stefan George. The quiet city is depicted as threatened by Spanish invaders. Some citizens call for surrender, hoping that the city will continue to prosper under foreign rule. Others feels that the population is exhausted from the struggle to maintain independence and favor community building (what in Galicia was known as "organic work") until the appearance of a new generation ready to cast off imperial domination. A third group asks how future generations will be able to expel the Spanish if today's citizens do not provide them with an example of resistance. Finally, a call is made to find another land where a new Brugge can be built. Those who take this last option are condemned to eternal wandering as a penance for treason. Their punishment can only be lifted when independence is gained. The poem expresses the émigré's guilt over leaving the homeland. The trauma of emigration also runs through *Zodiak*, a collection of poems written in the years 1921–36 and republished in 1941. The final cycle, "Pomona militans," is dedicated to Dontsov. Pomona, the Roman goddess of the harvest, represents Ukraine. She has been treacherously captured by Vertum, but defends herself with weapons in hand. One poem, "Usta netsilovani" (Unkissed Lips), is a legend that describes three fairies who provide gifts at the birth of a knight. One gives glory, one beauty and manliness, while the third constricts his heart "so that it will never get in his way. . . in battle."

Volynskyii rik (Volhynian Year, 1948) is dedicated to Mosendz's daughter, who remained with her mother in Bratislava after the war. The author invites his child to travel into the past with him and learn about the world of the *khutir* (homestead), and the customs and traditions of Volhynia, where he spent his childhood. Ancient legends and myths are recalled, such as the children of rusalkas (nymphs), who hide and play in the chimney during snowstorms, the six-winged bird, and various pagan deities. The poem ends by announcing that in the age of the atom and the Superhuman, which has begun, human beings will "understand the cosmos to the farthest stars." But readers are reminded that peace cannot be built on compulsion and violence. A prophet and leader will appear not "in the thunder of storms, not in the roar of the lion" but in "the quiet words . . . of our devoted hearts" (Mosendz 1948, 71–72). This new tone and message are representative of Mosendz's writings in the postwar period.

His professor and friend, Vasyl Ivanys, has left a candid account of the writer's intellectual development. He describes Mosendz's enthusiastic, pro-Hitler mood in 1938 on the eve of Carpatho-Ukraine's declaration of independence:

> Having studied Hitler's *Mein Kampf* [. . .] I replied that Hitler was a fanatical, conceited primitive, who would cause a great deal of trouble in Ukraine, would plunder Germany and would be defeated by the democrats. This was prior to the invasion of Poland. This "prophecy" was immediately answered by a highly critical letter from L. M. [Leonid Mosendz] which stated that I "had grown soft," had lost "my political orientation," had become a "rotten intellectual," and so on. His faith in vozhdism [the leader cult] had not been shaken. [. . .] Each of his letters breathed a romantic vozhdism. Dr. D. Dontsov was his god.
>
> However, Hitler's cohorts quickly turned nach Osten and in fifteen days squashed "aristocratic" Poland and embraced "father" Stalin. Dr. Dontsov after a short term in Bereza-Kartuzka [concentration camp] moved to Berlin and it appeared that the time had come for him to demonstrate action. But after walking the Berlin sidewalks for a couple of weeks, he quietly moved off to Romania to the cares of the R. [Rusov] family. I discovered this in a letter from L. M., in which he wrote: "the spiritual creator of an ideology at the decisive moment deserted the youth that had been enthralled by him. Dontsov is a corpse. I have written this to him and will have no more to do with him." [. . .] And he kept his word. In 1945 in the café Beranek in Prague

he accidentally met Dontsov sitting at a table, but asked not to be introduced and left. In all his later letters he often recalled this vozhd of his with disdain. (Letter from V. Ivanys to Petro Danyliuk, 19 October 1954, UM, Danyliuk Collection)

The unfinished novel *Ostannii prorok* (Last Prophet, 1960), which describes the life of the Israelite Yehokhanan, can be read as a meditation on the evolution of revolutionary nationalism. It describes a nation that finds itself in a state of moral decay under foreign subjugation. Difficult choices have to be made on the path to political liberation and moral rebirth. The book incorporates much biblical history, drawing on the author's lifelong interest in biblical studies. In the early 1920s Mosendz had considered becoming a priest, and in the years 1923–25, while attending the Academy of Economics in Poděbrady, he attended the meetings of a branch of the North American Ukrainian Gospel Union, which advocated reforming the teachings of traditional churches.

In the novel, Yehokhanan learns the teachings of the Pharisees, who represent conservative thought. After becoming disillusioned with them, he joins the zealots, who are fighting for independence from Roman occupation and against their own turncoats. The zealots deliberately inflame social antagonisms, because they realize that hatred is the soil that nourishes their movement. The boy gradually comes to understand the relationship between various classes and parties. Eventually, he meets the Essenes. It appears that the author was preparing readers for Yehokhanan's adherence to this sect, which practices nonviolence and asceticism. The narrative demonstrates Mosendz's disillusionment with the politics of organized nationalism and the behavior of its leadership.

Oleh Olzhych was the youngest member of the OUN's émigré leadership. In 1937 he was appointed by Konovalets as the organization's authority on cultural matters and became its leading literary theorist. He was born in Zhytomyr in 1907 and grew up near Kyiv. His father Oleksandr Oles was one of the great lyrical poets of the prewar years and a descendant of Cossack gentry. Although trained as a veterinarian, Olzhych's father had to take various jobs in order to survive; from 1909 to 1919, for example, he worked in a slaughterhouse near Kyiv. He was appointed the UNR's cultural attaché in Bucharest in 1919 and then emigrated. Olzhych and his mother remained in Kyiv, where they survived by bartering family belongings for food. In 1923 they were allowed to leave for Prague, thanks to the intervention of the bolshevik leaders Christian Rakovsky and Dmytro Zatonsky. Olzhych studied at Charles University, the Ukrainian Pedagogical Institute, and the Ukrainian Free University, graduating from the latter in 1930 with a doctorate in archaeology. He conducted archaeological expeditions throughout Eastern Europe, publishing the results of his research in German, Czech, French, English, and Ukrainian journals. In the 1930s he maintained contact with Harvard scholars, took part in archaeological excavations organized by them in Serbia, and was invited to lecture in the United States and Italy. A particular interest was Trypillia and the painted pottery of the Neolithic Age found in Galicia. This was the subject of his PhD thesis, written in Czech and completed in 1930, and of a monograph published in German in 1937.[1] Olzhych's scholarly research enabled him to link contemporary Ukrainian culture to the ancient past and also to challenge some Nazi theorizing. He disputed the theory, popular in the Third Reich, that Indo-Germanic tribes had invaded Eastern Europe, bringing weapons and "Aryanizing" the people. His research also led him to the conclusion that "the people of the painted ceramics" belonged to at least three races (Videiko 2008, 69). Olzhych joined the OUN in 1929 and soon became widely known as an accomplished poet. Outraged that his son was writing poems glorifying violence and bloodshed, his father wrote these lines: "The phials contain blood instead of wine. And the stooping fraternity, liberty and love Make their way to Golgotha." The son referred to his father as a poet "for high-school girls and telephone operators" (Antonovych-Rudnytska 1985, 111). However, the two were reconciled during the war.

Olzhych was active in the attempt to establish Carpatho-Ukraine, and in 1941–44 he headed the OUN-M's underground in Eastern Ukraine. He created the Ukrainian National Council in Kyiv in these years, bringing together a range of parties, social groups, and professions. When Melnyk was arrested by the Germans in January 1944, Olzhych took over the organization's leadership. The Gestapo arrested him on 25 May 1944, in Lviv, where he had been hiding in a friend's apartment. At the time he was preparing a collection of documents dealing with Nazi crimes. The collection fell into their hands (Vynar 2008, 43, 175–88). Prior to his arrest he had often spoken of the Gestapo and German rule as "a mob of racists, cut-throats, and gangsters" (Shumelda 1985, 85). While being tortured in Sachsenhausen prison, he was either murdered or committed suicide. His body was found hanged on 10 June. Ten days before his arrest, on 15 May, Shukhevych had proposed to him that the Melnyk faction should enter the UPA and, probably, the UHVR. Olzhych was in favor of accepting the proposition but was outvoted at a meeting of the OUN-M leadership (G. Motyka 2006b, 129).

A modest, scholarly man who made a conscious decision to fully devote himself to politics when asked to be the OUN's spokesman on culture, Olzhych, like Teliha, gained cult status after his death. His achievements as the OUN's leading cultural activist were considerable. By drawing together scholars and activists, many of whom were not members of the organization, he was able to initiate many publications, to encourage the work of the Prague theater Apollo Militans and the Flying Stage (Letiucha Estrada), which was active in Carpatho-Ukraine and then under the name Experimental Studio (Eksperymentalna Studiia) in Prague. He directed research into a number of fields and attempted to create a Ukrainian Scientific Institute in the United States (Maruniak 1985, 77–79). He is the author of around thirty programmatic articles whose authority was not disputed by the OUN-B, even after the split of 1940. These articles make the case that Ukrainian culture has ancient origins. In the distant past it drew from Mediterranean sources, but in later periods it was influenced by interaction with peoples from the east and north. Trypillia, the Antes, Kyivan Rus, and the Cossack baroque are salient moments in its development. According to Olzhych, the culture has preserved ancient myths, rituals, and folk beliefs that are of great power and beauty, and which contemporary authors with a pantheistic sensibility, like the Soviet writer Vasyl Mysyk, have explored. Contemporary Ukrainians have a strong sense of identity, which stems from their connection to this ancient past and their liberationist drive. An essay comparing Russian and Ukrainian émigré poets contrasts the passive, tragic, and self-lacerating tone of the first with the determined, forward-looking tone of the second. In the early 1930s Olzhych did not reject modernism, only "pseudo-modernisms," which he equated with futurism, cubism, and surrealism in art, and formalism in music. He described these movements as products of the demoralization that gripped Europe following the traumatic experiences of revolution and war; they reflected the "literary chaos of cosmopolitan postwar Europe in its worst social decay" (Olzhych 2007, 226). The coming Ukrainian art would, in his opinion, reject these movements.

In his essays Olzhych often collated conservative cultural values and bolshevism: both were for him the products of outdated liberal and democratic forms of thinking, which are being overtaken by a vigorous new Nationalist culture. He argued that Soviet Russia only speculates on the old revolutionary slogans; it has passed into a hypocritical phase in which the shimmy and foxtrot are no longer entertainments of the bourgeois-minded NEPman (the businessman produced by the New Economic Policy of 1923–28) but of every communist bureaucrat (ibid., 185). The best element in bolshevism was the fanatical utopian dreamer, who provided the movement with its revolutionary elan. Now this dreamer has been silenced: "Bolshevism, as long as it was vital, linked itself to the romantic period of War Communism [the political and economic system that existed while the bolsheviks fought to establish their rule, 1918–21] and enjoyed certain achievements" (ibid., 225). When Olzhych surveyed contemporary Ukrainian literature and art, he was particularly drawn to Soviet writers of the 1920s. Although he classified bolshevism as materialistic, intellectualist, irreligious, and dogmatic, he was clearly inspired by the faith of its revolutionaries and by the achievements of the Cultural Renaissance in Ukraine that appeared after the policy of Ukrainianization was declared in 1923. This literature, in his view, was idealistic, intuitive, and mystical. It included the strong, self-confident voices of Bazhan, Khvylovy, and Yanovsky. Counterparts to these voices, he argued, could be found in the forceful new literature being produced outside the Soviet Union, especially in the writings of Lypa, Malaniuk, Daragan, Mosendz, Chyrsky, and Hryva (ibid., 197–98).

Olzhych described the new Nationalist creativity of the future as innovative and visionary, and declared that in this respect it could learn from the early bolshevik fanatics, the prophets and propagandists who were not proletarians but déclassé elements in the intelligentsia. These doctrinaires and dreamers were possessed by planetary ideas and romanticized civil war. Out of a materialistic worldview they unexpectedly created a superstructure that was, he argued, in its essence voluntaristic and romantic. This human trait in communism provided it with all its drive but was in fundamental conflict with its mechanistic ideology. Olzhych also found much to admire in the history of Ukrainian literature, praising many nineteenth-century figures, including the early feminist Marko Vovchok.

Ukraine, with its deeply emotional attachment to self-assertion and self-realization, would, he felt, be the harbinger of a new mode of thinking and feeling. Its modernism, he suggest in numerous passages written in the late 1930s and early 1940s, is best expressed through a "militarized neoclassicism" (ibid., 186). This sensibility blends a clearly articulated world view with a dynamic form. The new literature will be "closer to Homer than to Zola" (ibid., 262). It will be classical in its simplicity and distinctness but will not be weighed down by artificial solemnity. It will draw on European sources and high culture. The martial aspect of this neoclassicism will be evident in its strength of spirit and internal harmony. It will be inspired by knightly virtues, heroism, an implacable and unrepenting commitment to the nation, all of which are required in the "stern new age" (ibid., 192). Above all, this literature will be driven by a great faith and love.

One of his best essays is "V avanhardi heroichnoi doby" (In the Avant-Garde of the Heroic Age, 1938). It makes the point that the new culture will not be forced on people but will be driven by spiritual needs. Europe, he says, is splitting from the pressure of two volcanic islands that have arisen out of its depths in the north and east. Ukraine will be the third volcanic island, the avant-garde of a new human civilization (ibid., 263). In spite of this gesture toward freely developing cultural forms, Olzhych's entire critical output from 1935 to 1941 aimed to show that a radical, authoritarian nationalism—the integral nationalism of the OUN—was the only alternative to democracy, liberalism, socialism, communism, and conservatism. Already in 1936, in an essay on contemporary Ukrainian culture entitled "Obloha kultury" (The Siege of Culture, 1936), he identified liberalism, communism, and conservatism as "three reactionary spiritualities" (ibid., 224). Liberalism he associated with the chaos of freethinking and the idea of "science for science's sake," or free enquiry. He also linked it to European "cosmopolitanism." Communism, he argued, was mechanistic, leveling, and wedded to a dead theory. Conservatism was outdated and rapidly becoming indistinguishable from liberalism. In his view, both bolshevism and conservatism blended into liberalism—an idea that he developed most extensively in "V avanhardi heroichnoi doby" (1938), which is a full-scale attack on liberalism and democracy. In it he states: "Communism is tightly entwined with and takes sustenance from demo-liberalism" (ibid., 258).

Written in 1941 on the eve of the German-Soviet war, the essay "Ukrainska istorychna svidomist" (Ukrainian Historical Consciousness) states: "A nation that closes itself within boundaries, that does not yearn for spiritual and state expansion, that has no *imperial* tendencies—is not vital" (ibid., 268). He spoke of militancy and the martial ethos as traits of "Ukrainian consciousness" throughout the ages. The sword had been the symbol of medieval knights and Cossacks: "Militarism is a universal worldview and a morality that forms an individual and a people. It does not see in the enemy a criminal or monster, but another human being, placed in an adversarial position by the profound, creative, and tragic wisdom of life. This is how knightly *ethics and virtues* originate. A militaristic worldview ennobles life, calling forth courage, steadfastness, soldierly camaraderie, a sense of higher duty and honour" (ibid., 272).

Olzhych took Italian fascism as a guide, but developments in Germany exerted an influence. In 1935 Hitler had ranted against modernism, singling out dadaism, cubism, and futurism as "primitive forms of expression," insisting that great art should direct its attention to the "good and beautiful" and always follow "eternal principles." The turn against expressionism came in the same year. In 1937 Goebbels opened the Exhibition of Degenerate Art in Munich, which in terms of official visitor figures remains "the world's most 'successful' exhibition of modern art ever mounted" (Griffin 2007, 27). This anti-exhibition was designed to vilify aesthetic modernism. In 1938 a Degenerate Music Exhibition began in Dusseldorf, and on 20 March 1939 the Degenerate Art Commission ordered over a thousand paintings and almost four thousand

watercolors and drawings to be burned in Berlin's central fire station (ibid.).
These events were paralleled by the opening of the Great German Art Exhibition
and the Music Festival, both of which were designed to showcase acceptable
works. Nonetheless, as has been seen, modernism and functionalism were
strongly in evidence in art and industrial design, notably in the planned major
steel and glass constructions and the autobahns, whose nine thousand bridges
and overpasses were the style's most notable aesthetic success (Spotts 2009,
393). Three thousand kilometers of road had been completed by 1938, and the
network was hailed by the German press as "the single greatest masterpiece of
all times and places" (ibid., 392). In 1935 in an essay dealing with fascist art,
Olzhych distanced himself from futurism in art and architecture and modernism in music, which he saw as too concerned with abstraction and "empty"
experimentation (Olzhych 2007, 211). He felt that this kind of avant-gardism was
not in the true spirit of fascism, which for him was "severe" and "responsible,"
whereas futurism represented mere play with the senses and was excessively
negative toward past cultural achievements. The ideal was a purposeful and
organized art that could project a vision of the nation's future. He quoted with
approval Mussolini's words that art had to be modern but allied to tradition, that
it had to combine past and future. He also approved of art's link to action
through a commitment to politics, sport, war, and construction.

Olzhych rejected an amateurish or intellectually undemanding approach to
the study of folk customs or beliefs. In the deepest pagan past and biblical records
he searched for a myth of origins that would describe the Ukrainian character
and point the way to a future rebirth. He found this myth in Dazhboh and
Japheth. In "Ukrainska istorychna svidomist" (Ukrainian Historical Consciousness,
1941) he wrote: "We have searched for the idea that throughout history has served
Ukrainian spirituality as a myth, a stimulus for history-creating efforts. And we
have found it in the pagan dawn of our past in 'Dazhboh's grandchildren'" (ibid.,
274). This legend, he wrote, was the original myth of the people's divine origins.
The Christian metamorphosis of this original myth, he suggests, is to be found in
the idea of "Children born of Japheth."

Dazhboh was the chief god of pagan Rus. Japheth, one of Noah's three sons,
is mentioned in Genesis as having been assigned the lands of northern and
western Europe. The chronicles of Kyivan Rus, in particular the *Tale of Bygone
Years* in the Hypatian codex, describe the Slavs as descended from Japheth.
Subsequently the *Synopsis*, which was first published in Kyiv in 1678, picked up
this idea: "The Rus, or rather the Rossian people are Slavs as well, for they
derive from their ancestor Japheth, and their language derives from a common

language. Upon receiving their 'glorious' name for their 'glorious' deeds in times of old, they began to be called Rossians from the dissemination of their tribes" (Rothe 1983, 145–51; quoted in Kohut 2008–09, 285). The word "glorious" (*slava*) is a play on the word "Slav"; phonetic similarities of this kind were often used at the time to indicate historical links. Later, in the eighteenth century, Cossack chronicles developed this genealogy, claiming that the Cossack-Rus people were descended from Japheth's oldest son Gomer (ibid., 289–90).

Olzhych uses the myths of Dazhboh and Japheth to project the idea of a powerful nation driven by a desire for conquest and expansion. In his earlier 1935 essay on fascism, he had written: "Fascism today realizes that its future art ought to be imperialistic, expansionist, synthetic, powerful, clear, and uncompromising; however [. . .] there are still no works worth talking about" (Olzhych 2007, 188). Nationalist art is envisaged as heroic, idealistic, voluntaristic, active, monumental, dynamic, and expressive (ibid., 203). It should revive and express the national tradition (ibid., 212). In one of his last articles, "Ukrainska kultura" (Ukrainian Culture, 1942), he again calls heroism and glory the culture's guiding ideals, and speculates that the warlike Antes were the early progenitors of the Ukrainian race. The same foundation myth for the *rid* (genus or race) also appears in "Natsionalistychna kultura" (Nationalist Culture, 1940). Here Dazhboh and Japheth are once more presented as two aspects (pagan and Christian) of the same phenomenon: they are the nation's mythical founders, represent its blessed origins, and encode its fundamental character. The subsequent era of Cossackdom was inspired by this myth. According to Olzhych, therefore, Japheth and Dazhboh represent a myth of origins that provides the required mystical sense of common ancestry and destiny.

Olzhych produced three books of poetry: *Rin* (River Gravel, 1935), *Vezhi* (Towers, 1940), and the posthumously published *Pidzamcha* (By the Castle, 1946). His work illustrates the neoclassical ideal of lucid and firm ideas, disciplined metrical form, and refined imagery and diction. Many poems are set in the bronze or iron age; Greeks, Romans, Gauls, Goths, Vikings, and the warriors of Kyivan Rus appear often. An imagery of forests and stones, animals and sky dominates his verse, and his themes are the love of man and woman, parting, community, journeys, courage, and death. He aims for an elevated, epic tone, one that is serious and laconic. In "Neznanomu voiakovi" (To an Unknown Soldier, 1935) he produces a moving tribute to military life and to service for the good of the nation. This poem contains the following lines: "There was a time of frivolous thoughts— One reception after another, Then Horodok glittered on the ploughed field With the heartless cold of a knife blade. Oh, society of pale pink half-words, Of cheering scholarly nonsense, Stout and stupid parliamentary patriots And culture's many honorees!" As counterpoint to this decadence, he gives the following bracing lines: "Oh, believe in the bright fire of courage, And you will throw off, like a torn rag, The weakness, the doubt and the vanity of life" (ibid., 55). As with Teliha, some lines reveal a premonition of martyrdom, or a death wish. In 1930 he wrote: "How magnificent that we shall not be given The chance to live to thirty!" (ibid., 83). He also wrote: "The final moment will be unbearably blinding For a burned heart that yearned for a sweet miracle" (ibid., 75).

These lines capture a soldier's desire for action, for the moment of self-sacrifice, sometimes expressed as a wish to be led into combat by a Joan of Arc or a Saint George. An important feature of this writing, as Derzhavyn has pointed out, is the freely chosen path of self-sacrifice (Derzhavyn 2009b, 648). More than commitment to a cause, it appears to be a requirement of the writer's spirit. In one poem he welcomes "barbaric time" as an opportunity to show "eternal virtues." Heroic conduct expresses a worldview, a way of life. Therefore, Hannibal and Rome are both described as heroes and worthy antagonists. The seven-headed dragon who holds a princess captive informs the reader that he is prepared to die in combat rather than give up the prisoner he loves. In this, he too is heroic. Olzhych's poetry, as almost every commentator has noted, is a severe, ascetic world, in which unflinching conviction rules. Hordynsky called him the poet of a Ukrainian Sparta and indicated that his laconic verse was based on the elimination of everything inessential (quoted in Ilnytskyi 1995, 288). The result is a "sculpted" poetry that can be grand and magnificent but can simultaneously breathe the coldness of cenotaphs. Regular hexameters, the occasional carefully chosen archaic word inserted into common diction, the avoidance of artificial or easily achieved emotional effects—all give the reader the impression of monumentalism, of reading a work that aims at permanence and is meant to survive the changing fashions of time. But the sense of power and control that his poetry communicates, as Livytska-Kholodna has noted, makes Olzhych unemotional: "he is always dry, cold, enduring. He does not suffer; he teaches and builds" (Livytska-Kholodna 2009, 801). There is something awe-inspiring in this image of the dedicated builder, but, she says, "I find it frightening to consider what kind of world would have emerged if Olzhych had been its co-creator" (ibid., 801).

A much gentler portrait of a shy, sensitive, and highly intuitive man emerges from the memoirs of Maria Antonovych-Rudnytska, who has also published the poetry he wrote for her. Admirers of his verse have indicated Olzhych's gift for imaginatively connecting the ancient to the present, his ability to "link the two margins of time," as Malaniuk put it (quoted in Ilnytskyi 1995, 288). By reconstructing a scene from an earlier epoch and giving the lyrical hero the persona of a figure from this period, Olzhych allows the reader to enter another time and place in which myth and legend rule. But it is also a strangely familiar world in which the behavior and feelings of a soldier are convincingly portrayed and the museum *panneau* comes to life. In one poem, entitled "Archaeology" (*Arkheolohiia*), an encased museum display appears to utter the words "I was killed in a just battle, And buried by a caring family." This is followed by a vision: "I once lived in a simple hut By a lake with bright banks." It is not clear whether the voice comes from within the encased exposition or is that of the lyrical hero. When the poem was first published in *Vistnyk* in 1933, these words were not placed within quotation marks. The confusion appears to be deliberate; the contemporary speaks with the same intonations and expresses the same concerns as the fallen warrior. This manner, which allows Olzhych to successfully open windows or doorways to other worlds, accounts for the enduring power of his poetry.

9

YURII LYPA

Yurii Lypa was raised in Odesa, where he began his university studies in 1917. His father was a well-known writer and public figure who had served thirteen months in a tsarist prison for criticizing the imperial regime and who in 1917 was appointed commissar of Odesa by the new Ukrainian government. Yurii served in the UNR army in the years 1917–18, participating in the battles for Odesa. He emigrated with his father to Poland, where both were interned as prisoners of war. After release, Yurii completed Poznan University in 1929 and then worked as a doctor. He published widely—poetry, prose, essays, cultural-historical studies, and two books on medicine. His studies of Ukraine were influenced by the political geographer Stepan Rudnytsky, the classicist Tadei Zelinsky (Tadeusz Zielinski), and the historian Vadym Shcherbakivsky, with whom he corresponded. Throughout the 1930s Lypa lived in Warsaw. Here, in 1940 he created the Ukrainian Black Sea Institute, which investigated political and economic issues in the Black Sea littoral. It produced dozens of works in the following two years, some of which were destroyed during the war before they could even leave the printer. As the German front retreated, he had the opportunity of traveling west, but chose to return to Ukraine, where he worked for the Ukrainian Insurgent Army (UPA), training medical personnel, preparing leaflets, and tending to the wounded. He was arrested on 19 August 1944, and his body was discovered two days later. He had been tortured by the NKVD, who, as his daughter has recounted, used the method of castration for which they were known (Lypa 2007, 2, 388).

Lypa made his literary reputation with the poetry collections *Svitlist* (Light, 1925), *Suvorist* (Sternness, 1931), and *Viruiu* (Credo, 1938). In the later 1930s he ceased to treat poetry seriously and spoke ironically of his poetic persona in the third person: "my brother the poet" (Livytska-Kholodna 2009, 794). He also produced the novel *Kozaky v Moskovii: Roman iz XVII-ho stolittia* (Cossacks in Muscovy: A Novel of the XVII Century, 1934) and the three-volume collection of short stories *Notatnyk: Noveli* (Notebook: Novellas, 1936–37). His collection of essays, *Bii za ukrainsku literaturu* (The Battle for Ukrainian Literature, 1935) is a manifesto of the revolutionary nationalist spirit in the arts. It was followed by four cultural-political studies that attempt to define Ukraine's role in the modern world: *Ukrainska doba* (The Ukrainian Age, 1936), *Pryznachennia Ukrainy* (The Destiny of Ukraine, 1938), *Chornomorska doktryna* (The Black Sea Doctrine, 1940, 1942, 1947), and *Rozpodil Rosii* (The Partitioning of Russia, 1941). Because of the quality and breadth of Lypa's achievement, he was viewed by many as the leading ideologist of Ukrainian integral nationalism.

The early Lypa was strongly influenced by voluntarism and irrationalism, and in the 1930s he continued to draw inspiration from Italian futurism and Mussolini's writings. In *Pryznachennia Ukrainy* Lypa quotes favorably the Italian leader on "preserving a dose of barbarism in oneself," of not fearing "cold, hunger, and struggle," and the maxim that "a nation that only thinks of comfort cannot be strong." He counterposed these ideas to "primitive, barrack-room Germanism" (a reference to Nazism) and "cheap, mechanistic Stalinism" (Lypa 1953, 12). The style of his *Bii za ukrainsku literaturu* (1935) is assertive, impatient with the rationalistic and appreciative of unusual personal qualities. It is in keeping with his love of individualism and admiration for the rugged, self-sufficiency of the Ukrainian farmer from the southern Steppe. The author rejects passivity; a "dreamy person," he says, "brings chaos, not a worldview" (Lypa 1935, 25). However, he also recognizes that some expressions of individualism, such as neologisms of the futurists, are empty gestures. They are the cheap effects of half-baked avant-gardists and bohemians, among whom he lists the Soviet writers Valeriian Polishchuk and Mikhail Semenko. In 1919 in Kamianets-Podilsk, Lypa and Polishchuk headed the literary group Avanhard (Avant-garde), but came to blows over the latter's evolution toward pro-Soviet positions (Lypa 2007, 2, 382). In *Bii* Lypa defines "anarchy of feelings" as a curse, arguing that literature requires strong sentiments and a sense of the age's rhythms. Contemporary writing, he feels, has shifted from quietism to turbulence and the search for new values (Lypa 1935, 90).

The reading of Western literatures, especially French and English, gradually brought a strong dose of rationalism to Lypa's thinking. He developed a pithy, lucid style reminiscent of French essayists like André Maurois and André Malraux, and his cultural critiques, even when speculative, are always grounded in historical research. His later essays try to synthesize cultural history, to trace patterns, and to systematize. Lypa's literary tastes and his view of tradition were broad. Unlike Dontsov, he admired nineteenth-century writers like Borys Hrinchenko and Kvitka-Osnovianenko. Lypa argued that only by grasping the past as a whole could one perceive the outline of Ukraine's future development. He viewed tradition as acquired over the millennia and was interested in all aspects of the country's cultural legacy, including legal history, relations with the outside world, and traditions of social justice. Accordingly, he lamented the destruction by bolshevism of long-established values that formed the basis of a Ukrainian worldview, among them the importance of family life, the tradition of "not killing without a trial," respect for womanhood, and the privileging of moral over material values. His studies are often a form of cultural anthropology that explores the influence of origins on later developments. In the later 1930s the scholar and anthropologist within him largely displaced the earlier irrationalist.

Lypa viewed mythology as inextricably interwoven with ancient rituals and customs. It was not, he insisted, invented in the contemporary period, "like myths of the German type" (Lypa 1953, 184). German racists were bent on developing a political mythology that would relegate Ukrainians and other Slavs to servility. The Nazis were preparing for a total war, teaching their nation "the style of marching columns" and instilling in them a faith in their own moral sanctities. In order to survive this onslaught, Ukrainians needed to develop their own sense of mission and to rely on their own stock of myths. The task was difficult because few synthetic cultural histories existed. Lypa accordingly attempted in his own writings to provide such a synthetic treatment of national mythology and perceived historical mission. His *Pryznachennia Ukrainy* suggests that in the future, alongside the Anglo-Saxon, Roman, and Germanic, a fourth great "race" will arise in Europe, "the Pontic Ukrainian" (ibid., 300). The term "race" is used to describe a political, not a biological, identity. It represents a method of thinking and feeling, an attachment to a collective past. "Race," he says, "is a great spiritual community in the moral and emotional dimension" (ibid., 125). At the time the word was commonly used in this manner as a synonym for nation.[1]

Lypa's political writings, like his fiction, emphasize the Ukrainian population's ethnic and biological diversity, the product of numerous waves of migration and the coming together of many ethnic groups and cultures over time. He links this diversity to an optimistic faith in the resilience of ordinary people, whose core values and common psychology have repeatedly enabled them to recover from oppressive rule. This resilience is expressed in the wisdom of passive resistance; aware that cells can regenerate, seeds can lay dormant for many years before germinating, Ukrainians have remained confident of their ability to outlive invaders.

Lypa is sometimes assimilated to a racist discourse. Selected pieces from his texts have been used to support the views of groups on the extreme right.[2] The writer engaged in a discussion of the contemporary population's anthropological origins, but he was quick to point out that history, culture, and psychology were more important in shaping identity than these origins. The term "race" meant for him a nation with roots in an *ethnie* — more correctly, several *ethnies*. He used it to demonstrate the existence of a stable Ukrainian identity, a strong collective "ego" that has resisted attempts to manipulate and "re-engineer" it. When he invoked Mendelian genetics in this regard, it was to reject both Hitler's plans for Eastern Europe, and Stalin's pseudosciences, especially the linguistics of Nikolai Marr (who suggested that the languages of the Soviet Union would fuse into one) and the biology of Trofim Lysenko (who argued that acquired characteristics could be passed from one generation to another through heredity). After 1935 all Soviet research into genetics inspired by Johann Gregor Mendel was curtailed. Stalin felt that the work of Darwin and Mendel was too "deterministic." Eventually in 1948 he outlawed the study of genetics as a "bourgeois pseudoscience." Mendel's work, which was first published in 1865 but only became influential at the beginning of the twentieth century, paved the way for the study of genes and the discovery of DNA. Lypa discusses the contemporary fascination with genes and blood groups in his *Pryznachennia Ukrainy* (originally published in 1938) and his *Rozpodil Rosii* (published in 1941 under German occupation). In both books he informs that the main blood groups in Ukraine, as in most of Europe (A, AB, O) differ from the main blood groups in Russia and Siberia (B), and goes on to say that in cases of intermarriage, the first blood group tends to remain dominant. He concludes that "biological anthropology indicates that Russian [*moskvynskoi*] blood is related to the blood of Finno-Mongolian peoples and not to the Western and Southern neighbours" (Lypa 1953, 156). Although he tended to phrase this cautiously, as a tentative finding of foreign and Soviet researchers, it was clearly an attempt to distinguish Ukrainians from Russians, to emphasize the strength of "Ukrainian genes," and to affirm, as he stated in 1937, that "all paths were open" to Ukrainians (Lypa 1937, 10).

His views on race and nation are most pithily stated in the brochure *Ukrainska rasa* (Ukrainian Race, 1937). In it he acknowledges his debt to the historian Vadym Shcherbakivsky, who had focused his studies on the territory that is today's Ukraine and on the history of its various peoples. Lypa explicitly rejects the "biblical" or "purely genealogical" approach to race, which, he says, has nothing in common with science. The concept of race has recently entered scholarship "not as a question of limitation, exclusiveness, something along the lines of Hitler's Germans" (ibid., 19). On the contrary, he says, in the years after 1917–21 the self-image of Ukrainians expanded; they now see themselves as a large people with many and various subgroups. The closest analogy to this kind of self-awareness can be found among the many groups who call themselves British or American (ibid., 20). The traditional focus on language, songs, and embroideries is therefore simplistic and misleading, unless connections are made to the cultures of the Mediterranean, the Hellenes and Rome, the Vikings and Ostrogoths, the Hittites, and so on (ibid.). Lypa may have been influenced by the work of Ksenofont Sosenko, who had learned from Wilhelm Schmidt and Wilhelm Koppers. The latter two scholars were influential in developing comparative cultural anthropology and the idea of Kulturkreise—cultural spheres that originated in antiquity but then expanded and interacted with one another.[3]

Passages in Lypa's writings are used by contemporary right-wing groups to demonstrate his adherence to a "blood and soil" racism. However, when these passages are read alongside others in the same texts, they produce a different argument. For example, the section "Solidaryzm rasy" (Solidarity of the Race) is sometimes lifted from his *Pryznachennia Ukrainy* without reference to the section "Tsilist, vidpornist i nastup rasy" (The Wholeness, Resistance, and Advance of Race).[4] In the latter section, the author lists many prominent figures in Ukrainian history who were not of "Ukrainian" origin. Spiritual-psychological factors were, according to the author, the key to their integration. These factors include respect for the people, empathy for their psychology and traditions, and a refusal of "denationalization" (Lypa 1953, 164–68). In a couple of respects this passage flatly opposes the writings of the OUN. Lypa comments that contrary to what "pure Nationalism would demand" Ukrainians have retained their identity in far-flung places like the Amur and Bessarabia, where they had no elite to guide them (ibid., 167). Their traditions were sufficiently strong to preserve a sense of identity. The statement might be contrasted with the OUN's belief that a leadership had to "forge" a nation out of an amorphous "ethnographic mass," turning "iron into tempered steel" ("*Realna*" 1933, 11, 14). Confident in the wisdom of the masses, Lypa does not dismiss those among his countrymen who in the 1920s supported Lev Trotsky or Mykola Skrypnyk in factional struggles among bolsheviks. These were strategies of survival in Soviet conditions. In a similar fashion, Lypa refuses to dismiss the many nineteenth-century intellectuals who devoted themselves to building a Ukrainian spirit, a process he describes as driven by an admirable, stubborn, "ant-like" instinct of construction (Lypa 1953, 241). He argues that the socialists should not simply be blamed for the defeat of 1917–20 but also praised for the struggle they put up: "Many who died for Ukrainian socialism were strong characters who can only be treated with respect." Readers are asked to recall that socialist and collectivist myths played a role in Christianity and the humanist renaissance. It was only the "perversity of Marxism" that injected class hatred into them (ibid., 257–58). Needless to say, these views were anathema to the OUN, who presented themselves as belonging to a "new world," a new breed of Ukrainian. They viewed Soviet Ukrainian leaders like Skrypnyk as agents of Moscow, and the Ukrainianization policy as a "spiritual enslavement" that was a greater threat to the nation than open chauvinism because it masked the reality of denational-ization ("*Realna*" 1933, 11).

Lypa makes anti-Jewish comments when discussing Jews who in his opinion did the bidding of the Russian majority in the Communist Party. In these instances he is less forgiving than he is toward Skrypnyk and other Soviet Ukrainian leaders, who are viewed as at least attempting to resist the pressures of the Moscow center. However, when he discusses Jews in his *Pryznachennia Ukrainy*, he makes the point that according to a number of scholars, they do not constitute a separate race in purely biological terms: like other distinct peoples, they have over the centuries assimilated individuals from various racial groups. He goes on to describe the positive attitude toward Jewish traders held by Kyivan princes like Sviatopolk and Yaroslav the Wise, the importance of Jews in the development of the Cossack state (including the administration of Bohdan Khmelnytsky), and the positive role played by many Jews in modern Ukrainian literature and politics (Lypa 1953, 151–52). He reminds Dontsov that the latter defended the Jews against antisemitic Ukrainian nationalists in 1911 and against Kyiv's antisemites in 1906, and laments the fact that the Russian Black Hundreds infected the tsarist administration in Ukraine with their views and spread fabri-cations like the *Protocols of the Elders of Zion* (ibid., 152).

Lypa devotes attention to the popular wisdom encoded in myths. The folk tale of Kyrylo Kozhumiaka teaches that solidarity is expected of all, from a prince to a lowly tanner. On the request of the ruler Volodymyr, the tanner (Kozhumiaka or Kozhemiaka) rescues Kyiv, the Eternal City, from a dragon who represents the enemy. In Lypa's view, this tale characterizes the demo-cratic spirit of Ukrainians. The myth of Japheth indicates the culture's enor-mous self-confidence at the time it was settling the Steppe. In the seventeenth century Ukrainians carried their religion and identity on their banners as they moved into new territories. As in Olzhych's work, the figure of Japheth is inter-preted as a myth of origins, one that had already appeared in Inokentii Gisel's seventeenth-century *Synopsis* as the ideological justification for Cossack expan-sionism. Gisel, according to Lypa, portrayed the Cossack elite as the sons of Japheth, inheritors of great military traditions. Another myth of origins dates back to the earliest days of Christianity in Ukraine. It is that of St. Andrew planting a cross on the hills of Kyiv and prophesying that a great city would arise there. Lypa interprets this as a demonstration of the Ukrainian people's desire "to hold their own dialogue with God," to possess "a mystery for their race alone" and a church that could spread unity and love among the people (ibid., 294, 298). Such positive myths are prominent in his poetry; they challenge the tone of Dontsov's *Natsionalizm*, which, he says, represents a "brilliant lyrical reaction to the passivity of Ukrainians" but offers no deeper synthesis of Ukrainian thought. It merely mirrors the bolshevism that it attacks, and in this sense constitutes Marxism's twin. Like bolshevism, it is driven by hatred and a need to bring about "the race's internal destruction" (ibid., 259). Dontsov's great achievement in the years 1922–32, Lypa says, was to expose Soviet propaganda, but after Stalin's terror opened the eyes of even the blindest, Dontsov could propose nothing that might challenge the Soviet ideal of "a new man." The editor of *Vistnyk* could not play a constructive role because he did not understand that the Ukrainian people had their own historical character, but viewed them as a hybrid species, a mixture of Polish and Muscovite elements, a bastard nation, from whose "defeatist" traditions he wished to sever himself (ibid., 278). The problem, argues Lypa, is Dontsov's inability to treat Ukraine as a developing historical organism. Instead, the editor of *Vistnyk* merely dismisses the people as unable to live up to his expectations.

Lypa points out that some important Ukrainian myths are of literary origin. For example, the story of Alexander the Great, which was widespread throughout Asia Minor, Mesopotamia, and Turkestan, was a favorite reading of the Cossack class and Kyiv's elite until the eighteenth century. It portrays the leader of the Greeks as modest and thoughtful, the embodiment of moral virtues. The contemporary interest in myth is, in his opinion, driven by a similar desire to ennoble but is best characterized as an oppressed people's need to create a counterhistory. His own imagined Ukraine is beautiful, mysterious, and terrible, an answer, Livytska-Kholodna thought, to Malaniuk's captive raped by invaders and to Dontsov's beast without a head (Livytska-Kholodna 2009, 796–97). In his *Ukrainska doba* (The Ukrainian Age, 1936) Lypa criticizes Dontsov for overwhelmingly stressing the negative, especially hatred of foreigners and contempt for native tradition. Every writer outside the *Vistnyk* group, he says, has been rejected by the editor, a fact that prompts the suggestion that a Ukrainian Dante, Shakespeare, or Kipling, if they appeared, would also be denounced as lacking "absolute dynamism." Dynamism for its own sake can be nothing but destructive. In fact, says Lypa, there is no way of living up to the editor's standards of "abstract dynamism" because these are not sensibly defined (Lypa 1936, 13). Dontsov responded to this essay by declaring that Lypa's desire to view his compatriots with a "loving heart" had placed him in the enemy camp (Dontsov 1936b, 382). The age demanded "the sharp sword of criticism, so that the rotten might be severed from the healthy, the old from the new, the puny from the strong" (ibid., 385). As has been seen, in this exchange both Teliha and Mosendz supported Dontsov. When Lypa responded in *Pryznachennia Ukrainy*, a review jointly written by Yendyk, O. Lahutenko and Dontsov attacked the book for rejecting German militarism and for an "eclectic, people-loving" worldview (Ie. L. D. 1938, 912). Dontsov later repeated this attack in his *Dukh nashoi davnyny*.

Pryznachannia Ukrainy, Lypa's most extensive critique of Dontsovism, refuses to dismiss the masses, whom the author praises for their resistance to bolshevism in 1917–20. More than other writers who were close to the OUN, Lypa was favorably disposed toward spontaneous revolts. Teliha, Olzhych, and Malaniuk, on the other hand, felt strongly that anarchy and individualism had been the bane of Ukraine's political history. The masses, in Lypa's view, always exhibited a remarkably strong sense of belonging to a collective and struggled to preserve their cultural, scholarly, and military elites. They have over the centuries demonstrated an extraordinary capacity for self-organization, mainly because of traditions that have been passed down through many generations. Like the Jews, who have maintained a sense of enduring presence in this world, Ukrainians sense their distinctiveness and deep-rooted identity. The tradition of solidarity, the people's moral conservatism and faith in its own myths are causes for optimism. In his view, moral conservatism is a good thing insofar as it strengthens resistance to the inhuman social experimentation of both Nazis and bolsheviks. He mentions that a *Vistnyk* writer once lamented that "Ukrainians have no inclination for Baltic or Ural mysticism, and it is not easy to 'shift them from their place'" (Lypa 1953, 197). Lypa responds that this immovability is a strength and states that the "Nietzschean bombast" of Malaniuk and Teliha, and the desire to discredit the past in favor of the present have both proven ineffective (ibid., 21, 242).

In short, whereas Dontsov looked back in anger, Lypa did so with appreciation. According to Lypa, strong voluntary associations had always been the Ukrainian strength. He saw the people as naturally opposed to regimentation and exploitation. Popular solidarity expressed itself in economic organizations (cooperatives, the *chumak* trading convoys), in education (the Prosvita society, Cossack brotherhoods), and in the military. Ukrainians had their own love of beauty, which was expressed in dress, music, and decoration, and in a Hellenic yearning for harmony and utopia. The individual was allowed to find his or her place within the greater collective. Lypa contrasts this with the approach of *Vistnyk* writers, whose "frenzied intolerance toward others shows how far they are from understanding real individualism" (ibid., 188). Ukrainians, he says, are resistant to the radical psychological experimentation favored by Vistnykites. The Don Quixote admired by the latter is superficial, because he believes that everything is clear and straightforward, and that "absolute dynamism" will solve all problems (ibid., 243).

The *chumaks* are Lypa's favorite example of self-organization. These traders traveled in wagon convoys sometimes 100–300 strong to the Black Sea and were organized for self-defense. In 1856 there were 17,500 *chumaks* in the Kyiv region alone and their convoys accounted for two-thirds of the transportation from the ports of the Black and Azov Seas. The *chumaks* acted as businessmen and financiers. Their struggle for civil rights and freedoms was part of the long struggle of Ukrainian merchant associations that reached into the distant past. A genius for self-organization also exhibited itself in the mass action during 1917–20, when powerful military organizations appeared spontaneously. The same genius expressed itself in the readiness of Ukrainians to form cooperatives and self-education networks. Even in artistic life Ukrainians have tended to prefer associative structures: the choir, the cooperative of kobzars, the Vertep, carol singers, and so on. Ukrainians, according to Lypa, reject great "experimenters" like Napoleon, Peter the Great, or Genghis Khan. Their heroes express the "yearnings and labor of many generations" (ibid., 177). Consequently the people despise tsars, despots, and führers.

For Lypa, psychology and cultural memory play a primary role in creating the national community. As the term "Pontic" implies, he considers the ancient cultures of the Black Sea littoral to be the foundation on which Ukrainian civilization has arisen. These cultures include the Trypillian, the Hellenic, and the Gothic. The Trypillia is the most ancient. The Pontic or Hellenic brought maritime traditions, trade, and the arts. The Gothic taught the values of military and political organization. All three have flowed into today's culture and civilization. This genealogy represents a different conception of Ukrainian history from that of the Vistnykites. Lypa calls Malaniuk "defeatist" for demanding that "the organic blossom of the centuries" be destroyed (ibid., 18). In Lypa's view it is precisely the organic and the unconscious that forms the foundation of national psychology, and it can be seen operating in collective reflexes that are immediately understood by everyone (ibid.). These collective rhythms, he says, have not been adequately understood by psychological theory. He rejects Dontsov's fulminations against the danger of unchanging elements in the nation, because these elements are precisely the ones driving the popular struggle. Bolshevik Russia's attacks on tradition and the Ukrainian way of life have mobilized the deepest survival instincts within ordinary people. Moscow sees the "organic" as its greatest enemy, a challenge to its wish to manufacture a mechanistic collective. Organic links between contemporary Ukraine and its ancient past do exist, argues Lypa, as the study of archaeology, banned or persecuted under the Soviets, reveals. Some studies show that the settlement and behavior patterns of the ancient and medieval world can be related to contemporary psychology.

These ideas are embodied in his fiction. His novel *Kozaky v Moskovii: Roman iz XVII-ho stolittia* (Cossacks in Muscovy: A Novel of the XVII Century, 1934) describes the adventures of a brave, enterprising group of Cossacks in Muscovy during Khmelnytsky's time. Their knightly ethos is contrasted with tsarism's brutality and xenophobia. Lypa shows that Latin was at the time not only part of the Kyiv elite's culture, but had penetrated the world of ordinary Cossacks and produced what he calls elsewhere "a fusion of the Rus and Roman spirit" (Lypa 1997, 114). Lypa himself had an expert knowledge of the Cossack state's literary language, with its strong admixture of Latin terms. He uses this language in the novel and in his poetry to popularize archaic elements. This was not a form of embellishment or ornamentation (his writing is laconic and direct) but represents, in Malaniuk's words, "the discovery of an entire epoch in the historical-linguistic process" (Malaniuk 2009, 622).

The travelers are happy to return to their own people, among whom individual and collective liberties are valued. They witness Khmelnytsky holding court in 1650, at the height of his power. One protagonist is deeply moved during a church service to God's glory and the "emperor of the great Rus." As he listens, he swells with pride and his private troubles dissolve. He has a vision of an enormous Cossack lion with its head above the clouds, which roars and stretches its "iron paw over its rich land" (Lypa 1934, 234). This idea of a powerful country unified under monarchical rule is meant to reassure readers of a strong identity able to deal with a threat from the north.

The three-volume prose collection *Notatnyk: Noveli* (Notebook: Novellas, 1936–37) is set in Southern Ukraine and draws on the author's experiences in the 1917–18 struggle for independence. The stories blend political realism with an idealism that draws on courtly love and medieval legends. The main protagonists often appear to be reincarnations of princesses, knights, St. George, or the heroes of folk tales. "Ruban," the opening story, describes a simple man of the soil who becomes a great partisan leader. He is part of the partisan forces associated with Kholodny Yar, Vovche Horlo, and Chorny Lis—the great hiding places of revolutionaries over the centuries. Ruban's army consists of villagers who are implacable opponents of bolshevism. They command widespread support and exhibit a proud, unbending nature. These are not the cowed peasants of Russia, comments one bolshevik leader, who realizes that only after the

Ukrainian village has been terrorized and reduced to indigency like the Russian village, will bolshevism triumph and shape society in the way it desires (Lypa 1936, 1, 14). Ruban escapes a sadistic Cheka execution squad and vows to fight the invaders. He develops effective tactics and controls the countryside around Yelizavethrad (Elizavetgrad). Strict discipline is maintained among his fighters, while among the invading bolsheviks there are thieves, cocaine-sniffers, and outright sadists. Because Ruban is not interested in establishing a government, after he takes Yelizavethrad he merely eliminates foreign communists. He represents the freedom-loving southern homesteader whose ancestors escaped service to a lord in order to build independent lives and who has never known serfdom. This is the world in which the philosophy of anarchism has taken root. Lypa, who was sympathetic toward Nestor Makhno's anarchism, describes Ruban in terms that recall the latter. Even Zinoviev's brother, the reader is told, is leading an anarchist party among local people. The communists understand that they must break this "elemental peasant force" (ibid., 37). One of them, Finkelshtein, has a dream in which Ruban and his army of greens appear as a terrifying Goliath who crushes him. Finkelshtein, like the other bolsheviks, fears the Steppe, which constantly menaces them.

Ruban's forces include seasoned fighters of various nationalities, some of whom have come from distant parts of Ukraine. They draw strength from a rural resourcefulness and devotion to the land. The communist Upornikov, who is tracking Ruban, recognizes that these people are disciplined, hardened soldiers. The greens simply describe themselves as "the earth." As they leave the city, they sing the folk song "Yarema" as an act of self-affirmation. Ruban allies himself with the UNR armies, but cannot stomach the world of military bureaucracy, provisioning, government, and subordination. Eventually he leaves, although his soldiers remain. Serbetsky, the senior officer in the UNR, comments that strong characters like Ruban have to learn hierarchy and obedience: "Because we are faced with great issues. We have to carve and adapt our Rubans. The time for romantic wildness is over. Everything has to be ploughed, built up, planned out. We will construct railways, lay out highways, connect everything, uniting it into one. We will throw bridges across rivers and marshes. We will awaken the city and the village; we will set a fast pace, an implacable one. Enough of thatched roofs—we will have metal in the villages. Enough of cherry orchards—we will make everyone a competitor, a racehorse. We will straighten and tidy the villages all along the highways" (ibid., 65–66).

And yet, this same Serbetsky is moved to tears by the loss of Ruban. "People are hay," he says, "people are straw, but I have lost a haymaker, I need the haymaker" (ibid., 69). It becomes clear that Serbetsky, whose grandparents were *chumaks*, grasps the importance of freedom to Ruban and understands his contempt for bureaucracies, governments, and intellectuals. He spends two days trying to convince the rebel leader to join the army: "I explained to him the great world that is emerging before us, Ukrainians. I explained that the days of salt trading and Cossackdom are over [. . .], that we have no greater task than to entrench ourselves on our own land, to root ourselves here, to establish our own justice. I told him as a brother that here in this human sea, in this dangerous storm, we must gain control of the elements for [the creation of] a strong state, the strongest" (ibid., 70).

Serbetsky understands that his failure to convince Ruban represents an inability to integrate part of Ukraine, and comments: "I tell you, gentlemen [. . .] that with the Rubans of this world one could build empires" (ibid., 71). Eventually Ruban is captured by the Whites, who are unable to recruit him. The Russian general finds this puzzling: "Your attachment to Petliura is strange. Chimeras, folk tales, kobzas, banduras . . . What chance does he have against all of Russia?" When Ruban replies that he will not go "against his own people," the general hangs him in Yelizavethrad's marketplace with a board attached to him on which is written: "Here hangs Ruban, destroyer of the Russian people" (ibid., 76).

The story is deeply ambivalent toward peasant revolts, which are both admired for their strength and criticized for their political impotence. Although capable of breaking down the old, they are incapable of engaging in the crucial task of state building.

"Koval Suprun" (Suprun the Blacksmith) has a similar structure. Here the main protagonist understands the city as exploitative and perverted, a place that produces wars and oppression. He is a gifted inventor and constructor, able to manufacture bicycles and equipment almost out of nothing: "I can set up a water-pump. I can make a steam kitchen. Maybe I could even make a steam engine [. . .] You just have to push me, set me onto something, and I'll do it. Just show me what. I can do anything!" (ibid., 2, 7). His skills make him capable of surviving in the modern world. After reading Shevchenko he becomes convinced that the Ukrainian nation needs to awaken from its dream and recognize that it is being plundered. Conscripted into the Russian fleet, he becomes a revolutionary leader and directs his anger against the city, but like Ruban, he fails to understand the need to become part of the urban world: "The village did not wage war; it destroyed. In the same way as it once scattered the nests of wintering snakes, drove braying foxes from their dens, dug pits with sharp stakes for clumsy bears. It destroyed without thinking; it destroyed enthusiastically" (ibid., 26). However, even after the various imperial government officials have been driven out, the hated city culture endures. When Suprun's revolutionary sailors discover the library of a Frenchman who is hiding in an estate abandoned by the lord, Suprun's reaction is to destroy the books:

> He was destroying the content of the lives in these wasps' nests. He bent down, grabbed the nearest volume in his right hand, and opened it with a single blow on the back, the way children break open water-melons on the floor. Holding the candle high, he looked, waiting for an appearance.
>
> He made out separate words on the yellowed paper, names and illustrations. Images of new and old uniforms danced before his eyes, battles and maps, lawmakers with rolls of papers in their hands, cold masks, busts [. . .]
>
> Most often in those books he found fauns and satyrs, giggling indecent gods entwined in garlands. Among the artificial red roses, lascivious young ladies and gentlemen peered with cunning, wicked, cat-like faces. They lisped sweetly, jumped gracefully, wove themselves into mathematical formulas, history, natural sciences, and veterinary manuals. (Ibid., 33)

In order to "drive out the old," he orders the books burned. They represent the foreign and exploitative. When news of the tsar's abdication arrives, he raises a white flag, announces that the snakes have been squelched and that a "blessed new world" has arrived (ibid., 36). The story is both a celebration and critique of the greens, after the manner of Soviet authors like Khvylovy, Yanovsky, and Pidmohylny. It expresses the plight of a generation that fought heroically for a better world only to be disenchanted.

"Zustrich literatoriv" (Meeting of Writers) strikes a note of contempt for unengaged intellectuals. An old writer meets a novice. Fighting is going on in the streets and countryside. The young man is a typical lyricist, "like most Ukrainian writers," but the old writer has become convinced that the days of this kind of literature are over:

> "I am a descendant of our old Ukrainian gentry, the Ukrainophiles, the Ukrainian radicals, the end of a small rivulet that trickles and murmurs to this day but can no longer be a stream. Today—listen to these bullets—the people are speaking. It is he, who has lived until now like a sleepwalker, a colossal sleepwalker who under foreign rule has been taking control of more and more lands. He has now begun to speak.
>
> I am no historian but I think that after gaining the sea, filling all contested surrounding lands, marking firm boundaries, the giant sleepwalker has awoken, and the time has come for his greatest achievement and creative work—the state. We are beginning, maybe on a grand scale for the first time since Batyi's invasion . . . As for me? My creativity? It was linked to my time. My time, however, was a small one, a small time." (Ibid., 1, 87)

The old writer laments that the intellectuals of his day tilted at windmills, wrote about oppressed peasants, lived like aesthetes, each on his or her own Mount Athos. Writers must find the contemporary world "perhaps in heroes, perhaps in the courageous, perhaps merely in bandits, but always in people" (ibid.). In the final paragraph, the young writer leaves his scattered papers and jottings, and sets off with a message for an army commander. In this way he completes the mission of a wounded soldier unable to travel any farther and joins the military struggle.

Modernist influences are evident in the narrative style, which is fast paced, focused on action, and full of strong impressions. The meaning is revealed only after the reader has pieced together fragmented scenes and dialogues. There are surrealistic dream sequences and moments of distorted perception. In "Hryniv," for example, the sick and dying hero has an out-of-body experience during which he appears to relive his youth in Galicia. He approaches several young ladies and asks them to join him in a dignified aristocratic dance but is informed by them that he has died.

Biological vitality is a feature of Lypa's characterization. His main protagonists are driven by an overpowering life energy, and his mass uprisings are treated as natural phenomena. Sexuality is viewed unsentimentally. In "Hannusia" the woman spends a short time with a handsome fighter who visits the village. The liaison is viewed as natural and inevitable: "These people probably treat the life of woman in this way: they throw her across the saddle in front of them without laughter, and speak without pity. They ride and their eyes show alarm. Then suddenly one of them turns pale, leans sideways and falls from the stirrups somewhere in the Steppe, and the horse carries off the life of the woman hanging across the saddle, further and further" (ibid., 123). Descriptions like these drew Teliha's charge of erotomania.

Although machismo is admired, it is subjected to a critique. In his essays Lypa advances a cult of womanhood. He dismisses the futurists and bohemians, who live in a café culture and view sexuality as merely animal attraction. Men, he says, have to "master" their instincts (Lypa 1935, 141). He encourages gallantry and celebrates woman as muse, patriot, and mother. However, he indicates that war leaves no time for sentimentality. In "Bliashanky" (Tin Cans), a woman attaches herself to a group of UNR fighters. She carries with her tin cans, with which she plans to minister to them if they catch typhoid. Although they tolerate her presence for a while, they eventually send her away. As he drives her off, a young soldier sees in her the image of his own mother. "Kinnotchyk" strikes a similar note: the soldier leaves the woman who has nursed him back to health when he meets up with his fellow soldiers, his true comrades.

Lypa's construction of Ukrainian womanhood is an important part of his fiction. The story "Hryniv" celebrates Odesa as a multicultural city and contains a hymn to its women:

> Sometimes it seemed to him, the seafarer, that women emerged before him one by one like islands half-gilded by the sun's rays. They blossomed in a greeting and disappeared again into greyness, silence, eternal immobility in the running, moving sea. Each was a loud resonance of the Southern nature, a sincere reflection of the surrounding world—and in this way he grasped this world.
>
> Ukrainian women looked with Scythian, silent eyes, allowed no boldness in their words, defended themselves and did not react to advances. When they selected someone, they opened up to the chosen one suddenly, without preludes, without words, like a hot, stormy, pitiless natural force. Hryniv got to know them, the local young ladies full of naïve freshness and the strength of their womanhood, young ladies who were themselves somewhat bemused by the strength and excess of joy with which their steps rang.
>
> There were intellectuals among them, heads radiant with passion, in which socialism mixed with piracy. There were sharp-tongued, cheerful officers' wives, who valued only courage and play. There were many light-footed, agile, petite, bosomy women of the independent homesteads, who look the same throughout Ukraine. And there were simple settler women, perhaps descendants of proud Cossack generations, who were passionate in their domestic vigilance, faithful to family and husband, cold in defeat, explosive in victory.
>
> Sometimes there was a hint of another local bloodline, one that stemmed from vengeful and ambitious Greeks, lazy and attractive Moldavians, or flinty and naïve Tatars. Hryniv met tall, dark-blonde urbanites from Kyiv with fluid graceful movements, coquettish Podillians noisy in their chattering, thin-nostrilled, aquiline-nosed, trusting ladies from Kuban Cossack villages, and bright-lipped, mocking women from beyond the seas. The blood of Genoa, Hellas, Iran or Asia Minor flowed in the veins of more than one. In their fragrant breath and quiet laughter Hryniv heard the music of distant seas and gardens. (Lypa 1936–37, 3, 53–54)

The Ukrainian woman is here synthesized out of fragments in a manner typical of modernism. Diversity is celebrated and appropriated. Hryniv the flaneur searches in womanly charms for connections to the mysterious, mythical world of the Ukrainian south. The women are culture creators engaged in building, protecting, and developing the city, homestead, settlement, and village. Their civilizational role and connection to nature make them powerful. Their passion is an elemental force, frank and unabashed.

The writer's ideas on women and femininity were expressed in his "Ukrainska zhinka" (Ukrainian Woman, 1938), an essay published in Milena Rudnytska's newspaper *Zhinka*. In it Lypa interprets the Ukrainian marriage tradition as a union of equals, a partnership and alliance. He refers to the folk song in which the word *druzhyna* (spouse, partner, ally) is used to signal a friend equal before God. This differs from the "chaos and primitivism" of other cultures, which emphasize the satisfaction of physiological needs. The Ukrainian woman is an integral part of the heroic, martial tradition. Many women have defended the honor and glory of Ukraine by taking the place of their fallen brothers, and many have demonstrated their ability to die "like warriors." He points out that the line of warriorlike women in Ukrainian history stretches from sixteenth-century Volhynian amazon-princesses like Maria Holshanska, Hanna Mylska, and Hanna Borzobohata-Krasenska to Matviienko, who led revolutionary partisans in the independence struggle. He admires the strong personalities of the artist Maria Bashkirtseva, and the writers Natalia Kobrynska and Olena Pchilka—all pathblazers of Ukrainian culture.

However, this is not woman's main role: "Even the Amazons, this proto-Ukrainian tribe that lived alone and devoted itself to war and hunting, did not, according to Hellenic descriptions, retreat permanently from the world and did not remain military professionals. Even they eventually found fine, remarkable boys, with whom they fell in love and whom they married" (ibid.). Lypa therefore allows women to be both amazon warriors and mothers. Women possess a superior understanding of love, which they use to guide men and shield them from instinct's dangers, to "arrange harmoniously the brutality and irregularity caused by the eruption of feelings" (ibid.). This role has been sanctified by custom and tradition. He praises America for allowing women to play leading roles in government and politics while still enabling them to raise children. In short, the experience of motherhood gives women a spiritual strength, endurance, and understanding that men do not possess.

He claims for Ukrainian women a "greater individuality" than allowed in many other nations and a greater awareness of passion. The woman in "Hryniv" understands that her lovers are fated to die in combat, but this only makes her love greater; it is "perhaps the deepest love, a love filled with bitterness" (Lypa 1936–37, 3, 67). Female students who bring food and clothing to Ukrainian prisoners also act with dignity when they are executed by the Russian White Army.

Lypa views culture as the product of two poles, the masculine and feminine, each of which is equally valuable and necessary. Men and women each have their job to do: "It is not possible, for example, to describe the Zaporozhians as exclusively a military organization (the masculine element), because they were also simultaneously one of the best organized economic-trade enterprises (the female element)" (Lypa 1938, 4). This view of women contradicts Nazi mythology, what he calls the "Baltic, mystical" beliefs that obscure Ukrainian realities. In the Ukrainian tradition women have always had a special role: to "cement, steady, and balance Ukrainian spiritual life" (ibid.,). Since the time of Trypillia and its matriarchal civilization, the woman and mother have been at the center of Ukrainian spirituality. Man's equal, she plays the key role in shaping a harmonious culture responsive to community needs.

Lypa expressed admiration for Maria Dontsova, Dontsov's wife, whom he met in 1924. They corresponded regularly over the next three years. From Lviv she sent him packages of sweetbreads, chocolates, drinks, and sausage. On 24 April 1924, after one such gift he wrote: "Your greeting could have made me rejoice greatly. Creative cookies, fragrant paska-breads—this is too much. But the package contained only a slip of paper with "Dontsova" written on it—this is too little. In any case I will never forget this. At least as long as I continue eating it. And with my appetite these days that will take a long time. I do not have time to think about eating [. . .] P.S. Madam Mariika, I am very grateful to you for your attention, for your support, for the expedited present, but—could you not do this in some other way?" (TsDAVO, f. 3849, op. 1, spr. 17, ark. 62). Throughout 1924 Lypa played the role of the gallant knight, writing amusing, sometimes flirtatious letters: "I silently kiss the tips of your all-knowing (poetry, culinary art and . . .) fingers" (ibid., 60, 60b), "I think you could be close to me, but I have left many and will leave many more" (ibid., 63b, 64). He signed one letter: "Your Grace's footstool" (ibid., 65). That summer she invited him to spend time with her in the mountains "without any consequences!" and he agreed to do so "without consequences" (ibid., 66). Lypa described his English and French lessons, his desire to learn the tango, his tennis playing and rowing, and his search for writers who used a vigorous, forceful language and had a broad worldview. He told her that he found more of this in medieval literature's apocrypha and Alexandrines than in contemporary writing (BN, f. 3849, op. 1, spr. 18, ark. 56, 56b). In Maria Dontsova he appears to have found a sophisticated and graceful modern woman who acted both as friend and courtly lover.

The final chapter in Lypa's evolution took place during the war. In the week following Poland's defeat in September 1939, he headed the Ukrainian Aid Committee (Ukrainskyi Dopomohovyi Komitet) in Warsaw, which liaised with the German occupation and tried to help escapees from Soviet-controlled territories, but he soon resigned this position. He appears to have tried to influence German attitudes by publishing his cultural-political studies, which stress the strategic importance of Ukraine and its potential as a state power. In 1943–44 he wrote a series of articles for *Krakivski visti*. Even though the newspaper was subject to German censorship and compelled to print propaganda, its writers often used coded language to convey messages of hope in desperate times. Lypa's serialized essay "Mizh dvoma svitohliadamy" (Between Two Worldviews) belongs to this category. In a manner that recalls Oswald Spengler's *Decline of the West* (1922) he develops the idea of successive cultural cycles. The earlier world of the Homestead, which represented a strong moral order based on tradition and custom, died in 1917. A new world and historical cycle, which he calls the Leap, has arrived. Technology has displaced literature, philosophy, and romantic folklore. The imperatives are education, catching up with the West, and the acceleration of life. The new world has given rise to Ukrainian cooperatives, credit unions, scholars, and scientists. Writers like Yanovsky, Mykola Kulish, and Malaniuk have given it literary form. Lypa writes that concepts like international proletarian solidarity, or fascism's pan-European union conceal "an emotional anticipation of reward, of heaven, to be won in a single leap" (Lypa 1943–44, 31 December 1943.) This represents a description of modernity's political and cultural drive. However, this new world has now produced a desperate struggle for survival. Readers are informed that they must try to endure and hope for a better future. A third worldview is only beginning to emerge, one that he calls the Metropolis. It looks with equanimity at the Homestead's individualism and the logical pursuits of the Leap. While the people of the Homestead were excited by lyrical feelings, and those of the Leap by revolutionary pathos, the people of the Metropolis obtain their greatest satisfaction from mass rhythms, from working steadily in harmony. This world is driven by the vision of a new rightful order and a liberated family. Will the promised land of the Metropolis ever come? Millions have been sent to Siberia by Moscow, and millions more have been sent to work in Germany. The present looks long and dark, but other nations have survived greater losses. (Lypa here suggests, but does not mention, the genocide of the Jews). What is happening to Ukrainians, he consoles, has happened to every great people that has emerged stronger from a catastrophic experience. Civil wars tore Rome apart, but from them emerged the Roman Empire; internecine strife and destruction preceded England's conquest of great spaces. Ukraine, he insists, will one day be the cornerstone of the new Metropolis. Although years of war have deadened human feelings, "precisely because we are people, the humane will shine forth again with even greater force than in previous worldviews" (ibid., 14 January 1944). These last articles offer hope that a better civilization will spring from the ruins of war, that the people "will regenerate from below," with "a desire for their own Metropolis" (ibid.).

The historian Mykhailo Antonovych made some perceptive comments about Lypa in 1945. He wrote that the writer evolved to the point where he had no need to abuse Ukrainian socialists, or Drahomanov, or Lypynsky, but was able to extract what was valuable from these people and to understand that they all represented various paths taken by the same process of development. Antonovych described Lypa's ideas as a "synthetic Ukrainianness" (TsDAHO, f. 269, op. 2, spr. 33, ark. 111). Lypa belonged to a generation that viewed its identity without needing to look through the eyes of other "brotherly" peoples. As a consequence, "they perceived and digested foreign influences differently from people who had suddenly discovered that they were Ukrainian during 1917–20. Dontsov still had to use fierce chauvinism to try and convince himself that he was Ukrainian. Lypa could be nothing else [but a Ukrainian]; he found chauvinism meaningless; he was already looking for the nation's mission" (ibid.).

ULAS SAMCHUK

Ulas Samchuk grew up in Volhynia and joined the UVO in the early 1920s. In 1924 he attempted to cross the border into Soviet Ukraine, hoping to participate in the Ukrainianization campaign. He was arrested by Polish authorities and imprisoned for half a year, an experience that is portrayed in his novel *Kulak*. In 1927 he deserted from the Polish army and made his way to Germany, where he attended Breslau (Wroclaw) University, then moved to Prague, where he enrolled in the Ukrainian Free University. Here he wrote his best works: *Mesnyky* (Avengers, 1931–32); *Kulak* (1929–35; as a separate book 1937); *Hory hovoriat* (The Hills Speak, 1932–33; as separate book 1934); *Vidnaidenyi rai* (Heaven Rediscovered, 1936); *Volyn* (Volhynia, 1934–38); and *Maria* (1952). *Volyn* gained him recognition as the leading Ukrainian prose writer outside the Soviet Union. *Iunist Vasylia Sheremety* (Vasyl Sheremeta's Youth, 1946–47) was also written in the 1930s but published after the war. Although never formally a member of the OUN, he published in the organization's periodicals. His *Mesnyky* (Avengers) appeared anonymously in the years 1931–32 in *Surma* and separately under the pseudonym Olha Volynianka as a publication of the UVO. In 1938–39 he worked for the Carpatho-Ukrainian state. Like Olzhych, Chyrsky, Horlis-Horskyi, and other literary figures who moved to the territory to support the drive for independence, he gave lectures and wrote for newspapers. When in 1941 Germany invaded the Soviet Union, he accompanied Olena Teliha into Ukraine and worked as the first editor of *Volyn*, the Ukrainian newspaper in Rivne. In his wartime editorials, articles, and speeches he attempted to rally the population to anti-Soviet positions and the cause of independence.

His fiction records the development of the new Nationalist ideology. *Mesnyky* describes six men and one woman who participate in revolutionary work on behalf of the national cause. In attempts to trigger an uprising, they set fires and attack a Polish army barrack. Each individual recounts their suffering at the hands of Poles or bolsheviks. Sacred space is important: the setting is "the ancient Ukrainian land of Volhynia," and the ravine in which the outlaws hide is where the Derevliany tribe and a medieval prince once lived. An old monastery recalls a distant age. However, that time has long faded from memory and "our once invincible, strong, broad-shouldered men" are now slaves who have dutifully borne "the yoke of their shameful subjection for centuries" (Samchuk 2009, 320). The contemporary revolt is compared to battles with Tatar invaders, the eighteenth-century revolts of the *haidamakas*,[1] and the war with the bolsheviks. In all these cases the ravine was a place of refuge for those who sought to avenge atrocities committed against their people. In this way the stories suggest the inevitable transformation through violence of "pariahs, forgotten by God and man" into a people who can take its rightful place among European nations. The message is that the foreigners who rule this broken people with contempt have to be removed.

Kulak narrates a psychological transformation. The main protagonist is a hard new man. His roots lie in a rural or small-town community, but he is enthralled by the glamorous European city and desperately wishes his own country to join this modern world. A fervent leftist, he wants to participate in Soviet Ukraine's cultural construction but is captured by border guards and spends time in a Polish jail. Here he learns from other prisoners about bolshevik reality. Transformed by this experience, he turns his talents to self-development, becomes a successful businessman, and runs into conflict with his former communist comrades. In this way the novel records a generation's evolution from socialist to nationalist views. It is clear to the hero Lev that the towns and cities need to become Ukrainian, and the people need to be organized. One source of strength and self-confidence lies in the kulak, a word Samchuk uses to mean independent rather than rich peasant. In this way he challenges communist usage, in which it was a term of abuse for any private farmer. James Mace explains: "The regime always identified the kulaks as its main enemy in the countryside, an omnipresent foe whose role in the Bolshevik world view was comparable to that of the Jews in Nazi ideology: evil incarnate" (Mace 1983, 282). During the collectivization of agriculture in 1929–31, the "liquidation of the kulaks as a class" was the stated goal. Hundreds of thousands were thrown off their land, deported, or killed. According to Anne Applebaum, over two million were exiled to remote regions between 1930 and 1933 (Applebaum 2003, 64).

Samchuk describes how fellow prisoners insist that the nation requires a psychological reconstruction. The artist Pavlovsky tells the hero that it has to pass through a cleansing fire: "We need despots and rulers. Brilliant despots, but fools repeat that we are democrats" (Samchuk 2009, 141–42). What is required is not a bolshevik revolution of "a million plebeians" but a revolution that will give "a single master" (ibid., 142). The prisoners argue the uselessness of mass meetings in which no clear decision is reached. Ultimately, only the well-drilled communist infiltrators and demagogues benefit from such meetings. In the meantime, foreign interests continue to profit from Ukrainian labor.

Under the influence of Maria, the daughter of a businessman, the hero, Lev, begins to change. She encourages him to dress for success, to smoke, to learn social skills, and to get his way. He acquires German and later English. Eventually he sets up a successful forestry and paper business that competes internationally. The workers initially agree to take wages lower than those offered elsewhere, but after the firm has been successfully launched, their wages rise and they work "the normal eight hours" (ibid., 249). The corporate message is extended to the nation; at stake is the country's rebirth. Lev learns a great deal from Hilda, an elegant, strong-willed German, with whom he has an affair: "He wanted above all to learn how to live. Loudly and fully, with all his nerves" (ibid., 221). However, the obsession with self-perfection and profit threatens to destroy his marriage and distances him from the common people. He fails to deal with the discontent that has been fomented by his former communist friends.

The novel admits the strength of communist ideology in both Galicia and Volhynia in the 1920s. The Nationalists were struggling to challenge this ideology, and *Kulak* was in many ways a propaganda exercise that aimed to replace the communist with the Nationalist dream of renewal. The stated goal is urbanization and modernization. As Lev climbs the social ladder he meets talented, strong-willed individuals from other nations who are beginning to take his own nation seriously. He sees that economic struggles have a national dimension: Russian, German, English, and Jewish interests and capital are arraigned against his firm. In an impassioned speech toward the end of the novel, he says: "One must go forward, act, be strong during storms. The main thing is strength during storms. Precisely now we must stay afloat. Around us there is so much enmity, hatred. Everyone is against us, as though part of a conspiracy [. . .] Something great and dangerous is growing here. This will be the end of those parasites, those millions of loafers who have crawled here from all over the world to sponge off our people's impotence and misfortune" (ibid., 305). Toward the novel's end, as people contemplate the forest fire that has destroyed the firm, their veins and muscles feel the flow of a "ruthless, animal power" that makes them want to throw themselves onto the fire, to strangle it, and then to regrow the million trees that had been destroyed (ibid., 315).

The protagonists in Samchuk's novels of the 1930s are attracted to discipline, hard work, and self-improvement, but also to passion and irrational commitment.

Lev is driven by a Faustian urge to achieve, conquer opposition, and impose his will. An elemental drive seems to link him to universal, amoral forces. However, the drive makes him into a monomaniac. His wife turns against him. Friends, supporters, and his own mother caution him against hardening his heart to the point of losing all feelings and humanity. In the end he recoils from amoralism and fanaticism and restores his relationship with his wife and trusted colleagues. It becomes clear that neither force alone nor blind, fanatical desire are sufficient. They have to be tempered by wisdom, experience, and the cooperation of others.

A review in *Vistnyk* drew attention to the fragmentary style that made demands on readers, compelling them to reconstruct events from conversations, stories, and confessions. The novel's first part was judged to be the most successful, especially Lev's revolt against those who avoid politics or wait out events, and his own decision to leave for the city and bend the future to his will (-kyi 1937, 842). The reviewer avoided mentioning the critique of monomania and fanaticism. Although the novel occasionally focuses on the protagonist's ecstatic moments, the framework is the social and political context that ultimately explains human motivation. Even while Ukrainians are urged to develop a national egoism, the narrative demonstrates how this egoism can take both healthy and unhealthy forms. It also introduces the central myth in Samchuk's work: the strong, enduring man who has sprung from the soil.

The author favored the bildungsroman, or novel of personal development. When they began corresponding in 1926, Samchuk admitted to Dontsov that Russian writers and Thomas Mann's *Tonio Kroger* had been strong influences (BN, 83986, 34). The fact that in numerous novels Samchuk made the man from the homestead his main hero and savior of the nation irritated other Nationalist writers. In a letter to Dontsov on 10 February 1934, Lypa dismissed Samchuk as a "self-satisfied muzhik" (BN, 83984, 136). The Tolstoyan message of slow change and peasant endurance was not appreciated by Dontsovians. In the postwar period Samchuk was criticized by Rostyslav Yendyk, who saw all history as a struggle for "the space that provides nourishment" and that "must be taken from another by force" (Iendyk 1955, 85). He justified violence in the name of self-preservation, and in a long tirade he charged Samchuk with breaking from this prewar ideology and advancing realism in place of romanticism, democratic views in place of elitism. Yendyk continued to keep faith with the amoral and irrational core of Dontsovism: "The creation of the new world comes out of ecstasy and frenzy; common sense can only lead at a time like this to nihilism. This ecstasy travels joyfully toward its goal and either conquers or perishes. [. . .] Dontsov's ideas, like his means of expression, are fervent. His love is passionate, his hatred haughty. He often renounces objectivity, but substitutes it with deep faith and conviction" (ibid., 175).

Kulak shows the dangers of this negative sublime. In the conclusion, after Lev decides to rebuild the business destroyed by fire, he meets a man who has worked eight years in a factory and is now returning to work his own land (Samchuk 2009, 317). Lev is inspired by the old man's commitment to slow, steady labor, faith in his own abilities, and connection to the earth. There is nothing ecstatic or frenzied about the hunched Shabelian, but the reader senses that this worker's quiet strength and sober understanding of life guarantees the nation's survival and future success. The ending demonstrates Samchuk's admiration for the laboring individual and his rejection of the Dontsovian contempt for the masses.

Samchuk's collection *Vidnaidenyi rai* is set in Prague. Each story describes the musings of a young Ukrainian in love with the city, who wishes that his own country could one day compete with the sophistication he finds around him. The style reveals the writer's search for a dynamic form: it is fragmentary, full of rapidly flowing, distorted perceptions. Although the reader senses a mood of resentment against British and American power, the focus is on the charms of this democratic haven in interwar Europe and its rich cultural life.

Maria is an experiment with the epic style. Dedicated to the mothers who died of hunger in 1932–33, it recounts the life of one such woman. The first two parts describe life in the early twentieth century; the third deals with the famine. The village suffers from epidemics of typhoid and scarlet fever, from the burdens of war and revolution. The author shows sympathy for the broken lives of these rural people, who continue to draw inspiration from the beauty of the land and the dignity of their rites and traditions. When Dontsov published the second edition of his *Dukh nashoi davnyny* in 1952, he singled out Samchuk as an "ideologist of the mob" who expounded "a Svejkian ideal" (Dontsov 1951, 92–93). This may well have been aimed at *Maria*. The novel blames the devastating famine on the perverted "modernization" of the bolsheviks, who sacrifice millions of agricultural workers in order to extract a surplus. The ending, a descent into madness and cannibalism, would have been viewed unfavorably by Dontsov, who saw little value in accounts of victimhood. Moreover, the novel deconstructs Ukrainian masculinity. A central theme is the relationship of the main protagonist to the men in her life: her two husbands, Hnat and Kornii, and her son Maksym.

Hnat is taciturn, withdrawn, and diffident in relations with others, especially with women. Devoted to Maria, he is devastated when she divorces him. Eventually he becomes a monk and spends his life in prayer. During the famine he guards the swine, a job that enables him to "steal" crusts of bread from the animal feed, which he then distributes at night to villagers. Having suffered a broken leg in childhood, he walks with a limp, perhaps an indication of his inadequate masculinity. In the end he suffers a mental collapse, publicly rages against the bolshevik regime, and is dragged away by soldiers. The bold and physically strong Kornii is Maria's great love. She only marries Hnat after learning that Kornii has been conscripted into the tsarist navy for seven years. Kornii returns from his naval service a brutal, insensitive boor, who insists on speaking Russian. Nonetheless, Maria lives with him while her husband is away convalescing from an injury. When she becomes pregnant, Kornii insists on an abortion, which is conducted in barbaric fashion by an old woman in the village. Gradually, under the influence of Maria and his work on the land, the persona of the brutal sailor disappears. Kornii no longer describes affairs with black women or visits to Hamburg brothels or "Athenian nights" in St. Petersburg: "His vagabond-proletarian habits faded away. The earth drew him into itself and filled his veins, mind and entire being with firm habits. He already senses this. His sailoring is a thing of the past and he is becoming a human being. Slowly he is forgetting how to curse and is returning to his native language" (Samchuk 1952, 115). Kornii says of his earlier condition: "A sailor cannot be a good man." He tells his wife: "The land makes one gentle, whereas the sea tempers one" (ibid., 123). Earlier he loved Maria "as an animal," and wanted to murder her and her former husband. While he was a sailor, he roared with laughter when talking about women with his comrades and thought: "Maria's like that too. Today she's mine, tomorrow she's the devil's." But now he understands that a girl from the land cannot be like that: "A girl from the land is faith; a girl from the sea is treachery" (ibid., 124). Militarism and imperial power are linked here to the atavistic in human nature; they transform a civilized peasant into an uncouth military man. The authentic life is to be found in enjoying "the fullness of existence," a phrase that occurs in a passage describing Maria, Kornii, and his old mother around the table on Christmas Eve. Their faces show the calm glow of happiness: "We," say Maria's eyes, "do not demand a lot of happiness. Our happiness lies in the fullness of existence, but several times each year we collect it into one great visible happiness, which radiates from our eyes, our lips, our souls" (ibid., 120).

For some Nationalists this description of simple harmony raised the specter of sentimentality and retreat into domesticity. By emphasizing the superiority of love, family, and pleasure it represented a challenge to the cultivation of military hardness. In passages like these the aesthetics of the sublime retreats in favor of a beauty that is connected with charm, pleasure, and the furtherance of life. The sublime's uncompromising, distant perspective, its contempt for petty deeds and small people, is forgotten when the world of domesticity and pleasure reasserts itself. Even in the midst of terrible circumstances, Samchuk insists on presenting this counteraesthetic of pleasure, the joys of a life lived close to the soil. One passage is an ode to the land:

> On a Sunday morning after the Spring sowing, when everything is coming up and the rye and wheat are beginning to sway, Kornii goes into the field. He sees everything here as filled with God. Kneel and pray. The sun, enormous and eternal, the sun of the field and countryside, has come out from behind distant horizons and is rising to the heights. Kornii takes large firm steps along the country path between the meadows, looks at the slow, cat-like, grey-green swaying of the rolling fields, listens to the tireless ringing banter of the sunny birds above him, breathes into his strong peasant lungs the crystal-clear fragrant air. There is no end to it all. There is no boundary. The wind, warm and gentle, sails over the grain fields flattening them; small white clouds like lilies in an enormous azure pond, touched by the sun, sail off and somewhere in the distance fall behind the oak forest's black wall. (Ibid., 155–56)

The novel shows war from the perspective of women and the village. Forced recruitment leads to brutalization and death. The quartering of armies results in robbery and destruction. The arrival of the bolsheviks brings additional insults: soldiers stand in church without removing their caps during services, smoking and laughing; their comrades rob the monastery. Maria's communist son Maksym destroys the icon in his mother's home, saying: "I have executed your idol" (ibid., 178). During a wedding, after drinking a great deal, he announces: "Socialism has brought a new life. Woman will no longer be man's slave. She will sleep with anyone she likes. Weddings are unnecessary. That's all superstition, dreamed up by the priests. .. There's no such thing as love or anything like that. There's only the satisfaction of sexual needs" (ibid., 186–87). His father, Kornii, throws him out. But collectivization has brought thousands of young fanatics like him, who rob and abuse the "peasants." The Komsomol youth conduct an enthusiastic campaign to strip a church and turn it into a cinema, but since they know nothing about farming, they make a mess of the sowing and blame the disastrous harvest on sabotage by "enemies."

   In the modernist sublime, female beauty is often associated with weakness, sentimentalism, and the ideology of love. Accordingly, the narrative of romance gets reworked into a story of the modern Tarzan, noble savage, or careless warrior. *Maria* asks the reader to consider to what extent sexual and personal freedom should be embraced. The author does not deny the heroine's charms, nor her sexuality. Her decision to marry Hnat is explained by the desire to revenge herself "on someone or other" when snubbed by Kornii, but she then ignores her husband, dresses finely, stays out late, and sleeps with other men (ibid., 87). She remains passionately attracted to Kornii, and when he returns she leaves her husband and asks for a divorce. Nor is the female body denied: the whole introductory scene describing Maria as a baby enjoying life at her mother's breast represents a calm acceptance and enjoyment of the flesh.

Hory hovoriat! was serialized in *Samostiina dumka*, the OUN's journal published in Chernivtsi, the capital of Bukovyna. It describes the region of the Carpathian mountains controlled by Hungary before the First World War, in which the population has begun to identify itself as Ukrainian. The Chokan brothers—Pavlo, Yura, and Dmytro—join the cause of independence. So does Mariika, Pavlo's lover. At first she only identifies herself as a Hutsul, but by the end of the story she has been transformed from a quiet, fearful girl into a woman who fights with the men to defend her land and people. When her husband, an officer in the Hungarian army, tries to kill her as a Ukrainian spy, she strangles him.

An incursion by Russian troops who trample and poke out the eyes of Shevchenko's portrait convinces the local population that these are not "our people." However, the Hungarians also refuse to grant autonomy to the Ukrainians. After reading Shevchenko's *Kobzar*, Dmytro becomes a patriot. However, Kiti, whom Dmytro loves, remains a Hungarian. She is convinced "that everything good in the world is Hungarian, that Hungary is the entire world, that Ukrainian is the language of muzhiks, while all Hungarians are dukes and princes" (Samchuk 1944, 189). Babchynsky, a member of the upper class, says: "A Hutsul will always be a Hutsul. He has to be kept on a leash, like a dog" (ibid., 113). Unlike him, Kiti understands that local people have to be part of any administration and cannot be beaten into submission. She is torn between devotion to a view of the country as her Hungarian homeland and her love for Dmytro.

Identity choices constitute an important part of the narrative. They interweave the political and the personal. The Ukrainian population is exploited by a non-Ukrainian upper class and by mercantile interests controlled by non-Ukrainians, mainly Hungarians and Jews. Yura has an affair with the beautiful Jewish seamstress Esterka. After being politicized and radicalized in the 1917 revolution, he speaks to the crowd, telling them that rapacious invaders have taken the best land: "Our people were pushed back onto the high crests, onto the cliffs, where there is only moss and stone. We were not seen in the lowlands, but only came down there to work, to visit the taverns and churches, and then went back to our holes like wildlife. Meanwhile in the valleys palaces were built for rich gentlefolk, taverns multiplied, and new crowds of foreigners appeared" (ibid., 96). Nonetheless, Yura and the brothers hold back the angry mob set on lynching members of the upper class, and they try to build a responsible and fair administration.

The novel is a version of palingenesis, the regenerative myth. This is made clear in the final lines: "The earth itself shuddered and shook itself hungrily. In the endless heavens it saw its Maker breathing the sun's rays, inspired by a terrible power of action. It revived" (ibid., 194). This vision is related to an earlier one in which Dmytro sees the angel of the apocalypse. Together these visions suggest a transformation that will occur on the day of judgment.

Surrealistic moments, especially dream sequences and visions, recur. The injured Dmytro, as he lies wounded and sleeping, sees the following:

> The dead. Angels with trumpets. In front of me a handkerchief, white as snow, with three bloody marks on it. And each mark looks at me as though it was a living eye. I turn around. At that moment some tender, warm hands embrace my head, placing it on something soft and pleasant. And I know that Parania is embracing me, I know, although I cannot see her. I begin to reach for her, because she is far from me. I try to raise my arms to embrace her, but they are so heavy that I lack the strength. I lose hope and let them drop.
>
> Then I see a large room. Not really a room. More a church. The cupola is very high and on it, as though on heaven's vault, there are shining stars. They burn and glimmer. There are books all around by the walls, from the floor up to the very vault. Thick, bound with string, with "War" written on them in large black letters.
>
> Various columns come next, which open onto further halls. I walk through them carefully. On the walls I see large portraits whose eyes have been poked out. Ah, this is a museum. Yes, yes. Over there are our back-packs, rifles, machine guns, helmets. I search for the people. No one anywhere. Where have the people gone? (Ibid., 55)

The passage conveys the disorientation of war and wounding as depicted in expressionist writings. In fact the entire narrative structure is made up of inter-spliced fragments. The various stories of the brothers and their lovers are intercut in cinematographic fashion, without introductions or explanations. The novel shares these modernist features with *Mesnyky*, *Vidnaidenyi rai*, and *Kulak*.

Samchuk witnessed the horrors of the German occupation. He was shocked by the assassination of Senyk-Hrybivsky and Stsiborsky on 30 August 1941 and by the strife within the OUN. The same issue of the Prague journal *Proboiem* that carried news of the murders included an article by him denouncing émigrés "who at first sight appear normal but who excitedly relate old wives tales about how they will enter Kyiv, whom they will allow in, whom they will not, how they will take all the ministerial posts, what a fantastic life they will lead and how rich they will get. Taking a closer look at these knights one concludes that if they ever get to Kyiv they should first see a psychiatrist" (Samchuk 1941, 535). The writer tried to douse inflamed imaginations. He suggested that his countrymen should study European technology: "We should not fear that this will bring us down from the clouds to earth. We should also not fear that this will disturb our Cossack Steppe traditions, eclipse the days when one could blithely and easily breathe the clean air of open spaces and sing sad songs about long-horned cattle or Sahaidachny, weep pure innocent tears while sitting on a stone by the Nenasytny Rapids." This world, he warned, now belonged to museums. The West was advancing in terrifying steel machines, "the real West, the one that flies and sails across oceans and fights with aircraft" (ibid., 537).

After the war, Western intellectuals depicted fascism as a disease. Karl Jaspers in Germany in his *The Question of German Guilt* (1946) wrote of Nazism as a foreign accretion, and projected an authentic German culture that would counteract the worldview of the Nazis. The Ukrainian intelligentsia in emigration—in particular the organization MUR (Mystetskyi Ukrainskyi Rukh—Artistic Ukrainian Movement), which was created in the Displaced Persons (DP) camps—mounted a similar attack on the writers around Dontsov and *Visnyk* in an attempt to purify and heal the national psychology by exorcising dangerous myths. A key term became modernism. Recognizing Western modernism was equated with accepting diversity and complexity, and European civilization's humanist values. In the years 1946–48 the new emigration began conceptualizing and articulating its wartime experience in poetry, prose, and drama. In 1946–47 Samchuk published the novel *Iunist Vasylia Sheremety* (although he indicates that much of it had been written before the war). Like his earlier works, it shows a boy's transformation into a Ukrainian patriot in the years 1922–23 and contains many autobiographical elements. He is part of a cohort that attends the Ukrainian gymnasium (high school) in Kamianets. Vasyl prefers Jack London and Hamson to Nadson and Turgenev, who are too sweet and honeyed, and he is aware that "one cannot live only off sweet things" (Samchuk 1946–47, 1, 129). He has been prepared by the revolutionary underground to carry out an assassination, but he refuses the assignment at the last minute. Instead he dreams of crossing the ocean and becoming a millionaire in America, then funding educational institutions, including a high school,

university, and libraries. A mystical moment occurs in a glade. He finds himself
calling his ancestors:

> "Come follow me all you oppressed, slaves, serfs, persecuted, downtrodden.
> Come all you who lack speech and whose eyes are covered in cataracts.
> Come my comrades paralyzed by your heritage, who throw yourselves from
> fire to fire and burn your wings, then prostrate yourselves before the impla-
> cable. Come you sons of muzhiks, black as the earth and grey as fresh wood.
> Come to me, sit on this grave stone, and it will dictate to you the real law, the
> law of life and the law of death. And you will go into the world and will build
> laboratories, will find death-carrying machines, and will forge paths to glory."
> (Ibid., 139–41)

Vasyl realizes that he is the product of many generations and that he carries
within himself their hopes for the future. He feels the desire to be strong, but
senses also the weight of the "ten speechless generations" that have preceded
him (ibid., 34). He laments the fact that he has only once been on a train, has
not seen a big city, a streetcar, or a real factory, the sea, mountains, the Steppe,
volcanoes. He dreams of "spiritual fullness," a higher, richer "style of life" (ibid.,
36). The pull of modernity is ambiguously linked here to the ancestral past. The
hero realizes that he has the strength to "open all exits, unlock the rusty locks of
ages," and to lift the cataracts from his eyes, but he is also aware that the most
important thing is not to be unfaithful to himself, to the strength that his ancestors possessed, and to their desire to endure (ibid., 48). When he returns to the
family farm during the summer vacation, he recognizes that although he is now
detached from rural life, his role is to speak for these people in the wider world.

In the postwar period Samchuk published *Ost: Roman u 3 tomakh* (Ost: A
Novel in Three Volumes). The first volume was subtitled *Moroziv khutir* (The
Moroz Homestead, 1948). The second appeared under the title *Temnota:
Roman u 2-okh chastnakh* (Darkness: A Novel in Two Parts, 1957), and the third
appeared at the end of his life as *Vtecha vid sebe* (Escape from Oneself, 1982).
The saga follows the fortunes of the Moroz family from before the 1917 revolution to life in postwar North America. It records the revolutionary period of
1917–20, the interwar years, the Second World War, and emigration. Like his
memoirs, in particular *Na bilomu koni* (On a White Horse, 1965) and *Na koni
voronomu* (On a Black Horse, 1975), the trilogy attempts to portray the experience of an entire generation.

The first part of the trilogy is one of his best books. It is set during the revolutionary turmoil of 1917–20. The Moroz children, Sopron, Ivan, Petro, Andrii and
Tetiana, are products of the *khutir* (homestead) built by their grandfather on the

banks of the Dnieper near Kaniv, Ukraine's heartland. Each sibling holds a different political attitude. Sopron, the oldest, works in Siberia and has a pan-Russian orientation. He opposes the empire's breakup. His views bear some resemblance to Afohen, the local schoolteacher, who also belongs to the older generation, considers himself a Little Russian (which suggests a regional identity with no hint of political separatism) and refuses to be called a Ukrainian. He laments the loss of the old regime and old traditions. This generation's world is captured in the painting on the walls of the home. They are by Repin, Serov, Izhakevych, Krasytsky, Kuindzhi, and Pymonenko—nineteenth-century classics famous for their pastoral landscapes, romanticized portraits, and historical scenes.

The second brother, Ivan, holds to a philosophy of organic growth, fears fanaticism, anarchy, and disorder. He is the apotheosis of the Ukrainian home-steader and illustrates Viacheslav Lypynsky's ideas as expressed in *Lysty do brativ khliborobiv* (Letters to Brother-Farmers, 1921–25). The scholar held that the individual closely linked to the land was most concerned with the existence of a Ukrainian state because he needed peace and order and would always be an opponent of chaos and anarchy. Agriculturalists, whether large or small, had similar interests and would give the state a firm foundation.

The three younger siblings are part of the urban environment and profess more radical ideas. Petro, an artist and professor in Kyiv's Academy of Art, is a Petliura supporter. After the revolution he and his sister Tetiana leave for Prague. The youngest and most intellectual, Andrii, becomes a writer and moves to the capital Kharkiv. The conflict between Andrii, a representative of the new urban intelligentsia, and Ivan, a representative of the rural leadership, is at the book's core. Ivan works on the homestead. He is constantly drawn back to it through three decades of political and social turmoil. A gradualist in every-thing, he resists the message of political revolution.

Sopron and Ivan voice some opposition to the idea of a literature written in Ukrainian, criticizing it as superficial, village-centered, and retrograde. They think it has a narrow range of genres and topics and a limited public. By contrast, the younger siblings are already saturated in the new intellectual and artistic medium, and the next generation, represented by the boy Vasyl, already consumes a steady diet of Ukrainian authors. Both Sopron and Ivan, however, agree on the need to break with nostalgic images of a rural, unchanging Ukraine, which act as a brake on required socioeconomic reforms. Although Ivan opposes all revolu-tions, he is no peasant traditionalist but understands the need for a moderniza-tion of the agricultural economy and the wider culture.

A series of debates between Ivan and Andrii make this clear. The older brother defends a united Russia as the best way of securing Ukraine's development against the encroachment of German capitalism. Andrii, on the other hand, supports the idea of independence and the creation of a modern intelligentsia. When challenged by Ivan, who complains that he is asking for the sky, Andrii insists that this is precisely what people should demand; they should not be denied their dreams and ideals. Where Ivan sees a recipe for chaos and confusion, Andrii sees a leap toward something far better. He denies the progressive nature of the link to Russia, which, in his opinion, is not a benevolent and tolerant state run by a kindly shepherd-tsar, but a power with a messianic drive that denies Ukraine's aspirations. While agreeing that Ivan's critique has merit (insofar as the culture and language lack depth), he says this is precisely why rapid development is needed. In any case, the process of radical change has already begun and is affecting young people and minorities like the Jews.

Samchuk's traditionalist sympathies come through in a nostalgic depiction of a disappearing life. He recalls familiar scenes: unchanging landscapes, family meals, community meetings, Christmas celebrations, and church gatherings. The novel reflects a complex attitude toward modern political and cultural change. For example, on the one hand, it describes the pull of ten centuries of Christmas traditions. On the other hand, it emphasizes the importance of Faustian ambition and a new art. The young generation now associates Ukraine with the modern, and there can be no going back to the pastoral idyll. When asked how he can support a culture that has "no geometry" (meaning that the subject has always been taught in Russian), Andrii replies that it is precisely for that reason that he supports it: only with support will it develop to its full potential.

Both Ivan and Andrii have a Dostoevskian contempt for Kropotkin's anarchist views and for revolutionary phraseology in general. They recognize the need for constructive intellectual and manual labor and see through the demagogic calls for destruction. This places them not in the socialist camp with its abstract ideal of the working person, and still less in the anarchist world, which refuses to consider the role of the state. They realize that ignorance is widespread and that a fundamental change is required in the mass psyche. They also realize that some people have been seduced by false doctrines spread by Lenin and the October Revolution.

However, there is another alternative, a national revolution. Marusia and Vodiany are leaders of the local anti-bolshevik resistance. Although Ivan has strong reservations, he is gradually drawn into helping the latter. By the end of the book, three concepts of how to resist bolshevism emerge: Ivan's work on the land, which represents turning one's back on politics, Vodiany's armed struggle, and Andrii's work within the existing political system. The three approaches share a skepticism toward abstract theorizing, a faith in the power of practical activity, and a confidence in the greater wisdom of nature. But the central myth is that of the homestead, which represents an entire civilization. Samchuk shows how the spirit of this *khutir* ethos, carried by the siblings to various places, continues to shape their lives and pursuits. Raisa Movchan has argued that *Moroziv khutir*, by focusing on the homestead myth and endowing it with an almost metaphysical significance, represents a transformation of the realist narrative "within the force field of modernism" (Movchan 2008, 455).

Temnota (Ignorance) begins in the year 1928. Ivan has remained on the homestead. Andrii is now a famous writer in Kharkiv, Petro an artist in Kyiv, Sofron a mechanic in Siberia, Tetiana a physician in Prague. Andrii's play brings him fame. He meets Gorky, Alexei Tolstoi, and various Soviet leaders. The novel describes the "grandiose experiment" of collectivization, and the social engineering that results in the famine of 1932–33 and the Gulag. Andrii expresses the main message when he states that the enormous human sacrifices were in no way required. The last book, *Vtecha vid sebe*, is a retrospective glance at the immediate postwar years, a time when each protagonist must decide whether to return to the Soviet Union from the DP camps in the American or British zone of Germany or to emigrate to North America, Australia, or other European countries.

These last two books are considerably weaker artistically, although they provide some excellent dialogue—often the best aspect of Samchuk's prose—and powerful moments that overturn false assumptions about the war experience. Several Jewish characters appear in this postwar fiction. In *Moroziv khutir*, Yankel, a butcher, turns up with the bolshevik forces. Later a Jewish commissar appears. *Temnota* portrays two Jewish members of the GPU, Rokyta and Shuster, who have grown up in poverty in Ukraine and are now part of the bolshevik inquisition. However, the most interesting is Petrov, a high official in the GPU. He understands Andrii and sympathizes with him politically. During the mass arrests he helps Andrii rescue Ivan from prison. Ivan has to agree to organize production in the Gulag, where thousands work under his control. Andrii becomes the author of a successful play about collectivization, just as the brutal campaign is beginning. The two brothers are therefore implicated in the Stalinist system. In this way Samchuk complicates the description of Soviet reality, distancing himself from the Manichaean world of prewar narratives.

The figure of Sashko further confounds expectations. He appears in the third volume as a Ukrainian artist of Jewish origins, whose father was an important figure in the secret police. Like everyone else he has now "burned the old gods" and created a new persona. He embraces his Ukrainian identity, marries Vira, and settles in New York. Sashko explains to Vera how racist ideas governed

Nazi politics, and what the Germans planned for Ukraine. It was to be "an African colony." Transformed into "a Niemandsland," it was to be "called Ost, divided into latifundia and presented, along with ourselves, to their own meritorious" (Samchuk 1982, 37). He sees clearly that a new Ukrainian identity has to be created and points to the Jews as an example of the power in tradition and dream. After a hiatus of two thousand years they are building a new state with its capital in Jerusalem. The Holocaust has hardened the determination of Jews to succeed, and Ukrainians are learning from them that spiritual resolve and self-sacrifice can overturn thousands of years of history.

Sashko's decision to become a Ukrainian surprises the old man Ivan Moroz, this Ur-Ukrainian, with the deepest roots in the homestead, but Sashko reacts angrily to the charge that "cosmopolitans" usually prefer to identify with Russian culture. Instead he accuses people like Ivan of faithfully serving imperial overlords. Jewish utopian revolutionary thought (in the figure of Marx) is counterposed to Ukrainian servility and conservatism. Both are found wanting and seen as responsible for the disaster of the Soviet state. Sashko's openness to the new, symbolized by his commitment to abstract art, wins him success in the West and points toward the development of a new Ukrainian sensibility. Even Ivan finally concedes that a return to Ukraine to rebuild the family nest along traditional lines is a fantasy.

A particular event during his youth is the key to understanding Sashko's metamorphosis. A number of his schoolteachers who lectured in Ukrainian were arrested in the 1930s, among them a Jewish professor of physics called Feldman. Sashko at the time refused to use Ukrainian, which he considered "spoiled" or "bad" Russian. However, his professor insisted that, since they lived in the capital of the second largest Soviet republic, they should know its language. When his teacher disappeared in the Great Terror, Sashko's eyes were suddenly opened to "the powerless, the exiled, the hungry," and he understood that the most terrible threat to people came from theories ruthlessly applied by fanatics. Salvation, he now realized, had to come from good deeds.

Samchuk's agitational journalism during the war centered on the need to affirm the nation's vitality. "Ukraine will survive!" became a mantra. The slogan was conceived as a response to Hitler's ideas about Lebensraum and the planned elimination of Ukrainians. Berkhoff reports that under German occupation, as the first editor of the Rivne newspaper *Volyn*, Samchuk wrote several editorials that many regarded as covert criticisms of German policy. "Suspecting (wrongly) that he was the general district's leading Melnykite, the Security Police arrested him in February 1942 and kept him locked up for two months" (Berkhoff 2004, 151). Later, Samchuk wrote that the Ukrainian partisan movement had been released too soon and produced "only a great massacre of civilians, without any results for us" (Samchuk 1975, 160). His literary works are not antisemitic, as the prewar *Volyn* shows. It describes a childhood spent with close Jewish friends. However, Samchuk's writings under German occupation were not something he could be proud of, and he carried a burden of guilt in the postwar period.

On 1 September 1941, the first issue of Volyn appeared. It contained an article entitled "Zavoiovuimo misto" (Let Us Conquer the City) in which Samchuk wrote: "All that element that has populated our towns, whether a Jewish or a Polish influx, has to disappear from our towns. The problem of Jewry is in process of being solved and it will be solved in the framework of a general reorganization in the New Europe. The empty space that may be created must immediately and irrevocably be filled by the real owners and masters of this land, the Ukrainian people." In subsequent issues he praised Hitler and called for supporting the German army. Scattered throughout this journalism of 1941 and early 1942 are references to the "Jewish-bolshevik" regime. On 27 November in "Pidniatyi mech" (The Raised Sword), he questioned why England did not take the opportunity of fighting alongside Hitler. On 2 December in "Nasha shkola" (Our School), he attempted to justify the closing of schools: "On the other hand one has to understand that the closing of our schools is temporary, that as soon as better times appear, the schools will immediately be reactivated." On 25 December he wrote "Vyderzhaty" (To Hold On), which is a cry for the nation to hang on in desperate times. The best of Samchuk's articles indirectly try to instill a sense of pride and a will to endure, and signal to readers the maximum that can be gained from the current situation without incurring the wrath of the German authorities.

Frantz Fanon has argued that the human personality is under cultural pressure to apprehend the world from a preassigned viewing position. A black man who has been raised on a steady diet of Gallic culture perceives himself more as "French" than "black." After leaving the colonies and arriving in France, he may be subjected to a violent corporeal redefinition from which it is not easy to remain psychically aloof. Fanon describes going to a film in Paris and feeling himself being observed, seen through images of a stereotypically menial blackness (Silverman 1996, 27). A screen of "blackness" creates unflattering images that have been imposed by others, and the black individual refuses to identify with them. The situation of Samchuk and many Nationalists might be compared to this. In the 1930s they developed an image of themselves as heroic, assertive, and uncompromising Ukrainians. During the war they were treated as subhuman, a nameless people predestined for minimal education and menial labor, a stateless ethnographic mulch for the colonizing superrace. Wendy

Lower has documented aspects of this German attitude toward the OUN (Lower 2005, 38–40, 94–96). In this situation Samchuk's journalism alternates between instilling notions of heroism and self-reliance, agonizing over the nation's fate, and fulfilling German directives.

Andrii Zhyviuk has pointed out that Samchuk was walking a line between collaboration and opposition, trying to play off pro- and anti-Ukrainian Germans and to work with different tendencies in the Nationalist movement. He is adamant that while Samchuk was editor, the newspaper *Volyn* "never took collaborationist positions in the way that it is charged with doing" and accepts only that it had to compromise by explaining official German policies (Zhyviuk 1996, 270). Some have argued that Samchuk's articles were both anti-bolshevik and anti-fascist (Rusnak 2005, 3–7). However, most readers of the articles, all of which were signed by the author, would probably disagree. Even his supporters have called a number of them "odious" (Zhyviuk 2008a, 7). The support of Germany and the portrayal of bolshevism as inextricably linked to Jewishness runs through the writings of 1941. In surveying the destruction in Ternopil, his comment on 30 November 1941 is: "All this occurred because of the will of the sons of Israel, who could find no better way of saving their native Soviet Union than by setting fire to the town as soon as the German army entered" (Zhyviuk 2008b, 157). After the war Samchuk claimed that he tried to write in a way that allowed readers to read between the lines and understand his critique of the Germans. It is not possible to square this statement with his apotheoses of Hitler, the attacks on England, the support of Japan, the defense of ruthless German methods in the village and the attacks on Jews. On 22 March 1942 he wrote the editorial for which he was imprisoned and which ended his editorship, "Tak bulo—Tak bude" (That Was How It Was—That Is How It Will Be). It said: "On the map of Europe a new space is being drawn, which takes the name of Ukraine." After quoting Hitler's words about the German soldier having to overcome not only enemy armies but the "enormous, seemingly inexhaustible flow of blood of the most primitive nationalities," the article delivers an impassioned defense of the Ukrainian nation's right to exist. It argues that this nation is "perhaps not overly civilized," but still represents a force to be reckoned with, and, he hints, it could turn its anger against the East or West. Such a direct critique of Hitler and German policies was unacceptable to the military occupation.

In this context the positive portrayal of Jews in his later works can be considered a form of expiation and atonement. *Choho ne hoit ohon* (What Fire Cannot Heal, 1959), the story of a young Jewish woman who tries to hide her identity during the occupation, has been called "an act of repentance" for his statements, or silences, during the Holocaust (Gon 2010a, 284). The narrative describes the actions of a Ukrainian, a former officer in the Polish army, who serves in the militia organized by the Germans. He tries to save Shpryndzia, for whom he feels a romantic attraction, and to rescue her family from the Jewish ghetto to which they have been sent.

One constant in Samchuk's evolution is the idea that Ukraine must modernize and join the new technological age. The Westerner, he wrote in his wartime journalism, was a radically different creature, led not just by "untrammelled instincts," but also by "a free mind and free spirit" (Zhyviuk 2008b, 52). Ukrainians, he said, need "fantasists of the machine, fantasists of factory chimneys, fantasists of autostradas, fantasists of railway development. We need great, brave, and powerful economists" (ibid., 65). Samchuk, like other Nationalists, was willing to pay a price to achieve this dream of modernization and catch up with other nations. In the months that followed the German invasion, he realized how misplaced his hopes had been.

11

A CHANGE OF HEART: YURII KLEN'S "ADVENTURES OF THE ARCHANGEL RAPHAEL" (1948)

Klen's evolution as a literary figure is particularly instructive because in Soviet Ukraine in the 1920s he was a supporter of Mykola Zerov's neoclassicism, then in Germany in the 1930s he aligned himself with *Vistnyk*, during which time he celebrated Faustian voluntarism and urged the implantation of a new, dynamic spirit into the Ukrainian body as a kind of unavoidable radical surgery. His collection *Karavely* (Caravels, 1943), which contains poems written between 1926 and 1943, is full of conquistadores, Vikings, and adventurous medieval raiders. Finally, at the end of his life—certainly by 1946–47, but probably already in 1943, when he began writing his epic poem *Popil imperii* (Ashes of Empire), which is a picture of two ruthless empires in collision—he decisively rejected the *Vistnyk* group and returned to his earlier neoclassicism. In this final stage, Europe once again figures in his work as personifying the wisdom of ages and providing the distancing perspective required for a critique of contemporary political engagements. Some critics have attempted to completely identify Klen's writings with a Dontsovian inspiration (see Bahan 2004; Ivanyshyn 2004). This influence is clearly evident in his work of the thirties, even though most poems maintain a high degree of neoclassicist restraint and maintain a distance from the heat of contemporary events. However, it is also clear that at the end of the war, Klen reassessed his collaboration with Dontsov, and in the postwar period joined MUR, which strongly criticized *Vistnyk*'s entire tone and philosophical underpinning. Klen's change of heart is inscribed into his "Pryhody Arkhanhela Rafaila" (Adventures of the Archangel Raphael, 1948), which was written in the last year of his life and is perhaps his best short story. It presents a key to understanding the writer's complex evolution and the dilemmas of radical nationalism.

Klen (real name Osvald Burghardt) was born into a family of German origin. After spending some time studying in Germany, in 1921 he finished Kyiv University, where he studied English, German, and Slavic literatures. He began writing in Russian under the influence of the symbolists. When he joined the neoclassicists, he translated European authors into Ukrainian. Arrested by the bolsheviks in 1921, he was released as a result of the intervention of the writer Vladimir Korolenko. This experience, during which he witnessed the execution of non-communists who were shot in the prison corridor and dragged out in pairs, left an indelible mark and was recorded in one of his best poems, "Prokliati roky" (Cursed Years, 1937). When in the early 1930s sweeping arrests began to take Klen's closest friends, including the great lyricist and fellow neoclassicist Maksym Rylsky, he emigrated with his family to Germany, a privilege that he was allowed as an "ethnic German." He lectured on Slavic literatures in the University of Münster until 1941. Although his debut as a Ukrainian poet occurred in 1925 (all his previous work had been in Russian or German), it was in Germany that he secured his reputation as a Ukrainian writer. During the thirties he contributed regularly to *Visnyk*. Mobilized into the German army in 1939, Klen served as a translator on the eastern front. After being demobilized in 1942, he taught in Germany and Prague and then edited the journal *Litavry* in Austria.

A couple of essays written in the same year as the story "Archangel Raphael" provide a way of understanding the text. The first is called "Mid zveniashchaia" (Sounding Brass). The human being, according to Klen, has been placed on earth by God and given the capacity and freedom to create new worlds, but also the ability to destroy the existing one. The main challenge facing humanity is spiritual: without love, life is meaningless and hollow—the noise of "sounding brass." The phrase is taken from the Bible: "Though I speak with the tongues of men and of angels, and have not charity, I am become as sounding brass, or a tinkling cymbal" (1 Corinthians 13). Klen quotes Christ: what does it profit a man if he gains the whole world and suffers the loss of his own soul? The writer's concern is that humanity has lost all interest in love and personal salvation. The Nazi philosophy, he states, was built precisely on the absence of all love—on egoism and hatred, and Hitler, who viewed moral principles as "weakness and treachery," was driven by the idea that the more foreigners that could be destroyed, the more space would be left for Germans (Klen 1957a, 217). The second essay, entitled "Bii mozhe pochatysia" (The Battle May Begin), is a contribution to the great postwar émigré debate concerning the nature and direction of Ukrainian literature. The writer feels that, having unlocked the secrets of the atom, "the human being now interferes in the world-making process, and has turned from a magical, Faustian individual into a demiurge." Unfortunately, the dangerous technical possibilities at humanity's disposal have not been accompanied by a corresponding growth in self-awareness, which can best be achieved by looking deeply into the long tradition provided by literature and art. Klen accordingly directs Ukrainians to study the European and Western tradition in all its fullness (Klen 1953, 11 October, 4–5).

In the eponymous story, the Archangel Raphael takes the body of a human being. He is impressed by the fact that human genius is capable of remarkable achievements, such as unlocking the structure of the atom, penetrating to an understanding of primary forms, and reworking these into something entirely new. But the angel recognizes that in emotional terms, humans remain selfish and naive. They have been presented with a crucial, hitherto undreamed-of capacity for transforming the world, because once the alchemy of recreating and recombining atoms into new form-structures has been mastered, matter itself can be reshaped. However, this brilliant achievement has also brought with it a terrible destructive power. The atomic bomb, which had shortly before been detonated in Hiroshima and Nagasaki, and the horrors of the Second World War were no doubt on the author's mind. The narrator suggests that human beings need to examine anew the meaning and purpose of their existence on Earth.

A supreme power and leading cultural role belong to the artist-creator. The two archangels, Raphael and Michael, are amazed by humanity's achievements:

> If a human being, walking alongside the archangels, had been gifted with their sight, their ability to see things that were invisible to the ordinary eye, this human being would have been astonished to see on the surfaces of large towns, alongside familiar towers, churches and spires, buildings that had never stood there and whose presence completely changed the external appearance and living memory of the town. These buildings differed from the others because of a kind of transparency, which seemed to allow light to pass through them, as though they were built of glass or formed from thick fog that gave off reflections with a phosphorescent glow.
>
> These building were never built, but had been created in the fantasy of architects, who wanted to beautify the town with them. They were unrealized projects, materializations of powerful, brilliant ideas that had not been translated into stone and steel. Alongside buildings that could be touched as real objects, these seemed to be fantastic structures made out of patterns and dreams. The gaze of the archangels rested longer on these than on any others. As they were moving along the bare steppe, an entire city of such

transparent-patterned buildings suddenly grew up around them, a never-achieved plan of some builder, worked out to the smallest details.

"Look," said Michael, "those wonderful chimeras bear witness to the eternal human striving. Even what they have not created by hand, but only in their imaginations, exists like the real, the immovable, and acts as a prophecy before God concerning their yearnings, aspirations and drive for the unattainable." (Klen 1957c, 64)

Klen encourages the reader to think in terms of the long perspective of human history, especially as it is available to us through the Greco-Roman classics and the Judeo-Christian tradition. The great writers of the past enable us to see beyond the chaos and disillusionment of the present day and to establish a framework for interpreting human history. They provide something akin to the Archangel Raphael's steadying, celestial perspective. This European experience is not a form of mystical escapism, not a search for the Holy Grail, but a promise of understanding based on the collective experience of the best minds. The above passage appears to reaffirm faith in the importance of the past for an awareness of present and future developments. However, the passage can also be read as a genuflection to the Dontsovian precept that the "best people" have to lead by providing visions of a future that is as yet invisible to ordinary individuals. The never-before-seen structures made out of patterns and dreams recall the imperative to create the radically new not by imitating nature, but by bending the material world to the designer's will. This is precisely what Dontsov, writing in 1926, admired about futurism: it gave free reign to the creative ego (Dontsov 1926, 127). In this same passage Dontsov dismissed vulgar, provincial taste (his term is "Provencale") by suggesting that it cannot see into the future but can only appreciate the already visible, repeated forms that conform to the already established laws. But the passage could also be read as a defense of political and artistic modernism.

Klen's views have roots in the Christian literature of the Middle Ages. The Archangel Michael describes people in this way: "unfinished, unperfected, ever changing, sometimes lifted by impulse to inaccessible heights, sometimes, dragged into the abyss by the whirlpool of the Fall, they speed in the stream of a ceaseless becoming" (Klen 1957c, 59). However, their greatness lies in the fact that they continually strive for self-perfection. "Is it not strange," says Raphael, "that of all the creatures made by the Lord, it is given only to human beings to die, that only human beings are defined by the struggle for change, for self-perfection, the desire to create their lives out of falls and flights, and to transfer from one generation to another the aspiration for even higher flight, for even greater falls?" (ibid., 61) Two paths are available to humanity, says Michael: to "become the universe's shame or to justify its secret hopes" (ibid., 62). When Raphael takes the bodily form of the Soviet citizen Vertoprakh, he sacrifices some of his omniscient perspective in order to understand the time-bound human world. He experiences all the wretched details of earthly existence, its physical pains and biological impulses, its vulgarity and egoism, and the sordid personal and political ambitions that lead to the shameful manipulation of others. Paradoxically, his attempts to do good lead in almost all cases to evil. However, he does succeed in bringing love into the world, and this selfless feeling redeems his time on earth; it is his greatest triumph and his legacy.

The brutishness that Klen describes is a consequence of humanity's loss of the higher perspective once provided by religion, the Christian worldview, and the tradition of European humanism. His story is built on a Christian frame-work, which includes the Last Judgment, heaven and earth, and the promise of salvation in the next world. Life on earth, when governed by this higher perspective, holds out the promise of decency, generosity and mutual respect. Only this promise affords the preconditions for the observance of legal and social forms. The narrator, who appears to be speaking for the author, wishes to drive lusts and passions into a place where they can be controlled and tamed, in much the same way that Raphael tames the dissolute, polluted, and unruly body of Vertoprakh. The Soviet citizens that the archangel meets care nothing for faith, civilization, or spiritual values. They are ruled by material interests and carnal passions, and their behavior is only kept in check by fear of political authorities. Like Raphael, the narrator stands above this maelstrom of personal and political passions; he views the world through the lens of eternity, or at least through the distancing perspective that European literature and spiritual faith provide.

Klen draws on medieval Christian anthropology, which saw human nature as located somewhere between the angelic and the bestial. Saint Augustine used the angel-beast contrast to describe the human being; Pascal and many later Christian writers also took it up. According to this view, human beings are pulled between their desire to rise up toward ever-greater perfection and the animal-like temptation to surrender to their lower instincts. Such a contradictory nature defines the Raphael-Vertoprakh duality. The existence of a heaven, to which Raphael is eventually recalled, suggests the biblical doctrine of the resurrection of the flesh. The tragedy of the human condition, the reader is made to feel, lies in the fact that it has lost sight of this supreme metanarrative of the Fall and Resurrection. Michael says: "Timelessness exists only for us. The past, the present and the future are always before our eyes and we do not differentiate between them. People, captured by the stream of becoming, pass everything through the aperture of the present; they soar between the two non-existences. Being tri-dimensional themselves, they see only tri-dimensional space" (ibid., 60).

At another level the story is an amusing sociopolitical satire. It exposes the general slovenliness of Soviet life and reveals the state's paranoid fear of its own citizenry, which leads it to suspect conspiracy in even the most harmless events. The story also contains hints of the *Visnyk* philosophy. For example, Raphael makes a decision to enter Vertoprakh's body with surprising suddenness: "he said to himself that if he considered the consequences of his actions too long he would never dare perform the deed, because reflection paralyzes action and makes life questionable" (ibid., 66). Action, not reflection, was the *Vistnyk* motto; the world had to be changed. There is, however, also a suggestion of the limitations attached to such voluntarism. After all, Raphael's good intentions lead to much suffering and disaster, and he cannot alter the underlying laws of causality to which all life is subordinated. Still, in the long run, the fact that he changes the life of one individual and leaves a legacy of love offers hope that eventually human nature and society may be improved.

A writer steeped in the literature of the past, Klen accepted the achievement of former civilizations. Culture was for him a completed achievement as much as a task for the future. He therefore tended to focus on the constant and unchanging, the search for lessons to be learned from antiquity and recurring cultural forms, and he was suspicious of claims that a human and spiritual metamorphosis could be brought about in response to the pressures of history and new ideas. Destiny for him was not an apocalyptic and transforming moment, but a slow process of gaining self-awareness, one that involved understanding the past, the road already traveled. Only then, he felt, would humanity become aware of its own nature and change its behavior.

Klen's story demonstrates a rejection of the radical social and cultural experimentation of bolshevism and Stalin's rule. In its respect for the humanist values of the European heritage, it can also be read as a rejection of Nazism. However, radical nationalist and fascist views had their attractions for modernists with a deep awareness of tradition. While living in Germany, Klen appears to have been seduced by the style and rhetoric of fascist politics. It is an aspect of his life that is not well known and rarely discussed. The view of Klen as a European humanist and a defender of universal values is contradicted by Hordii Yavir, the pseudonym under which he wrote reports from Germany for *Vistnyk*. They begin with a record of his impressions when listening to Hitler's election speeches in 1932–33 and the powerful effect these were having on the population. He concludes: "Those who read abroad about the 'brutality of nationalists,' the 'mocking of the people,' the 'repression of Jews,' are incapable of imagining the true picture of German reality"

(Iavir 1933, 817). He filed essays on Stephan George as an aristocrat of the spirit and on Oswald Spengler's cult of the will. He defended the politics of Germany, Italy, and Japan as the only countries capable of standing up to bolshevism by using ruthless, "bolshevik" methods. In this last article he says: "The Faustian tension and irrepressible yearning, as the spiritual force of the German individual, has entered into wonderful works of art. The forces of the medieval individual are at work even today. The liberal individual with his rationalism is foreign to us. The slogan 'freedom, equality, and fraternity' are empty and groundless. For us the freedom of the separate individual rests on the link to family, genus [*rodom*], people" (Iavir 1937, 878). The annexation of Austria in 1938 is greeted by the author as a new dawn for Europe and perhaps the world (Iavir 1938, 289). Two articles that Klen signed under his real name, Osvald Burghardt, deal with the brutalities of bolshevism, including the use of torture and concentration camps. They link Jews very directly to the worst atrocities of the regime. "Tsarstvo Satany" (Satan's Empire) is an account of the reports given by five hundred "ethnic Germans," most of whom spoke only Ukrainian or Russian, who had been expelled from the Soviet Union. When asked what percentage of the interrogators were Jews, "most replied ninety percent" (Burghardt 1938, 304). "Bolshevytska spadshchyna" (The Bolshevik Legacy) makes the point that the "army of commissars, lesser commissars and their lackeys was in large degree recruited from this race [the Jews]" (Burghardt 1939, 94). It goes on to say that Jews have "monopolized" the leading positions in the state, while talented Ukrainians have been pushed aside (ibid., 96).

These articles make it clear that Klen not only appropriated the vogue for elitism and voluntarism, along with the cult of ancient traditions, but welcomed the antiliberal, antidemocratic and antisemitic policies of Nazi Germany. This makes an explanation of his politics as driven by conjunctural factors (in other words, motivated by anti-bolshevism) much less convincing. Particularly surprising is his glorification of German expansionism, which, he must have known, held fatal consequences for the rest of Europe, including Ukraine. When, on the eve of the German invasion of the Soviet Union, Samchuk met a uniformed Klen in a Berlin café, the latter spoke of Germany taking the wrong course: "conquest instead of liberation." When asked whether Ukrainians could hope for anything, he replied that he was doubtful: "As you can see, this is a call for space, a delayed conquistadorism. . . Of course, we will get something. . . But never what we need" (Samchuk 1965, 19). Samchuk detected an ambiguity in Klen's attitude. His comment on this meeting was that Klen's "German blood and Ukrainian spirit, or rather heart, are now in great contradiction. He suffers because things have worked out this way, but he has no answer for why they did so" (ibid.). Whatever the real motivation for Klen's actions, his support of

Germany and his poetic glorification of conquest and conquerors—so evident in his collection of poetry *Karavely* (Caravels, published in Prague in 1944)—were soon disabused. Some insights into his life as a soldier-translator on the eastern front have been published. They reveal his attempts to deal humanely with people and to mitigate the cruelty of some German officers. It appears that he was removed from the front partly because of this, and also because he contracted pleurisy. In 1943 he began writing his great tragic epic *Popil imperii* (Ashes of Empire), which remained unfinished at the time of his death and was only published in 1957. At this time, his mood was one of retreat from authoritarianism and dreams of conquest. He saw himself in the figure of Archimedes, who in Syracuse made geometrical drawings in the sand, oblivious to events around him. When he warned a drunken Roman soldier not to touch these drawings, he was cut down by the latter, who had no understanding of their worth (Klen 1957b, 332). Klen's epic poem deals with the long suffering of Ukrainians throughout history, but it also describes the murder of Jews during the war. This makes him one of few contemporaries who attempted to describe both the cruelties of Stalin and Hitler, the Gulag, and the Holocaust.

With these facts in mind, his participation in MUR in 1946–47 and his postwar works can be seen as a rejection of the *Visnyk* period. In the immediate postwar years, MUR conducted a fierce polemic with Dontsov and his supporters. While Dontsov continued to castigate democracy, liberalism, and parliamentarism, Yurii Sherekh, MUR's leading critic, argued that contemporary Ukrainian literature was developing, as it had always done, within the European tradition of humane values (Sherekh 1947, 18). MUR publications, such as the flagship journal *Arka* (Arch, 1947–48) examined Ukrainian literature against the background of European developments. Sherekh and Yurii Kosach excoriated Dontsov and the Vistnykites for breaking with humanism, and in doing so, severing Ukrainian literature from its own mainstream and from world literature. Dontsov, in their minds, was not a "traditionalist" at all, in spite of his attempts to appropriate this epithet. They viewed him as the architect of a radical departure from the mainstream (Kosach 1946, 48–49). Several critics responded to these charges. Throughout 1947–48 every issue of *Orlyk* and other journals sympathetic to the Visnykites carried criticisms of MUR. It is noteworthy that in these responses Klen is always identified as a member of MUR and is no longer viewed as a supporter of the *Vistnyk* camp or of Dontsov.

Our best indication of Klen's attitude at the time can be found in his "Archangel Raphael." It suggests a return on the part of the author to a millennial perspective, a disappointment with efforts to rapidly transform humanity, and some degree of contrition concerning his own role in the world's iniquity. The story can be read, like Dostoevsky's *Idiot*, as the portrayal of a character who attempts to live a good life in circumstances that inevitably entangle him and bring about disastrous consequences. Raphael, like the Prince in Dostoevsky's novel, takes on Christ's role of suffering. Clearly autobiographical, the story captures the author's feelings of disorientation during the wartime and postwar years.

Klen began by supporting the ideals of Christian humanism and stressing the importance of studying classical authors. He moved in the 1930s and early 1940s to extolling heroic myths of conquest in line with Dontsov's desires, and ended by reaffirming an outlook of Christian tolerance and classical restraint. As a German who had first been educated in Russian and Western schools and had later assumed a Ukrainian identity, he presents a fascinating case study in identity politics. He was first a Russian poet, then a translator into Ukrainian, and from Ukrainian into German and Russian. Among his translations into Ukrainian are Shakespeare's *Hamlet* and *The Tempest*. When he emigrated to Germany, his name was removed from these translated texts, and there is little information on their stage history (Siryk 2004, 321). It is significant that throughout his life Klen acted as an interpreter who moved between cultures and identities. Much of his literary career was devoted to translating great literature into Ukrainian, and to explaining Ukraine's cultural identity to German and Russian readers. One constant throughout his life remained his Lutheran Christianity. Another was his reverence for European classics—especially Stefan George, Rainer Maria Rilke, Goethe, and Russian writers of the Silver Age. These were for a while combined with a political enthusiasm for German expansionism, and at other times with an anti-imperialism that recognized Ukraine's cultural potential and its legitimate drive for independence.

His liminal status is also evident in the way he straddles the divide between a radical, "engaged" nationalism and a cerebral, disengaged aestheticism. Although Klen vehemently rejected the militant bolshevik avant-garde, during his years in Germany he appears for a while to have been seduced by fascist rhetoric and the authoritarianism of Dontsov's *Vistnyk*. The puzzles of the writer's evolution are reflected in his biography, identity choices, and literary works.

12

DOKIA HUMENNA'S REPRESENTATION OF
THE SECOND WORLD WAR IN HER
NOVEL AND DIARY

Dokia Humenna's account of the Second World War is entitled *Khreshchatyi iar (Kyiv 1941–43: Roman-khronika)* (Khreshchatyk Ravine, Kyiv 1941–43: A Novel-Chronicle, 1956). It examines a number of sensitive topics, including wartime antisemitism and the suffering of Jews and focuses heavily on the early months of the German occupation of Kyiv, devoting half its pages to the period from June until December 1941. By describing the attitudes of Kyiv's population toward the Nationalists who arrived from Western Ukraine and the emigration, she challenged romanticized images of the impression they produced on "Eastern" Ukrainians and the role they played. This aspect of the book elicited strong reactions from reviewers and readers among postwar émigrés.[1]

The novel was based on a diary entitled "Materiial do povisty Hnizdo nad bezodneiu," (1941–43), which the author kept during the first two years of the war.[2] In it, Humenna occasionally expresses her views with greater frankness than in the novel, which was written in the years 1946–49 and published in 1956 in New York, the city to which the writer emigrated. In the novel some personal names that had appeared in the diary were altered, some opinions and descriptions modified, and some apparently fictional characters and scenes introduced. Discrepancies between the diary and novel are evident in the portrayal of Jews and indicate that the author was rethinking events.

Humenna's point of view can be characterized in general terms as that of a woman writer and civilian who is both anti-Soviet and anti-Nazi. After making her literary debut in the 1920s, she was heavily criticized in the early 1930s, effectively banned by the Soviet Writers' Union, and treated as a pariah by many

253

fellow writers.[3] However, although she remained defiant and suffered black-listing as a result, she was not imprisoned. In her early creative years, according to her own description, she was a true believer and youthful idealist who complained that a segment of the population, including the leadership of the Writers' Union, was living in luxury as a privileged caste: "The difference between me and some Voskrekasenko or Smiliansky [two minor writers] is that they did not believe in communism, while I did, and I spoke out when I saw the loathsomeness that profaned it. For this I was called a slanderer" (Humenna 1946, 18). In 1941, upon the outbreak of the German-Soviet war, she began to chronicle events in her diary. By that time the disillusioned and embittered writer viewed the entire Soviet system as hypocritical, corrupt, and brutally repressive, and was particularly scornful of leading writers. Her critique of literary life in the 1920s and 1930s would receive its fullest expression in the four-volume *Dity Chumats'koho Shliakhu* (1948), which was written in 1942–46 and published in Munich in the period of Displaced Person camps, and in her *Dar Evdotei* (1990). The wartime years were amazingly productive for the writer, who seems to have been released from silence and driven by a desire to bear witness to her generation's experience.

Humenna was not only anti-Nazi, she was critical of various nationalisms. She consistently opposed racism, authoritarianism, or elitism, whatever the regime or ideology. For example, she complained of the narrow-minded, caste-like attitudes of those Ukrainians who had arrived from Central European countries and Galicia in the wake of the Nazi invasion. She was angered by the self-appointed leadership in literature—Olena Teliha's circle. Humenna viewed them as newcomers who considered themselves "aristocrats of the spirit, Nietzscheans," and who assumed that they were predestined to play starring roles in the new Ukraine. She saw them as "half-baked" and "arrogant" (Humenna 1946, 145, 184). These first impressions recorded in her diary would be toned down in the novel, where she would point out, among other things, that Teliha died a heroic and tragic death at the hands of the Gestapo.

Humenna was also sympathetic toward a particular kind of feminism, one that was linked to her fascination with ancient cultures, especially the Trypillian (5,000–3,000 B.C.E) and the Scythian (700 B.C.E –200 C.E), and with the matri-archal traditions and goddess worship that have left strong traces in Ukraine. The author read widely on the subject of these ancient cultures, attended confer-ences on archaeology, and in the mid-1930s participated in the excavation of prehistoric sites. These interests receive a large degree of attention in the novel, where they are articulated by Mariana (the leading protagonist and the author's alter ego) who considers herself a "citizen of the millennia" and for whom the *longue durée,* an awareness of long-term historical structures, provides a distancing perspective on the tragic present and allows her to keep faith in humanity. The interest in ancient history and goddess worship would inspire several of Humenna's postwar works.[4] The diary indicates that the millennial view of cultural development is the frame through which the critique of racism and of contemporary nationalism is articulated. For example, the author dismisses a sense of national identity based on more recent Christian traditions as "lamentation over lost churches" (Humenna 1946, 215). Her field of vision takes in the civilizations that have existed in Ukraine over several millennia and whose ancient rituals underpin contemporary Christian rites: "I cannot make peace with a limited view of the national. I do not walk in the last ten centuries, as do the nationalists, but wander over the millennia. I see my own people in the Trypillians and in the future citizens of the universe. I want to find the thread that links the primitive and the highly intellectual" (ibid., 132). She focuses on the role of women in maintaining communal identities over centuries of disruptive change. Civilization and progress, she suggests, are dependent on the removal of egoism, the desire to think beyond the present day and beyond the satisfaction of immediate needs. This aspect of human nature, it is argued, has been the achievement of women. It is the result of motherly love and self-sacrifice: "She would not perhaps have considered herself, but having children who are a part of her, she found in herself a concern for tomorrow, for provisions, for the development of plants into future food . . . Therefore there are two poles. The male—separation, egoism, unclasping, destruction of another for one's own benefit. And the female—self-sacrifice, the feeling of unity, love" (ibid., 153–54).

And finally, one should add to this overview of Humenna's bedrock convictions a strong commitment to honesty, personal integrity, and outspokenness— all prerequisites for the kind of clear-sighted commentary that she admires in the greatest writers. It is from these positions that she heaps scorn on the toadyism of Soviet authors, the racism of the Nazis, and the snobbish arrogance of the nationalist intelligentsia that had arrived from Western Ukraine and emigration.

The diary and novel provide a wealth of marvelous eyewitness detail that illuminates events and gives life to various historical figures, such as Olena Teliha, Ulas Samchuk, Arkadii Liubchenko, and Leonid Pervomaisky; these appear under their own names in the diary and under thinly disguised pseudonyms in the novel. Relations between Ukrainians, Russians (who are mostly Russified Ukrainians), Jews, and returning émigrés are observed. However, the main focus is on the fluctuation of public opinion and the population's response to events: the initial Soviet retreat, the arrival of the Nazis in Kyiv, the massacre in Babyn Yar, and the subsequent return of the Red Army. All this takes place amidst swirling rumors, anecdotes, gossip, and newspaper reportage. The author presents the ebb and flow of opinion as the movement of a single organism, the expression of the city's mind with all its changing moods and evolving awareness. She demonstrates the difficulty of establishing facts in a confused situation and during a time when there are no reliable sources of information. Both the diary and the novel show people struggling to weigh news and hearsay and to evaluate personalities.

However, there are some substantive differences between the two accounts. Changes in the depiction of Jews and antisemitism illuminate Humenna's thinking and the process of writing the novel. The diary notes the escape from Kyiv of many Jews in the first days of the war. It is clear that they often feel like foreigners among non-Jews, who resent the Jews' relative affluence (which is revealed by their clothing, behavior, influential positions, and abandoned apartments) and the fact that they are leaving the city's defense to others. This resentment is sometimes phrased as a criticism of noncombatants, but there are other disquieting notes that suggest a deeper animosity and the imminence of anti-Jewish violence. The diary's account of the antisemitic mood is considerably harsher and less sentimental than the novel's. It documents a rapidly growing, menacing hatred. There is no evidence of the "sympathy and pity" for the Jews that was typical of the earlier philosemitic Ukrainian literature that appeared in the last decades of tsarist rule and during the Revolution of 1917–1920. When asked, "Why are you taking so long?" by a harbor worker, an infuriated old Jew snaps back: "Are you getting ready to throw me into the Dnieper?" (ibid., 9). People who remain in the city show hostility to all evacuees, to Jews in particular. While recording these attitudes, the author makes it clear that she herself considers that the privileged position of Jews has generated much of the opprobrium. She notes the anger directed "against those who have feathered their nests, grown rich, and are the first to leave" (ibid., 12), who are cursed in the market square, and who themselves feel that "our own people would kill us if they had a chance" (ibid., 19). The author comments:

> There is such a taboo placed on the word "Jew" that one cannot even dare to criticize them, especially in print. For some reason, the actions of a bad communist can be criticized sooner than those of a Jew. You are immediately accused of antisemitism for no reason. Now everyone is talking openly about them. However, psychologically there is pressure. One cannot write about the following subjects: that they are cowards and insolent, that they are not going to the front, that they have sullied wonderful ideas, grafted onto society and made bloom the idea of "getting a good spot," "weaseling one's way out," "avoiding," and "working something out." One Jew explains why Hitler does

not like them: because only the Jews can be the equals of Germans. This represents the idea of superiority, of possessing an exceptional nature. It is chauvinism, but no one dares to say so. (Ibid., 39)

Although the earlier quotations are retained in the novel, this last one, which appears to be a personal comment by the narrator, is omitted. The attitudes expressed are probably an accurate reflection of the mood among many who witnessed the privileged strata's frantic and often unseemly rush to catch boats, trains, and other transport moving eastward. In the diary, Humenna describes how she herself was forced to leave on a boat traveling down the Dnieper, how she stayed behind at a stop en route, and then returned to Kyiv. She informs the reader that she did so out of patriotic reasons—a desire to share and record the fate of her people—and also because of her wish to escape Stalin's regime. Animosity toward the members of the escaping literary elite who lived well while claiming to represent the common citizen is presented as a widespread phenomenon. Back in Kyiv, she notes in a passage also dropped from the novel that the vacated apartments of the affluent are now being taken over by working people: "The Communist Party with the help of the Jews has completely discredited itself and has no authority among the masses, has gone rotten, the people have rushed into a reaction" (ibid., 60). She is also motivated by a personal anger against the leaders of the Writers' Union, in particular Oleksandr Korniichuk, Illia Stebun, Ivan Le, and Sava Holovanivsky. She resents not only their privileged and pampered life but also the fact that many of these authors are of Jewish origin (including the last three mentioned) and that it is they who present the official face of Ukrainian literature. Although there is an occasional mention of ordinary, working-class Jews from outside the city, including some who do not plan to join the evacuation, the reader's overall impression is that the Jewish population, at least in Kyiv, consists of well-heeled urbanites, most of whom were quick to leave in the first days of war. Lacking is the kind of perspective provided by Vasily Grossman's famous lament over the death of ordinary people in his sketch "Ukraine without Jews" (1943): "Old men and women are dead, as well as craftsmen and professional people: tailors, shoemakers, tinsmiths, jewelers, housepainters, ironmongers, bookbinders, workers, freight handlers, carpenters, stove-makers, jokers, cabinetmakers, water carriers, millers, bakers, and cooks," and so on (quoted in Beevor and Vinogradova 2005, 252).

Humenna astutely observes how this antisemitism, inspired by a sense of social inequality and linked to rural resentment of the city's rich, quickly becomes entangled with base impulses: personal greed, the coveting of property and apartments, and the lust for violence. As the writer witnesses this moral degeneration, her attitude changes. When the Germans enter the city, she observes their brutality toward Jews, and at this point her views undergo a fundamental reassessment. She and her friends are disgusted by the propaganda posters portraying caricatures of Jews (Humenna 1946, 138). She is equally appalled by the pro-German newspapers, in particular *Nove ukraïnske slovo*, which describes all non-Aryans, including Ukrainians, as defective: "The newspaper and Shtepa's editorials are aimed at instilling a lack of faith in ourselves, our own powers, a lack of will and a slavish submissiveness, in full belief that our 'elder brother' will provide everything good. The Germanic peoples have been quickly promoted to this 'elder brother' status. Without them, it seems, through all of history we would not have made a single step forward" (ibid., 152). Such views reflect the colonial mentality that has been Ukraine's scourge. The colonized continue to pay homage to their oppressor; one colonialist has simply been supplanted by another. Humenna records comments overheard on the street to the effect that democracy is a product of Judaism: "They argue that there is no freedom, that the democratic idea is false, deceives people, that the entire liberal democratic movement is pernicious, a weapon in the hands of Judaism's rule, that Jews corrupt society by bringing on revolutions so that they themselves can rule" (ibid., 163). These views are dismissed. Instead, the author argues, there are systems of government far worse than democracy—aristocracy, monarchy, dictatorship, or blind obedience, for example.

Initially, the writer's anger toward Jews is based on their association with the Soviet "ruling class," but it softens substantially when confronted with the behavior of German troops, returning émigrés or individuals from Western Ukraine, some of whom are members of the OUN, and above all with the shock of the Holocaust. Humenna's reassessment of her attitude to the Jews is even more evident in the novel that was written in the three years following the war, while she was reflecting upon her recent experience. The most important change in the novel is the introduction of a narrative of Jewish suffering and loss. It is present in the diary, which records the Babyn Yar massacre of 29–30 September 1941, but the novel also introduces Jewish characters, including Roza, who is a friend of the main protagonist Mariana. The later account represents an attempt to grapple with the issues of antisemitism and complicity in the killings. It discredits not only Nazi attitudes but also those of nationalists who share these attitudes. Humenna asserts liberal-democratic values and solidarity among oppressed peoples.

The writer bears witness to the destruction of the city's Jews and attempts to give an honest account of what she sees and hears. In the diary she describes old, sick Jews left to die on the streets; she records her revulsion at casual comments, such as "it has become easier to breathe without the Jews" (ibid., 117), and at attempts to rationalize the taking of clothing belonging to Holocaust victims. The following is an overheard conversation: "Jews on one side, possessions on the other. The Germans took the best stuff and passed on the worse, saying 'Take it, Rus!' 'But, really, when you think about it, does it belong to the Jews? It belongs to the people, because the people worked for all of it. What was stolen has now been returned'" (ibid., 121). This is spoken by Zina, who was kept in high style by Kopelev, a Jew, who provided her with the finest clothing, much of which he came by during the "liberation of Western Ukraine" in 1939–41 at the time of the Hitler-Stalin pact. The above conversation from the diary is retained in the novel but displaced: it is used to expose the increasingly antisemitic views of Halyna, who continually adapts to whomever is in power. She holds that the Jews have brought persecution on themselves by conducting subversive work and by setting fire to buildings (Humenna 1956, 230). A typical conformist, she insists at various points that she is Russian, Ukrainian, and German (a Volksdeutscher), depending on what is convenient, and adjusts her opinions accordingly.

The diary reports the arrest of Jews in the weeks after Babyn Yar. The entry for 24 October 1941 reads: "Old people were being removed from the hospital. They walked as though in a funeral procession, slowly, supporting one another, with lowered heads. A second [group was composed of] mothers with children. The children did not want to go. The mothers pulled them along. Bystanders follow their progress. In the Jewish Market there was a group of Jews in their underwear. And the frosts have already begun" (Humenna 1946, 126).

On 25 September 1941, shortly after the city's fall and a few days before the massacre in Babyn Yar, she witnessed the following scene:

> The Germans took a Jewish woman from a building and beat her. Why? Someone, it appears, noticed that she had lit the stove and poured gas on it. She fell and said something. Then she got up, was surrounded by people, who shouted something at her, threw her to the ground, and then put her by the automobile. The Germans demanded something from her. Then the two who had beaten her ran into the same courtyard from which they had dragged her, while she sat on the wheel as though crucified, without her galoshes. The bystanders stood and waited. Then the German ran out, threw her out of the automobile onto the pavement and shot her. From the courtyard a second woman was pulled and dragged, almost naked, and also shot. Among the bystanders one could hear conversations about them being arsonists. (Ibid., 105–6)

These and similar passages are reproduced in the novel. They dispel any notion that Humenna avoided mentioning Babyn Yar or the Holocaust.[5]

The tone of narration is restrained, a conscious decision that is made explicit in a comment toward the end of the diary, when she was already considering writing the novel: "The tone has to be epic-philosophical, far from the daily rush, thoughtful, surprised by what everyone finds ordinary. Terrible events that breathe the heat of political situations must be transformed, given an entirely different tone within a broad historical framework. No incitement [in the manner] of the Black Hundreds, no rabid foaming at the mouth, but a solemn bell" (ibid., 263). Such an epic tone was also chosen by Vasily Grossman, who wrote in Russian but was of Jewish origin and came from Berdychiv in Ukraine. He used a restrained narrative voice in the most important Russian novel of the war, *Zhizn i sudba* (Life and Fate, 1980), which was only allowed to appear in Russia at the end of the Soviet period. In describing her tone, Humenna also uses the significant phrase "surprised by what everyone finds ordinary." Even in the midst of terrible events, her narrator does indeed find time to be stunned by the unexpected and beautiful, both in human character and in observed scenes. On one of the first nights of the war, thousands of people have been sent home from work, and they lie in a field watching the dark sky illuminated with red-green streams of anti-aircraft fire: "Although it was terrifying, it was very beautiful. These streaks, these wide, round tents of parachutes that descended in front of our eyes as though they were returning to their homes" (Humenna 1956, 12).

It should be noted that in 1941–43 Humenna, like many citizens, could not have been aware of the full extent of the Holocaust, a fact that accounts for her underestimating the scale of the killing, which became fully apparent to all observers only at the war's end. Having grasped the enormity of the event, she reconsidered some earlier views. Among the diary passages that did not make it into the novel is the following, recorded on 23 February 1943:

These pogroms, which are even reckoned as having destroyed tens of thousands of Jews, will not destroy the Jewish nation, but they have profoundly insulted the Jews, made martyrs of them, placed a crown of thorns on this nation's head, of which it is unworthy. "The Jews have been forgiven everything," says one Komsomol member, "because of the way they have been treated." — "The peasants worked day and night on their sugar beets and knew no rest, had no time to sleep or wash. And saw no sugar. At the same time some Leia or Khana consumed that sugar in the cities in the most varied forms." — "But you were not killed, and they [the Jews] were." Therefore, all the evil the Jews did to us has been justified, precisely because they were killed. (Humenna 1946, 253)

This and similar passages suggest a widespread attitude, not simply one that characterized, for example, members of the OUN. It was an attitude that was at first shared by the author, which explains the tension in her diary between horror at the Holocaust and sympathy for the suffering of Jews, on the one hand, and a residual anger at what she perceives to be their privileged position, on the other.

It is clear from the diary that Humenna initially planned to tell the story of anti-Ukrainian discrimination and prejudice. Her account provides many instances of these. For example, in 1943, as it becomes clear that Kyiv will be retaken by the Red Army, she describes how the city's mood becomes anti-Ukrainian and how Russian once more becomes the dominant language in official life, even in the editorial offices of *Nove Ukraïnske Slovo*. The author overhears the following: "Boors, I hate them. There is nothing worse than a Ukrainian. What did they lack under the tsar? They had fat back, bread. They could have studied, but did not want to." The Ukrainian language is now once more ridiculed: "What language?" says one character (Humenna 1946, 259–60). The author fears that under returning Soviet rule Ukrainian culture will again be reduced to the level of exotic folklore, denied high cultural expression, and allowed only a watered-down, sanitized, and standardized literature. She also fears the return of mass arrests and executions and the social experimentation that caused the famine of 1932–33.

When she came to write the novel, the author attempted to combine the narratives of Jewish and Ukrainian suffering. Her strategy was to link Hitlerism with Stalinism and to juxtapose the horrors of both regimes. Vasily Grossman later employed a similar strategy, drawing analogies between Hitler's destruction of the Jews and Stalin's destruction of the peasantry in his *Zhizn i sudba* and *Vse techet* (Forever Flowing, 1970). In the latter book one character says:

> I asked you how the Germans could kill Jewish children in gas chambers, how they could go on living after that. Could it be that there would be no retribution from God or from other people? And you said: only one form of retribution is visited upon an executioner—the fact that he looks upon his victim as something other than a human being and thereby ceases to be a human being himself [. . .] And nowadays I look back on the liquidation of the kulaks in a quite different light—I am no longer under a spell, and I can see the human beings there. But why had I been so benumbed? After all, I could see then how people were being tortured and how badly they were being treated! But what I said to myself at the time was "They are not human beings, they are kulaks." I remember and I think: Who thought up the word "kulak" anyway? Was it really Lenin? What torture was meted out to them! In order to massacre them, it was necessary to proclaim that kulaks are not human beings. Just as the Germans proclaimed that Jews are not human beings. (Grossman 1986, 143–44)

The catastrophes of the 1930s, including the famine, were never mentioned in Soviet literature and had been largely ignored in Europe and the United States. They were part of the larger story she wished to tell. The need to maintain this narrative of Ukrainian suffering but to intertwine it with the narrative of the Jewish tragedy led to most of the changes introduced in the novel. Both narratives had a powerful claim on the postwar reader's attention and their integration was not an easy task.

In the opening pages of the novel, war and the German invasion have just been announced on the radio. We meet Mariana and her Jewish friends in the apartment of the rabbi (Rebe) and Klara, who are planning to join the evacuation. The apartment's balcony overlooks Kyiv. Interior details suggest a comfortable and dignified life: a milky-white tablecloth, crystal glasses, and a gleaming piano. At the rabbi's request, Mariana agrees to deliver some written materials and photographs to a librarian for safekeeping. Soon after the occupation of Kyiv, Mariana helps her Jewish friend Roza hide her identity. When news of Babyn Yar spreads through the city, she meets the distraught Roza on the street:

> Roza stares with panic-stricken eyes. Mariana cannot give a full account of all those rumors circulating throughout Kyiv. Lvivska Street was full of people on the day that Kyiv's Jews were summoned there by the order in the azure-colored notice. They all believed that they were to be transferred somewhere, some brought an enormous amount of food with them, purchased little carts for this purpose, or hired baggage handlers. And no one thought that there were so many of them still left in Kyiv! There, on the corner of Dohtiarivska and Dorohozhytska their passports were taken away and thrown into a fire. Those who did not have the word "Jew" registered in their passports were pushed aside, in spite of protests and intentions of sharing a husband's or a wife's fate. Mariana told Roza this. No one comes back from there—she told her this too. But then, about how they were stripped to their underwear, how their things were thrown over the fence, how they were led to Babyn Yar beyond the cemetery, how there above the ravine the machine gun sprayed them with bullets, sweeping them into the ravine, how the Germans threw a couple of grenades and the earth covered thousands who were perhaps only wounded, perhaps still alive, how they were killed by an electrical current—all those rumors that made one's hair stand on end— Mariana could not tell Roza this. (Humenna 1956, 194–95)

After Babyn Yar the attitudes of Kyivites change completely. Many discover that acquaintances (whose Jewish background was often unknown to them) have disappeared. The abstraction "Jews" suddenly becomes a noun signifying particular colleagues and friends. Petty resentments toward the Jewish population turn to horror in the face of this unfathomable crime. As a result, some characters become violently antinationalistic, associating the national cause with the German invasion and the killing of Jews. One climactic scene is a furious discussion between Mariana and Vasanta, a childhood friend whose family had been arrested and exiled in the 1930s during Stalin's collectivization of agriculture. Vasanta has now adopted anti-Ukrainian, pro-Soviet views. Mariana, on the other hand, refuses to identify with either regime. She hopes for the survival of her people and the eventual return of political sanity.

In this way the novel interweaves Ukrainian and Jewish narratives. It also raises issues that entered public discourse only later in the century: political conformism, guilt felt by silent witnesses, and the need to construct a personal narrative for even the most traumatic events. One poignant moment that encapsulates many of these issues and is emblematic of Jewish-Ukrainian relations occurs when Mariana's friend Roza is removed from a public gathering. Roza and Mariana are present at a meeting of people who have lost their apartments through fire or bombing. Some well-dressed Jewish women are sitting or lying on the tables at the front, which raises complaints that "they have taken the best places again, while our children have to stand by the door" (ibid., 186). Roza sits with Mariana and holds her hand. Disturbed by the talk of expelling Jews from the city, Roza leaves the hall for some air. She attracts an admirer, a German soldier called Willi, who is a good-natured village lad of twenty-two. He gives her presents (perfume and his photograph) and distributes chocolates to the women. The women murmur that the officer should be informed of the presence of Jews. The words "we will not cover for them" and "my children are over there by the door; why can't they sit on the table too?" are overheard. When Willi returns, his attitude has changed. He asks in German whether there are any Jews in the room, and Roza acts as his translator. When informed that this is indeed the case, he demands their immediate departure. Those sitting on the tables leave in silence, without meeting anyone's eyes. An old man hiding under the table is discovered and removed. Throughout all this Roza and Mariana hold hands tightly. Willi comes up behind Roza and lashes her across the back with a whip. She too leaves with head lowered. The scene represents the lack of support for Jews, the jealousies and social antagonisms that were easily exploited to drive them out, and the difficulty of maintaining solidarity and protecting Jewish friends. This episode, like the meeting after Babyn Yar, is a reshaping of similar events recorded in the diary. But, in the novel both episodes become part of a narrative of destruction and loss, in which the friendship between a Ukrainian and Jew proves insufficient to prevent tragedy.

As the novel drives for closure, it attempts to recognize all sufferings. Throughout the novel Mariana has searched for people with whom she can speak freely—strong and upright citizens who will be part of the new Ukraine that must appear after the totalitarian regimes have gone. The members of her spiritual family include Ukrainians and Jews. The loss of the rabbi, Klara, and Roza therefore represent the destruction of part of this family. At the end of the novel's first section, Mariana returns to the deserted apartment of the rabbi and Klara. She also spends much of the remaining two sections first in the apartment of a Jewish family and then in Roza's. During this time she tries to reconstruct the lives of the former occupants and mourns their fate. Roza has been murdered by the Nazis. However, so has her friend Vasanta, the communist sympathizer, and so has Olena Teliha, the OUN member. Mariana's imagined nation includes all these, indeed all who throughout the millennia have lived in the land and suffered its "ruins, colonizations, fusions, cross-pollinations, subjugations" (ibid., 281). But she insists that the main inhabitant, who has always been rooted in the land, has survived past catastrophes and will survive the present horrors. Mariana feels that she is continuing the life of this eternal commoner. In this way, the novel grapples with the issue of who constitutes "family," what an inclusive identity should look like, and how a narrative of inclusiveness may be constructed. The writer's concept of community stretches racial and national categories to the point of dissolving them. In both the novel and the diary she invokes the Trypillians, Scythians, Polovtsians, Jews, and other races who have all blended into or left their mark on the people and culture of today's Ukraine.

This view of nation and patria differs from the uncomplicated concept of one homogeneous ethnos to which some nationalists subscribe. Moreover, Humenna does not idolize or romanticize the "folk." She is aware of what the common people, in spite of their wonderful, edifying traditions, are capable. The following remarkable scene in the novel is an eyewitness account told by a character named Hnat:

> "One day two very well brought up young men came to the house—courteous, rosy-cheeked, with innocent blue eyes . . . obviously from a nice family. They asked very modestly for permission to have breakfast. They were so polite and modest that they asked for nothing; they had everything they needed. During breakfast all the men in the small town were ordered to gather at once in the square, so the old man had to run off without eating anything. The polite young men offered to help the people of the house by taking breakfast to their father. You can immediately tell an old, time-honored culture with its respect for elders.

They left, and then the women and children were also told to gather. In the middle of the square all the men of the small town and village were standing in line surrounded by SS platoons. Every tenth man was selected and told to stand aside. The father was among them. These selected men were to be hanged. Ukrainian policemen were to do this, but they shook with fear; their hands trembled; one fainted; another began to cry. They were unable to do it. Then the two polite young men with innocent blue eyes, well-bred specialists in hanging, pushed aside the incompetent, useless policemen and expertly, professionally, and quickly hanged those who had been selected, including the old man. The people, women and children were surrounded to prevent them from running away and to force them to watch their relatives being hanged. There were cries to the heavens, sobbing; people went mad; turned grey.

How do you like my story? It is true, because that old man, hanged by the sentimental-romantic youths, was my father." (Ibid., 362–63)

This passage is particularly interesting for the way it exposes instrumental rationality, the technological approach to the machinery of destruction. Industrialized mass murder is possible once it can be reduced to bureaucratic, technical problems that become the focus of ordinary people involved in its execution. The passage also raises many questions concerning human responsibility, motivation, and the capacity for violence. How could these young men act with so little reflection? What had prepared them for such moral indifference? Although the episode does not specifically refer to the killing of Jews, it supports the explanation of the Holocaust as the product of instrumental rationality.

It is worth mentioning that Humenna does not focus at all on another view of violence, one that sees it as redemptive, as a way of galvanizing a debased mass. This last view of violence was implied in the works of Dmytro Dontsov and the writers grouped around the journal *Vistnyk* in the 1930s. As has been seen, Yurii Sherekh and the writers in MUR attacked the *Vistnyk* ideology in postwar years. They rejected the apotheosis of the will as born of weak reasoning, and criticized the cult of vitality and amoral enthusiasm (Sherekh 2003, 212). In their view, such attitudes had prepared the ground for a break with normative forms of behavior and provided a justification for extreme transgression. Humenna's position was close to Sherekh's. Her depiction of violence in the above passage was probably meant as a critique of Dontsov and the OUN's ideology at the beginning of the war. Innocent, untroubled minds, such as those of the two blue-eyed boys, might have taken the writings of Dontsov or the OUN as a license to kill—one sanctioned by higher goals and articulated by leading intellectuals.

Humenna's writings are the first by a Ukrainian eyewitness to describe the Holocaust in Kyiv. They predate by fourteen years Anatoli Kuznetsov's *Babi Yar*, which caused a sensation when it appeared in English translation in 1970, a year after the author escaped to the United Kingdom.[6] She deserves credit for portraying public attitudes toward the Holocaust, for problematizing the issue of violence and the question of who forms part of the nation. Her account contrasts, say, with Ulas Samchuk's memoirs, which hardly mention Jews, or Arkadii Liubchenko's diary, which exhibits a virulent and racist antisemitism.[7] Humenna belongs to those intellectuals who were committed to a civic nationalism and a broadly conceived, pluralistic culture and identity. To convey this vision of community, she interwove a number of narrative threads and opposing views. The result is a novel of complex texture.

Today Humenna's sensibility resonates with many citizens of Ukraine who are concerned with the issues of democracy and diversity. Her book also still unnerves those who, out of a concern with national unity, fear the revelation of history's dark pages or disturbing complexities. When it first appeared the novel provided a challenge to the way war and the OUN were portrayed in émigré novels, such as those written by Ulas Samchuk or Stepan Liubomyrsky. Many ordinary readers were shocked. In a letter to Humenna, one correspondent complained that the author had done a grave disservice to the OUN youth of Western Ukraine, who had sacrificed everything

> in order to make their way secretly past enemy posts and to go on foot, often cold and hungry, to our golden-domed capital, or to other towns in Central and Eastern Ukraine. They went with a single purpose, to join the ranks of those who were fighting for and building a Ukrainian state, which in their imaginations and dreams was to be resurrected on their native soil. I know this youth well and bow my head before their idealism, dedication, and strength of spirit. They did not go to be bosses. They went to help in any way necessary. They took the steering wheel in their hands only where none of the local people were capable of doing so, and they acted as they knew best. These were not statesmen, diplomats; they were idealistic, completely dedicated youth. (UVAN, Archive of Dokia Humenna, Maria Lohaza, 14 April 1956)

Humenna replied:

> I would like to assure you that there is neither tendentiousness nor ridicule in the book, but only a desire to dispassionately fix the living, unvarnished picture of the contemporary reality in Kyiv. The words of my characters (in particular the ones you quote) are not my words, but those of typical individuals in Kyiv at that time. I am not able to force them to speak another

language, one desirable to nationalist romantics, a language of propaganda, because this would be a falsification of reality, and I tried to present this reality as truthfully as possible. [. . .] My main idea was that there existed various ideological tendencies in living Ukrainian reality and that we all need to search for a common Ukrainian path. How should I have presented this? By denying a voice to various tendencies, and immediately striking an iconic, propagandistic note? (Ibid., Humenna's reply)

Halyna Kovalenko, the widow of the writer Yevhen Pluzhnyk, who died in the Gulag in 1936, lived through the occupation of Kyiv. She praised the novel and particularly appreciated the depiction of the OUN's attempts to assert itself in the capital. Members of the organization, in her view, had been "deeply mistaken in their actions" toward the local population. They "forgot that it was an unpardonable mistake to order people around in the same tone that the Germans used." She continued:

Kyiv was not waiting for orders from abroad, but for the infusion of new forces, and these had no business showing off and acting as superiors in the way they did. [. . .] The Ukrainian "Ubermenschen" will rage against you, but all this will be as useless as it was in the past! The greatest mistake was of their own making—in cooperating with the occupation—and now there is no point in remonstrating. You deserve sincere and heartfelt thanks for fixing the real events of Kyiv in 1941–43 in a literary work. (Ibid., H. Kovalenko, 29 January 1956)

Current debates over contested memory rehearse many of these same arguments. Not the least of Humenna's achievements is the fact that her novel remains relevant, having stimulated early exchanges in a discourse that continues to rage.

CONCLUSION

You must not dare, for shame, to talk of mercy;
For your own reasons turn into your bosoms,
As dogs upon their masters, worrying you.
—Shakespeare, *Henry V*

The OUN's brand of authoritarian nationalism—sometimes called integral nationalism—has been condemned as an ideology of national egoism that encouraged violence against non-Ukrainians and was responsible for the killing of many innocent Jews, Poles, and Ukrainians. Amir Weiner has written: "The pursuit of ethnic purity and belief in aggression as the natural state of human relations constituted the core of the officially endorsed ideology of integral nationalism (*natsiokratiia*). The reading of the nation was unapologetically racial. Nationalist ideologues tried to draw the line between the Nazi blood-based concept of race and their own, which sought the spiritual and biological revival of the nation, but the result was nothing more than a semantic splitting of hairs with an ideology to which they confessed their affinity in any case" (Weiner 2001, 241). This is an influential view, but it is not the full story.

As the present account has tried to show, neither pursuit of ethnic purity, nor racism, nor acceptance of Nazi doctrine were central to the OUN's ideology, nor were they officially endorsed. Stsiborsky's *Natsiokratiia* (1935) does not mention any of these terms. Exploitative Russian and Polish landowners are mentioned twice (ibid., 95, 97), but so are exploitative Ukrainian landowners (ibid., 91). The key question of who constitutes the nation is left vague. It is only said that the nation's main groupings are the peasants and workers, and the intelligentsia that springs from them (ibid., 90). The words "blood" or "race" never occur.

Stsiborsky does admit the affinity of nationalism, any nationalism, with fascism (never with Nazism), because he applauds fascism's concern with national development and its hostility to communism, which he describes as an "absolute evil" bent on destroying national communities (ibid., 39). But Stsiborsky opposes dictatorships: "Any dictatorship that is based on permanent political terror and the repression of a people's spontaneous activity becomes an end in itself; it gradually shrinks the already limited social base that supports it" (ibid., 43). He applies this criticism to the fascist idea of permanent dictatorship; Mussolini's elite, he says, might in ten years' time become corrupt and self-serving (ibid., 59). Stsiborsky devotes an entire chapter to the question of dictatorship and concludes that there is danger in rule by any elite (ibid., 68). The issue is connected to the wider problem of a government's relationship to its governed: "Are the popular masses really only a 'mob' whose herd instinct, primitiveness, and riotousness prevent them from constructive work and condemn them to being only a blind tool in the hands of a governing minority? . . . Such ideas, which are now fairly common among the overly exalted idealizers of vozhdism [leadership cult], are diametrically opposed to the theory of political democracy and 'populist' currents related to it, which see the source of all truth in the masses alone (a classic example of this is the well-known phrase that in a conflict between the government and the masses, the fault is always on the side of the government). Comparing these different views, we believe that the truth lies somewhere in between" (ibid., 64). This is the authoritarian credo: the government has to remain in contact with the people and express its will, but only the government can sometimes decide what is best for the people. It is, however, also the dilemma of any government. Stsiborsky makes it clear that any dictatorship should be temporary, since there is no example in political history, he says, of a dictatorship that was "productive after serving the purpose for which it had been created" (ibid., 69). Stsiborsky envisages a republican system without political parties. In it people will be elected to a State Council by universal and secret ballot (ibid., 112, 115). This, he says, will put the Council in direct contact with the people, who will be organized in syndicates and social groups. The *vozhd* will be elected every seven years by a National Congress made up of a State Council, an All-Ukrainian Economic Council, representatives of syndicates and regional councils. The *vozhd*, says Stsiborsky, will be neither a dictator, not a "puppet-like" president of a democratic republic (ibid., 116). The text shows that the OUN's focus was on winning national independence through revolution and creating a strong state. The ambiguities around the term "nation" and "dictatorship" remained largely unresolved, perhaps deliberately.

Authoritarian nationalism (Stsiborsky's preferred this term to integral nationalism) itself went through a political evolution. As pointed out in chapter 2, the apogee of its totalitarian phase, according to Zaitsev, occurred with the publication in the autumn of 1939 of the "Outline of a Project of the Main Laws (Constitution) of the Ukrainian State," in which the first article states: "Ukraine is a sovereign, authoritarian, totalitarian state of occupational estates that bears the name Ukrainian State" (Zaitsev 2011, 211; 2013b, 21). Especially in the period 1938–41, when the OUN tried to cooperate with the Germans, it made public statements increasingly supportive of Germany and Hitler. The antisemitic current that had been present in the movement from the late 1920s emerged forcefully in 1938 in the organization's public pronouncements, which began indiscriminately linking Jews to the "primary" enemy—Moscow and Soviet communism. However, the top eschelon of the émigré leadership (Konovalets, Stsiborsky, Onatsky, Andriievsky, Martynets) in public statements and private correspondence disassociated itself from national socialism, racism, and German hegemonism. It also consistently rejected the fascist label.

Historians still debate whether the pre-1943 OUN can be described as fascist. Internal correspondence and published articles make it clear that the émigré leaders strongly admired Italian fascism because it conducted an anti-communist struggle and appeared to offer the promise of national unity, political and cultural rejuvenation. But the OUN's ultimate goal remained an independent state. Hence, members of the organization defined themselves as fighters for national liberation, not fascists. Focused on winning a state, they were much less interested in discussing the state's possible nature. The Third Extraordinary Congress, which took place in Ukraine on 21–25 September 1943, although not a complete reorientation and acceptance of Western democratic and liberal principles, was "certainly the beginning of a metamorphosis in the OUN's ranks" (Hrynevych 2012, 53). Ensuing events demonstrate that a large number of members genuinely embraced these principles.

Alexander Motyl therefore appears to be correct when he writes that "the Ukrainian nationalist movement's relationship to political ideology changed continually, proceeding from an apolitical militarism to authoritarianism to proto-fascism to democracy to social democracy. Thus, whereas nationalism as national liberation was a constant, the political ideology was variable" (Motyl 2013, 25 June).

Within the eight months that followed the outbreak of the German-Soviet war, most of the organization's leaders had been arrested by the Germans and many of its members murdered. In 1943 the organization was involved in a bloody struggle to expel the Polish population from Volhynia. From 1943 the underground OUN and UPA fought both Nazi and Soviet forces, as well as Polish partisans. Throughout this period it was continually adjusting and changing its ideology. And continued to do so after the war.

Different forms of nationalism were not allowed serious study in the Soviet Union, where it was standard procedure to equate them all with fascism and anti-semitism. This has eclipsed the fact that democratic nationalism was a different phenomenon from authoritarian nationalism, and the latter was itself a multifac-eted phenomenon that included competing currents. The focus on a particular period, event, or selected statements can obscure this reality. Democratic nation-alists pointed out that the OUN was fundamentally sectarian and cultish. Mykhailo Demkovych-Dobriansky wrote in a letter to Mykhailo Antonovych on 13 November 1940: "The Nationalists have made a sect out of a political organi-zation and a dogma out of a few principles of their 'world-view.' Whoever does not recognize these dogmas is a heathen, a heretic, condemned to destruction, lacking the right to live among people of the chosen faith" (quoted in Hrynevych 2012, 435).

Right-wing authoritarianism found adherents in a variety of currents (monar-chist, conservative, religious fundamentalist), and not only within regimes supportive of Hitler but also within democracies. Among Ukrainians it arose in a climate of moral nihilism created by the cynical acceptance of Realpolitik. The Ukrainian population, whether in Western Ukraine, emigration, or the Soviet Union, was vulnerable to the temptations of this politics of despair. After 1923 Europe appeared to have washed its hands of the Ukrainian question. The Holodomor, the Gulag, the German and Soviet invasions of East European countries in 1938–40, which were followed by mass deportations and murders, all contributed to a belief among many young people that violence was the norm and might was right.

But the political ideology of authoritarian nationalism was not homoge-neous. The OUN's ideology might profitably be compared with Dontsovism. Dontsov proposed an amoral voluntarism, in which ends justified means and action was elevated over thought, and he spread a cynical contempt for ordinary people. His brand of Realpolitik and glorification of national egoism offered no resistance to Nazi fanaticism; it could in fact be read as justifying it. This Dontsovian attitude helped to create an atmosphere that many commentators at the time described as a moral degeneration. Although not all members of the OUN leadership were Dontsovians, his "doctrine" played a baneful role in spreading fanaticism and hatred. Fed by the cruelties of war, it thrived in the years 1939–41. It should be recalled that unlike the war in the West, which was in many ways a more traditional conflict, the one in the East from the beginning ignored all conventions; it was a brutal war of extermination and enslavement.

This account has argued that all three main currents of Ukrainian nation-alism—the national democratic and the two versions of radical authoritarian nationalism (the OUN's and the Dontsovian)—can be distinguished, even though they influenced one another and at points blended into one another. They were able to interact in no small part because they shared a wider vision of modernity, according to which their country and people would rapidly catch up with Western economic and cultural progress. During the interwar years the broader democratic current viewed this modernization as occurring in a more evolutionary fashion; the OUN, in contrast, saw it as a forced march, which they, as the government, would lead. Dontsov introduced a frenzied tone and a xenophobia that was also a form of "self-hatred" insofar as it attacked almost all forms of traditionalism and hitherto accepted moral norms. He steered the interwar generation toward adulation of Western dictators and implied that the solutions to political and cultural problems were brutally simple.

Authoritarian nationalism operated in a wider force field dominated by a modernizing and modernist sensibility that embraced the paradigm of rupture and change, accepted new technologies and the idea of a transformed human character. Its sources were Nietzsche, Spengler, Sorel, Bergson, but also futurism, expressionism, and the avant-garde. Throughout their evolution authoritarian nationalists remained committed to the modernist ideal of rapid transformational change—societal, psychological, and political. This explains why more often than not their authors admired and borrowed from writers of the Cultural Renaissance, the great innovators in the Soviet Ukraine of the 1920s who were executed or silenced in the 1930s. In its militant rhetoric the literature of authoritarian nationalism sometimes resembles this Soviet writing, but there is nothing in the creative literature of the seven leading writers—Lypa, Olzhych, Samchuk, Mosendz, Klen, Teliha, or Malaniuk—that comes close to the crudeness of much Socialist Realist writing, or to the bloodthirsty rhetoric of some politically motivated works produced in this period by leading Soviet writers. These seven writers, at least, maintained a high level of literary decorum as a matter of principle. Although in the thirties the OUN's political rhetoric was often directed against the Polish state, perhaps surprisingly, in their creative literature these seven figures did not denounce Poland. In many ways they admired Polish nationalism and modeled their views upon it. The Poles had, after all, succeeded in winning a state in 1919, even if this had been achieved partly at Ukrainian expense. Opprobrium in their works is reserved for Muscovy, the Russian Empire, and the Soviet Union.

The three strands of nationalism drew from the same pool of myths. Like the audience in Shakespeare's *Henry V*, the Ukrainian reader delighted in the image of a conquering ruler, accepted the heroic tone, stirring message, and call to steel the spirit. St. George the warrior-saint and Kyrylo Kozhumiaka, the folk hero who defeats the dragon and rescues a captive maiden, were constantly present in the art and literature of this period as symbols of the struggle for liberation. But then they have always served this role in popular, patriotic, even children's literature. The same can be said of historical fiction. Just as English audiences have been stirred by the stories of Edward III, the Black Prince, and Henry V, the Ukrainian public was moved by narratives of Kyivan Rus and Cossackdom. Victories over Polovtsian and Pecheneg tribes, like the Battles of Agincourt and Cressy for English readers, fueled dreams of glory. Past greatness brought a sense of dignity to the lives of contemporaries and held out hope for improvement. By recounting inspiring episodes in history, these narratives offered images of a better future. Their purpose was also to define the nation's character and distinctive qualities, its preparedness for action. The entire interwar generation took part in this mythologizing and historicizing trend.

The myths of palingenesis or regenerative revolution, Rome, the healthy pagan or barbarian, and the transformed individual—each suggested that a successful future could be created by drawing strength from the ancestral past. By using these myths, the seven major writers discussed were most successful in articulating the OUN's belief system and giving it a mobilizing power. This patriotic note and mythmaking is also evident in the songs of the UPA, which provide another example of how this generation defined itself.[1]

Like all totalitarian movements (a label that in the 1930s was worn with pride by the OUN's ideologists), this one lived within its own fantasies and, until the experience of the war wrought a profound change, rejected the idea of cooperating or forming alliances with other parties or groups. It used terror against those among "the people" who disagreed publicly with the organization's tactics and opinions, frequently assassinating individuals who belonged to rival groups with a similar ideology, not to mention hostile organizations. This fiercely partisan attitude was to a degree reflected in the creative literature inspired by authoritarian nationalism. In contrast to the wider, democratic current, the work of the seven writers close to the OUN struck a more urgent note and introduced an apocalyptic tone. It sometimes voiced criticism of narrow-mindedness, arrogance, and brutality in "its own" ranks. Frequently, however, it ignored these, preferring to praise the virtues of single-mindedness, determination, and willfulness.

A critique of Dontsovism did take place within the OUN in the 1930s, but it is not to the organization's credit that the discussion was denied a public airing. Not until the postwar years was such a critique vigorously prosecuted in public by those who espoused liberal and democratic principles. These included figures like Sherekh, Kosach, and Humenna, and the leaders of the OUN-Z, the organization formed by those who broke with the OUN-B over the issue of

democracy. Those former supporters of the OUN who retreated from totalitarian positions, produced some of their best works in these years—works that
often served as public disavowals or, in part at least, as acts of atonement. Among
such texts one could mention Samchuk's *Moroziv khutir* (1948), Mosendz's
Ostannii prorok (unfinished at the author's death in 1948, published 1960), and
Klen's stories and epic poem *Popil imperii* (unfinished at the author's death in
1948, published 1957).

In Soviet writing the demonization of all forms of Ukrainian nationalism has
a long tradition, and would make an interesting study in itself. Soviet writers
considered almost any criticism of their state—and, from the 1930s, of the
Russian Empire—as "fascist" or "counterrevolutionary," while at the same time
they often made their own xenophobia into a form of patriotic ritual. Under the
impact of such attacks, discussions of nationalist ideology have sometimes
adopted a Manichaean approach and an eschatological tone. A study of the
interwar period and of the literature it produced suggests that such a simplified
view should be resisted. Even when one examines the seven pro-OUN writers,
it becomes clear that, in spite of similarities in their ideological development,
each responded to circumstances in quite different ways. Moreover, each elaborated a critique of the mythmaking that surrounded them.

The dominant trend throughout the 1930s was toward ever-greater authoritarianism: most European countries at this time developed anti-internationalist,
antiliberal, and often overtly antisemitic movements. The radical right believed
that only the fittest nations would survive, and the Communist Parties believed
in wiping the bourgeoisie and its supporters off the face of the earth. Accordingly,
both sides promoted soldierly virtues and commitment to a strong state, and
embraced the palingenetic myth. There were, however, many nuances. Although
numerous individuals admired the martial attitude and dreamed of a strong state,
they were not necessarily pro-fascist and antisemitic, or pro-communist and
Stalinist. A fascination with myth, medieval times, and Cossackdom, or with the
contemporary discourses around history, health, biology, and sexuality did not in
itself reveal a political proclivity.

Western democracies were in the 1930s and 1940s focused on the threat from
Hitler or Stalin. They generally showed little interest in the issue of Ukrainian
minorities or sympathy for the Ukrainian independence struggle. In the postwar
period they did not have to deal with Ukraine as a political factor in international relations. The Soviet Union was therefore able to conduct a brutal war
against the UPA and the resistance of the Western Ukrainian population with
relative impunity.[2] Although the Cold War produced a need for Ukrainian
experts (as a result of which the OUN-Z became a useful source of information

for the Americans), the Ukrainian question was viewed as the internal affair of a totalitarian regime and superpower. Nationalists were demonized by Soviet authorities, identified as "German-Ukrainian fascists," de-individualized and often referred to as animals (Weiner 2001, 168). State revenge was institutionalized by the USSR, a fact that set it apart from other countries. Arrests and deportations in the hundreds of thousands continued in the postwar period. While in the 1940s and 1950s pardons were being granted to French and German citizens, even those who had participated in wartime massacres, there was no such amnesty for Nationalists (ibid., 188).

Like its political ideology, the political orientation of revolutionary nationalism went through changes. The UVO, OUN, UPA, and UHVR evolved in response to international developments and searched for allies in different places. From 1921 the UVO's orientation was toward Germany, which provided financing on the understanding that the organization's activities would be directed against Poland, since the Weimar Republic was secretly rearming by cooperating with Soviet armed forces. The UVO and then the OUN also received funding from the Lithuanian government. It kept an office in Kovno and printed *Surma* there from 1928 to 1934 (Kentii 2005, 60). However, it did not renounce the principle of self-reliance. The Nazi accession to power and the German-Polish pact of 1935 eliminated the possibility of German support. Émigré leaders, however, realized that Germany remained the key player in Eastern Europe and that relations with it could not be avoided. They were divided on how to deal with the regime. Konovalets, when ejected from Geneva in 1936, moved to Rome partly to escape German pressure. He made attempts to establish contacts with British and French circles, as well as with the Italian and Japanese governments (V. Stakhiv 2005, 24–31). Commentators have written that while he was alive the OUN had no contacts with the SS intelligence service, the Sicherheitsdienst [Security Service], and the Gestapo (ibid., 47). Contacts with the Abwehr were reestablished in the spring of 1938 after a conspiratorial meeting near Vienna (Kentii 2005, 133). Following Konovalets's assassination, both factions of the OUN oriented themselves toward Germany, which they viewed as the only power capable of changing the status quo. Samchuk has written that the experience of earlier decades convinced Ukrainians that "only Germany could have an interest in Ukraine's emergence in an independent form." But, he added, "Slavic political amorphousness" made Ukrainians vulnerable to manipulation (Samchuk 1965, 63–64). After the Bandera faction failed to win German support for independence, it made several miscalculations: the mutual war of attrition between Germany and the Soviet Union was not fought to the expected stalemate; an OUN-led front of oppressed nations within the

Soviet Union could not be created; and the postwar conflict between the Western allies and the Soviet Union did not erupt as foreseen. At the end of the war the OUN-B did cooperate with British intelligence, and the OUN-Z with American. However, the idea that the OUN and UPA were obedient tools of fascist regimes or Western powers was a fantasy spread by Soviet propaganda. By the same token, the view that the OUN had support in all sectors of Ukrainian society or that its history did not have a dark side were also fantasies. These myths were exposed with the opening of the archives in the 1990s.

Nonetheless, in spite of their political miscalculations, the Nationalists were in the postwar years able to mount the longest and most determined war against Soviet rule since the Revolution of 1917–20 and the battles against collectivization in 1929–30. They succeeded, as one researcher put it, in engraving on the population's consciousness "a faith in the possibility of winning state independence and in the inevitable fall of the communist party regime in the USSR" (Kentii 2005, 16). It is this aspect of Nationalist history that many take pride in today. The OUN, like its figurehead Bandera, are for many contemporaries symbols of uncompromising patriotism and anticolonial resistance. Their idealization serves as psychological compensation for the forty years of Soviet rule and Russificatory policies that followed the war, or represents a reaction against the growth of contemporary Russian nationalism and Moscow's heavy-handed intervention into Ukraine's political affairs. However, as scholars have pointed out, this idealization has created a rift between "historical knowledge confined to academic and intellectual circles and narratives suggested to a broader audience" (Narvselius 2012, 490). The idealization marginalizes unwelcome facts, such as the OUN's embrace of a totalitarian ideology prior to 1943, the brutality of the war it unleashed against the Polish population of Volhynia in 1943, and its complicity in the killing of Jews. The last is evident in the antisemitic rhetoric that issued from the leadership in 1938–41 and encouraged violence, and the failure to condemn the killing of Jews that began when Germany invaded the Soviet Union on 22 June 1941. A glorification of the organization and its leader may be seen by some observers as tacit confirmation of what Eleonora Narvselius has called "a totalitarian principle that political transformations justify violence" (ibid., 477). Yaroslav Hrytsak is one of a number of historians who have written that immoral or criminal acts, which form a part of all national histories, need to be acknowledged, and their causes and consequences understood (Hrytsak 2004, 110–11). Only through full disclosure and informed debate will the misaligned, often conflicting narratives that at present characterize political, academic, and popular accounts of Ukrainian nationalism be surmounted.

NOTES

1. For a collection of exchanges on the OUN, see *Strasti za Banderoiu*, edited by T. S. Amar, I. Bachynskyi and Ia. Hrytsak (2007). On the Bandera debate, see Narvselius (2012). Discussions of the OUN have appeared regularly on the Web portal Zakhid.net of *Istorychna Pravda*: http://www.istpravda.com.ua; *Ukraina Moderna*: http://uamoderna.com; *Historian.in*: http://www.historians.in.ua; and in the journal *Krytyka*. A special issue entitled *Historical Memory and World War II in Russia and Ukraine* has been devoted to contested memory by the journal *Canadian Slavonic Papers*, 54.3–4 (2012): 401–510. See also the Web site *Memory at War*: www.memoryat-war.org.

2. Tomasz Stryjek has written a book on Ukrainian political thinkers (2000); Roman Wysocki (2003) and Robert Potocki (2003) have examined Poland's attitude toward its Ukrainian population in the 1930s, and the OUN in particular; Grzegorz Motyka has produced an important study of the OUN as a wartime partisan movement (2006b); and Andrzej A. Zięba has studied the interwar lobbying campaigns conducted in the West by the Ukrainian emigration (1993, 2010).

3. Franziska Bruder (2007) and Frank Golczewski (2010a) made extensive use of German archives to throw light on the organization's relationship with the Third Reich. Their work extends the exploration of German sources begun earlier by researchers like Volodymyr Kosyk (2009, 1993), Ihor Kamenetskyi (1974), and Dmytro Zlepko (1980, 1994).

4. Amir Weiner (2001), Kate Brown (2004), Karel C. Berkhoff (2004), Wendy Lower (2005), and Timothy Snyder (1999, 2003a, 2010a, 2010b).

5. Dieter Pohl (1997, 2007, 2010), Martin Dean (1996, 2000), John-Paul Himka (2011b), Marco Carynnyk (2011), and Taras Hunczak (2009). A collection of articles by Brandon and Lower (2010) includes work by several leading researchers in this field.

6. Ihor I. Iliushyn (2000, 2001, 2009) and Anatolii Kentii (2005).

7. Among them are Kostiantyn Kurylyshyn's description of the legal press under German occupation (2010) and Oleksandra Stasiuk's examination of the propaganda work conducted by the OUN and UPA (2006).

8. Vincent Shandor (1997), O. Pahiria (2009), Andrzej Małkiewicz (2001), and Maria Mandryk (2009).

9. See the collections of the OUN's internal documents by M. I. Serhiichuk (1996, 2009) and Volodymyr Viatrovych (2011). The minutes of the OUN's founding congress of 1929 have been edited by Volodymyr Muravsky (2006).

10. See in particular Voldymyr Prystaiko and Yurii Shapoval (1995, 1996, 1999), O. Rublov and Iu. Cherchenko (1994), Oleksandr Rublov (2004), Oleksandr Rublov and Natalia Rublova (2012), Oleksandr Ushkalov and Leonid Ushkalov (2010), and Vadym Zolotarov (2007). See Bertelsen and Shkandrij (2014), Shkandrij and Bertelsen (2013).

11. Archival sources available in Canada, Britain, and the United States have also been used by scholars. Among them are Karel Berkhoff, Richard Breitman, Martin Dean, Lubomyr Y. Luciuk, Marco Carynnyk, Orest T. Martynowych, and John-Paul Himka.

12. Earlier books, such as those by Mykola S[ydor]-Chartoryiskyi (1951), Yevhen Onatsky (1954, 1981–89), Zinovii Knysh (1959–67), Ivan Kedryn (1976), Ulas Samchuk (1965, 1975), Stepan Kasiian (1967), Volodymyr Kubiiovych (1975), Kost Pankivsky (1983), Vasyl Roman (1983), and the collection edited by Yurii Boiko (1974), are well known. Newer accounts by eyewitnesses—some of whom were members of the OUN—have now supplemented these. Among more recently published recollections are those of Hryhorii Stetsiuk (1988), Mykhailo Seleshko (1991), Yevhen Stakhiv (1995), Vincent Shandor (1997), Yurii Shevelov (2001), Volodymyr P. Stakhiv (2005), Roman Petrenko (1997, 2004), and Larysa Krushelnytska (2008). Ostap Tarnavsky has provided an account of literary life in Lviv during the war (1995).

13. Most notable is the work of Tomasz Stryjek (2000 and 2002), Zaitsev (2013a), and of Zaitsev, Behen, and Stefaniv (2011). The first version of Serhii Kvit's account (2000) praises "authoritarian doctrines" and denounces liberalism and modernity (to which, in the author's opinion, all centrist parties, including conservative ones, subscribe). Detractors of Dontsov and integral nationalism, are placed into an undifferentiated camp of liberals, leftists, totalitarians, "socialist realists," and postmodernists. At various points the account also condemns humanism, rationalism, and atheism. The revised second edition (2013) eliminates such passages but denies Dontsov's antisemitism and argues that the writer viewed totalitarian regimes as continuing European traditionalism and conservatism.

14. For a discussion of these, see Myroslav Shkandrij 2014 (forthcoming). "The Second World War and the OUN in Reader Responses to Dokia Humenna's *Khreshchatyi iar* (1956)," *Journal of Ukrainian Studies*.

15. Ihor Nabytovych (2001), Mykola Ilnytsky (1995, 2009), Lesia Kravchenko (2004), Raisa Movchan (2008), and Olesia Omelchuk (2011).

16. Other scholars who in different ways explore this line of inquiry include Matthew Affron and Antliff (1997), Mark Antliff (2007), Jeffrey Herf (1984), Richard Wolin (2004), and Frederic Spotts (2009).

CHAPTER 1. INTERWAR NATIONALISM, 1922–38

1. Some soldiers from Central or Eastern Ukraine were allowed to settle in Volhynia, Galicia, or the Chełm (Kholm) regions but forbidden to engage in any political or

community work. Since they were not given Polish citizenship, they were under threat of deportation to the Soviet Union if they violated this condition (Petrenko 2004, 22–23).

2. The French military urged the Allies to send arms and ammunition to Poland and recommended that a legion formed out of the Polish prisoners captured in the war should be sent to help resist a bolshevik invasion: "The Supreme Council assented to these expedients. The Poles were armed and the Polish divisions, equipped with the necessary artillery, were despatched to Warsaw under a General Haller. [. . .] Haller's Army, which was ready for war when it arrived, was immediately marched into Galicia, ostensibly to drive off the Bolsheviks, but in reality to conquer the country and annex it to Poland. The Supreme Council sent a message to General Haller ordering his withdrawal. Of this command he did not take the slightest notice. Subsequently he pretended that he had never received the telegram in time to act upon the instructions it conveyed" (Lloyd George 1938, vol. 1, 312). At the peace congress Poland rejected application of the principle of self-determination in the case of Galicia, stating: "In settling the boundaries of Poland, the principle of including within those boundaries only those territories where the Poles were in a large majority must not be accepted" (ibid., 313).

3. For an overview of interwar Western Ukraine, see Magocsi 2010, 626–51, and Budurowycz 1983.

4. On Schwartzbard's work as a Soviet agent, see V. Savchenko (2009).

5. See, for example, Chojnowski 1979, 173–205; Torzecki 1989, 146–64; and the more-recent works of Snyder 2005, and Zięba 1993, 80–86; 2008; and 2010, 650–89.

6. Knysh has written that the OUN's youth organizer, Ivan Gabrusevych, taught students how to use explosives and inflammatory materials and encouraged them to apply this knowledge during their summer vacation. He maintains that the Homeland Executive did not sanction the arsons and Yuliian Holovinsky made strenuous attempts to stop them (Knysh 1951, 15). Zięba disagrees with this assessment. He writes that "the OUN/UVO was clearly the main organizer of the sabotage," whose main goal was "to provoke the government and Polish organizations into a forceful reaction, so that this could be used in international propaganda" (2010, 372). The action, according to Zięba, had been prepared by Konovalets in Geneva and was inspired by Weimar Germany (ibid., 666–67). The plan was to discredit the Polish government and force the League of Nations to guarantee Galicia's autonomy, but also to consolidate German political and financial help. The OUN misjudged the League's reaction, which did not condemn Poland. However, Zięba's argument is contradicted by other witnesses, by internal OUN documents, and by the files of the Polish police, who could attribute only 14 of 180 acts of sabotage committed from August to October of 1930 to the UVO. In all likelihood the action was not planned or supported by the OUN, but the organization decided to take responsibility for it in order to gain political capital and to align itself with the spreading peasant discontent (Zaitsev 2013a, 251–55). For Polish authorities it was important to pin the action on the OUN and frame it as a German provocation so as to justify the Pacification.

7. It has been suggested that this move was a response to the imminent acceptance of the Soviet Union into the League of Nations. Warsaw wanted to deprive Moscow of the

opportunity to attack the treatment of Ukrainians and Belarusian in Poland (Budurowycz 1983, 488).

8. The OUN's clash with the Youth for Christ movement is described in Zaitsev, Behen, and Stefaniv 2011, 265–87.

9. On Nazaruk's critique, see Zaitsev, Behen, and Stefaniv 2011, 312–13; on the Church's criticism of "neo-nationalism," see 265–87. Other Catholic organizations created at this time include the Ukrainska Khrystyianska Orhanizatsiia (Ukrainian Christian Organization), which in 1930 became the Ukrainska Katolytska Orhanizatsiia (Ukrainian Catholic Organization); the Ukrainskyi Katolytskyi Soiuz (Ukrainian Catholic Union), which was formed in 1930; and the Katolytska Aktsiia (Catholic Action), which later became the Katolytska Aktsiia Ukrainskoi Molodi (Catholic Action of Ukrainian Youth). Many observers felt that the formation of the Ukrainian Catholic Party by Bishop Hryhorii Khomyshyn and the Ukrainian Catholic Union by Metropolitan Andrei Sheptytsky were direct responses by the Church to the actions of underground groups, both nationalist and communist.

10. Elected to the Sejm in 1928, Paliiv was arrested along with other deputies in 1930 and spent three years in prison. In the years 1939–43 he was not politically active, but in 1943 he helped to organize and served in the Ukrainian Division Galizien (Halychyna). He was killed at the Battle of Brody. The main ideologist of the Front Natsionalnoi Iednosti was Mykola Shlemkevych (pseudonym M. Ivaneiko). The party's "creative nationalism" was less radical and less inclined to violence than Dontsov's "active nationalism" and the OUN's "organized nationalism." Its main organ *Peremoha* (Victory, 1933–35) argued that Ukrainians should learn from the successes of Italian fascism but it also printed some of Rostyslav Yendyk's antisemitic and racist articles. From 1934 Paliiv and Shlemkevych fought the UNDO's politics of accommodation. They stressed the importance of "organic" work (community building, social and economic development) and opposed the OUN's terrorist tactics, arguing that the OUN, like the bolsheviks, was for ochlocracy, or the dictatorship of a party over the broad masses (Zaitsev 2013a, 329–74).

11. Zięba informs that the real author of this publication was Vasyl Koroliv-Staryi, who was commissioned to write it by the independent lobbyist Yakiv Makohin. Makohin ran an information bureau in London and was appalled by the OUN's terrorist tactics. Koroliv-Staryi, who lectured at the Ukrainian Academy of Economics in Poděbrady in Czechoslovakia, worked closely with Makohin (Zięba 2010, 636).

12. It has also been suggested that Holówko was assassinated by the OUN because he was a leading spokesman for a Polish-Ukrainian rapprochement and for the strategy of Prometheanism — neither of which was desired by Galician Ukrainians. Moreover, he worked closely with the UNR camp (supporters of the exiled government of the Ukrainian People's Republic) that constituted the OUN's main political rival in the émigré community. Zięba considers Konovalets responsible for the assassination and argues that the latter tried to distance himself from the action when its disastrous political consequences became clear. The OUN was henceforth firmly identified with terrorism and any support among Western states was permanently undermined. Moreover, the attempt to publicize the Pacification in the League of Nations and in

Western capitals was damaged, and Konovalets was told to leave Geneva. In Galicia the action exacerbated the conflict with Metropolitan Sheptytsky, the UNDO, and Dmytro Paliiv. In response to the assassination, both Onatsky and Andriievsky expressed a desire to resign from the organization-and to devote themselves to political lobbying in the Western press and with governments (Zięba 2010, 521, 581, 639–41).

13. Onatsky has described the international conference called in Geneva on 17 January 1931, and the cooperation at this conference between members of the OUN, the wider Ukrainian community, and international figures (Onatskyi 1981, 12–18).

14. At the Paris Peace Conference in November 1919 England's plan was for Eastern Galicia to become a mandate territory of the League of Nations under Polish administration. On 21 November the Supreme Council accepted the statute of autonomy for Eastern Galicia in spite of Polish objections. The statute took the form of a treaty between Poland on one side and America, England, France, Italy, and Japan on the other. The statute gave Poland a twenty-five-year mandate to govern and administer Eastern Galicia on condition that the territorial autonomy of the country, spelled out in subsequent articles, be respected. The Polish administration was under the control of the League of Nations. At the end of the twenty-five years the League would have the right to renew, withdraw, or change the mandate (Kuchabsky 2009, 318–19).

15. As a result of this agreement some students traveled to Italy for study and received stipends. They were restricted, however, to the study of Italian language and history, economics, and similar subjects, and not allowed to study military subjects. The OUN's contacts with Italian officials remained at the level of "mutually beneficial propagandistic activity" (Kovalchuk 2011).

16. See Shkandrij 2009, 150–65.

CHAPTER 2. THE WAR AND POSTWAR YEARS, 1939–56

1. When it became part of Czechoslovakia in 1919 the territory was called Subcarpathian Rus (Pidkarpatska Rus; in Czech, Podkarpatska Rus). It became known as Carpathian Ukraine after gaining autonomy, but in English-language publications is generally referred to as Carpatho-Ukraine.

2. The broadcasts lasted from 29 September 1938 to 22 September 1939 and were allowed by German intelligence, as part of a strategy to destabilize Czechoslovakia. See Havryliuk 1964.

3. Pro-Ukrainian Jewish voices did exist. See Shkandrij, 2009, 92–136, and Yohanan Petrovsky-Shtern, *The Anti-Imperial Choice: the Making and Unmaking of the Ukrainian Jew* (New Haven, CT: Yale University Press, 2009). It might be recalled that early Soviet Ukrainian historians of Jewish origin emphasized the role that Jews played in the victory of bolshevik rule in Ukraine. Moisei Ravich-Cherkassky in his *Istoriia Kommunisticheskoi Partii (b-ov) Ukrainy* (Kharkiv: Gosudarstvennoe izdatelstvo Ukrainy, 1923) did not hide the fact that the proportion of Ukrainians in the Red Army and the leadership of the Communist Party (bolshevik) of Ukraine was extremely small. He put forward the theory that this party had developed from three separate streams—Russian, Jewish, and Ukrainian—and said it was "undeniable that until

recently and in significant measure today" the party remained "largely a party of the
Russian or Russified proletariat" (11). M. G. Rafes in his *Dva goda revoliutsii na
Ukraine* (Moscow, 1920) argued that without the Jewish cadres the Right Bank of
Ukraine would not have been subdued. M. M. Popov in his *Narys istorii Komunistychnoi
partii (Bilshovykiv) Ukrainy*, 4th ed. (Kharkiv: Proletarii, 1930) also pointed out that
Russian and Jewish cadres were Russophile and that Ukrainians ceaselessly com-
plained about being marginalized (211). However, these texts concealed the fact that
Rafes, like many other leaders of the Jewish Bund, had in 1917–18 supported the
Ukrainian Central Rada and fiercely opposed the bolsheviks. From reading them it
was possible to form an impression of the Jewish population as pro-bolshevik in these
years.

4. See Griffin 2007, 247. For a discussion of racism in the OUN's ideology, see chapter 4.
5. These acronyms were quickly established, as were the terms "Banderites" and
   "Melnikites." In fact, the official acronym of the Bandera group was OUN-R, in which
   the "R" stood for "Revolutionaries," while the Melnyk group simply continued to call
   itself the OUN.
6. Although conservative estimates have put the number of people in the OUN-B expeditionary forces at around twelve hundred, Shankovsky says the figure was five thousand. Others have put the number even higher (Kentii 2005, 238).
7. Two battalions, named Nachtigall and Roland, were removed in the first weeks of the
   war after protesting German policy toward Ukraine. Nachtigall had reached Vinnytsia.
   On 1 December 1941 both formations were given the option of signing a contract to
   serve in the municipal police force for one year or be sent to Germany for forced labor.
   Reformed as the 201 Police Battalion, on 16 March 1942 these soldiers were sent to a
   region near Minsk for guard and antipartisan duties. After the year was completed,
   most of the 650 men refused to renew the contact. Soldiers were allowed to return to
   Galicia, but officers were imprisoned or kept under house arrest and told to report
   regularly to the Gestapo. Many soldiers and officers soon disappeared into the underground, where they joined the partisans (G. Motyka 2006b, 114–15, Hunczak 2009). A
   Bukovynian force (popularly known as the Bukovynian Battalion) entered Kyiv in the
   wake of the German advance as the 115 Battalion. It was then reformed as the 118
   Battalion and used for clearing demolished buildings on Khreshchatyk Street. In
   August 1942, it was again reconstituted as the 115 Battalion and sent to Belarus for
   antipartisan fighting. Transferred to France in 1944, it immediately deserted on 27
   June, joined the French underground, and fought the Germans as the Second
   Ukrainian Shevchenko Battalion (Dereiko 2003; Petrenko 2004, 68–69).
8. Motyka has argued that the Bandera faction had most to gain from the assassinations.
   He also considers the Bandera faction responsible for the assassination of Yaroslav
   Baranovych on 11 May 1943, and for Roman Sushko's killing on 14 January 1944 (G.
   Motyka 2006b, 128–29). Kentii appears to agree with this assessment (Kentii 2005,
   245–46).
9. Berkhoff calculates that most Schuma were Ukrainians, but there were also Russians
   and members of other nationalities. Some Schuma battalions were designated as
   Latvian, Lithuanian, Cossack, or Polish, and there were ethnic German, Estonian,

Uzbek, Azerbaijani, and Central Asian units. There were also battalions made up only of Reich Germans, who collectively "killed even more people than the Einsatzgruppen did" (Berkhoff 2004, 42).

10. For a list of members in this body, see Serhiichuk 1996, 240–42.

11. On the Polish-Ukrainian conflict, see Snyder 1999 and 2003a, Iliushyn 2001 and 2009; G. Motyka 2006b, 298–413; Viatrovych 2011, 21–142; Berkhoff 2004, 287–99. On Ukrainian losses, see Hud 2006, 348, 375.

12. On the historical background, see Beauvois 1993 and Hud 2006. The latter points out that as a result of interwar colonization, the number of Poles in Volhynia tripled from 100,000 to 360,000 (320) and that government repression in 1937–39 led to a "renaissance" of the Orthodox Church (333).

13. The complexities of this conflict and various explanations of how the fighting began are reviewed in Iliushyn 2011.

14. For a review of the literature in Polish, see the Zbrodnia Wolynska site: http://www.zbrodniawolynska.pl/czytelnia, and for a review of the literature in Ukrainian, see the Istorychna Pravda site: http://www.istpravda.com.ua/articles/2013/06/21/126702/. A trilingual (Polish, Ukrainian, English) collection of essays on the subject has been published by Alexandra Zińczuk, ed., 2012. The publication was financed by Poland's Ministry of Foreign Affairs.

15. On 20 June 2013 the Polish Senate passed a resolution to call the events in Volhynia "an ethnic cleansing with the features of a genocide."

16. On the SB's atrocities, see Grzegorz Motyka 2006a and Berkhoff 2004, 287, 297–98. The atrocities and participation of the OUN's secret police are also attested by members of the UPA and OUN. See, for example, Shumuk 1998, 132.

17. Berkhoff has written: "It seems clear that early in 1943, the leadership of the Bandera faction decided to kill all Poles in the Ukrainian-dominated land between the Buh River and the pre–1939 border, lands that the Polish government-in-exile and the Polish underground had continued to claim for the Polish state" (Berkhoff 2004, 291). However, the source quoted in support of this statement, Taras Bulba-Borovets's *Armiia bez derzhavy*, 1981, 251, 253, 272, is problematic. Borovets was pushed out of Volhynia in 1943 and his army forcibly absorbed into the OUN-controlled UPA. His writings, although resolutely anti-Banderite, are unreliable in a number of respects, including the dating of events, his relations with the Germans, and his treatment of Jews and Poles. On his relations with the OUN-B, see Dziobak 1995, 42–49; on his relations with Poles, see 49–50.

18. Bandera's response to this debate can be followed in his *Perspektyvy ukrainskoi revoliutsii* (1999). Although in 1946 he spoke of a "monoparty system in state life" as "inappropriate for the needs of full and healthy national development" (39), on all other occasions he avoided speaking of the political nature of a future Ukrainian state. In 1950 he came out against the slogan "For a democratic order in Ukraine" as harmful (146) and denounced "various conjuncturalists" who since 1945 had supported democratic principles (158). In 1954 he wrote that the Western Representation of the UHVR was "slipping toward Marxism" (305) and said that the OUN-Z was promoting "antinationalist and pro-Marxist positions" (307). His writings defend the proclamation of a

renewed Ukrainian statehood on 30 June 1941, and deny that the language used expressed a friendly tone toward Germany (92–94). However, the OUN-B rarely made available the proclamation's full text, which spoke of close cooperation with "National Socialist Greater Germany" under Adolph Hitler.

CHAPTER 3. DMYTRO DONTSOV

1. Olesia Omelchuk writes that the *LNV* was financed through a fund of the Sichovi Striltsi (Sich Sharpshooters) Regiment that had been commanded by Konovalets. The later *Vistnyk* was financed by the family of Dontsov's wife, Maria Bachynska (Omelchuk 2011, 6).
2. Volodymyr Martynets wrote to Dontsov on 18 July 1930: "If you, Doctor, had at the time paid more attention to order in the political party around *Zahrava* and purged it of undesirable elements, then we would not have witnessed these undesirable elements outgrowing you, demolishing the party, and leaving you completely alone" (TsDAHO, f. 269, Dokumenty provodu OUN; quoted in Kentii 2005, 62).
3. For recent treatments of these dichotomous structures, see Golczewski 2010a, 512–20, Krupach 2009, and Zaitsev 2013a, 155–237. An insightful critique of Dontsov's political thought was produced by Sosnovsky, a leader of the postwar OUN-B, who emphasized the organization's evolution in the forties and fifties away from Dontsovism and Dontsov's inability to accept this fact (Sosnovskyi 1974). Zaitsev stresses Dontsov's mythmaking and admiration for the Roman Catholic Church's ability to inspire and discipline the masses (Zaitsev 2011 and 2013b). Kvit's apologia for Dontsov avoids dealing with the racist and pro-Hitler statements made in the late 1930s and early 1940s, but has the merit of drawing attention to the writer's style, which is viewed as a form of modernism (Kvit 2013). This work is a complete revision of the first edition (2003–04 and 2000).
4. Mudry's later evolution demonstrates the difficulty of conducting a democratic politics in undemocratic times. In 1944 he was part of a delegation mandated by the OUN to hold talks with the Gestapo and SD, and in July of that year he became a vice president of the UHVR, the governing body of the UPA (Kentii 48).
5. These statements were made in Dontsov 1937, 288–89; and 1939b, 328, 333–35. Zaitsev has also pointed out that in the last issue of *Vistnyk* published before the war Dontsov published, under a pseudonym, an article popularizing those passages of *Mein Kampf* that speak of the Jewish danger to the Aryan race (Zaitsev 2013a, 230). For the article, see A. R. "Zhydivske pytannia i natsionalsotsilizm," *Vistnyk* 9 (1939): 630–41.

CHAPTER 4. THE ORGANIZATION OF UKRAINIAN NATIONALISTS

1. The Decalogue read: "I am the Spirit of eternal nature [*stykii*] that preserved You from the Tatar deluge and placed You on the border of two worlds to create the new life: 1. You will win a Ukrainian State or die in the struggle. 2. You will allow no one to stain your Nation's glory or honor. 3. Remember the great days of our Liberation struggle. 4. Be proud that you are a descendant of the struggle for the glory of Volodymyr's

Trident. 5. You will avenge the death of the Great Knights. 6. Do not speak about the cause with whomever you can, but only with whom you should. 7. You will not hesitate to do the most dangerous act, if the good of the cause demands this. 8. You will greet your Nation's enemies with hatred and resolute struggle. 9. Neither requests, not threats, nor tortures, nor death will force you to reveal a secret. 10. You will strive to augment the power, glory, riches, and territory of the Ukrainian State." In their initial forms, point 7 read: "You will not hesitate to do the greatest crime [*zlochyn*], if the good of the Cause demands this"; point 8 read: "with deceit" rather than "with resolute struggle" (Mirchuk 1968, 126), and point 10 read: "You will strive to augment the power, glory, riches, and territory of the Ukrainian State even by means of subjugating foreigners" [*navit shliakhom ponevolennia chuzhyntsiv*] (Golczewski 2010a, 598). For the Twelve Character Traits and Forty-Four Principles of Conduct, see Mirchuk 1968, 127–30.

2. Zaitsev informs that in 1924 the Polish Ministry of Internal Affairs issued an order to deport Dontsov as a danger to civil order, but upon Dontsov's request the order was canceled. The editor made an agreement with Polish security services and the ministry, who agreed to stay the order for deportation if he changed his hostile attitude toward Poland. Zaitsev thinks it probable that Dontsov made certain promises and "from that moment carefully avoided acting in any way that might raise suspicion that he had links to nationalist organizations of an anti-Polish character, and refrained from publishing works overtly hostile to Poland" (Zaitsev 2013a, 165). Dontsov was arrested and interned by the Poles on 2 September 1939, the day after Germany invaded Poland. The Polish state was quickly overrun and almost all the prisoners were freed two weeks later when the Soviet Union invaded Poland from the east on September 17.

3. For a bibliography, see Havryliuk 1964.

4. See Miroslav Shkandrii, "Radio Vienna: Radioperedachi Organizatsii Ukrainskikh Natsionalistov" (Radio Vienna: Broadcasts by the Organization of Ukrainian Nationalists, 1938–39), *Forum*, 2014 (forthcoming).

5. Transcripts of the broadcasts, which began on 29 September 1938 and ended on 5 August 1939, are available in UCEC, Mykhailo Seleshko Archive, OUN B3 (c) and B4 (a) Ea–4–8, and in OUN B4 (a) Ea–4–9. Initially directed against the Soviet Union and Poland, the broadcasts were a concession to the OUN by the German military intelligence, who were aware that a war with Poland or the Soviet Union might occur and wanted to have some influence over the OUN, with whom they could trade for information concerning conditions in these two states. Until September 1939, the broadcasts were often agitational, aimed at exposing the repressive nature of the two regimes. After the signing of the Molotov-Ribbentrop pact on 23–24 August 1939, criticism of the Soviet Union ceased. The inclusion of an anti-Jewish component in the broadcasts may have been a "payment" to the Germans in return for continued radio broadcasts, military training, and the promise of future support.

6. Nitskevych had been sent to Bulgaria in 1933 to investigate the possibility of publishing *Rozbudova natsii* there should the situation in Czechoslovakia lead to the journal's closing. He reported that the strong influence of Russian nationalists on the government would make this difficult, but stayed on as an organizer of community events through which he tried to spread the organization's ideas. He was arrested by the

Soviet secret police near Sofia in 1944 and sentenced to death by a military tribunal, but since his role in the OUN could not be established and he had never lived on Soviet territory, this was commuted to twenty years of hard labor. He was released in 1956 and rehabilitated in 1964. He died in 1969. (Zhyviuk 2010, 229, 233–34).

7. In 1928 Konovalets wrote: "In Proskuriv the Sich Riflemen came face-to-face with the terrible evidence [*iavyshche*] of Jewish pogroms. We arrived in Proskuriv three days after the brutal killings [*rizni*]. Upon arrival I instructed Captain Bisyk to conduct an investigation. Together with the appointed town commander, H. Hladky, Captain Bisyk was able to collect very extensive materials on the causes of the pogrom, those chiefly responsible, the perpetrators, the development of the pogrom, and the losses to the city and Jewish population. I hope that the archive has not been lost and that this extraordinarily interesting material about the Proskuriv pogrom will, God grant, be made public" (Konovalets (1928), 4: 158).

CHAPTER 5. NATIONALIST LITERATURE BETWEEN MYTH AND MODERNISM

1. For a summary of these discussions, see Ilnytskyi 1995, 196–211, and Nabytovych 2001, 57–69.

2. Like him, Osyp Boidunyk, Yuliian Vassyian, Stepan Lenkavsky, and Zenon Pelensky also received four-year sentences. Pelensky was released in 1933 after his appeal was upheld. He quit the organization in the following year.

3. See Peter L. Berger, *The Sacred Canopy: Elements of a Sociological Theory of Religion* (Garden City, NY: Doubleday, 1967).

4. *My* may not have been as apolitical as the editors make out. Mykhailo Antonovych in his correspondence with Volodymyr Miiakovsky in 1945 suggested that the literary venture was a project of the UNR emigration. He says that the Roman Smal-Stotsky led the action, along with Andrii Kryzhanivsky (who used the pseudonym Dolengo). The idea was to attract young people who were showing disenchantment with Dontsov and *Vistnyk* (TsDAHO, f. 269, op. 2, spr. 33, ark. 111, 41b).

5. For a description of the literary scene in Lviv during the interwar period, the Soviet occupation of 1939–41, and the German occupation of 1941–44, see Ostap Tarnavsky's *Literaturnyi Lviv, 1995*.

6. For other articles in this debate, see P. Z., "Za ridne mystetstvo," *Krakivski visti*, 1 February 1942; ZET, "Ukrainske mystetstvo na novykh shliakhakh," *Krakivski visti*, 14 February 1942; Mykhailo Ostroverkha, "Za natsionalnyi kharakter mystetstva," *Krakivski visti*, 21 January 1943; Sviatoslav Hordynskyi, "Shche pro mystetsku krytyku," *Krakivski visti*, 25 July 1943; Damian Horniatkevych, "Sche na temu mystetskoi krytyky," *Krakivski visti*, 1 August 1943; Mykhailo Ostroverkha, "Nolens volens," *Krakivski visti*, 10 August 1943; Damian Horniatkevych, "Shche do problem mystetskoi krytyky," *Krakivski visti*, 13 August 1943.

7. Walter Benjamin, "Paris, Capital of the Nineteenth-Century," in *Reflections: Essays, Aphorisms, Autobiographical Writings*, trans. by E. Jephcott (New York: Harcourt Brace Jovanovich, 1978), 157. See also Graeme Gilloch, *Myth and Metropolis: Walter Benjamin and the City* (Cambridge, UK: Polity Press, 1996); Lutz Koepwick, *Walter Benjamin and the Aesthetics of Power* (Lincoln: University of Nebraska Press, 1999).

8. Myron Levytsky is a central figure in the development of a modern, often decolike graphic art. After studying at the Oleksa Novakivsky Art School in Lviv in 1931–33 and the Kraków School of Fine Art in 1933–34, he illustrated many books and became the editor-publisher of the journal *My i svit* (We and the World) in 1938–39. In 1942–43 he worked for Ukrainske vydavnytstvo (Ukrainian Publishers) and together with three other outstanding graphic artists—Mykola Butovych, Yakiv Hnizdovsky, and Edvard Kozak— taught at the Lviv Art-Industrial School. He then worked as a war correspondent for *Do peremohy* (To Victory), the newspaper of the Ukrainian Division "Halychyna" (Galicia). He moved to Canada in 1949.

CHAPTER 6. THE MYTH OF PALINGENESIS

1. Ihor Sviatoslavych (1151–1202) was prince of Novhorod-Siverskyi and Chernihiv and is the hero of the epic poem *Slovo o polku Ihorevi* (The Tale of Ihor's Campaign). Danylo Romanovych (1201–64) was prince of Volhynia and Galicia, and king of Rus from 1253. Prince Oleh ruled the Rus state in the early tenth century. According to the Rus chronicles, during a campaign against Byzantium, he nailed his shield to the gates of Constantinople. Sviatoslav Ihorevych (942?–72) was Grand Prince of Kyiv and gained fame for his courage in battle and military victories. Volodymyr Monomakh (1053–125) was Grand Prince of Kyiv (1113–25). Roman Mstyslavych (c. 1160–1205) united Galicia and Volhynia, creating the powerful Galician-Volhynian principality and capturing Kyiv in 1204. He founded the Romanovych dynasty of 1199–1340.

CHAPTER 7. OLENA TELIHA

1. Dudnyt zemlia pid kolamy vahonu,

Doshch iskor zolotykh u teplomu vikni.
Znykaie y rozplyvaietsia v pivtonakh
Tvii obraz mov u sni.

Tomu hodynu mozhe
Bulo tse: iakyis strakh
Spershu (chy stanetsia?) y tryvozhne
Zapytannia v ochakh.

I—nahlyi shal,
Shcho zatopyv nam mozok,
Shcho nache konei chval
Sploshenykh, ponis nas dykym skokom
V terpkyi y solodkyi vyr . . .

II
Dudnyt zemlia pid kolamy vahonu
I nykne spomyn . . . Mov koshmar

Ohydna zmora znov tiazhyt nad mnoiu:
Vdovoleno-tupykh ochei desiatky par,

Iz zadu, speredu, z bokiv, naproty–
V pivtemriavi zadushnoho kupe,
Banalnist triiumfuiucha holoty
Vykhyliuie lytse svoie hydke.

Zhar v holovi . . . Hyien chortiachyi rehit,
Liashchyt u vyskakh (strinu vas, iak nalezhyt),
Zasmuchuie khaos . . .

III
I os.
Peron . . . I postat ta strunka,
Rozsmishana, dytyniacha holivka,
Pidnesena do proshchannia ruka,
I pohliad . . . Lysh na khvylku

Ta vzhe znyka khaos.
Ia bachu berih znovu,
I cholo stomleneie khtos
Vuzkoiu laskaie rukoiu . . .

I znovu—v inshyi vyr
Shchos tiahne i manyt
Pirnuty strimholov
Soit benie, ma petite,
Merci, ia pryidu znov.

2. Kudy b mene khymerna dolia ne kydala,
   Ziavlialas z vitrom vesnianym—vona!
   Khoch iak by tam Ii i nazyvaly,
   To vse buly razom: vona y vesna!

CHAPTER 8. LEONID MOSENDZ AND OLEH OLZHYCH

1. For a study of Olzhych's contribution to archaeology and a bibliography of his publications and speeches, see Mykhailo Videiko and Serhii Kot (2008), and Liubomyr Vynar
(2008). For information on the PhD thesis and monograph in German, see Vynar
2008, 41–42, 77.

CHAPTER 9. YURII LYPA

1. A glance at the terminology of Western European scholars, historians, and politicians
is instructive. Lloyd George, for example, wrote the following: "The emancipated

races of Southern Europe were at each other's throats in their avidity to secure choice bits of the carcases of dead Empires. Pole and Czech were fighting over Teschen. The Poles and the Ukrainians had both pounced on Galicia, whilst Roumanians and Serbs were tearing up Hungary and Austria. [. . .] Where races were mixed near frontiers, the snarling and clawing were deafening. [. . .] These areas were the mangrove swamps where the racial roots were so tangled and intermingled that no peacemakers could move inside them without stumbling" (Lloyd George 1938, vol. 1, 306–7).

2. See, for example, the Web site of the Social-Nationalist Nasha Vatra (Our Fire), which has three excerpts from Lypa: http://www.vatra.cc/nasha-vatra, accessed 9 August 2013.

3. Sosenko's works include *Pradzherelo ukrainskohi relihiinoho svitohliadu* (Ancient Sources of the Ukrainian Religious Worldview), Lviv, 1923; and *Kulturno-istorychna postat staroukrainskykh sviat Rizdva i Shchedroho Vechora* (Cultural-Historical Profile of Old Ukrainian Feasts of Christmas and Epiphany Eve), Lviv, 1923. Schmidt founded the periodical *Anthropos* in 1906. He was director of the Museo Missionario-Etnologica Lateranense in Rome in the years 1927–39 and the Anthropos Institute at St. Augustin near Bonn in the years 1932–50. Koppers worked with Schmidt in editing *Anthropos*. He was head of the University of Vienna's Institute of Ethnology in the years 1929–38 and 1945–51.

4. See the Web site of Nasha Vatra (Our Fire), where this passage from *Pryznachannia Ukrainy* (1938) has been slightly changed and an introduction added that is not in the published book. The earlier passage that contradicts the image of Lypa as a racist is not quoted. Lypa's statements criticizing the OUN and Dontsov are also omitted, as are passages from his *Rozpodil Rossii* that deals with race, blood groups, and genes on page 34. Published in 1941 under German occupation, this book was confiscated. See http://www.vatra.cc/rasa/yuriy-lypa-solidaryzm-rasy.html, accessed 9 August 2013.

CHAPTER 10. ULAS SAMCHUK

1. *Haidamakas* was the name given to rebels who banded together to fight Polish rule in Right-Bank Ukraine. Many were peasants in revolt against serfdom. There were extensive revolts in 1734 and 1750, but the largest, known as Koliivshchyna, swept much of Southern Ukraine in 1768.

CHAPTER 11. A CHANGE OF HEART

Note: Originally published in *Canadian Slavonic Papers* 51.4 (2009): 513–24.

CHAPTER 12. DOKIA HUMENNA'S REPRESENTATION OF THE SECOND WORLD WAR IN HER NOVEL AND DIARY

Note: An earlier version of this article appeared in *Harvard Ukrainian Studies*. I am grateful to Halyna Hryn for finding the second issue of the journal *Kerma*, in which several pages of Humenna's diary were published, and to Marta Olynyk and Roman Koropetsky for suggesting improvements to the article.

1. For a discussion of these, see Myroslav Shkandrij 2014 (forthcoming).

2. Humenna, "Materiial do povisty Hnizdo nad bezodneiu," UCEC, Dokia Humenna Archive. This version of the diary appears to have been typed around 1946–47 in preparation for its reworking into the novel. Two later versions of her diary can be found in the Dokia Humenna papers in the archives of UVAN (Ukrainska Vilna Akademiia Nauk). See Dokiia Humenna Papers, Ukrainian Academy of Arts and Sciences in the United States, New York. The first of these is entitled "Shchodennyk, 1923–49" (Diary, 1923–49), and its five books bear the date 1990 on the cover. The second is entitled "Dar Evdotei" (Evdoteiia's Gift). It covers the same period and also appears to have been completed in 1990. Both these versions add some details to the descriptions of 1941–43 in the earlier diary, but also drop some passages. Dokia Humenna's two-volume *Dar Evdotei: Ispyt pamiati* was published in 1990, but it covers only the years up to 1940. See Humenna 1990.

3. For biographical information on Humenna based on her correspondence with Volodymyr Zhyla, see the latter's "Dokiia Humenna ta ii doistorychnyi zhanr v literaturi," *Verkhovyna: Literaturna mozaika* 17 (2002): 12–20. The best source on her early career is her *Dar Evdotei*.

4. Humenna's *Skarha maibutnomu: Roman* (New York: Slovo, 1964), contains many of the same characters as *Khreshchatyi iar* but is set in the immediate prewar years. In it, Mariana, who at one point has a vision of herself as a Cimmerian princess from the Bosphorus, links her personality and appearance to this ancient ancestry. Two other works are introductions to the archaeology and ancient history of Ukraine: Humenna, *Blahoslovy, Maty! Kazka-esei* (New York: Slovo, 1966); and Humenna, *Rodynnyi albom* (New York: Slovo, 1971).

5. This is suggested by Herbert Tiedemann in "Babi Yar: Critical Questions and Comments," www.vho.org/GB/Books/dth/fndbabiyar.html.

6. It had appeared in censored form in the journal *Iunost* in 1966. The translation of the uncensored version appeared as Anatoli Kuznetsov, *Babi Yar: A Document in the Form of a Novel*, trans. David Floyd (London: Jonathan Cape, 1970).

7. Ulas Samchuk, *Na bilomu koni* (New York: Suchasnist, 1965; 2nd ed., Winnipeg: Volyn, 1972); Samchuk, *Na koni voronomu: Spomyny i vrazhennia* (Winnipeg: Volyn, 1975; 2nd ed., Lviv: Litopys chervonoi kalyny, 2000); Arkadii Liubchenko, *Shchodennyk Arkadiia Liubchenka* (Lviv: M. P. Kots, 1999).

CONCLUSION

1. For a compilation of the UPA's songs, for example, see Lavryshyn 1996.

2. The Soviet "dirty war" against the UPA included torture, atrocities by special MGB troops dressed as UPA soldiers, and the use of poison gas. The film *Zachyneni dveri: Sluzhba bezpeky OUN* (Closed Doors: The Security Service of the OUN), directed by Vitalii Zahoriuiko (2012), makes these points. It was reported that in order to prevent information concerning these tactics from becoming better known, in January 2012 the Yanukovych government began discussing the possibility of permanently destroying "damaged" archival documents dealing with the UPA. See the television news program *Vikna-novyny*, 30 January 2012.

ARCHIVAL SOURCES

BN   Biblioteka narodowa, Warsaw.

          Archiwum im. Tarasa Szewczenki, Archiwum Dmytra Doncowa.

DAKhO   State Archive of Kharkiv Oblast (Derzhavnyi Arkhiv Kharkivskoi Oblasti), Kharkiv.

HDA SBU   Sectoral State Archive of the Security Service of Ukraine (Haluzevyi Derzhavnyi Arkhiv Sluzhby Bezpeky Ukrainy), Kyiv.

KhLM   Kharkiv Literary Museum (Kharkivskyi Literaturnyi Muzei), Kharkiv.

LAC   Library and Archives Canada, Ottawa.

          Manuscript Division. Kaye, Vladimir Julian (Kisilewsky). London Diaries MG31-D69, l 36–41.

NTSh   Shevchenko Scientific Society (Naukove Tovarystvo im. Shevchenka), New York.

          Archive of Vasyl Mudryi.

          Archive of Yevhen Onatsky.

          Archive of Ivan Kedryn-Rudnytsky.

          Archive of Mykola Ostroverkha.

PA   Provincial Archives of Alberta, Edmonton.

          Archive of Michael Chomiak.

SBU KhO   Archive of the Security Service of Ukraine of Kharkiv Oblast (Arkhiv Upravlinnia Sluzhby Bezpeky Ukrainy Kharkivskoi Oblasti), Kharkiv.

TsDAHO   Central State Archive of Civic Organizations (Tsentralnyi Derzhavnyi Arkhiv Hromadskykh Obiednan Ukrainy), Kyiv.

TsDALIM   Central State Archive of Literature and Art (Tsentralnyi Derzhavnyi Arkhiv Literatury i Mystetstva), Kyiv.

TsDAVO   Central Archives of Higher State Organs and Government of Ukraine (Tsentralnyi Arkhiv Vyshchykh Orhaniv Vlady ta Upravlinnia Ukrainy), Kyiv.

UCEC   Ukrainian Cultural and Education Centre (Oseredok), Winnipeg.

          Archive of Dokia Humenna.

Archive of Yevhen Konovalets.

Archive of Yevhen Onatsky.

Archive of Mykhailo Seleshko.

UM   University of Manitoba, Archives of the Ukrainian-Canadian Experience.
Danyliuk Collection.

UVAN   Ukrainian Academy of Arts and Science in the United States (Ukrainska
Vilna Akademiia Nauk), New York.

Archive of Dokia Humenna.

BIBLIOGRAPHY

Adamson, Walter L. 1997. "Futurism, Mass Culture, and Women: The Reshaping of the Artistic Vocation, 1909–1920." *Modernism/Modernity* 4.1: 89–114.

Affron, Matthew, and Mark Antliff, eds. 1997. *Fascist Visions: Art and Ideology in France and Italy*. Princeton, NJ: Princeton University Press.

Amar, T. S., I. Bachynskyi, and Ia. Hrytsak, eds. 2007. *Strasti za Banderoiu*. Kyiv: Hrani-T.

Andriienko-Danchuk, P. 1975. "Zhyva Pravda (U 70-richchia pysmennytsi Dokii Humennoi)." *Promin* 1: 5–8.

Andriievskyi, D. 1928. "Rozbudova natsii," 74–88. In V. Roh, ed., *Ukrainskyi natsionalimz: Antolohiia*. Vol. 1. Kyiv: Ukrainska vydavnycha spilka im. Iu. Lypy, 2009. (Orig. in *Natsioonalna dumka* [Prague] 7–8 [1928].)

———. 1935. *Ukrainskyi natsionalizm 1917–1919 r.r. Osnovni element pravosvidomosty ukrainskoho narodu*. Chernivtsi: Nakladom avtora.

Antliff, Mark. 2007. *Avant-Garde Fascism: The Mobilization of Myth, Art, and Culture in France, 1909–1939*. Durham, NC: Duke University Press.

Antliff, Mark, and Patricia Leighten. 2001. *Cubism and Culture*. London: Thames and Hudson.

Antonenko-Davydovych, Borys. 1924. *Lytsari absurdu. Drama na 4 dii*. Kharkiv: Chervonyi shliakh.

Antonovych-Rudnytska, M. 1985. "Iz spomyniv pro Olzhycha." *Ukrainskyi istoryk* 22.1–4: 101–11.

Applebaum, Anne. 2003. *Gulag: A History*. New York: Doubleday.

Aragon, Loius. 1970. *Nightwalker (Le Paysan de Paris)*. Englewood Cliffs,NJ: Prentice-Hall.

Archard, David. 1995. "Myths, Lies and Historical Truth: A Defence of Nationalism." *Political Studies* 43: 472–81.

Armstrong, John. 1963. *Ukrainian Nationalism*. New York: Columbia University Press.

———. 1968. "Collaborationism in World War II: The Integral Nationalist Variant in Eastern Europe." *Journal of Modern History* 40: 396–410.

B., N. 1933. "Pravuvannia ta nasylkstvo." *Rozbudova natsii* 11–12: 252–53.

Bahan, Oleh. 2004. "Iurii Klen: Neoklasyk chy neoromantyk?" In L. Kravchenko 2004, 9–28.

———. 2008. "Filosof-voin." *Den.* 3 October: www.inosmi.ru/world/20081003/244412.html.

———. 2009. "Vistnykivstvo iak ponadchasovyi fenomen: Ideolohiia, estetyka, nastroi-evist." In L. Kravchenko et al. 2009, 6–48.

Bandera, S. 1999. *Perspektyvy ukrainskoi revoliutsii.* Kyiv: Instytut natsionalnoho dezhavoznavstva. (Orig. pub. Munich: Vydannia Orhanizatsii Ukrainskykh Natsionalistiv, 1978.)

Barash, Jeffrey Andrew. 2008. *The Symbolic Construction of Reality: The Legacy of Ernst Cassirer.* Chicago and London: University of Chicago Press.

Bartov, Omer, and Eric D. Weitz, eds. 2013. *Shatterzone of Empires: Coexistence and Violence in the German, Habsburg, Russian, and Ottoman Borderlands.* Bloomington and Indianapolis: Indiana University Press.

Beauvois, Daniel. 1993. *La Bataille de la terre en Ukraine, 1863–1914: Les Polonais et les conflits socio-ethniques.* Lille, France: Presses universitaires de Lille.

Beevor, Antony, and Luba Vinogradova, eds. 2005. *A Writer at War: Vasily Grossman with the Red Army, 1941–1945.* Toronto: Alfred A. Knopf Canada.

Behen, Oleh, Oleksandr Zaitsev and Vasyl Stefaniv. 2011. "Katolytska krytyka ukrainskoho 'neonatsionalizmu,'" 287–318. In Zaitsev, Behen, Stefaniv 2011.

Benjamin, Walter. 1978. "Theological Political Fragment." In *Reflections.* New York: Harcourt Brace.

———. 1996. *Selected Writings, Volume 1: 1913–1926.* Cambridge, MA: Harvard University Press.

Berkhoff, Karel C. 2004. *Harvest of Despair: Life and Death in Ukraine under Nazi Rule.* Cambridge, MA: Belknap Press of Harvard University Press.

Berkhoff, Karel. C., and Marco Carynnyk. 1999. "The Organization of Ukrainian Nationalists and Its Attitude toward Germans and Jews: Iaroslav Stateko's 1941 Zhyttiepys." *Harvard Ukrainian Studies* 23.3–4: 149–84.

Berry, Ellen E., and Anesa Miller-Pogacar, eds. 1995. *Re-entering the Sign: Articulating New Russian Culture.* Ann Arbor: University of Michigan Press.

Bertelsen, Olga, and Myroslav Shkandrij, 2014. "The Secret Police and the Campaign Against Galicians in Soviet Ukraine, 1929–34." *Nationalities Papers: The Journal of Nationalism and Ethnicity* 42.1: 37–62.

Bhabha, Homi. 1994. "Of Mimicry and Man: The Ambiguity of Colonial Discourse," 85–93. In his *The Location of Culture.* New York: Routledge.

Birchak, Volodymyr. 1940. *Karpatska Ukraina: Spomyny i perezhyvannia.* Prague: Natsiia v pokhodi.

B-k, O. 1936. "Na marginesi kampanii proty Zahalnoho Zbory T-va 'Prosvita.'" *Holos nat-sii* (Lviv), 2 August.

Blumenberg, Hans. 1985. *Work on Myth (Studies in Contemporary German Social Thought).* Cambridge: MIT Press.

Bohush, V. [real name Makar Kushnir]. "Rosiisko-zhydivske panuvannia ta rolia rosiiskoi kultury na Radianskii Ukraini." *Rozbudova natsii* 1–2 (1929): 85–93.

Boichuk, Bohdan. 2009a. "Dvi shtrykhy," 685–93. In Ilnytskyi 2009. (Orig. in *Suchasnist* 1 [1980].)

———. 2009b. "Rozmova z Nataleiu Livytskoiu-Kholodnoiu," 809–21. In Ilnytskyi 2009. (Orig. in *Suchasnist* 3 [1985].)

Boidunyk, Osyp. 1974. "Iak diishlo do stvorennia Orhanizatsii Ukraiinskykh Natsionalistiv," 359–79. In Boiko 1974.

Boiko [Blokhyn], Iurii. 1946. "Kudy idemo?" *Ridne slovo* 11.2: 44–54.

———. 1947. "Odvertyi lyst do Iuriia Sherekha." *Orlyk* 11: 19–23.

———. 1950. *Problemy istoriosofii ukrainskoho nasionalizmu.* Na chuzhyni, n.p.

———. 1951a. *Na holovnii magistrali.* Na chuzhyni: n.p.

———. 1951b. *Osnovy ukrainskoho natsionalizmu.* Na chuzhyni: n.p.

———. 1971–81. *Vybrane.* 3 vols. Munich: I. Iu. Boiko.

———. 1992. *Shliakh natsii.* Paris, Kyiv, Lviv: Ukrainske slovo. (Orig. pub. 1944.)

Boiko, Iurii, ed. 1974. *Ievhen Konovalets ta ioho doba.* Munich: Vydannia fundatsii im. Ievhena Konovaltsia.

Bokush, B. 1929. "Rosiisko-zhydivske panuvannia ta rolia rosiiskoi kultury na Radianskii Ukraini." *Rozbudova natsii* 1–2: 85–93.

Bolianovs'kyi, Andrii. 1999. "Cooperation between the German Military of the Weimar Republic and the Ukrainian Military Organization, 1923–1928." *Harvard Ukrainian Studies* 23.1–2: 73–84.

Boshko, Volodymyr. 1926. "Navkolo novoho shliubnoho kodeksu." *Literatura i revoliutsiia* 2.2: 110–13.

Boyd Whyte, Iain. 1994. "Sublime," 138–46. In Keith Hartley, ed., *The Romantic Spirit in German Art, 1790–1990.* London: Thames and Hudson.

Brandon, Ray, and Wendy Lower, eds. 2010. *The Shoah in Ukraine: History, Testimony, Memorialization.* Bloomington and Indianapolis: Indiana University Press.

Bratkivskyi, Iu. 1929. "Pered novymy boiamy." *Bilshovyk Ukrainy* 4: 71–87.

Braum, Emily. 2000. *Mario Sirone and Italian Modernism: Art and Politics under Fascism.* Cambridge: Cambridge University Press.

Breitman, Richard, et al. 2005. *U.S. Intelligence and the Nazis.* Cambridge: Cambridge University Press.

Brown, Kate. 2004. *A Biography of No Place: From Ethnic Borderland to Soviet Heartland.* Cambridge, MA: Harvard University Press.

Bruder, Franziska. 2007. *"Den ukrainischen Staat erkämpfen oder sterben!" Die Organisation Ukrainischer Natsionalisten (OUN) 1929–1948.* Berlin: Metropol Verlag.

Buck-Morss, Susan. 1993. *The Dialectics of Seeing: Walter Benjamin and the Arcades Project.* Cambridge, MA: MIT Press.

Budurowycz, Bohdan. 1983. "Poland and the Ukrainian Problem, 1921–1939." *Canadian Slavonic Papers* 25.4: 473–500.

Bulba-Borovets, Taras. 1946. *Kredo revoliutsii: Korotkyi narys istorii, ideolohichnko-maralni osnovy ta politychna platforma Ukrainskoi Nationalnoi Revoliutsiinoi Armii.* Paris: Nakladom Polit. Viddilu UNRA.

———. 1981. *Armiia bez derzhavy: Slava i trahediia ukrainskoho povstanskoho rukhu: Spohady.* Winnipeg: Nakladom Tovarystva Volyn.

Burghardt, Osvald [Iurii Klen]. 1938. "Tsarstvo Satany." *Vistnyk* 4: 301–5.

———. 1939. "Bolshevytska spadshchyna." *Vistnyk* 2: 94–99.

BUTRO. 1938. "Ukrainska zhinka i ii zavdannia." *Holos*, 23 January.

Bykovsky, Lev. 1955. "Publitsystyka Iuriia Lypy." *Rozbudova derzhavy* 1: 57–58 and 2: 115–21.

Carynnyk, Marco. 2011. "Foes of Our Rebirth: Ukrainian Nationalist Discussions about Jews, 1929–1947." *Nationalities Papers* 39.3: 315–52.

Cassirer, Ernst. 1961. *The Myth of the State*. New Haven, CT: Yale University Press.

———. 1979. "The Technique of Modern Political Myths" (1945). In Verene 1979.

Chekmanovsky, Antin. 1938. *Viky plyvut nad Kyievom*. Lviv: Batkivshchyna.

Cherchenko, Iu. ed. 2007. *Dokumenty i materialy z istorii Orhanizatsii Ukrainskykh Natsionalistiv. Vol. 2, pt 2. Lystuvannia Ie. Konovaltsia z D. Andriievskym (1927–1934 rr.)*. Kyiv: Vyd. imeni Oleny Telihy.

———. 2010. *Dokumenty i materialy z istorii Orhanizatsii Ukrainskykh Natsionalistiv*. Vol. 2, pt. 1, 1931–1934. Kyiv: Vyd. imeni Oleny Telihy,.

Cherchenko, Iu., and O. Kucheruk, eds. 2005. *Dokumenty i materialy z istorii Orhanizatsii Ukrainskykh Natsionalistiv*. Vol. 1, 1927–1930. Kyiv: Vyd. imeni Oleny Telihy.

Cherevatenko, Leonid. 1994. "Ia kamin z Bozhoi prashchi," 351–424. In Olzhych 1994.

Cherin, Hanna. 1974. "Pamiati Iuliiana Vassyiana." *Samostiina Ukraina* 7–8: 11–14.

Cherniava, Ivan. 1932. *Na skhodi–my!: Film pyideshnoho*. Lviv: Vydavnytstvo "Strybozhets."

———. 1935. *Liudy z chornym pidnebinniam*. Lviv: Vydavnytstvo, Ukrainska kultura.

Chernova, O. 1956. "Hromadianka tysiacholit." *Svoboda*, 3 May.

Chojnowski, A. 1979. *Koncepcja polityki narodowosciowej rzadów polskich w latach 1921–1939*. Wroclaw, Warsaw, Krakow: Zaklad Narodowy im. Ossolinskich.

Cicero. 1969. *Selected Political Speeches*. Harmondsworth, UK: Penguin Books.

Connor, Walker. 1994. *Ethnonationalism: The Quest for Understanding*. Princeton, NJ: Princeton University Press.

Danylenko-Danylevsky, O.K. 1964. "Nova mozaika heroiv. Roman *Skarha maibutnomu* pysmennytsi Dokii Humennoi." *Ukrainski visti*, 13 December.

Dashkevych, Iaroslav. 1993. *Ukraina vchora i nyni: Narysy, vystupy, ese: Do Druhoi mizhnarodnoi konferentsii ukrainistiv*. Kyiv: B.v.

Dean, Martin. 1996. "The German Gendarmerie, the Ukrainian Schutzmannschaft and the 'Second Wave' of Jewish Killings in Occupied Ukraine: German Policing at the Local Level in the Zhitomir Region, 1941–1944." *German History* 14.2: 168–92.

———. 2000. *Collaboration in the Holocaust: Crimes of the Local Police in Belorussia and Ukraine, 1941–44*. New York: St. Martin's Press.

Delzell, Charles F., ed. 1970. *Mediterranean Fascism, 1919–1945*. New York: Harper & Row.

Demo, A. 1938. "Fragmenty na temy mystetstva," 94–106. In *Almanakh: Na sluzhbi natsii*. Paris: n.p.

Dereiko, Ivan. 2003. "Vid kolaboratsii do rezystansu: diialnist 115/62-ho Ukrainskoho Batalionu shutsmanshaftu na terenakh Bilorusi i Frantsii v 1942–44 rr." *Z arkhiviv VUChK GPU NKVD KGB* 1: 179–93.

Derzhavyn, Volodymyr. 1950. "Poetychna tvorchist Oleny Telihy." *Samostiina Ukraina* 3.3 (March): 11–14. (Reprinted in Teliha 2008, 414–25).

———. 2009a. "Natsionalna heroinia," 638–47. In Ilnytskyi 2009. (Orig. pub. in *Promin*, 10 November 1948.)

———. 2009b. "Oleh Olzhych–Poet natsionalnoho heroizmu," 648–61. In Ilnytskyi 2009. (Orig. pub. as introduction to Oleh Olzhych, *Velychnist* [Chicago, 1969].)

Diadiuk, Myroslava. 2011. *Ukrainskyi zhinochyi rukh u mizhvoiennii Halychyni: Mizh hendernoiu identychnistiu ta natsionalnoiu zaanhazovanistiu.* Lviv: Astrolabiia.

Dolenga, Sviatoslav [real name Andrii Kryzhanivskyi]. 1938. *Dontsovshchyna.* Warsaw: Variak.

Dontsov, Dmytro. 1910. *Shkola a relihiia (Referat vyholoshenyi na zizdi Ukrainskoi Akademichnoi Molodi u Lvovi v lypni 1909 r.).* Lviv: Nakladom Ukrainskoho Studentskoho Soiuza.

———. 1921. *Pidstavy nashoi polityky* Vienna: Vydavnytstvo Dontsovykh.

———. 1923. "Pro molodykh." *Literaturno-naukovyi vistnyk* [Richnyk 22, tom. 81] 4: 267–80.

———. 1925. "Ukrainsko-sovitski psevdomorfozy." *Literaturno-naukovyi vistnyk* 12: 321–36.

———. 1926. *Natsionalizm.* Lviv: Nove zhyttia.

———. 1927. "Shatost malorosiiskaia." *Literaturno-naukovyi vistnyk* 3: 265–75.

———. 1928. "Za zavtrishnii den." *Literturno-naukovyi vistnyk* 1: 83–87.

———. 1933 [under pseudonym O.V.]. Review of Ivan Cherniava, *Na Skhodi–My. Vistnyk* 3: 232–34.

———. 1934a. "Ukrainske vacuum i ridna kultureniia." *Vistnyk* 2: 137–46.

———. 1934b. "Sancho Panza v nashii diisnosti." *Vistnyk* 7–8: 574–601.

———. 1935a. "Galvanizatory trupiv." *Vistnyk* 7–8: 592–611.

———. 1935b. "Poputchykam (vidpovid)." *Vistnyk* 12: 912–21.

———. 1936a. *Patriotyzm.* Lviv: Kvartalnyk Vistnyka.

———. 1936b. "Vony i my." *Vistnyk* 5: 370–88.

———. 1937. "Nerozryta mohyla." *Vistnyk* 4: 283–302.

———. 1938a. "Mizh molotom a kovadlom." *Vistnyk* 5: 371–86.

———. 1938b. "Pamiati velykoi buntarky (Lesia Ukrainka)." *Vistnyk* 2: 92–99.

———. 1938c. "Shliakhom veletniv." *Vistnyk* 10: 734–39.

———. 1939a. "Berezen 1939." *Vistnyk* 4: 298–305.

———. 1939b. "Zahadka III-oi imperii." *Vistnyk* 5: 326–42.

———. 1942. *De shukaty nashykh historychnykh tradytsii.* Lviv: Ukrainske vyd-vo.

———. 1951. *Dukh nashoi davnyny.* 2nd ed. Munich-Montreal: n.p. (Orig. 1943.)

———. 1953. *Poetka vohnennykh mezh: Olena Teliha.* Toronto: Vydannia O. Tiazhkoho.

———. 1957. *Vid mistyky do polityky.* Toronto: Spilka vyzvolennia Ukrainy.

———. 1958. "Moderna literatura rozkladu." *Literatura i mystetstvo*, supplement to *Homin Ukrainy*, 26 July.

———. 1967. *Khrestom i mechem: Tvory.* Toronto: Liga vyzvolennia Ukrainy.

———. 2002. *Rik 1918, Kyiv.* Kyiv: Tempora. (Orig. pub. Toronto, 1954.)

Dziobak, Volodymyr. 1994–95. "Taras Borovets i 'Poliska sich.' *Z Uiv VYChK-GPU-NKVD-KGB* 1 (1994): 124–39; 1–2 (1995): 39–59.

-enko, Hr. 1958. "Dumky, shcho pryishly z Khreshchatoho Iaru." *Ameryka*, 16 May.

Fishbein, Moisei. 2009. "The Jewish Card in Special Operations Against Ukraine." Conference Paper delivered at University of Illinois at Urbana-Champaign, June 24–27, http://eng.maidanua.org/node/977.

Fiut, Alexander. 2009. *Zustrichi z Inshym*. Kyiv: Akta. (Orig. *Spotkania z Innym*. Kraków: Wydawnictwo Literackie, 2006.)

Franklin, Simon, and Emma Widdis, eds. 2004. *National Identity in Russian Culture: An Introduction*. Cambridge: Cambridge University Press.

Fritzsche, Peter. 1996. "Nazi Modernism." *Modernism/Modernity* 3.1: 1–22.

Frost, Laura. 2002. *Sex Drives: Fantasies of Fascism in Literary Modernism*. Ithaca and London: Cornell University Press.

Gabor, Vasyl, ed. 2006. *Dvanadtsiatka: Naimolodsha lvivska bohema 30-kh rokiv: Antolohiia urbanistychnoi prozy*. Lviv: Piramida.

Gat, Azar, with Alexander Yakobson. 2013. *Nations: The Long History and Deep Roots of Political Ethnicity and Nationalism*. Cambridge: Cambridge University Press.

Gay, Peter. 1968. *Weimar Culture: The Outsider as Insider*. New York and Evanston: Harper & Row.

Geisler, Michael E., ed. 2005. *National Symbols, Fractured Identities: Contesting the National Narrative*. Hanover, NH: University Press of New England.

Gellately, Robert. 2007. *Lenin, Stalin, and Hitler: The Age of Social Catastrophe*. New York: Vintage Books.

Gellner, Ernest. 2006. *Nations and Nationalism*. 2nd ed. Ithaca: Cornell University Press. (Orig. pub. 1983.)

Gentile, Emilio. 1994. "The Conquest of Modernity: From Modernist Nationalism to Fascism." *Modernism/Modernity* 1.3: 55–87.

———. 1996. *The Sacralization of Politics in Fascist Italy*. Cambridge, MA: Harvard University Press.

———. 1997. "The Myth of National Regeneration in Italy. From Modernist Avant-Garde to Fascism," 25–45. In Affron and Antliff 1997.

———. 2003. *The Struggle for Modernity: Nationalism, Futurism, and Fascism*. Westport, CT: Praeger.

———. 2006. *Politics as Religion*. Princeton, NJ: Princeton University Press.

Gillerman, Sharon. 2012. "A Kinder Gentler Strongman? Sigmund Breitbart in Eastern Europe," 197–209. In Benjamin Maria Baader, Sharon Gillerman, and Paul Lerner, eds., *Jewish Masculinities: German Jews, Gender, and History*. Bloomington, IN: Indiana University Press.

Gillis, John R., ed. 1994. *Commemorations: The Politics of National Identity*. Princeton, NJ: Princeton University Press.

Golczewski, Frank. 2010a. *Deutsche und Ukrainer 1914–1939*. Paderborn, Germany: Ferdinand Schöningh.

———. 2010b. "Shades of Grey: Reflections on Jewish-Ukrainian and German-Ukrainian Relations in Galicia," 114–55. In Brandon and Lower 2010.

Gon, Maksym. 2010a. "'Ievreiske pytannia' v retseptsii chasopysu 'Volyn' (1941–1943 rr.)." Katastrofa ievopeiskoho ievreistva pid chas Druhoi svitovoi viiny. Refleksii na mezhi tysiacholit. Zbirnyk naukovykh prats, 279–85. Kyiv: Instytut iudaiky; Natsionalna biblioteka im. Vernadskoho, 2000.

———. 2010b. "Ukrainskyi natsionalizm i ievrei." *Ukraina moderna* 5: 251–68.

Greenfeld, Liah. 1992. *Nationalism: Five Roads to Modernity.* Cambridge, MA: Harvard University Press.

Griffin, Roger. 1991. *The Nature of Fascism.* New York: St. Martin's Press.

——. 2007. *Modernism and Fascism: The Sense of a Beginning under Mussolini and Hitler.* Houndmills, UK, and New York: Palgrave Macmillan.

——. 2008. "Modernity, Modernism, and Fascism. A 'Mazeway Resynthesis.'" *Modernism/Modernity* 15.1: 9–24.

Grossman, Vasily. 1986. *Forever Flowing. A Novel.* New York: Harper & Row.

Hałagida, Igor. 2005. *Prowokacja "Zenona." Geneza, Przebieg a Skutki MBP o Kryptonimie "C–1" Przeciwo Banderowskiej Frakcji OUN i Wywiadowi Brytyjskiemu (1950–1954).* Warsaw: Instytut Pamięci Narodowej.

Havryliuk, M., ed. 1964. *Bibliohrafiia prats Profesora Ievhena Onatskoho, 1917–1964.* Buenos Aires: Spilka ukrainskykh naukovtsiv, literatoriv i mystsiv.

Herf, Jeffrey. 1984. *Reactionary Modernism: Technology, Culture, and Politics in Weimar and the Third Reich.* Cambridge: Cambridge University Press.

Himka, John-Paul. 2010. "The Organization of Ukrainian Nationalists and the Ukrainian Insurgent Army: Unwelcome Elements of an Identity Project." *Ab imperio* 4: 83–101.

——. 2011a. "Debates in Ukraine over Nationalist Involvement in the Holocaust, 2004–2008." *Nationalities Papers* 39.3: 353–70.

——. 2011b. "The Lviv Pogrom of 1941: The Germans, Ukrainian Nationalists, and the Carnival Crowd." *Canadian Slavonic Papers* 53.2–4: 209–44.

——. 2012. "Ukrainian Memories of the Holocaust: The Destruction of Jews as Reflected in Memoirs Collected in 1947." *Canadian Slavonic Papers* 54.3–4. 427–42.

——. 2013. "Ethnicity and the Reporting of Mass Murder: *Krakivsiki visti*, the NKVD Murders of 1941, and the Vinnytsia Exhumantion," 378–98. In Bartov and Weitz 2013.

Hnatiuk, Olia. 2010–11. "Doktor Faust: Motyvy istoriosofii Osvalda Shpenhlera v literaturni publitsystytsi Dmytra Dontsova." *Journal of Ukrainian Studies* 35–36: 193–206.

Hnatyshak, M. 1930. "Syntetychnyi teatr." *Rozbudova natsii* 7–8 (1930): 168–74. (Also *Samostiina dumka* 1 (1933): 19–23).

——. 1936. "Odno zavdannia suchasnoi ukrainskoi literatury." *Shliakh natsii* 2 (June): 20–24.

Holkeskamp, Karl-Joachim. 2006. "History and Collective Memory in the Middle Republic," 480–81. In *A Companion to the Roman Republic*, ed. Nathan Rosenstein and Robert Morstein-Marx. Oxford: Wiley Blackwell Publishers.

Horodynskyi, Orest. 2004. "Iurii Klen—voiakom." In L. Kravchenko 2004, 360–77.

Horlis-Horskyi, Iurii [real name Horodianyn-Lisovskyi]. 2010. *Kholodnyi Iar: Spohady osavula 1-ho kurenia polku haidamakiv Kholodnoho Iaru.* 12th ed. Kyiv: Istorychnyi klub "Kholodnyi Iar" and Vinnytsia: DP "Derzhavna kartohrafichna fabryka." (Orig. pub. 1934, 1937.)

Horyn, Mykhailo. 1991. "My mriialy pro nezalezhnu derzhavu." *Zustrichi* 2: 38–49.

Hryhorovych. M. 1924. *Iak Irlandiia zdobula sobi voliu.* Katerynoslav-Leipzig: Ukrainske vydavnytstvo v Katerynozlavi.

Hrynevych, Vladyslav. 2012. *Nepryborkane Riznoholossia: Druha Svitova Viina i Suspilno-politychni nastroi v Ukraini, 1939-cherven 1941 rr.* Kyiv-Dnipropetrovsk: Lira.

Hrytsai, Ostap. 1934a. "Mesnyky." *Samostiina dumka* 4.2: 164–68.

———. 1934b. "Plaie pozharom sertse moie." *Rozbudova natsii* 1–2: 1–4.

Hrytsak, Iaroslav. 2004. *Strasti za natsionalizmom: Istorychni esei.* Kyiv: Krytyka.

Hud, Vasyl. 2006. *Zahybel Arkadii: Etnosotsialni aspekty ukrainsko-polskykh konfliktiv XIX-pershoi polovyny XX stolittia.* Lviv: Natsionalna Akademiia Nauk Ukrainy, Lvivskyi Natsionalnyi Universytet imeni Ivana Franka.

Humenna, Dokia. 1946. "Materiialy do povisi Hnizdo nad bezodneiu." Ukrainian Cultural and Educational Centre (Oseredok), Winnipeg, Archive of Dokia Humenna.

———. 1948. *Dity chumatskoho shliaku. Roman u 4 knyhakh.* Munich: Vydavnystvo "Ukrainska trybuna."

———. 1956. *Khreshchatyi iar (Kyiv 1941–43: Roman-khronika.* New York: Slovo.

———. 1966. *Blahoslovy, Maty! Kazka-esei.* New York: Slovo.

———. 1971. *Rodynnyi albom.* New York: Slovo.

———. 1990. *Dar Evdotei: Ispyt pamiati.* 2 vols. Baltimore-Toronto: Smoloskyp.

Hunczak, Taras. 2001. "Problems of Historiography: History and Its Sources." *Harvard Ukrainian Studies* 25.1–2: 129–42. (The issue in fact appeared in 2004.)

———. 2009. "Shukhevych and the Nachtigall Batallion: Soviet Fabrications about the Ukrainian Resistance Movement." *Day*, 28 July and 15 September: http://www.day.kiev. ua/277652/ and /280054/.

Hutchinson, John. 1994. *Modern Nationalism.* Fontana Press.

Iakovenko, Serhii. 2006. *Romantyky, estety, nitsheantsi: Ukrainska ta polska literaturna krytyka rannoho modernizmu.* Kyiv: Krytyka.

"Iaku garantiiu Dilo daie v imeni OUN? Vidhuk endetskoho Kuriera Lvivskoho na stattiu Dila." 1933. Dilo. 4 November.

Iavir, Hordii [Iurii Klen]. 1933. "Z nimetskykh vrazhin (Reportazh z Nimechchyny)." *Vistnyk* 11: 813–17.

———. 1934. "Stefan George." *Vistnyk* 2: 116–22.

———. 1936. "Prognozy Shpenglera." *Vistnyk* 6: 425–29.

———. 1937. "Amaliekytiany, amorytiany i gibeonity (Dopys z Nimechchyny)." *Vistnyk* 12: 877–78.

———. 1938. "12 bereznia (Dopys z Nimechchyny)." *Vistnyk* 4: 287–89.

Ie. L. D. [R. Iendyk, O. Lahutenko, and D. Dontsov] 1938. "Nenko-sharovarnytska heopolityka." *Vistnyk* 12: 902–22.

Iendyk, Rostyslav. 1934. *Antropologichni prykmety ukrainskoho narodu.* Lviv: Prosvita.

———. 1935. *Adolf Hitler.* Lviv: Knyhozbirnia Vistnyka.

———. 1937. *Rehit Aridnyka.* Lviv: Vydavnytstvo "Vynne hrono."

———. 1949. *Vstup do rasovoi budovy Ukrainy: Osnovni pytannia z zahalnoi i suspilnoi antropolohii ta evheniky Ukrainy.* Munich: Nakladom Nuk. Tov. im. T. Shevchenka.

———. 1955. *Dmytro Dontsov: Ideoloh ukrainskoho natsionalizmu.* Munich: Ukrainske vydavnytstvo.

Iliushyn, I. I. 2000. *OUN-UPA i ukrainske pytannia v roky Druhoi svitovoi viiny (V svitli polskykh dokumentiv).* Kyiv: Natsionalna Akademiia Nauk Ukrainy, Instytut Istorii Ukrainy.

———. 2001. *Protystoiannia UPA i AK (Armii Kraiovoi) v roky Druhoi svitovoi viiny na tli diialnosti polskoho pidpillia v Zakhidnii Ukraini.* Kyiv: Natsionalna Akademiia Nauk Ukrainy.

———. 2009. *Ukrainska Povstanska Armiia i Armiia Kraiova: Protystoiannia v Zakhdnii Ukraini (1939–1945 rr.).* Kyiv: Kyievo-Mohylianska Akademiia.

———. 2011. "Mynule pid slidstvom." *Krytyka* 5–6 (May–June 2011): 27–30.

Ilnytskyi, Mykola. 1995. *Vid 'Molodoi Myzy' do 'Prazkoi shkoly.'* Lviv: Insytut ukrainoznavstva im. I. Krypiakevycha.

———, ed. 2009. *Poety prazkoi shkoly: Sribni surmy: Antolohiia.* Kyiv: Smoloskyp.

Ilnytzkyi, Roman. 1958. *Deutschland und die Ukraine, 1934–1945.* 2 vols. Munich: Osteuropa-Institut.

Inzh. D. 1933. "Pravuvannia a nasylstvo." *Rozbudova natsii* 11–12: 251–54.

Iuryniak, A. 1965. "Slushni i neslushni skarhy Mariany Veresoch (Skarha maibutnomu i Khreshchatyi iar Dokii Humennoi)." *Ukrainski visti.* 21 March.

Ivanys, Vasyl. 1961. *Rodovid L. M. Mosendza i ioho ostanni lysty.* Neu Ulm: Ukrainski visti.

Ivanyshyn, Petro. 2004. "Natsionalisychnyi typ literaturnoi hermenevtyky (Na bazi poemy Iu. Klena "Prokliati roky")." In L. Kravchenko 2004, 80–89.

"Iz lystiv do redaktsii" 1932. *Rozbudova natsii* 11–12, 316–18.

Kalytskyi, H. 1929. "Ukrainska literatura v svitli natsionalizmu." *Rozbudova natsii* 3–4: 100–109; 5: 153–66.

Kamenetskyi, Ihor. 1974. "Ukrainske pytannia v nimetskii zovnishnii politytsi mizh dvoma svitovymy viinamy," 851–82. In Boiko, ed. 1974.

Kandyba, Oleh [Olzhych]. 1939. "Voiaky–budivnychi," 33–51. In *Karpatska Ukraina v borotbi. Zbirnyk.* Vienna: Vydannia Ukrainskoi presovoi sluzhby.

Karbovych, Zynovii [Iaroslav Stetsko]. 1939. "Zhydivstvo i my." *Novyi shliakh,* 8 May.

Kasiian, Stepan. 1967. *Vohon rodytssia z iskry . . .* Toronto: Surma.

Kedryn, Ivan [Kedryn-Rudnytsky]. 1976. *Zhyttia-Podii-Liudy: Spomyny i komentari.* New York: Chervona kalyna.

Kedryn-Rudnytsky, Ivan. 1974. "Vydatna indyvidualnist," 341–56. In Boiko 1974.

Kentii, Anatolii. 2005. *Zbroinyi chyn ukrainskykh natsionalistiv, 1920–1956: Istorykoarkhivni narysy.* Vol. 1. Kyiv: Derzhavnyi komitet arkhiviv Ukrainy.

Khmuryi, V. 1929. *Anatol Petrytskyi: Teatralni stroi.* Kharkiv: Derzhevne Vydavnytstvo Ukrainy.

Khomyshyn, H. 1933. *Ukrainska problema.* Stanislawów: n.p.

Khromeychuk, Olesya. 2012. "The Shaping of 'Historical Truth': Construction and Reconstruction of the Memory and Narrative of the Waffen SS 'Galicia' Division." *Canadian Slavonic Papers* 54.3–4: 443–67.

Khvylovy, Mykola. 1986. *The Cultural Renaissance in Ukraine: Polemical Pamphlets, 1925–1926.* Edmonton: Canadian Institute of Ukrainian Studies.

Kirkconnell, Watson. 1939. *Canada, Europe, and Hitler.* Toronto: Oxford University Press.

———. 1944. *Seven Pillars of Freedom.* London: Oxford University Press.

Klen, Iurii. 1935. "Shche raz pro sire, zhovte i pro Vistnykovu kvadryhu." *Vistnyk* 6: 419–26.

———. 1936. "Slovo zhyve i mertve." *Vistnyk* 11: 828–34.

——. 1953. "Bii mozhe pochatysia." *Ukrainskyi samostiinyk* 39 (27 September): 3; 40 (4 October): 3; 41 (11 October): 4–5.

——. 1957a. "Mid zveniashchaia," Tzpo. 214–17. In Klen 1957d, 3.

——. 1957b. "Pro henezu poemy 'Popil imperii,'" 331–33. In Klen 1957d, 2.

——. 1957c. "Pryhody arkhanhela Rafaila," 57–93. In Klen 1957d, 3. (Orig. pub. 1948.)

——. 1957d. *Tvory.* 4 vols. Toronto: Fundatsiia imeny Iuriia Klena.

Knysh, Zynovii. 1951. *Dukh, shcho tilo rve do boiu . . . (Iuliian Holovinskyi, Kraiovyi Momandant U.V.O.).* Winnipeg: n.p.

——. 1952. *Ustrii Orhanizatsii Ukrainskykh Natsionalistiv (Porivnialna studiia).* Winnipeg-Buenos Aires: n.p.

——. 1959. *Pered pokhodom na skhid. Spohady y materiialy do diiannia Orhanizatsii Ukrainskykh Natsionalistiv u 1939–1941 rokakh.* Vol. 1. Toronto: Sribna Surma.

——. 1960. *Pered pokhodom na skhid. Spohady y materiialy do diiannia Orhanizatsii Ukrainskykh Natsionalistiv u 1939–1941 rokakh.* Vol. 2. Toronto: Sribna Surma.

——. 1965. *Sprava Skhidnykh Torhiv u Lvovi.* Toronto: Sribna Surma.

——. 1967. *Dalekyi prytsil: Ukrainska viiskova orhanizatsiia v 1927–1929 rokakh.* Toronto: Sribna Surma.

——. 1983. *Z taiemnykh dokumentiv polskoi okupatsii Zakhidnoi Ukrainy.* Toronto: Sribna surma.

Koepnik, Lutz. 1999. "Fascist Aesthetics Revisited." *Modernism/Modernity* 6.1: 51–74.

Koestler, Arthur. 1976. *The Ghost in the Machine.* London: Hutchinson.

Kohut, Zenon E. 2008–09. "From Japheth to Moscow: Narrating Biblical and Ethnic Origins of the Slavs in Polish, Ukrainian, and Russian Historiography (Sixteenth–Eighteenth Centuries)." *Journal of Ukrainian Studies* 33–34: 279–92.

Kolodzinskyi, Mykhailo. 1957. *Ukrainska voienna doktryna. Chastyna persha.* Toronto: Nakladom T-va Kolyshnikh Voiakiv UPA v Kanadi i ZDA.

Kompaniiets, Oksana. 1936. *Lesia Ukrainka v 23 rokovyny smerty.* Lviv: Desheva knyzhka.

"Kongres Mizhnarodnoho Zhinochoho Rukhu." 1929. *Rozbudova natsii* 6–7: 249–50.

Konovalets, Ievhen. 1928. "Prychynky do istorii roli Sichovykh Striltsiv v Ukrainskii revoliutsii." *Rozbudova natsii* 1: 18–23; 2: 60–64; 3: 104–10; 4: 153–58; 5: 199–204; 6: 241–44.

Konrad, Mykola. 1933. "Tserkva i natsionalism." *Dilo,* 4 May.

Kordiuk, Bohdan. 1974. "Ievhen Konovalets—Viiskovyi i politychnyi orhanizator," 959–73. In Boiko 1974.

Kosach, Iurii. 1946. "Vilna ukrainska literatura," 47–65. In MUR. *Mystetskyi ukrainskyi rukh. Zbirnyk II.* Munich-Karlsfeld: n.p.

Kostelnyk, Havryil. 1919. *Hranytsi demokratyzmu.* Lviv: Khrystiianska biblioteka.

Kostiuk, H. 1966. "Ukrainska emihratsiina khudozhnia proza za 1965 rik (Deiaki dumky i pidsumky)." *Novi dni,* May: 5–10.

Kosyk, Volodymyr. 1993. *Ukraina i Nimechchyna u Druhii svitovii viini.* Paris, New York, Lviv: Naukove tovarystvo imeni Tarasa Shevchenka u Lvovi. (Orig.: Wolodymyr Kosyk. *L'Allemagne national-socialiste et L'Ukraine.* Paris: Publications de l'Est Europeen, 1986).

——. 2009. *Spetsoperatsii NKVD-KGB Proty OUN: Borotba Moskvy proty ukrainskoho natsionalizmu 1933–1943.* Lviv: Halytska vydavnycha spilka.

Koval, Valentyn. 1995. "Ziznannia ubyvtsi (Iak bulo zdiisneno zamakh na polkovnyka Ie. Konovaltsia)." *Z arkhiviv VUChK GPU NKVD KGB* 1–2: 302–11.

Kovalchuk, V. M. 2011. "Italiiskyi vektor diialnosti OUN u 1930-kh rr.": www.vuzlib.com/ content/view/1659/52, accessed 13 July 2011.

Kovba, Zhanna. 2005. "U poshukakh vlasnoi vidpovidalnosty." *Krytyka* 9.9: 19–21.

Kowalewski, Z. M. 1993. "Kwestia Polska w powojennej strategii Ukraińskiej Powstańcyej Armii." In Michał Pulawski, ed., *Ukraińska myśl polityczna w XX wieku: Materialy y miedzynarodowej konferencji naukowej zorganizowanej pzez Instztutu Historii Uniwersytetu Jagiellońskiego i Fundacje św. Włodzimierza Chrzciciela Rusi Kijowskiej w Krakowie 28–30 maja 1990.* Kraków: Zeszyty Naukowe Uniwersytetu Jagiellońskiego, nr. 1088 (Prace Historyczne z. 107).

Kravchenko, Lesia, ed. 2004. *Tvorchist Iuriia Klena v konteksti ukrainskoho neoklasytsyzmu ta visnykivskoho neoromantyzmu. Zbirnyk naukovykh prats.* Drohobych: Vidrodzhennia.

———, et al. 2009. *Vistnykivstvo: literaturna tradytsiia ta idei: Zbirnyk naukovykh prats, prysviachenykh pam'iati Vasylia Ivanyshyna.* Drohobych: KOLO.

Kravchenko, Victor. 1946. *I Chose Freedom: The Personal and Political Life of a Soviet Official.* New York: Charles Scribner's Sons.

Kravtsiv, Bohdan. 1960. "Leonid Mosendz i ioho 'Ostannii prorok,'" v–xxxii. In Leonid Mosendz, *Ostannii Prorok.* Toronto: Vydano Dilovym Komitetom dlia Vyd. Tvoriv L. Mosendza.

Krawchenko, Bohdan. 1985. *Social Change and National Consciousness in Twentieth-Century Ukraine.* Oxford: Macmillan in Association with St. Antony's College.

Krivava knyha: Materiialy do polskoi invazii na ukrainski zemli Skhidnoi Halychyny 1918–1919. roku. 1919–21. 2 vols. Vienna: Vydannia Uriadu Zakhidno-Ukrainskoi Narodnoi Respubliky, vol. 1, 1919; vol. 2, 1921.

Kruglov, Alexander. 2010. "Jewish Losses in Ukraine, 1941–1944," 272–290. In Brandon and Lower 2010.

Krupach, Mykola. "Dmytro Dontsov ta Ievhen Malaniuk: Pershe polemichne perekhrestia," 49–58. In L. Kravchenko et al. 2009.

Krushelnytska, Larysa. 2008. *Rubaly lis: Spohady halychanky.* 3rd ed. Lviv: Vydavnytstvo Astroliabiia.

Krychevskyi, Roman. 1962. *Orhanizatsiia Ukrainskykh Natsionalistiv v Ukraini, Orhanizatsiia Ukrainskykh Natsionalistic Zakordonom: ZCH OUN i prychynok do isto-rii ukrainskoho natsionalistychnojo rukhu.* New York: Vydannia politychnoi rady odno-dumtsiv OUN v SShA.

Kubiiovych, Volodymyr. 1975. *Ukraintsi v Heneralnii hubernii, 1939–1941. Istoriia Tsentralnoho komitetu.* Chicago: Vyd. Mykoly Denysiuka.

Kuchabsky, Vasyl. 2009. *Western Ukraine in Conflict with Poland and Bolshevism, 1918–1923.* Edmonton: Canadian Institute of Ukrainian Studies. (Orig. pub. *Die Westukraine im Kampfe mit Polen und dem Bolschewismus in den Jahren 1918–1923* [1934].)

Kudelya, Serhiy. 2011. "The Impact of Collectivization on Insurgency Mobilization in Western Ukraine after World War II." Paper presented at Annual Danyliw Research Seminar on Contemporary Ukraine, Ottawa, 20 October.

Kurylyshyn, Kostiantyn. 2010. *Ukrainske zhyttia v umovakh nimetskoi okupatsii (1939–1944 rr.): Za materialamy ukrainskoi lehalnoi presy.* Lviv: Natsionalna Akademiia Nauk Ukrainy.

Kuznetsov, Anatoli. 1982. *Babi Yar: A Document in the Form of a Novel.* Penguin Books. (Orig. London: Jonathan Cape, 1970.)

Kvit, Serhii. 2003–04. "Dmytro Dontsov: Ideolohichnyi portret." *Vyzvolnyi shliakh* 56.4 (2003): 51–65; 56.5 (2003): 58–73; 56.6 (2003): 58–74; 56.7 (2003): 55–66; 57.1 (2004): 77–85; 57. 2 (2004): 25–42. (Orig. pub. under separate cover, Kyiv 2000.)

Kvit, Serhii. 2013. *Dmytro Dontsov: Ideolohichnyi portret.* 2nd revised and enlarged edition. Lviv: Halytska vydavnycha spilka. (Orig. pub. under separate cover, Kyiv 2000. Then republished in *Vyzvolnyi shliakh* 56.4 (2003): 51–65; 56.5 (2003): 58–73; 56.6 (2003): 58–74; 56.7 (2003): 55–66; 57.1 (2004): 77–85; 57. 2 (2004): 25–42.)

-kyi, S. 1937. "Kulak." *Vistnyk* 11: 842–43.

LaCapra, Dominick. 2001. *Writing History, Writing Trauma.* Baltimore and London: Johns Hopkins University Press.

Lavrinenko, Iurii. 1956. "Kyiv 1941–43 v dzerkali odniiei dushi." *Ukrainska literaturna hazeta* 2.4 (April): 3.

Lavryshyn, Zenovii, ed. 1996. *Litopys Ukrainskoi Povstanskoi Armii.* Vol. 25. Lviv: Vydavnytstvo Litopys UPA.

Lenkavskyi, Stepan. 1928. "Filosofski pidstavy 'Natsionalizmu' Dontsova." *Rozbudova natsii* 7–8: 272–76.

Levynskyi, Volodymyr. 1936. *Ideolog fashyzmu: Zamitky do ideologii Dmytra Dontsova.* Lviv: Nakladom Hromadskoho holosu.

Liakhovych, Ievhen. 1932. "Tserkva i my." *Rozbudova natsii* 11–12: 280–83.

———. 1974. "Diialnist OUN u Londoni v 1933–1935 rokakh," 907–25. In Boiko 1974.

Lista, Giovanni, and Ada Masoero, eds. 2009. *Futurismo 1909–2009. Velocita + Arte + Azione.* Milan: Skira.

Liubchenko, Arkadii. 1999. *Shchodennyk Arkadiia Liubchenka.* Lviv, New York: Vydavnytstvo M. P. Kots.

Livytska-Kholodna, Nataliia. 1980. "Vydavnytstvo Variah." *Suchasnist* 11: 3–16.

———. 1990. "Spomyn pro kortkyi period zhyttia Oleny Telihy." *Suchasnist* 10: 81–95.

———. 2009. "Iurii Lypa, iakoho ia znala," 790–802. In Ilnytskyi 2009. (Orig. *Suchasnist* 1 [1987].)

Lloyd George, David. 1938. *The Truth about the Peace Treaties.* 2 vols. London: Victor Gollancz.

Lower, Wendy. 2005. *Nazi Empire-Building and the Holocaust in Ukraine.* Chapel Hill: University of North Carolina Press.

Luciuk, Lubomyr Y., and Marco Carynnyk, eds. 1990. *Between Two Worlds: The Memoirs of Stanley Frolick.* Toronto: Multicultural History Society of Ontario.

Lypa, Iurii. 1934. *Kozaky v Moskovii: Roman iz XVII-ho stolittia.* Warsaw: Narodnii stiah.

———. 1935. *Bii za ukrainsku literaturu.* Warsaw: Narodnii stiah.

———. 1936. *Ukrainska doba.* Warsaw: Narodnii stiah.

———. 1936–37. *Notatnyk: Noveli.* 3 vols. Lviv: Narodnyi stiah. Vols. 1, 2: 1936; vol. 3: 1937.

———. 1937. *Ukrainska rasa.* Warsaw: Narodnii stiah.

———. 1938. "Ukrainska zhinka." *Zhinka* 7–8 (April): 2–4.

———. 1943–44. "Try suchasni ukrainski svitohliady." *Krakivski visti,* 31 December 1943; 1, 3, 5, 13, 14 January 1944.

———. 1953. *Pryznachennia Ukrainy.* 2nd facsimile ed. New York: Hoverlia. (Orig: Lviv: Nakaldom Vydavnychoi Kooperatyvy "Khortytsia," 1938.)

———. 1997. "Selianskyi korol." *Kurier Kryvbasu* 85–86 (September): 119–32.

———. 2007. *Vseukrainska trylohiia.* Vol. 2. Kyiv: Mizhrehionalna Akademiia upravlinnia personalom (MAUP).

Lysiak-Rudnytskyi, Ivan. 1973. "Natsionalizm," 233–49. In his *Mizh istoriieiu i politykoiu: Statti do istorii ta krytyky ukrainskoi suspilno-politychnoi dumky.* Munich: Suchasnist.

Lysiansky, Borys. 1942. "Pidvalyny maibutnoho." *Krakivski visti,* 21 January.

Mace, James E. 1983. *Communism and the Dilemmas of National Liberation: National Communism in Soviet Ukraine 1918–1933.* Cambridge, MA: Harvard University Press.

MacIntyre, Alasdair. 1985. *After Virtue: A Study in Moral Theory.* Rev. ed. 1981. London: Duckworth.

Magocsi, Paul Robert. 2010. *A History of Ukraine: The Land and Its Peoples.* 2nd ed. Toronto: Toronto University Press.

Malaniuk, Ievhen. 1930. "V richnytsiu Chuprynkovi." *Literaturno-naukovyi vistnyk* 11: 970–74.

———. 2008. *Notatnyky (1936–1968): Dokumentalno-khudozhnie vydannia.* Kyiv: Tempora.

———. 2009. "Iurii Lypa–poet," 614–27. In Ilnytskyi 2009. (Orig. *Nashe zhyttia* 7 [1947].)

Mali, Joseph. 1999. "The Reconciliation of Myth: Benjamin's Homage to Bachofen." *Journal of the History of Ideas* 60: 165–187.

———. 2008. "The Myth of the State Revisited: Ernst Cassirer and Modern Political Theory," 135–62. In Barash 2008.

Małkiewicz, Andrzej. 2001. "Dwudniowe państwo–Karpacka Ukraina w marcu 1939 r," 117–24. In *Łemkowie, Bojkowie, Rusini–historia, współeczność, kultura materialna i duchowa.* Vol. 3, ed. Stefan Dudra et al. Głogów: Wydawnictwo Druk-Ar.

Maltz, Moshe. 1993. *Years of Horror—Glimpse of Hope: The Diary of a Family in Hiding.* New York: Shengold.

Mandryk, Maria. 2006. *Ukrainskyi natsionalizm: Stanovlennia u mizhvoiennu dobu.* Kyiv: Vydavnytstvo imeni Oleny Telihy.

———. 2009. "Karpatska heopolitychnyi chynnyk 1938–1939 rr. u systemi mizhnarodnoi dyplomatii." *Z arkhiviv VUChK GPU NKVD KGB* 2: 22–85.

Marples, David. R. 2007. *Heroes and Villains: Creating National History in Contemporary Ukraine.* Budapest, New York: Central European University Press.

Martynets, V. 1928. "My i ukrainski politychni partii." *Rozbudova natsii* 6: 235–41.

———. 1937a. *Zabronzovuimo nashe mynule!* Paris: Ukrainske slovo.

———. 1937b. *Za zuby i pazuri natsii.* Paris: Ukrainske slovo.

———. 1938. *Zhydivska probliema v Ukraini.* N.p.: n.p. (Also in *Ideia v nastupi,* 24–47, n.p.: n.p., 1938.)

———. 1949. *Ukrainske pidpillia vid U.V.O. do O.U.N. Spohady i materiialy do peredistorii ta istorii ukrainskoho orhanizovanoho natsionalismu.* Winnipeg: Ukrainian National Federation.

——. 1954. *Ideolohiia orhanizovanoho i t. zv. Volevoho natsionalizmu. Analitychno-porivnialna studiia.* Winnipeg: Novyi Shliakh.

Martynowych, Orest T. 2011. "Sympathy for the Devil: The Attitude of Ukrainian War Veterans in Canada to Nazi Germany and the Jews, 1933–1939," 173–220. In Rhonda L. Hinther and Jim Mochoruk, eds., *Re-Imagining Ukrainian Canadians: History, Politics, and Identity.* Toronto: University of Toronto Press.

Maruniak, V. 1985. "Kulturna referentura PUN v rokakh 1937–1942." *Ukrainskyi istoryk* 22.1–4: 75–80.

Masiukevych, Dr. M. 1931. "Pidstavy rozvytku natsii." *Rozbudova natsii* 11–12: 292–96.

Mazepa, I. 1922. *Bolshevyzm i okupatsiia Ukrainy: Sotsiialno-politychni prychyny nedozrilosty syl ukrainskoi revoliutsii.* Lviv: Dilo.

——. 1946, 1949. *Pidstavy nashoho vidrodzhennia.* 2. vols. N.p.: Prometei.

——. 1950. *Ukraina v vohni i buri revoliutsii.* 3 vols. N.p.: Prometei.

Mazower, M. 1999. *Dark Continent: Europe's Twentieth Century.* 14th ed. London: Penguin Books.

McCole, John. 1993. *Walter Benjamin and the Antinomies of Tradition.* Ithaca: Cornell University Press.

Megas, Osyp. 1920. *Tragediia Halytskoi Ukrainy: materiialy pro polsku invaziiu, polskivarvarstva s polsku okupatsiiu Skhidnoi Halychyny za krovavi roky 1918, 1919, 1920.* Vol. 1. Winnipeg: Kanadiiskyi farmer.

Melnyk, Volodymyr. 1993. "Zhyvyi holos dalekoi epokhy: Sproba litportreta Dokii Humennoi." *Kyiv* 11: 112–15.

Miller, David. 1993. *On Nationality.* Oxford: Oxford University Press.

Mirchuk, Petro. 1953. *Ukrainska povstanska armiia, 1942–1952.* Munich: n.p.

——. 1968. *Narys istorii Orhanizatsii Ukrainskykh Natsionalistiv.* Vol. 1. Munich: Ukrainske vydavnytstvo.

——. 1969, "Khto i proty iakoho natsionalizmu pochav 'novyi nastup'? (Vidpovid na zakydy D-ra D. Dontsova)." *Shliakh peremohy,* 27 April.

Mosendz, Leonid. 1936a. "Marginalii do 'Ukrainskoi doby' Iu. Lypy." *Vistnyk* 9: 728–30.

——. 1936b. "Narodzhennia Don Kikhota." *Samostiina dumka* 6–8: 334–43.

——. 1936c. *Zasiv: Povist.* Cernauti (Chernivtsi): Samostiina dumka.

——. 1937. *Liudyna pokirna (Homo lenis): Opovidi.* Lviv: Ivan Tyktor.

——. 1940. *Vichnyi korabel (Lirychna drama).* Prague: Kolos.

——. 1948. *Volynskyi rik: Poema.* Munich: Ukrainska trybuna.

——. 1960. *Ostannii prorok.* Toronto: Vydano Dilovym Komitetom dlia Vyd. Tvoriv L. Mosendza.

Motyka, Grzegorz. 2006a. "Służba Bezpeky OUN-B (Służba Bezpieceństwa OUN-B). Z warsztatów badawczych." *Pamięć i Sprawiedliwość: biuletyn Głównej Komisji Badania Zbrodni przeciwko Narodowi Polskiemu Instytutu Pamięci Narodowej* 5:1; available online at http://www. zbrodiawolynska.pl/_data/assets/pdf_file/0017/3950/Grzegorz_Motyka_Sluzba_Bezpeky_OUN_B.pdf.

——. 2006b. *Ukraińska partyzantka, 1942–1960: Dyiałalność Organiyacji Ukraińskich Nacjonalistów i Ukraińskiej Powstańcyej Armii.* Warsaw: Instytut Studiów Politycznych Pan, Oficyna Wydawnicza Rytm.

Motyka, M. 1929. "'Zovsim novoho typu ukraintsi' . . ." *Bilshovyk Ukrainy* 7–8: 70–79.

Motyl, Alexander J. 1980. *The Turn to the Right: The Ideological Origins and Development of Ukrainian Nationalism, 1919–1929.* Boulder, CO: *East European Quarterly*; New York: distributed by Columbia University Press.

———. 1985. "Ukrainian Nationalist Political Violence in Inter-War Poland, 1921–1939." *East European Quarterly* 19.1 (1985): 45–55.

———. 2013. "On Nationalism and Fascism." *World Affairs.* 10, 14, and 25 June: http://www.worldaffairsjournal.org/blog/alexander-j-motyl/nationalism-and-fascism-part-1.

Movchan, Raisa. 2008. *Ukrainskyi modernism 1920-kh: portret v istorychnomu interieri.* Kyiv: Stylos.

Muravskyi, Volodymyr, ed. 2006. *Kongres Ukrainskykh Natsionalistiv 1929 r.: Dokumenty i materialy.* Lviv: Natsionalna Akademiia Nauk Ukrainy et al.

Mykolyn, Iu. 1956. "Povist pro Kyiv 1951 roku (Dumka chytacha)." *Svoboda*, 6 July.

Mylianych, Iu. 1929. "Zhydy, sionizm i Ukraina." *Rozbudova natsii* 8–9: 271–76.

Myron, Dmytro. 2009. "Ideia i chyn Ukrainy," 171–98. In Viktor Roh, ed., *Ukrainskyi natsionalizm: Antolohiia.* Vol. 1. Kyiv: Ukrainska vydavnycha spilka im. Iuriia Lypy.

Mytsiuk, O. 1929. "Fashyzm (Dyskusiina stattia)." *Rozbudova natsii* 8–9: 262–70.

———. 1932. "Zhydivska ekonomika na Ukraini za doby reaktsii (1882–1917)." *Rozbudova natsii* 5–6: 118–31.

———. 1933. *Agraryzatsiia zhydivstva Ukrainy na tli zahalnoi ekonomiky.* Prague: Nakladom avtora.

Nabytovych, Ihor. 2001. *Leonid Mosendz–Lytsar sviatoho gralia: Tvorchist pysmennyka v konteksti ievropeiskoi literatury.* Drohobych: Vidrodzhennia.

Narvselius, Eleonora. 2012. "The 'Bandera Debate': The Contentious Legacy of World War II and Liberalization of Collective Memory in Western Ukraine." *Canadian Slavonic Papers* 54.3–4: 469–90.

Na vichnu hanbu Polshchi. 1931. Prague: Rozbudova natsii.

Nazaruk, Osyp. 1924. *Do istorii revoliutsiinoho chasu na Ukraini. Ukrainski politychni partii, ikh soiuzy i teorii.* Winnipeg: n.p.

Nesina, Olena. 1969. "Shche pro Blahoslovy maty." *Novi dni*, May: 23–25.

Nietzsche, Friedrich. 1967. *The Birth of Tragedy and the Case of Wagner.* New York: Vintage Books.

Nykorovych, S. I. 1933. "Shchob zakinchyty paperovu viinu!" *Samostiina dumka* 5–6: 174–76.

O.-ko. 1958. "Pro dvi knyzhky." *Ukrainets.* 23 February.

Olzhych, Oleh. 1994. *Neznanomu Voiakovi: Zapovidane zhyvym.* Kyiv: Fundatsiia imeni O. Olzhycha.

———. 2007. *Poeziia, Proza.* Kyiv: Vydavnytstvo imeni Oleny Telihy.

———. 2009. *Vybrani tvory.* Kyiv: Smoloskyp.

Omelchuk, Olesia. 2009. "Fantazii pro Ukrainu," 739–52. In Ilnytskyi 2009. (Orig. *Slovo i chas* 1 [2005].)

———. 2011. *Literaturni idealy ukrainskoho vistnykivstva (1922–1939). Monohrafiia.* Kyiv: Smoloskyp.

Onatskyi, Ievhen. 1928. "Lysty z Italii, 1." *Rozbudova natsii* 1.3: 93–96.

———. 1929. "Fashyzm i my (Spryvodu statti prof. Mytsiuka)." *Rozbudova natsii* 12: 397–401.

———. 1933. "Nationalizm i indyvidualizm." *Rozbudova natsii* 7–8: 159–61.

———. 1934a. "Kult uspikhu." *Samostiina dumka* 9–10: 715–27. (Also *Rozbudova natsii* 7–8 [1934]: 162–68.)

———. 1934b. "Mezhy myloserdiam i zhorstokistiu." *Samostiina dumka* 1: 71–73.

———. 1938. " Zahostrennia zhydivskoi problemy (Z moioho rymskoho shchodennyka)." *Novyi shliakh*, 8 November.

———. 1949. *U vavylonskomu poloni (Spoyny).* Buenos Aires: n.p.

———. 1954. *U vichnomu misti. Zapysky ukrainskoho zhurnalista: Rik 1930.* Buenos Aires: Vydavnytstvo Mykoly Denysiuka.

———. 1974. "Ievhen Konovalets i PUN pered problemoiu rozbudovy OUN v Ukraini," 665–700. In Boiko 1974.

———. 1981. *U vichnomu misti: Zapysky ukrainskoho zhurnalista: Roky 1931–1932.* Vol. 2. Toronto: Novyi shliakh.

———. 1984. *U vichnomu misti: Zapysky ukrainskoho zhurnalista: 1933 Rik.* Vol. 3. Toronto: Novyi shliakh.

———. 1989. *U vichnomu misti: Zapysky ukrainskoho zhurnalista: 1934 Rik.* Vol. 4. Toronto: Novyi shliakh.

Ordivskyi, S. [Hryhorii Luzhnytskyi] 1939. *Chorna ihumena:Istorychna povist z XVII st.* Lviv: Ivan Tyktor.

Orest, M. 1948. "Zapovit Iu. Klena." *Orlyk* 3.2 (February): 5–7.

Orhanizatsiia Ukrainskykh Natsionalistiv, 1929–1954. 1955. Paris: Persha Ukrainska Drykarnia u Frantsii.

Orshan, Iaroslav [Orest Chemerynsky]. 1938a. *De stoimo?* Paris: n.p.

———. 1938b. *Doba natsionalizmu.* Paris: n.p. (Also as "Doba natsionalizmu," 21–43. In *Almanakh v avangardi.* N.p.: n.p., 1938.)

Ostroverkha, Mykhailo. 1934. *Musolini: Liudyna i chyn.* Lviv: Knyhozbirnia Vistnyka.

———. 1938. *Nova imperiia: Italiia i fashyzm.* Lviv: Biblioteka "Dorohy."

———. 1946. *Nihil novi: mirkuvannia na mystetski temy.* Stuttgard: Nakladom KEP.

———. 1958. *Na zakruti: Osin 1939 roku.* New York: Nakladom avtora.

P., M. 1942. "Mystetstvo ta krytyka u nas." *Krakivski visti*, 21–22 February.

Pahiria, O. 2009. "Nevidomi lysty delehatsii uriadu Karpatskoi Ukrainy do uriadu Uhorshchyny." *Z arkhiviv VUChK GPU NKVD KGB* 1: 49–70.

Paneyko, Basil. 1931. "Galicia and the Polish-Ukrainian Problem." *Slavonic and East European Review* 9.27 (March): 67–87.

Pankivskyi, Kost. 1983. *Roky nimetskoi okupatsii, 1941–1944.* 2nd ed. New York: Naukove tov-vo im. Shevchenka. (Orig. pub. 1965.)

Pasternakova, Mariia. 1963. *Ukrainska zhinka v khoreohrafii.* Winnipeg-Edmonton: Nakladom Soiuzu Ukrainok Kanady.

Paul, Gerhard, ed. 2002. *Die Täter der Shoah: Fanatische Nationalsozialisten oder ganz normale Deutsche?* Göttingen: Wallstein Verlag.

Pavlychko, Solomiia. 1999. *Dyskurs modernizmu v ukrainskii literaturi.* Kyiv: Lybid.

Pelenskyi, Zenon. 1928. "Pax Americana." *Rozbudova natsii* 6: 229–35, and 7–8: 290–97.

———. 1974. "Mizh dvoma konechnostiamy," 502–24. In Boiko 1974.

Petrenko, Roman. 1997. *Za Ukrainu, za ii voliu (Spohady). Litopys Ukrainskoi Povstanskoi Armii.* Vol. 27. Toronto-Lviv: Vydavnytstvo Litopys UPA

——— 2004. *Slidamy armii bez derzhavy.* Kyiv, Toronto: Ukrainska Vydavnycha Spilka.

Petryshyn, M. [real name Vasyl Koroliv-Staryi] 1932. *Buduiut chy ruinuiut? (Z pryvodu diialnosty organizatsii ukrainskykh natsionalistiv).* Prolom: n.p.

Pohl, Dieter. 1997. *Nationalsozialistische Judenverfolgung in Ostgalizien 1941–1944.* Munich: R. Oldenbourg Verlag.

———. 2002. "Ukrainische Hilfskräfte beim Mord an dem Juden," 205–34. In Paul 2002.

———. 2007. "Anti-Jewish Pogroms in Western Ukraine—A Research Agenda," 305–13. In *Shared History–Divided Memory: Jews and Others in Soviet-Occupied Poland, 1939–1941,* ed. Eleazar Barkan, Elizabeth A. Cole, and Kai Struve. Leipzig: Leipziger Universitätsverlag.

———. 2010. "The Murder of Ukraine's Jews under German Military Administration and in the Reich Commissariat Ukraine," 23–76. In Brandon and Lower 2010.

Portnov, Andrii. 2008. *Nauka u vyhnanni: Naukova i osvitnia diialnist ukrainskoi emihratsii v mizhvoiennii Polshchi (1919–1939).* Kharkiv: KhIFT.

Potocki, Robert. 2003. *Polityka państwa polskiego wobec zagadnienia ukraińskiego w latach 1930–1939.* Lublin: Instytut Europy Śródkowo-Wschodniej.

Prohrama vynarodovlennia ukraintsiv i bilorusyniv v Polshchi. ca. 1938. Lviv: Biblioteka UNO (Ukrainskoi Narodnoi Obnovy).

Prystaiko, Volodymyr, and Iurii Shapoval. 1995. *Sprava "Spiky Vyzvolennia Ukrainy": Nevidomi dokumenty i fakty.* Kyiv: Intel.

———. 1996. *Mykhailo Hrushevskyi i DPU-NKVD: Trahichne desiatylittia, 1924–1934.* Kyiv: Ukraina.

———. 1999. *Mykhailo Hrushevskyi: Sprava "UNTs" i ostanni roky (1931–1934).* Kyiv: Krytyka.

Rafes, M. G. 1920. *Dva goda revoliutsii na Ukraine.* Moscow: n.p.

Ravich-Cherkasskii, M. 1923. *Istoriia Kommunisticheskoi Partii (b-ov) Ukrainy.* Kharkiv: Gosudarstvennoe izdatelstvo Ukrainy.

"Realna" chy vyzvolna polityka? (Rozmova na chasi). 1933. Prague: Vydannia Rozbudovy natsii.

Rebet, Daria. 1974. "Natsionalistychna molod i molodechyi natsionalizm," 482–501. In Boiko 1974.

Rebet, Lev. 1964. *Svitla i tini OUN.* Munich: Ukrainskyi samostiinyk.

Rev, Istvan. 2005. *Retroactive Justice: Prehistory of Post-Communism.* Stanford, CA: Stanford University Press.

Revyuk, Emil, ed. 1931. *Polish Atrocities in Ukraine.* New York: United Ukrainian Organizations of the United States.

Riabchuk, Mykola. 2006. "Kutura pamiati ta polityka zabuttia." *Kultura* 10.1–2: 18–20.

Riabenko, Serhii. 2012. "Slidamy 'Lvivskoho pohromu' Dzhona-Pola Khymky." Istorychna pravda. 20 February: http://www.istpravda.com.ua/articles/2013/02/20/112766.

Roh, V., ed. 2009. *Ukrainskyi natsionalizm: Antolohiia.* Vol. 1. Kyiv: Ukrainska vydavnycha spilka im. Iu. Lypy.

Roman, Vasyl. 1983. *Moia pratsia i borotba (Spohady chlena OUN)*. Munich: Nakladom avtora.

Romaniuk, Mykhailo. 2009. *Petro Fedun—"Poltava"—providnyi ideoloh OUN ta UPA*. Toronto-Lviv: Litopys UPA.

Romulius. 1956. "Pro velyki mity." *Svoboda*, 21 April.

Roth, Joseph. 1985. *The Radetzky March*. Woodstock, New York: Overlook Press. (Orig. German pub. 1932.)

Rothe, Hans, ed. 1983. *Sinopsis, Kiev 1681: Facsimile miteiner Einleitung*. Cologne: Bohlau.

Rubchak, Bohdan. 2009. "Sertse nadvoie rozderte (Frahment)," 694–705. In Ilnytskyi 2009. (Orig. introduction to Natalia Livytska-Kholodna, *Poezii star ii novi* [1986].)

Rublov, Oleksandr. 2004. *Zakhidnoukrainska intellihentsiia u zahalnonatsionalnykh politychnykh ta kulturnykh protsesakh (1914–1939)*. Kyiv: Instytut Istorii Ukrainy, Natsional'na Akademiia Nauk Ukrainy.

Rublov, O. S., and Iu. A. Cherchenko. 1994. *Stalinshchyna i dolia zakhidnoukrainskoi intelihentsii: 20–50 roky XX st.* Kyiv: Naukova dumka.

Rublov, Oleksandr, and Natalia Rublova, eds. 2012. *Ukraina-Polshcha 1920–1939 rr.: Z istorii dyplomatychnykh vidnosyn USSR z Druhoiu Richchiu Pospolytoiu. Dokumenty i materialy*. Kyiv: Dukh i litera.

Rudling, Per. A. 2011. *The OUN, the UPA and the Holocaust: A Study in the Manufacturing of Historical Myths*. The Carl Beck Papers in Russian and East European Studies, no. 2107. Pittsburg: University of Pittsburg.

Rusnak, Iryna. 2005. "Povertsaiuchys do problemy kolaboranstva . . . ublitsystyka Ulasa Samchuka 1941–1941 rr." *Ukrainska mova ta literatura* 5: 3–7.

———. 2009. "Zhyvyi dukh Ulasa Samchuka," 9–28. In Samchuk 2009.

Ryndyk, S. 1957. "Chuzhymy dorohamy." *Ukrainske zhyttia*. 23 November.

Samchuk, Ulas. 1941. "Sohodni i zavtra." *Proboiem* 9: 530–37.

———. 1944. *Hory hovoriat! Roman u 2-okh chastynakh*. Winnipeg: Nakladom Novoho shliakhu.

———. 1946–47. *Iunist Vasylia Sheremety*. 2 vols. Munich: Prometei. Vol. 1: 1946, vol. 2: 1947.

———. 1948. *Ost: Roman u 3 tomakh*. Regensburg: Vydannia Mykhaila Boretskoho.

———. 1952. *Mariia: Khronika odnoho zhyttia*. 3rd ed. Buenos Aires: Vydavnytstvo Mykoly Denysiuka.

———. 1959. *Choho he hoit ohon: Roman*. New York: Vydavnytstvo "Visnyk"—OOChSU.

———. 1965. *Na bilomu koni*. New York, Munich: Suchasnist. (2nd ed. Winnipeg: Volyn.)

———. 1975. *Na koni voronomu: Spomyny i vrazhennia*. Winnipeg: Volyn. (2nd ed. Lviv, Litopys chervonoi kalyny, 2000.)

———. 1980. *Na bilomu koni. Spomyny i vrazhennia*. 3rd ed. Winnipeg: Volyn.

———. 1982. *Vtecha vid sebe: roman*. Winnipeg: Volyn.

———. 2008. "Z Olenoiu Telihoiu na shliakhu do Kyieva," 287–317. In Teliha 2008. (Orig. Suchasnyk 1 [1948].)

———. 2009. *Kulak, Mesnyky, Vidnaidenyi rai*. Drohobych: Vidrodzhennia.

Savchenko, V. 2009. "Malovidomi fakty z biohrafii S. Shvartsbarda (do istorii spivrobitnytstva z orhanamy derzhavnoi bezpeky SRSR)." *Z arkhiviv VUChK GPU NKVD KGB* 1: 120–36.

Schneider, Herbert W. 1936. *The Fascist Government of Italy*. New York: D. Van Nostrand.

Scholem, G., and T. Adorno, eds. 1994. *The Correspondence of Walter Benjamin*. Trans. M. R. Jacobson and E. M. Jacobson. Chicago: University of Chicago Press.

Sciborsky, Mykola [Stsiborskyi]. 1940. *Ukraine and Russia: A Survey of Soviet Russia's Twenty-Year Occupation of Eastern Ukraine*. New York: Organization for the Rebirth of Ukraine.

Seleshko, Mykhailo. 1991. *Vinnytsia: Spomyny perekladacha komissii doslidiv zlochyniv NKVD v 1937–1938*. New York, Toronto: Fundatsiia im. O. Olzhycha.

Serhiichuk, M. I. 1996. *OUN-UPA v roky viiny: Novi dokumenty i materialy*. Kyiv: Dnipro.

———, ed. 2009. *Stepan Bandera u dokumentakh radianskykh orhaniv derzhavnoi bezpetky (1939–1959)*. 3 vols. Kyiv: Haluzevyi derzhavnyi arkhiv Sluzhby Bezpeky Ukrainy, Haluzevyi derzhavnyi arkhiv Sluzhby Zovnishnoi Rozvidky Ukrainy.

Sh., F. 1933. "Deshcho pro nimetskyi national-sotsializm." *Rozbudova natsii* 1–2: 30–34. (Also *Samostiina dumka* 5–6: 157–60.)

Shandor, Vincent. 1997. *Carpatho-Ukraine in the Twentieth Century: A Political and Legal History*. Cambridge, MA: Distributed by Harvard University Press for the Ukrainian Research Institute, Harvard University.

Shankovskyi, Lev. 1958. *Pokhidni hrupy OUN (Prychynky do istorii pokhidnykh hrup OUN na tsentralnykh zemliakh Ukrainy v 1941–1943 rr.)*. Munich: Ukrainskyi samostiinyk.

Shapoval, Iurii, Volodymyr Prystaiko, and Vadym Zolotarov. 1997. *ChK—DPU—NKVD v Ukraini: Osoby, fakty, dokumenty*. Kyiv: Abrys.

Shapoval, M. 1923. *Shliakh vyzvolennai: Suspilno-politychni narysy*. Prague, Berlin: Nova Ukraina.

———. 1928. *Velyka revoliutsiia (Z nahody 10-littia revoliutsii na Ukraini)*. Prague: Vilna spilka.

Shcherbakivskyi, V. 1941. *Formatsiia ukrainskoi natsii. Narys praistorii Ukrainy*. Prague: Vydavnytstvo Iuriia Tyshchenka.

Shenfield, Stephen D. 2001. *Russian Fascism: Traditions, Tendencies, Movements*. Armonk, NY: N. E. Sharpe.

Sheptytskyi, Andrei. 2009. *Pastyrski poslannia*. Vol. 2, 1918–1939. Lviv: Andrei.

Sherekh, Iurii [real name Shevelov]. 1947. "V oboroni velykykh (Polemika bez osib)," 11–26. In *MUR: Mystetskyi ukrainskyi rukh: Zbirnyk III*. Regensburg: Ukrainske slovo.

———. 1948. *Dumky proty techii: Publitsystyka*. N.p.: Ukraina.

———. 1952. "Reabilitatsiia liudyny (*Mana* Dokii Humennoi)." *Novi dni*, July: 11–14.

———. 1998. *Porohy i Zaporizhzhia: Literatura. Mystetstvo. Ideolohiia*. Vol. 3. Kharkiv: Folio.

———. 2003. Proshchannia z uchora ("Koly zh pryide spravzhnii den?"). In Vira Aheieva, ed., *Proza pro inshykh: Iurii Kosach: Teksty, interpretatsii, komentari*, 209–53. Kyiv: Fakt. (Orig. pub. 1952.)

Shevchuk, Hryhorii [Iurii Shevelov]. 2008. "Bez metalevykh sliv i bez zitkhan daremnykh," 403–14. In Ilnytskyi 2009.

Shevelov, Iurii (Iurii Sherekh). 2001. *Ia—Mene—Meni—(i dovkruhy): Spohady*. 2 vols. Kharkiv: Berezil.

Shkandrii, Miroslav [Myroslav Shkandrij]. 2014 (forthcoming). "Radio Vena: Radioperedachi Organizatsii Ukrainskikh Natsionalistov, 1938–39." *Forum*.

Shkandrij, Myroslav. 2009. *Jews in Ukrainian Literature: Representation and Identity*. New Haven, CT: Yale University Press.

———. 2014 (forthcoming). "The Second World War and the OUN in Reader Responses to Dokia Humenna's Khreshchatyi iar (1956)." *Journal of Ukrainian Studies*.

Shkandrij, Myroslav, and Olga Bertelsen. 2013. "The Soviet Regime's National Operations in Ukraine, 1929–34." *Canadian Slavonic Papers* 55.3–4: 417–48.

Shkvarko, I. 1947. *Proklynaiu: Z shchodennyka ukrainskoho politviaznia*. Winnipeg: Ukrainskyi holos.

Shlemkevych, M. 1956. *Halychanstvo*. New York, Toronto: Zhyttia i mysli.

Shnirelman, Victor. 2002. *The Myth of the Khazars and Intellectual Antisemitism in Russia, 1970s–1990s*. Jerusalem: Vidal Sassoon International Center for the Study of Antisemitism, Hebrew University of Jerusalem.

Shumelda, Iakiv. 1985. "Chomu zahynuv D-r Oleh Kandyba-Olzhych u kontsentratsi-inomu tabori." *Ukrainskyi istoryk* 22.1–4: 81–90.

Shumuk, Danylo. 1998. *Perezhyte i peredumane: Spohady i rozdumy ukrainskoho dysydenta-politviaznia z rokiv blukan i borotby pid trioma okupantamy Ukrainy (1921–1981 rr.)*. Kyiv: Vyd-vo imeni Oleny Telihy.

Silverman, Kaja. 1996. *The Threshold of the Visible World*. New York, London: Routledge.

Simpson, G. W. 1939. "The Ukrainian Problem," 1–7. In *The Ukrainian Cause on Radio Waves*. Saskatoon, CA: Ukrainian National Federation.

Siryk, Liudmyla. 2004. "Iurii Klen—Poet i perekladach." In L. Kravchenko 2004, 310–24.

Smith, Anthony D. 1988. "The Myth of the 'Modern Nation' and the Myths of Nations." *Ethnic and Racial Studies* 11.1 (1988): 1–26.

———. 1991. *National Identity*. Harmondsworth: Penguin Books.

Smolii, V. I., ed. 2002. *Politychnyi teror i teroryzm v Ukraini XIX-XX st. Istorychni narysy*. Kyiv: Naukova dumka.

Snyder, Timothy. 1999. "'To Resolve the Ukrainian Problem Once and For All': The Ethnic Cleansing of Ukrainians in Poland 1943–1947." *Cold War Studies* 1.2: 86–120.

———. 2003a. "The Causes of Ukrainian-Polish Ethnic Cleansing 1943." *Past and Present* 179 (May): 197–234.

———. 2003b. *The Reconstruction of Nations: Poland, Ukraine, Lithuania, Belarus 1669–1999*. New Haven, CT: Yale University Press.

———. 2005. *Sketches from a Secret War: A Polish Artist's Mission to Liberate Soviet Ukraine*. New Haven, CT, and London: Yale University Press.

———. 2010a. *Bloodlands: Europe Between Hitler and Stalin*. New York: Basic Books.

———. 2010b. "Life and Death of Western Volhynian Jewry, 1921–1945," 77–113. In Brandon and Lower 2010.

Sobornakrovi, 2011. Documentary film: http://www.youtube.com/watch?v=eabM36WDNOQ.

Sokhah, P., and Potichnyi, P., eds. 2002. *Litopys UPA. Nova seriia*. Vol. 4. *Borotba proty UPA i natsionalistychnoho pidpillia: Informatsiiini dokumenty TsK KP(b)U, obkomiv partii, NKVS-MVS, MDB-KGB, 1943–1959. Knyha persha, 1943–1945.* Kyiv, Toronto: Nationalna Akademiia Nauk Ukrainy et al.

Sorel, Georges. 1969. *Reflections on Violence.* Trans. T. E Hulme and J. Roth. New York: Collier Books.

Sosnovskyi, Mykhailo. 1974. *Dmytro Dontsov: Politychnyi portret.* New York, Toronto: Naukove Tovarystvo imeni Shevchenka.

———. 1991. "Mykola Mikhnovskyi i Dmytro Dontsov—rechnyky dvokh kontseptsii ukrainskoho nationalizmu." *Zustrichi* 2: 122–29.

Spotts, Frederic. 2009. *Hitler and the Power of Aesthetics.* Woodstock and New York: Overlook Press.

Stakhiv, Ievhen. 1995. *Kris tiurmy, pidpillia i kordony: povist moho zhyttia.* Kyiv: Rada.

Stakhiv, Volodymyr P. 2005. *Pro ukrainsku zovnishniu polityku, OUN ta politychni vbyvstva Kremlia: Zbirka vybranykh prats.* Hadiach: Hadiach.

Starosolskyi, Volodymyr. 1922. *Teoriia natsii.* Vienna: Ukrainskyi sotsiolohichnyi instytut.

Stasiuk, Oleksandra. 2006. *Vydavnycho-propahandyvna diialnist OUN (1941–1953).* Lviv: Tsentr doslidzhennia vytzvolnoho rukhu, Instytut ukrainoznavstva im. I. Krypiakevycha.

Statiev, Alexander. 2010. *The Soviet Counterinsurgency in the Western Borderlands.* Cambridge: Cambridge University Press.

Stefaniv, Vasyl. 2011. "Pidtrymka dukhovenstvom HKTs ukrainskoho vyzvolnoho rukhu," 231–48. In Zaitsev, Behen, Stefaniv 2011.

Steiner, Wendy. 2001. *The Trouble with Beauty.* London: William Heinemann.

Stercho, Petro. 2009. *Karpato-Ukrainska derzhava: Do istorii vyzvolnoi borotby karpatskykh ukraintsiv u 1919–1939 rokakh.* Kyiv: Vydavnytstvo Oleny Telihy. (Orig. pub. 1965.)

Sternytskyi, V. 1933. "Problema molodi v Nimechchyni." *Vistnyk* 5: 441–53.

Stetsiuk, Hryhorii. 1988. *Nepostavlenyi pamiatnyk: Spohady.* Winnipeg: Instytut Doslidiv Volyni.

Stetsko, Iaroslav. 1967. *30 chervnia 1941.* Toronto: Nakladom Ligy Vyzvolennia Ukrainy.

St-Martin, Armelle. 2006. "De l'alimentation chez Sade: Clivages sociaux et (in) distinction feminine." *Dalhousie French Studies* 76: 13–29.

———. 2007. "Sade's System of Perversity and Italian Medicine," 26–53. In Frederick Burwick and Kathryn Tucker, eds., *Marquis de Sade and the Scientia and Techne of Erotocism.* Newcastle: Cambridge Scholars Publishing.

———. 2009. "Fantasmes et metaphors pathologiques dans l'Histoire secrete d'Isabelle de Baviere." *French Review* 82.3: 529–44.

Straus, Renke. 1928. "Mussolini Talks about Jews." *Canadian Jewish Chronicle,* 14 September.

Stryjek, Tomasz. 2000. *Ukraińska idea narodowa okresu miedzywojennego: Analiza wybranych koncepcji.* Wroclaw: Wydawnyctwo Funna.

———. 2002. "Europejskość Dmytra Doncowa, czyli o cechach szezególnych ideologii ukraińskiego nacjonalizmu," 19–32. In Grzegorz Motyka and Dariusza Libionka, eds., *Antypolska Akcja OUN-UPA 1943–1944: Fakty i Interpretacje.* Warsaw: Instytut Pamieci Narodowej.

Stsiborskyi, Mykola. 1930. "Ukrainskyi natsionalizm i zhydivstvo." *Rozbudova natsii* 11–12: 266–73.

——. 1935. *Natsiokratiia.* Paris: n.p.

——. 1939. *Zemelne pytannia.* Paris: Ukrainska Knyharnia-Nakladnia.

——. 1940. *Ukraina v tsyfrakh.* Winnipeg: Nakladom Ukrainskoho natsionalnoho obied-
nannia.

——. 1958. "Na uvahu suchasnykam i nashchadkam." *Ukrainskyi prometei,* 12 June.

Sudoplatov, Pavel. 1995. *Special Tasks: The Memoirs of an Unwanted Eyewitness, a Soviet
Spymaster.* Boston: Little, Brown.

Sukhoversky, Mykola. 1997. *Moi spohady.* Kyiv: Smoloskyp.

Swystun, Wasyl. 1939. "Claims of the Ukrainians," 10–15. In *The Ukrainian Cause on
Radio Waves. Saskatoon, CA: Ukrainian Federation of Canada.*

Sycz, Mirosław. 1999. "Polish Policy toward the Ukrainian Cooperative Movements, 1920–
1939." *Harvard Ukrainian Studies* 23.1–2: 25–45.

S[ydor]-Chartoryiskyi, Mykola. 1951. *Vid Sianu po Krym (Spomyny uchasnyka III Pokhidnoi
Hrupy).* New York: Howerla.

Sytnyk, Mykhailo. 2009. "Krov na kvitakh," 771–78. In Ilnytskyi 2009. (Orig. *Orlyk* 2
[1948].)

Szporluk, Roman. 1988. *Communism and Nationalism: Karl Marx versus Friedrich List.*
New York, Oxford: Oxford University Press.

Tarnavskyi, Ostap. 1995. *Literaturnyi Lviv, 1939–1944.* Lviv: Prosvita.

Taylor, Brandon. 1990. "Post-Modernism in the Third Reich," 128–43. In Taylor and van
der Will 1990.

Taylor, Brandon, and Wilfried van der Will, eds. 1990. *The Nazification of Art.* Winchester,
UK: Winchester Press.

Teliha, Olena. 1936. Review of Iurii Lypa, *Ukrainska doba. Vistnyk* 8: 613–16.

——. 1937. "Syla cheres radist." *Vistnyk* 9: 649–59.

——. 1947. *Prapory dukha: Zhyttia i tvorchist Oleny Telihy.* Ed. O. Zhdanovych. N.p.: Na
chuzhyni.

——. 1977. *Zbirnyk.* Ed. O. Zhdanovych. Detroit, New York, Paris: Vydannia Ukrainskoho
Zolotoho Khresta v ZSA.

——. 2004. *Lysty. Spohady.* Kyiv: Vydavnytstvo imeni Oleny Telihy.

——. 2008. *Vybrani tvory.* 2nd ed. Kyiv: Smoloskyp.

Temliak, V. 1937. *Zavdannia novoho pokolinnia.* Lviv: Kvartanyk Vistnyka.

Teteryna, Daryna. 1998. Zhyttia i tvorchist Iuriia Boika-Blokhyna. Do 70-richchia diialnosti. Munich, Kyiv: Vydavnytstvo imeni Oleny Telihy.

"The Crisis of Democracy and the Slavonic World." 1931. *Slavonic Review* 9.27 (March):
509–24.

The Ukrainian Cause on Radio Waves. 1939. Saskatoon: Ukrainian National Federation of
Canada.

Tiedemann, Herbert. 2010. "Babi Yar: Critical Questions and Comments," 16 November:
www.vho.org/GB/Books/dth/fndbabiyar.html.

Tismaneanu, Vladimir. 1998. *Fantasies of Salvation: Democracy, Nationalism, and Myth
in Post-Communist Europe.* Princeton, NJ: Princeton University Press.

——. 2012. *The Devil in History: Communism, Fascism, and Some Lessons of the Twentieth
Century.* Berkeley, Los Angeles, London: University of California Press.

Torzecki, Ryszard. 1989. *Kwestia ukraińska w Polsce w latach 1923–1929 (na tle okresu miedzwojennego)*. Kraków: Wydawnictwo Literackie.

——. 1993. *Polacy i Ukraińcy: Sprawa ukraińska w czasie II Wojny Swiatowej na terenie II Rzeczypospolitej*. Warsaw: Polskie Wydawnictwo Naukowe.

Tselevych, V. 1933a. "Ne mozhna movchaty." *Dilo*, 3 June.

——. 1933b. "Treba protydiiaty." *Dilo*, 17 June.

Tudor, Henry. 1972. *Political Myth*. New York: Praeger Publishers.

Tvorydlo, M. 1933. "Demokratyzm chy avtorytaryzm?" *Dilo*, 3 January.

Ushkalov, Oleksandr, and Leonid Ushkalov, eds. 2010. *Arkhiv Rozstrilianoho Vidrodzhennia: Materialy arkhivno-slidchykh sprav ukrainskykh pysmennykiv 1920–1930-kh rokiv*. Kyiv: Smoloskyp.

U.V.O. 1929. N.p.: Vydannia propahandyvnoho viddilu Ukrainskoi Viiskovoi Organizatsii.

Vassyian, Iuliian. 1929. "Ideolohichni osnovy ukrainskoho natsionalizmu." *Rozbudova natsii* 3–4: 65–77.

——. 1957. *Odynytsia i suspilnist (Suspilno-filosofichni narysy)*. Toronto: Zoloti vorota.

——. 1958. *Suspilno-filosofichni narysy*. Chicago: Biblioteka Samostiinoi Ukrainy.

——. 1972, 1974. *Tvory*. 2 vols. Toronto: Ievshan-Zillia.

"V dobi zanepadu." 1930. *Novi shliakhy* 1: 93–106.

Verene, Donald Phillip, ed. 1979. *Symbol, Myth, and Culture: Essays and Lectures of Ernst Cassirer, 1935–1945*. New Haven, CT, and London: Yale University Press.

Viatrovych, Volodymyr. 2006. *Stavlennia OUN do ievrei: Formuvannia posytsii na tli katastrofy*. Lviv: Vydavnytstvo Ms.

——. 2011. *Druha polsko-ukrainska viina, 1942–1947*. Kyiv: Tsentr doslidzhen vyzvolnoho rukhu. Kyiv.

Viatrovych, Volodymyr, ed. 2011. *Polsko-Ukrainski stosunky v 1942–1947 rokakh u dokumentakh OUN ta UPA*. Vol. 1. Lviv: Lvivskyi natsionalnyi universytet, Tsentr doslidzhen vysvolnoho rukhu.

Videiko, Mykhailo, and Serhii Kot. 2008. *Naukova spadshchyna Oleha Olzhycha*. Kyiv: Informatsiino-analitychna ahentsiia Nash chas.

Vinch, Maikl. *"Odnodenna derzhava": Svidchennia anhliiskoho ochevydtsia pro podii Karpatskoi Ukrainy*. Kyiv: Tempora, 2012. (Orig. pub. Winch, Michael. *Republic for a Day: An Eye-Witness Account of the Carpatho-Ukraine Incident*. London: Robert Hale Limited 1939.)

Volynsky, Iu. 1934. "Vidrodzhennia mitu." *Rozbudova natsii* 1–2: 5–6.

Vretsona, Ievhen. 1974. "Moi zustrichi z polkovnykom," 466–81. In Boiko 1974.

Vynar, Liubomyr. 1951. "Ideolohiia D. Dontsova y sohodnishnyi svitohliad Ukrainskoi molodi." *Rozbudova derahavy: Biuleten* (Montreal) 1: 6–13.

——. 1964. "Pam'iati Ostapa Hrytsaia (V desiatylittia smerty)." *Svoboda*, 12 May.

——. 2008. *Oleh Kandyba-Olzhych: Doslidzhennia ta dzherela*. New York, Ostoh, Lviv: Ukrainske Istorychne Tovarystvo, Natsionalnyi Universytet "Ostrozka Akademiia."

Weber, Max. 1958. "Science as Vocation," 129–56. In *From Max Weber: Essays in Sociology*. Ed. H. H. Gerth and C. Wright Mills. New York: A Galaxy Book, Oxford University Press.

Weiner, Amir. 2001. *Making Sense of War: The Second World War and the Fate of the Bolshevik Revolution*. Princeton, NJ, and Oxford: Princeton University Press.

Wilson, Andrew. 1997. *Ukrainian Nationalism in the 1990s: A Minority Faith*. Cambridge: Cambridge University Press.

Wolin, Richard. 2004. *The Seduction of UnReason: The Intellectual Dance with Fascism From Nietzsche to Postmodernism*. Princeton, NJ: Princeton University Press.

Wysocki, Roman. 2003. *Organizacja ukraińskich nacjonalistów w Polsce w latach 1929– 1939. Geneza, struktura, program, ideologia*. Lublin: Wydawnictwo Uniwersztetu Marii Curii-Sklodowskiej.

Zabarevskyi, M. [real name Dmytro Doroshenko]. 1925. *Viacheslav Lypynskyi i ioho dumky pro ukrainsku natsiiu i derzhavu*. Vienna: Zakhodamy O. Zherebka.

Zaitsev, Oleksandr. 2011. "Sakralizatsiia natsii: Dmytro Dontsov i OUN," 151–230. In Zaitsev, Behen, and Stefaniv 2011.

———. 2012. "Ukrainskyi natsionalizm ta italiiskyi fashyzm (1922–1939)." *Ukraina moderna*: http://www.uamoderna.com/md/98-zaitsev,. posted 3 January.

———. 2013a. *Ukrainskyi intehralnyi natsionalism (1920–1930 – ti roky): Narysy intelektualnoi istorii*. Kyiv: Krytyka.

———. 2013b. "Ukrainian Integral Nationalism in Quest of a 'Special Path' (1920s–1930s)." *Russian Politics and Law* 51.5: 11–32.

Zaitsev, Oleksandr, Oleh Behen, and Vasyl Stefaniv. 2011. *Natsionalizm i relihiia: Hreko-Katolytska Tserkva ta ukrainskyi naatsionalistychnyi rukh u Halychyni (1920–1930-ti roky)*. Lviv: Vydavnytstvo Ukrainskoho Katolytskoho Universytetu.

"Zhertvy naivnosty chy provokatsiia? Shche z pryvodu protyrelihiinoi demonstratsii chastyny ukrainskoi molodi." 1933. *Dilo*, 5 May.

Zhulynskyi, Mykola. 2007. "Poklykanyi Ukrainoiu," 5–18. In Olzhych 2007.

Zhurzhenko, Tatiana. 2007. "The Geopolitics of Memory." *Eurozine*, 10 May: http://www. eurozine.com/articles/2007–05–10-zhurzhenko-en.html.

Zhyla, Volodymyr. 2002. "Dokiia Humenna ta ii doistorychnyi zhanr v literaturi." *Verkhovyna: Literaturna mozaika* 17: 12–20.

Zhyviuk, Andrii. 1996. "Karpatyka Ulasa Samchuka," 263–71. In Ulas Samchuk, *Hory hovoriat: Roman u 2-kh chastynakh*. Uzhhorod: MPP Grazhda-Vydavnytstvo Karpaty.

———. 2008a. "'Dokument doby, iakoi buv svidkom,'" 5–42. In Zhyviuk 2008b.

———, ed. 2008b. *Dokument doby: Publitsystyka Ulasa Samchuka 1941–1943 rokiv*. Rivne: VAT Rivenska drukarnia.

———. 2010. "Mizh endekamy i bilshovykamy: Mykola Nitskevych v ukrainskomu natsionalistychnomu rusi 1920–1940-kh rr." *Z arkhiviv VUTsK, GPU, NKVD, KGB* 2: 212–36.

Zieba, Andrzej A. 1993. "Pacyfikacja Małopolski Wschodniej w 1930 roku i jej echo wśród emigracji ukraińskiej w Kanadyie," 79–99. In *Przez dwa stulecia XIX i XX w: studia historyczne ofiarowane prof. Wacławowi Felczakowi*. Ed. Wojciech Frazik et al. Kraców: Wydawnictwo ITKM.

———. 2008. "Straczona szansa czy Syzyfowy Trud?" *Polska Akademija Umiejetnosti* XXI: 47–65.

———. 2010. *Lobbing dla Ukrainy w Europie miedzywojennej: Ukraińskie Biuro Prasowe w Londyhie oraz jego konkurenci politycyni (do roku 1932)*. Kraków: Ksiegarnia Akademicka.

Zińczuk, Alexandr, ed. 2012. *Pojednanije przez trudna pamieć, Wołyń 1943. Poiednannia cherez vazhku pamiat, Volyn 1943.* (Trans. as *Reconciliation Through Difficult Remembrance, Volyn 1943*) Warsaw: Panorama Kultur, 2012.

Zlepko, Dmytro. 1980. *Entstellung der polnisch-ungarischen Grenze (Oktober 1938 bis 15 Marz 1939).* Munich: R. Trofenik.

——. 1994. "Ukrainske pytannia v 1938–1939 rokakh i Tretii Reikh." *Zapysky Naukovoho Tovarystva im. Tarasa Shevchenka,* 228: 249–307.

Zolotarov, Vadym. 2007. *Sekretno-politychnyi viddil DPU USRR: Spravy ta liudy.* Kharkiv: Folio.

"Zvernennia Voiuiuchoi Ukrainy do vsiiei ukrainskoi emihratsii," 1984. In Ie. Shtendera and P. Potichnyj, eds. *Litopys Ukrainskoi Povstanskoi Armii.* Vol. 10, 21–33.Toronto: Litopys UPA.

INDEX